PROGRAMMING LANGUAGE
DESIGN CONCEPTS

D0074317

PROGRAMMING LANGUAGE DESIGN CONCEPTS

David A. Watt, University of Glasgow

with contributions by

William Findlay, University of Glasgow

John Wiley & Sons, Ltd

Copyright © 2004   John Wiley & Sons Ltd, The Atrium, Southern Gate, Chichester,
West Sussex PO19 8SQ, England

Telephone (+44) 1243 779777

Email (for orders and customer service enquiries): cs-books@wiley.co.uk
Visit our Home Page on www.wileyeurope.com or www.wiley.com

All Rights Reserved. No part of this publication may be reproduced, stored in a retrieval system or transmitted in
any form or by any means, electronic, mechanical, photocopying, recording, scanning or otherwise, except under
the terms of the Copyright, Designs and Patents Act 1988 or under the terms of a licence issued by the Copyright
Licensing Agency Ltd, 90 Tottenham Court Road, London W1T 4LP, UK, without the permission in writing of the
Publisher, with the exception of any material supplied specifically for the purpose of being entered and executed
on a computer system for exclusive use by the purchaser of the publication. Requests to the Publisher should be
addressed to the Permissions Department, John Wiley & Sons Ltd, The Atrium, Southern Gate, Chichester, West
Sussex PO19 8SQ, England, or emailed to permreq@wiley.co.uk, or faxed to (+44) 1243 770620.

This publication is designed to provide accurate and authoritative information in regard to the subject matter
covered. It is sold on the understanding that the Publisher is not engaged in rendering professional services. If
professional advice or other expert assistance is required, the services of a competent professional should be sought.

ADA is a registered trademark of the US Government Ada Joint Program Office.

JAVA is a registered trademark of Sun Microsystems Inc.

OCCAM is a registered trademark of the INMOS Group of Companies.

UNIX is a registered trademark of AT&T Bell Laboratories.

Other Wiley Editorial Offices

John Wiley & Sons Inc., 111 River Street, Hoboken, NJ 07030, USA

Jossey-Bass, 989 Market Street, San Francisco, CA 94103-1741, USA

Wiley-VCH Verlag GmbH, Boschstr. 12, D-69469 Weinheim, Germany

John Wiley & Sons Australia Ltd, 33 Park Road, Milton, Queensland 4064, Australia

John Wiley & Sons (Asia) Pte Ltd, 2 Clementi Loop #02-01, Jin Xing Distripark, Singapore 129809

John Wiley & Sons Canada Ltd, 22 Worcester Road, Etobicoke, Ontario, Canada M9W 1L1

Wiley also publishes its books in a variety of electronic formats. Some content that appears
in print may not be available in electronic books.

Library of Congress Cataloging-in-Publication Data

Watt, David A. (David Anthony)
   Programming language design concepts / David A. Watt ; with
contributions by William Findlay.
      p. cm.
   Includes bibliographical references and index.
   ISBN 0-470-85320-4 (pbk. : alk. paper)
    1. Programming languages (Electronic computers) I. Findlay, William,
1947- II. Title.

QA76.7 .W388 2004
005.13 – dc22

                                                2003026236

British Library Cataloguing in Publication Data

A catalogue record for this book is available from the British Library

ISBN 0-470-85320-4

Typeset in 10/12pt TimesTen by Laserwords Private Limited, Chennai, India
Printed and bound in Great Britain by Biddles Ltd, King's Lynn
This book is printed on acid-free paper responsibly manufactured from sustainable forestry
in which at least two trees are planted for each one used for paper production.

To Carol

Contents

Preface

The first programming language I ever learned was ALGOL60. This language was notable for its elegance and its regularity; for all its imperfections, it stood head and shoulders above its contemporaries. My interest in languages was awakened, and I began to perceive the benefits of simplicity and consistency in language design.

Since then I have learned and programmed in about a dozen other languages, and I have struck a nodding acquaintance with many more. Like many programmers, I have found that certain languages make programming distasteful, a drudgery; others make programming enjoyable, even esthetically pleasing. A good language, like a good mathematical notation, helps us to formulate and communicate ideas clearly. My personal favorites have been PASCAL, ADA, ML, and JAVA. Each of these languages has sharpened my understanding of what programming is (or should be) all about. PASCAL taught me structured programming and data types. ADA taught me data abstraction, exception handling, and large-scale programming. ML taught me functional programming and parametric polymorphism. JAVA taught me object-oriented programming and inclusion polymorphism. I had previously met all of these concepts, and understood them in principle, but I did not *truly* understand them until I had the opportunity to program in languages that exposed them clearly.

Contents

This book consists of five parts.

Chapter 1 introduces the book with an overview of programming linguistics (the study of programming languages) and a brief history of programming and scripting languages.

Chapters 2–5 explain the basic concepts that underlie almost all programming languages: values and types, variables and storage, bindings and scope, procedures and parameters. The emphasis in these chapters is on identifying the basic concepts and studying them individually. These basic concepts are found in almost all languages.

Chapters 6–10 continue this theme by examining some more advanced concepts: data abstraction (packages, abstract types, and classes), generic abstraction (or templates), type systems (inclusion polymorphism, parametric polymorphism, overloading, and type conversions), sequencers (including exceptions), and concurrency (primitives, conditional critical regions, monitors, and rendezvous). These more advanced concepts are found in the more modern languages.

Chapters 11–16 survey the most important programming paradigms, comparing and contrasting the long-established paradigm of imperative programming with the increasingly important paradigms of object-oriented and concurrent programming, the more specialized paradigms of functional and logic programming, and the paradigm of scripting. These different paradigms are based on different selections of key concepts, and give rise to sharply contrasting styles of language and of programming. Each chapter identifies the key concepts of the subject paradigm, and presents an overview of one or more major languages, showing how concepts were selected and combined when the language was designed. Several designs and implementations of a simple spellchecker are presented to illustrate the pragmatics of programming in all of the major languages.

Chapters 17 and 18 conclude the book by looking at two issues: how to select a suitable language for a software development project, and how to design a new language.

The book need not be read sequentially. Chapters 1–5 should certainly be read first, but the remaining chapters could be read in many different orders. Chapters 11–15 are largely self-contained; my recommendation is to read at least some of them after Chapters 1–5, in order to gain some insight into how major languages have been designed. Figure P.1 summarizes the dependencies between the chapters.

Examples and case studies

The concepts studied in Chapters 2–10 are freely illustrated by examples. These examples are drawn primarily from C, C++, JAVA, and ADA. I have chosen these languages because they are well known, they contrast well, and even their flaws are instructive!

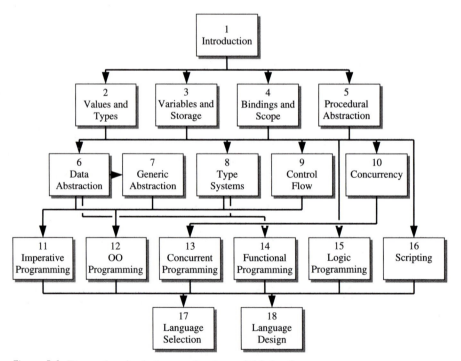

Figure P.1 Dependencies between chapters of this book.

The paradigms studied in Chapters 11–16 are illustrated by case studies of major languages: ADA, C, C++, HASKELL, JAVA, PROLOG, and PYTHON. These languages are studied only impressionistically. It would certainly be valuable for readers to learn to program in all of these languages, in order to gain deeper insight, but this book makes no attempt to teach programming *per se*. The bibliography contains suggested reading on all of these languages.

Exercises

Each chapter is followed by a number of relevant exercises. These vary from short exercises, through longer ones (marked *), up to truly demanding ones (marked **) that could be treated as projects.

A typical exercise is to analyze some aspect of a favorite language, in the same way that various languages are analyzed in the text. Exercises like this are designed to deepen readers' understanding of languages that they already know, and to reinforce understanding of particular concepts by studying how they are supported by different languages.

A typical project is to design some extension or modification to an existing language. I should emphasize that language design should not be undertaken lightly! These projects are aimed particularly at the most ambitious readers, but all readers would benefit by at least thinking about the issues raised.

Readership

All programmers, not just language specialists, need a thorough understanding of language concepts. This is because programming languages are our most fundamental tools. They influence the very way we think about software design and implementation, about algorithms and data structures.

This book is aimed at junior, senior, and graduate students of computer science and information technology, all of whom need some understanding of the fundamentals of programming languages. The book should also be of interest to professional software engineers, especially project leaders responsible for language evaluation and selection, designers and implementers of language processors, and designers of new languages and of extensions to existing languages.

To derive maximum benefit from this book, the reader should be able to program in at least two contrasting high-level languages. Language concepts can best be understood by comparing how they are supported by different languages. A reader who knows only a language like C, C++, or JAVA should learn a contrasting language such as ADA (or *vice versa*) at the same time as studying this book.

The reader will also need to be comfortable with some elementary concepts from discrete mathematics – sets, functions, relations, and predicate logic – as these are used to explain a variety of language concepts. The relevant mathematical concepts are briefly reviewed in Chapters 2 and 15, in order to keep this book reasonably self-contained.

This book attempts to cover all the most important aspects of a large subject. Where necessary, depth has been sacrificed for breadth. Thus the really serious student will need to follow up with more advanced studies. The book has an extensive bibliography, and each chapter closes with suggestions for further reading on the topics covered by the chapter.

Acknowledgments

Bob Tennent's classic book *Programming Language Principles* has profoundly influenced the way I have organized this book. Many books on programming languages have tended to be *syntax-oriented*, examining several popular languages feature by feature, without offering much insight into the underlying concepts or how future languages might be designed. Some books are *implementation-oriented*, attempting to explain concepts by showing how they are implemented on computers. By contrast, Tennent's book is *semantics-oriented*, first identifying and explaining powerful and general semantic concepts, and only then analyzing particular languages in terms of these concepts. In this book I have adopted Tennent's semantics-oriented approach, but placing far more emphasis on concepts that have become more prominent in the intervening two decades.

I have also been strongly influenced, in many different ways, by the work of Malcolm Atkinson, Peter Buneman, Luca Cardelli, Frank DeRemer, Edsger Dijkstra, Tony Hoare, Jean Ichbiah, John Hughes, Mehdi Jazayeri, Bill Joy, Robin Milner, Peter Mosses, Simon Peyton Jones, Phil Wadler, and Niklaus Wirth.

I wish to thank Bill Findlay for the two chapters (Chapters 10 and 13) he has contributed to this book. His expertise on concurrent programming has made this book broader in scope than I could have made it myself. His numerous suggestions for my own chapters have been challenging and insightful.

Last but not least, I would like to thank the Wiley reviewers for their constructive criticisms, and to acknowledge the assistance of the Wiley editorial staff led by Gaynor Redvers-Mutton.

David A. Watt
Brisbane
March 2004

PART I

INTRODUCTION

Part I introduces the book with an overview of programming linguistics and a brief history of programming and scripting languages.

Chapter 1

Programming languages

In this chapter we shall:

- outline the discipline of *programming linguistics*, which is the study of programming languages, encompassing concepts and paradigms, syntax, semantics, and pragmatics, and language processors such as compilers and interpreters;
- briefly survey the *historical development* of programming languages, covering the major programming languages and paradigms.

1.1 Programming linguistics

The first high-level programming languages were designed during the 1950s. Ever since then, programming languages have been a fascinating and productive area of study. Programmers endlessly debate the relative merits of their favorite programming languages, sometimes with almost religious zeal. On a more academic level, computer scientists search for ways to design programming languages that combine expressive power with simplicity and efficiency.

We sometimes use the term **programming linguistics** to mean the study of programming languages. This is by analogy with the older discipline of *linguistics*, which is the study of natural languages. Both programming languages and natural languages have *syntax* (form) and *semantics* (meaning). However, we cannot take the analogy too far. Natural languages are far broader, more expressive, and subtler than programming languages. A natural language is just what a human population speaks and writes, so linguists are restricted to analyzing existing (and dead) natural languages. On the other hand, programming linguists can not only analyze existing programming languages; they can also design and specify new programming languages, and they can implement these languages on computers.

Programming linguistics therefore has several aspects, which we discuss briefly in the following subsections.

1.1.1 Concepts and paradigms

Every programming language is an artifact, and as such has been consciously designed. Some programming languages have been designed by a single person (such as C++), others by small groups (such as C and JAVA), and still others by large groups (such as ADA).

A programming language, to be worthy of the name, must satisfy certain fundamental requirements.

A programming language must be ***universal***. That is to say, every problem must have a solution that can be programmed in the language, if that problem can be solved at all by a computer. This might seem to be a very strong requirement, but even a very small programming language can meet it. Any language in which we can define recursive functions is universal. On the other hand, a language with neither recursion nor iteration cannot be universal. Certain application languages are not universal, but we do not generally classify them as programming languages.

A programming language should also be reasonably *natural* for solving problems, at least problems within its intended application area. For example, a programming language whose only data types are numbers and arrays might be natural for solving numerical problems, but would be less natural for solving problems in commerce or artificial intelligence. Conversely, a programming language whose only data types are strings and lists would be an unnatural choice for solving numerical problems.

A programming language must also be ***implementable*** on a computer. That is to say, it must be possible to execute every well-formed program in the language. Mathematical notation (in its full generality) is not implementable, because in this notation it is possible to formulate problems that cannot be solved by any computer. Natural languages also are not implementable, because they are imprecise and ambiguous. Therefore, mathematical notation and natural languages, for entirely different reasons, cannot be classified as programming languages.

In practice, a programming language should be capable of an acceptably *efficient* implementation. There is plenty of room for debate over what is acceptably efficient, especially as the efficiency of a programming language implementation is strongly influenced by the computer architecture. FORTRAN, C, and PASCAL programmers might expect their programs to be almost as efficient (within a factor of 2–4) as the corresponding assembly-language programs. PROLOG programmers have to accept an order of magnitude lower efficiency, but would justify this on the grounds that the language is far more natural within its own application area; besides, they hope that new computer architectures will eventually appear that are more suited for executing PROLOG programs than conventional architectures.

In Parts II and III of this book we shall study the ***concepts*** that underlie the design of programming languages: *data* and *types*, *variables* and *storage*, *bindings* and *scope*, *procedural abstraction*, *data abstraction*, *generic abstraction*, *type systems*, *control*, and *concurrency*. Although few of us will ever design a programming language (which is extremely difficult to do well), as programmers we can all benefit by studying these concepts. Programming languages are our most basic tools, and we must thoroughly master them to use them effectively. Whenever we have to learn a new programming language and discover how it can be effectively exploited to construct reliable and maintainable programs, and whenever we have to decide which programming language is most suitable for solving a given problem, we find that a good understanding of programming language concepts is indispensable. We can master a new programming language most effectively if we understand the underlying concepts that it shares with other programming languages.

Just as important as the individual concepts are the ways in which they may be put together to design complete programming languages. Different selections of key concepts support radically different styles of programming, which are called **paradigms**. There are six major paradigms. *Imperative programming* is characterized by the use of variables, commands, and procedures; *object-oriented programming* by the use of objects, classes, and inheritance; *concurrent programming* by the use of concurrent processes, and various control abstractions; *functional programming* by the use of functions; *logic programming* by the use of relations; and *scripting languages* by the presence of very high-level features. We shall study all of these paradigms in Part IV of this book.

1.1.2   Syntax, semantics, and pragmatics

Every programming language has syntax, semantics, and pragmatics. We have seen that natural languages also have syntax and semantics, but pragmatics is unique to programming languages.

- A programming language's **syntax** is concerned with the *form* of programs: how expressions, commands, declarations, and other constructs must be arranged to make a well-formed program.

- A programming language's **semantics** is concerned with the *meaning* of programs: how a well-formed program may be expected to behave when executed on a computer.

- A programming language's **pragmatics** is concerned with the way in which the language is intended to be used in practice.

Syntax influences how programs are *written* by the programmer, *read* by other programmers, and *parsed* by the computer. Semantics determines how programs are *composed* by the programmer, *understood* by other programmers, and *interpreted* by the computer. Pragmatics influences how programmers are expected to design and implement programs in practice. Syntax is important, but semantics and pragmatics are more important still.

To underline this point, consider how an expert programmer thinks, given a programming problem to solve. Firstly, the programmer decomposes the problem, identifying suitable program units (procedures, packages, abstract types, or classes). Secondly, the programmer conceives a suitable implementation of each program unit, deploying language concepts such as types, control structures, exceptions, and so on. Lastly, the programmer codes each program unit. Only at this last stage does the programming language's syntax become relevant.

In this book we shall pay most attention to semantic and pragmatic issues. A given construct might be provided in several programming languages, with variations in syntax that are essentially superficial. Semantic issues are more important. We need to appreciate subtle differences in meaning between apparently similar constructs. We need to see whether a given programming language confuses distinct concepts, or supports an important concept inadequately, or fails to support it at all. In this book we study those concepts that are so important that they are supported by a variety of programming languages.

In order to avoid distracting syntactic variations, wherever possible we shall illustrate each concept using the following programming languages: C, C++, JAVA, and ADA. C is now middle-aged, and its design defects are numerous; however, it is very widely known and used, and even its defects are instructive. C++ and JAVA are modern and popular object-oriented languages. ADA is a programming language that supports imperative, object-oriented, and concurrent programming. None of these programming languages is by any means perfect. The ideal programming language has not yet been designed, and is never likely to be!

1.1.3   Language processors

This book is concerned only with high-level languages, i.e., programming languages that are (more or less) independent of the machines on which programs are executed. High-level languages are implemented by *compiling* programs into machine language, by *interpreting* them directly, or by some combination of compilation and interpretation.

Any system for processing programs – executing programs, or preparing them for execution – is called a **language processor**. Language processors include compilers, interpreters, and auxiliary tools like source-code editors and debuggers.

We have seen that a programming language must be implementable. However, this does not mean that programmers need to know in detail how a programming language is implemented in order to understand it thoroughly. Accordingly, implementation issues will receive limited attention in this book, except for a short section ("Implementation notes") at the end of each chapter.

1.2   Historical development

Today's programming languages are the product of developments that started in the 1950s. Numerous concepts have been invented, tested, and improved by being incorporated in successive programming languages. With very few exceptions, the design of each programming language has been strongly influenced by experience with earlier languages. The following brief historical survey summarizes the ancestry of the major programming languages and sketches the development of the concepts introduced in this book. It also reminds us that today's programming languages are not the end product of developments in programming language design; exciting new concepts, languages, and paradigms are still being developed, and the programming language scene ten years from now will probably be rather different from today's.

Figure 1.1 summarizes the dates and ancestry of several important programming languages. This is not the place for a comprehensive survey, so only the major programming languages are mentioned.

FORTRAN was the earliest major high-level language. It introduced symbolic expressions and arrays, and also procedures ("subroutines") with parameters. In other respects FORTRAN (in its original form) was fairly low-level; for example, control flow was largely effected by conditional and unconditional jumps. FORTRAN has developed a long way from its original design; the latest version was standardized as recently as 1997.

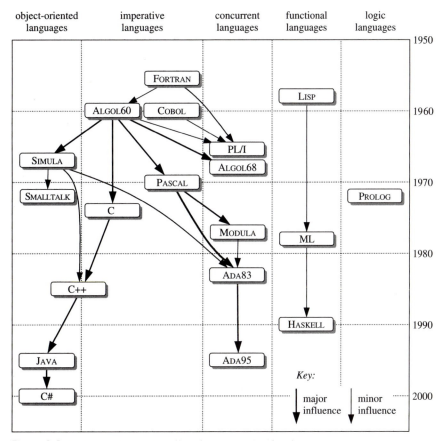

Figure 1.1 Dates and ancestry of major programming languages.

COBOL was another early major high-level language. Its most important contribution was the concept of data descriptions, a forerunner of today's data types. Like FORTRAN, COBOL's control flow was fairly low-level. Also like FORTRAN, COBOL has developed a long way from its original design, the latest version being standardized in 2002.

ALGOL60 was the first major programming language to be designed for communicating algorithms, not just for programming a computer. ALGOL60 introduced the concept of block structure, whereby variables and procedures could be declared wherever in the program they were needed. It was also the first major programming language to support recursive procedures. ALGOL60 influenced numerous successor languages so strongly that they are collectively called *ALGOL-like languages*.

FORTRAN and ALGOL60 were most useful for numerical computation, and COBOL for commercial data processing. PL/I was an attempt to design a general-purpose programming language by merging features from all three. On top of these it introduced many new features, including low-level forms of exceptions and concurrency. The resulting language was huge, complex, incoherent, and difficult to implement. The PL/I experience showed that simply piling feature upon feature is a bad way to make a programming language more powerful and general-purpose.

A better way to gain expressive power is to choose an adequate set of concepts and allow them to be combined systematically. This was the design philosophy of ALGOL68. For instance, starting with concepts such as integers, arrays, and procedures, the ALGOL68 programmer can declare an array of integers, an array of arrays, or an array of procedures; likewise, the programmer can define a procedure whose parameter or result is an integer, an array, or another procedure.

PASCAL, however, turned out to be the most popular of the ALGOL-like languages. It is simple, systematic, and efficiently implementable. PASCAL and ALGOL68 were among the first major programming languages with both a rich variety of control structures (conditional and iterative commands) and a rich variety of data types (such as arrays, records, and recursive types).

C was originally designed to be the system programming language of the UNIX operating system. The symbiotic relationship between C and UNIX has proved very good for both of them. C is suitable for writing both low-level code (such as the UNIX system kernel) and higher-level applications. However, its low-level features are easily misused, resulting in code that is unportable and unmaintainable.

PASCAL's powerful successor, ADA, introduced packages and generic units – designed to aid the construction of large modular programs – as well as high-level forms of exceptions and concurrency. Like PL/I, ADA was intended by its designers to become the standard general-purpose programming language. Such a stated ambition is perhaps very rash, and ADA also attracted a lot of criticism. (For example, Tony Hoare quipped that PASCAL, like ALGOL60 before it, was a marked advance on its successors!) The critics were wrong: ADA was very well designed, is particularly suitable for developing high-quality (reliable, robust, maintainable, efficient) software, and is the language of choice for mission-critical applications in fields such as aerospace.

We can discern certain trends in the history of programming languages. One has been a trend towards higher levels of abstraction. The mnemonics and symbolic labels of assembly languages abstract away from operation codes and machine addresses. Variables and assignment abstract away from inspection and updating of storage locations. Data types abstract away from storage structures. Control structures abstract away from jumps. Procedures abstract away from subroutines. Packages achieve encapsulation, and thus improve modularity. Generic units abstract procedures and packages away from the types of data on which they operate, and thus improve reusability.

Another trend has been a proliferation of paradigms. Nearly all the languages mentioned so far have supported *imperative programming*, which is characterized by the use of commands and procedures that update variables. PL/I and ADA support *concurrent programming*, characterized by the use of concurrent processes. However, other paradigms have also become popular and important.

Object-oriented programming is based on classes of objects. An *object* has variable components and is equipped with certain operations. Only these operations can access the object's variable components. A *class* is a family of objects with similar variable components and operations. Classes turn out to be convenient reusable program units, and all the major object-oriented languages are equipped with rich class libraries.

The concepts of object and class had their origins in SIMULA, yet another ALGOL-like language. SMALLTALK was the earliest pure object-oriented language, in which entire programs are constructed from classes.

C++ was designed by adding object-oriented concepts to C. C++ brought together the C and object-oriented programming communities, and thus became very popular. Nevertheless, its design is clumsy; it inherited all C's shortcomings, and it added some more of its own.

JAVA was designed by drastically simplifying C++, removing nearly all its shortcomings. Although primarily a simple object-oriented language, JAVA can also be used for distributed and concurrent programming. JAVA is well suited for writing *applets* (small portable application programs embedded in Web pages), as a consequence of a highly portable implementation (the *Java Virtual Machine*) that has been incorporated into all the major Web browsers. Thus JAVA has enjoyed a symbiotic relationship with the Web, and both have experienced enormous growth in popularity. C# is very similar to JAVA, apart from some relatively minor design improvements, but its more efficient implementation makes it more suitable for ordinary application programming.

Functional programming is based on functions over types such as lists and trees. The ancestral functional language was LISP, which demonstrated at a remarkably early date that significant programs can be written without resorting to variables and assignment.

ML and HASKELL are modern functional languages. They treat functions as ordinary values, which can be passed as parameters and returned as results from other functions. Moreover, they incorporate advanced type systems, allowing us to write *polymorphic* functions (functions that operate on data of a variety of types). ML (like LISP) is an impure functional language, since it does support variables and assignment. HASKELL is a pure functional language.

As noted in Section 1.1.1, mathematical notation in its full generality is not implementable. Nevertheless, many programming language designers have sought to exploit subsets of mathematical notation in programming languages. ***Logic programming*** is based on a subset of predicate logic. Logic programs infer relationships between values, as opposed to computing output values from input values. PROLOG was the ancestral logic language, and is still the most popular. In its pure logical form, however, PROLOG is rather weak and inefficient, so it has been extended with extra-logical features to make it more usable as a programming language.

Programming languages are intended for writing application programs and systems programs. However, there are other niches in the ecology of computing. An operating system such as UNIX provides a language in which a user or system administrator can issue commands from the keyboard, or store a command script that will later be called whenever required. An office system (such as a word processor or spreadsheet system) might enable the user to store a script ("macro") embodying a common sequence of commands, typically written in VISUAL BASIC. The Internet has created a variety of new niches for scripting. For example, the results of a database query might be converted to a dynamic Web page by a script, typically written in PERL. All these applications are examples of *scripting*. Scripts ("programs" written in scripting languages) typically are short and high-level, are developed very quickly, and are used to glue together subsystems written in other languages. So scripting languages, while having much in common with imperative programming languages, have different design constraints. The most modern and best-designed of these scripting languages is PYTHON.

Summary

In this introductory chapter:

- We have seen what is meant by programming linguistics, and the topics encompassed by this term: concepts and paradigms; syntax, semantics, and pragmatics; and language processors.

- We have briefly surveyed the history of programming languages. We saw how new languages inherited successful concepts from their ancestors, and sometimes introduced new concepts of their own. We also saw how the major paradigms evolved: imperative programming, object-oriented programming, concurrent programming, functional programming, logic programming, and scripting.

Further reading

Programming language concepts and paradigms are covered not only in this book, but also in TENNENT (1981), GHEZZI and JAZAYERI (1997), SEBESTA (2001), and SETHI (1996). Programming language syntax and semantics are covered in WATT (1991). Programming language processors are covered in AHO et al. (1986), APPEL (1998), and WATT and BROWN (2000).

The early history of programming languages (up to the 1970s) was the theme of a major conference, reported in WEXELBLAT (1980). Comparative studies of programming languages may be found in HOROWITZ (1995), PRATT and ZELCOWITZ (2001), and SEBESTA (2001). A survey of scripting languages may be found in BARRON (2000).

More detailed information on the programming languages mentioned in this chapter may be found in the references cited in Table 1.1.

Exercises

Note: Harder exercises are marked *.

Exercises for Section 1.1

1.1.1 Here is a whimsical exercise to get you started. For each programming language that you know, write down the shortest program that does *nothing at all*. How long is this program? This is quite a good measure of the programming language's verbosity!

Table 1.1   Descriptions of major programming and scripting languages.

Programming language	Description
ADA	ISO/IEC (1995); www.ada-auth.org/~acats/arm.html
ALGOL60	Naur (1963)
ALGOL68	van Wijngaarden et al. (1976)
C	Kernighan and Ritchie (1989); ISO/IEC (1999)
C++	Stroustrup (1997); ISO/IEC (1998)
C#	Drayton et al. (2002)
COBOL	ISO/IEC (2002)
FORTRAN	ISO/IEC (1997)
JAVA	Joy et al. (2000); Flanagan (2002)
LISP	McCarthy et al. (1965); ANSI (1994)
HASKELL	Thompson (1999)
ML	Milner et al. (1997)
MODULA	Wirth (1977)
PASCAL	ISO (1990)
PERL	Wall et al. (2000)
PL/I	ISO (1979)
PROLOG	Bratko (1990)
PYTHON	Beazley (2001); www.python.org/doc/current/ref/
SIMULA	Birtwhistle et al. (1979)
SMALLTALK	Goldberg and Robson (1989)

Exercises for Section 1.2

*1.2.1 The brief historical survey of Section 1.2 does not mention all major programming languages (only those that have been particularly influential, in the author's opinion). If a favorite language of yours has been omitted, explain why you think that it is important enough to be included, and show where your language fits into Figure 1.1.

*1.2.2 FORTRAN and COBOL are very old programming languages, but still widely used today. How would you explain this paradox?

*1.2.3 Imperative programming was the dominant paradigm from the dawn of computing until about 1990, after which if was overtaken by object-oriented programming. How would you explain this development? Why has functional or logic programming never become dominant?

PART II

BASIC CONCEPTS

Part II explains the more elementary programming language concepts, which are supported by almost all programming languages:

- values and types
- variables and storage
- bindings and scope
- procedural abstraction (procedures and parameters).

Chapter 2

Values and types

Data are the raw material of computation, and are just as important (and valuable) as the programs that manipulate the data. In computer science, therefore, the study of data is considered as an important topic in its own right.

In this chapter we shall study:

- *types* of *values* that may be used as data in programming languages;
- *primitive*, *composite*, and *recursive types*;
- *type systems*, which group values into types and constrain the operations that may be performed on these values;
- *expressions*, which are program constructs that compute new values;
- how values of primitive, composite, and recursive types are represented.

(In Chapter 3 we shall go on to study how values may be stored, and in Chapter 4 how values may be bound to identifiers.)

2.1 Types

A ***value*** is any entity that can be manipulated by a program. Values can be evaluated, stored, passed as arguments, returned as function results, and so on.

Different programming languages support different types of values:

- C supports integers, real numbers, structures, arrays, unions, pointers to variables, and pointers to functions. (Integers, real numbers, and pointers are *primitive values*; structures, arrays, and unions are *composite values*.)
- C++, which is a superset of C, supports all the above types of values plus objects. (Objects are composite values.)
- JAVA supports booleans, integers, real numbers, arrays, and objects. (Booleans, integers, and real numbers are primitive values; arrays and objects are composite values.)
- ADA supports booleans, characters, enumerands, integers, real numbers, records, arrays, discriminated records, objects (tagged records), strings, pointers to data, and pointers to procedures. (Booleans, characters, enumerands, integers, real numbers, and pointers are primitive values; records, arrays, discriminated records, objects, and strings are composite values.)

Most programming languages group values into *types*. For instance, nearly all languages make a clear distinction between integer and real numbers. Most languages also make a clear distinction between booleans and integers: integers can be added and multiplied, while booleans can be subjected to operations like *not, and*, and *or*.

What exactly is a type? The most obvious answer, perhaps, is that a type is a set of values. When we say that v is a value of type T, we mean simply that $v \in T$. When we say that an expression E is of type T, we are asserting that the result of evaluating E will be a value of type T.

However, not every set of values is suitable to be regarded as a type. We insist that each operation associated with the type behaves uniformly when applied to all values of the type. Thus {*false, true*} is a type because the operations *not, and*, and *or* operate uniformly over the values *false* and *true*. Also, $\{\ldots, -2, -1, 0, +1, +2, \ldots\}$ is a type because operations such as addition and multiplication operate uniformly over all these values. But {13, *true, Monday*} is not a type, since there are no useful operations over this set of values. Thus we see that a type is characterized not only by its set of values, but also by the operations over that set of values.

Therefore we define a **type** to be a set of values, equipped with one or more operations that can be applied uniformly to all these values.

Every programming language supports both *primitive types*, whose values are primitive, and *composite types*, whose values are composed from simpler values. Some languages also have *recursive types*, a recursive type being one whose values are composed from other values of the same type. We examine primitive, composite, and recursive types in the next three sections.

2.2   Primitive types

A **primitive value** is one that cannot be decomposed into simpler values. A **primitive type** is one whose values are primitive.

Every programming language provides built-in primitive types. Some languages also allow programs to define new primitive types.

2.2.1   Built-in primitive types

One or more primitive types are built-in to every programming language. The choice of built-in primitive types tells us much about the programming language's intended application area. Languages intended for commercial data processing (such as COBOL) are likely to have primitive types whose values are fixed-length strings and fixed-point numbers. Languages intended for numerical computation (such as FORTRAN) are likely to have primitive types whose values are real numbers (with a choice of precisions) and perhaps also complex numbers. A language intended for string processing (such as SNOBOL) is likely to have a primitive type whose values are strings of arbitrary length.

Nevertheless, certain primitive types crop up in a variety of languages, often under different names. For example, JAVA has **boolean**, **char**, **int**, and **float**, whereas ADA has Boolean, Character, Integer, and Float. These name differences are of no significance. For the sake of consistency, we shall use Boolean,

Character, Integer, and Float as names for the most common primitive types:

$$\text{Boolean} = \{\textit{false}, \textit{true}\} \tag{2.1}$$
$$\text{Character} = \{\ldots, \text{'a'}, \ldots, \text{'z'}, \ldots, \text{'0'}, \ldots, \text{'9'}, \ldots, \text{'?'}, \ldots\} \tag{2.2}$$
$$\text{Integer} = \{\ldots, -2, -1, 0, +1, +2, \ldots\} \tag{2.3}$$
$$\text{Float} = \{\ldots, -1.0, \ldots, 0.0, \ldots, +1.0, \ldots\} \tag{2.4}$$

(Here we are focusing on the set of values of each type.)

The Boolean type has exactly two values, *false* and *true*. In some languages these two values are denoted by the literals **false** and **true**, in others by predefined identifiers `false` and `true`.

The Character type is a language-defined or implementation-defined set of characters. The chosen character set is usually ASCII (128 characters), ISO LATIN (256 characters), or UNICODE (65 536 characters).

The Integer type is a language-defined or implementation-defined range of whole numbers. The range is influenced by the computer's word size and integer arithmetic. For instance, on a 32-bit computer with two's complement arithmetic, Integer will be $\{-2\,147\,483\,648, \ldots, +2\,147\,483\,647\}$.

The Float type is a language-defined or implementation-defined subset of the (rational) real numbers. The range and precision are determined by the computer's word size and floating-point arithmetic.

The Character, Integer, and Float types are usually *implementation-defined*, i.e., the set of values is chosen by the compiler. Sometimes, however, these types are language-defined, i.e., the set of values is defined by the programming language. In particular, JAVA defines all its types precisely.

The **cardinality** of a type T, written $\#T$, is the number of distinct values in T. For example:

$$\#\text{Boolean} = 2 \tag{2.5}$$
$$\#\text{Character} = 256 \quad \text{(ISO LATIN character set)} \tag{2.6a}$$
$$\#\text{Character} = 65\,536 \quad \text{(UNICODE character set)} \tag{2.6b}$$

Although nearly all programming languages support the Boolean, Character, Integer, and Float types in one way or another, there are many complications:

- Not all languages have a *distinct* type corresponding to Boolean. For example, C++ has a type named **bool**, but its values are just small integers; there is a convention that zero represents *false* and any other integer represents *true*. This convention originated in C.

- Not all languages have a *distinct* type corresponding to Character. For example, C, C++, and JAVA all have a type **char**, but its values are just small integers; no distinction is made between a character and its internal representation.

- Some languages provide not one but several integer types. For example, JAVA provides **byte** $\{-128, \ldots, +127\}$, **short** $\{-32\,768, \ldots, +32\,767\}$, **int** $\{-2\,147\,483\,648, \ldots, +2\,147\,483\,647\}$, and **long** $\{-9\,223\,372\,036\,854\,775\,808, \ldots, +9\,223\,372\,036\,854\,775\,807\}$. C and

C++ also provide a variety of integer types, but they are implementation-defined.

- Some languages provide not one but several floating-point types. For example, C, C++, and JAVA provide both **float** and **double**, of which the latter provides greater range and precision.

EXAMPLE 2.1   JAVA and C++ integer types

Consider the following JAVA declarations:

```
int countryPop;
long worldPop;
```

The variable countryPop could be used to contain the current population of any country (since no country yet has a population exceeding 2 billion). The variable worldPop could be used to contain the world's total population. But note that the program would fail if worldPop's type were **int** rather than **long** (since the world's total population now exceeds 6 billion).

A C++ program with the same declarations would be unportable: a C++ compiler may choose $\{-65\,536, \ldots, +65\,535\}$ as the set of **int** values!

If some types are implementation-defined, the behavior of programs may vary from one computer to another, even programs written in high-level languages. This gives rise to portability problems: a program that works well on one computer might fail when moved to a different computer.

One way to avoid such portability problems is for the programming language to define all its primitive types precisely. As we have seen, this approach is taken by JAVA.

2.2.2   Defined primitive types

Another way to avoid portability problems is to allow programs to define their own integer and floating-point types, stating explicitly the desired range and/or precision for each type. This approach is taken by ADA.

EXAMPLE 2.2   ADA integer types

Consider the following ADA declarations:

```
type Population is range 0 .. 1e10;

countryPop: Population;
worldPop: Population;
```

The integer type defined here has the following set of values:

$$\text{Population} = \{0, \ldots, 10^{10}\}$$

and its cardinality is:

$$\#Population = 10^{10} + 1$$

This code is completely portable – provided only that the computer is capable of supporting the specified range of integers.

In ADA we can define a completely new primitive type by *enumerating* its values (more precisely, by enumerating identifiers that will denote its values). Such a type is called an **enumeration type**, and its values are called **enumerands**.

C and C++ also support enumerations, but in these languages an enumeration type is actually an integer type, and each enumerand denotes a small integer.

EXAMPLE 2.3   ADA and C++ enumeration types

The following ADA type definition:

```
type Month is (jan, feb, mar, apr, may, jun,
       jul, aug, sep, oct, nov, dec);
```

defines a completely new type, whose values are twelve enumerands:

$$Month = \{jan, feb, mar, apr, may, jun, jul, aug, sep, oct, nov, dec\}$$

The cardinality of this type is:

$$\#Month = 12$$

The enumerands of type Month are distinct from the values of any other type. Note that we must carefully distinguish between these enumerands (which for convenience we have written as *jan, feb*, etc.) and the identifiers that denote them in the program (jan, feb, etc.). This distinction is necessary because the identifiers might later be redeclared. (For example, we might later redeclare dec as a procedure that decrements an integer; but the enumerand *dec* still exists and can be computed.)

By contrast, the C++ type definition:

```
enum Month {jan, feb, mar, apr, may, jun,
       jul, aug, sep, oct, nov, dec};
```

defines Month to be an integer type, and binds jan to 0, feb to 1, and so on. Thus:

$$Month = \{0, 1, 2, \ldots, 11\}$$

2.2.3 Discrete primitive types

A **discrete primitive type** is a primitive type whose values have a one-to-one relationship with a range of integers.

This is an important concept in ADA, in which values of *any* discrete primitive type may be used for array indexing, counting, and so on. The discrete primitive types in ADA are Boolean, Character, integer types, and enumeration types.

EXAMPLE 2.4   ADA discrete primitive types

Consider the following ADA code:

```
freq: array (Character) of Natural;
...
for ch in Character loop
    freq(ch) := 0;
end loop;
```

The indices of the array freq are values of type Character. Likewise, the loop control variable ch takes a sequence of values of type Character.

Also consider the following ADA code:

```
type Month is (jan, feb, mar, apr, may, jun,
    jul, aug, sep, oct, nov, dec);
length: array (Month) of Natural :=
    (31, 28, 31, 30, 31, 30, 31, 31, 30, 31, 30, 31);
...
for mth in Month loop
    put(length(mth));
end loop;
```

The indices of the array length are values of type Month. Likewise, the loop control variable mth takes a sequence of values of type Month.

Most programming languages allow only integers to be used for counting and array indexing. C and C++ allow enumerands also to be used for counting and array indexing, since they classify enumeration types as integer types.

2.3 Composite types

A **composite value** (or *data structure*) is a value that is composed from simpler values. A **composite type** is a type whose values are composite.

Programming languages support a huge variety of composite values: tuples, structures, records, arrays, algebraic types, discriminated records, objects, unions, strings, lists, trees, sequential files, direct files, relations, etc. The variety might seem bewildering, but in fact nearly all these composite values can be understood in terms of a small number of structuring concepts, which are:

- Cartesian products (tuples, records)
- mappings (arrays)
- disjoint unions (algebraic types, discriminated records, objects)
- recursive types (lists, trees).

(For sequential files, direct files, and relations see Exercise 2.3.6.)

We discuss Cartesian products, mappings, and disjoint unions in this section, and recursive types in Section 2.4. Each programming language provides its own notation for describing composite types. Here we shall use mathematical notation that is concise, standard, and suitable for defining sets of values structured as Cartesian products, mappings, and disjoint unions.

2.3.1 Cartesian products, structures, and records

In a **Cartesian product**, values of several (possibly different) types are grouped into tuples.

We use the notation (x, y) to stand for the pair whose first component is x and whose second component is y. We use the notation $S \times T$ to stand for the set of all pairs (x, y) such that x is chosen from set S and y is chosen from set T. Formally:

$$S \times T = \{(x, y) \mid x \in S; y \in T\} \tag{2.7}$$

This is illustrated in Figure 2.1.

The basic operations on pairs are:

- **construction** of a pair from two component values;
- **selection** of the first or second component of a pair.

We can easily infer the cardinality of a Cartesian product:

$$\#(S \times T) = \#S \times \#T \tag{2.8}$$

This equation motivates the use of the notation "$\times$" for Cartesian product.

We can extend the notion of Cartesian product from pairs to tuples with any number of components. In general, the notation $S_1 \times S_2 \times \ldots \times S_n$ stands for the set of all n-tuples, such that the first component of each n-tuple is chosen from S_1, the second component from $S_2, \ldots$, and the nth component from S_n.

The **structures** of C and C++, and the **records** of ADA, can be understood in terms of Cartesian products.

EXAMPLE 2.5 ADA records

Consider the following ADA definitions:

```
type Month is (jan, feb, mar, apr, may, jun,
    jul, aug, sep, oct, nov, dec);
type Day_Number is range 1 .. 31;
type Date is
    record
        m: Month;
        d: Day_Number;
    end record;
```

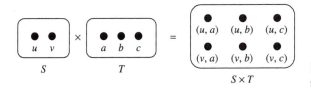

Figure 2.1 Cartesian product of sets S and T.

This record type has the set of values:

$$\text{Date} = \text{Month} \times \text{Day-Number} = \{jan, feb, \dots, dec\} \times \{1, \dots, 31\}$$

This type's cardinality is:

$$\#\text{Date} = \#\text{Month} \times \#\text{Day-Number} = 12 \times 31 = 372$$

and its values are the following pairs:

$(jan, 1)$	$(jan, 2)$	$(jan, 3)$	$\dots$	$(jan, 31)$
$(feb, 1)$	$(feb, 2)$	$(feb, 3)$	$\dots$	$(feb, 31)$
$\dots$	$\dots$	$\dots$	$\dots$	$\dots$
$(dec, 1)$	$(dec, 2)$	$(dec, 3)$	$\dots$	$(dec, 31)$

Note that the Date type models real-world dates only approximately: some Date values, such as $(feb, 31)$, do not correspond to real-world dates. (This is a common problem in data modeling. Some real-world data are too awkward to model exactly by programming language types, so our data models have to be approximate.)

The following code illustrates record construction:

```
someday: Date := (m => jan, d => 1);
```

The following code illustrates record component selection:

```
put(someday.m + 1);  put("/");  put(someday.d);
someday.d := 29;  someday.m := feb;
```

Here someday.m selects the first component, and someday.d the second component, of the record someday. Note that the use of component identifiers m and d in record construction and selection enables us to write code that does not depend on the order of the components.

EXAMPLE 2.6   C++ structures

Consider the following C++ definitions:

```
enum Month {jan, feb, mar, apr, may, jun,
    jul, aug, sep, oct, nov, dec};
struct Date {
    Month m;
    byte d;
};
```

This structure type has the set of values:

$$\text{Date} = \text{Month} \times \text{Byte} = \{jan, feb, \dots, dec\} \times \{0, \dots, 255\}$$

This type models dates even more crudely than its ADA counterpart in Example 2.5.

The following code illustrates structure construction:

```
struct Date someday = {jan, 1};
```

The following code illustrates structure selection:

```
printf("%d/%d", someday.m + 1, someday.d);
someday.d = 29;  someday.m = feb;
```

A special case of a Cartesian product is one where all tuple components are chosen from the same set. The tuples in this case are said to be **homogeneous**. For example:

$$S^2 = S \times S \tag{2.9}$$

means the set of homogeneous pairs whose components are both chosen from set S. More generally we write:

$$S^n = S \times \ldots \times S \tag{2.10}$$

to mean the set of homogeneous n-tuples whose components are all chosen from set S.

The cardinality of a set of homogeneous n-tuples is given by:

$$\#(S^n) = (\#S)^n \tag{2.11}$$

This motivates the superscript notation.

Finally, let us consider the special case where $n = 0$. Equation (2.11) tells us that S^0 should have exactly one value. This value is the empty tuple (), which is the unique tuple with no components at all. We shall find it useful to define a type that has the empty tuple as its only value:

$$\text{Unit} = \{()\} \tag{2.12}$$

This type's cardinality is:

$$\#\text{Unit} = 1 \tag{2.13}$$

Note that Unit is *not* the empty set (whose cardinality is 0).

Unit corresponds to the type named **void** in C, C++, and JAVA, and to the type **null record** in ADA.

2.3.2 Mappings, arrays, and functions

The notion of a **mapping** from one set to another is extremely important in programming languages. This notion in fact underlies two apparently different language features: arrays and functions.

We write:

$$m : S \to T$$

to state that m is a mapping from set S to set T. In other words, m maps every value in S to a value in T. (Read the symbol "$\to$" as "maps to".)

If m maps value x in set S to value y in set T, we write $y = m(x)$. The value y is called the *image* of x under m.

Two different mappings from $S = \{u, v\}$ to $T = \{a, b, c\}$ are illustrated in Figure 2.2. We use notation such as $\{u \to a, v \to c\}$ to denote the mapping that maps u to a and v to c.

The notation $S \to T$ stands for the set of all mappings from S to T. Formally:

$$S \to T = \{m \mid x \in S \Rightarrow m(x) \in T\} \tag{2.14}$$

This is illustrated in Figure 2.3.

Let us deduce the cardinality of $S \to T$. Each value in S has $\#T$ possible images under a mapping in $S \to T$. There are $\#S$ such values in S. Therefore there

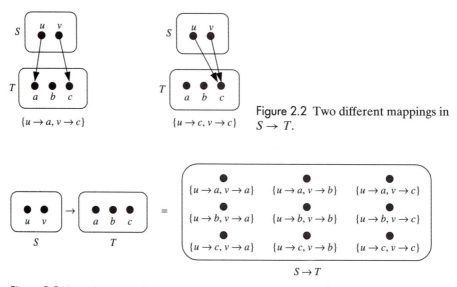

Figure 2.2 Two different mappings in $S \to T$.

Figure 2.3 Set of all mappings in $S \to T$.

are $\#T \times \#T \times \ldots \times \#T$ possible mappings ($\#S$ copies of $\#T$ multiplied together). In short:

$$\#(S \to T) = (\#T)^{\#S} \tag{2.15}$$

An **array** is an indexed sequence of components. An array has one component of type T for each value in type S, so the array itself has type $S \to T$. The **length** of the array is its number of components, which is $\#S$. Arrays are found in all imperative and object-oriented languages.

The type S must be finite, so an array is a *finite* mapping. In practice, S is always a range of consecutive values, which is called the array's **index range**. The limits of the index range are called its **lower bound** and **upper bound**.

The basic operations on arrays are:

- **construction** of an array from its components;
- **indexing**, i.e., selecting a particular component of an array, given its index.

The index used to select an array component is a computed value. Thus array indexing differs fundamentally from Cartesian-product selection (where the component to be selected is always explicit).

C and C++ restrict an array's index range to be a range of integers whose lower bound is zero.

EXAMPLE 2.7   **C++ arrays**

Consider the C++ declaration:

```
bool p[3];
```

The indices of this array range from the lower bound 0 to the upper bound 2. The set of possible values of this array is therefore:

$$\{0, 1, 2\} \to \{false, true\}$$

The cardinality of this set of values is 2^3, and the values are the following eight finite mappings:

$\{0 \to false, 1 \to false, 2 \to false\}$ $\{0 \to true, 1 \to false, 2 \to false\}$
$\{0 \to false, 1 \to false, 2 \to true\}$ $\{0 \to true, 1 \to false, 2 \to true\}$
$\{0 \to false, 1 \to true, 2 \to false\}$ $\{0 \to true, 1 \to true, 2 \to false\}$
$\{0 \to false, 1 \to true, 2 \to true\}$ $\{0 \to true, 1 \to true, 2 \to true\}$

The following code illustrates array construction:

```
bool p[] = {true, false, true};
```

The following code illustrates array indexing (using an **int** variable c):

```
p[c] = !p[c];
```

JAVA also restricts an array's index range to be a range of integers whose lower bound is zero. JAVA arrays are similar to C and C++ arrays, but they are in fact objects.

ADA allows an array's index range to be chosen by the programmer, the only restriction being that the index range must be a discrete primitive type.

EXAMPLE 2.8   ADA arrays

Consider the ADA type definitions:

```
type Color is (red, green, blue);
type Pixel is array (Color) of Boolean;
```

The set of values of this array type is:

$$Pixel = Color \to Boolean = \{red, green, blue\} \to \{false, true\}$$

This type's cardinality is:

$$\#Pixel = (\#Boolean)^{\#Color} = 2^3 = 8$$

and its values are the following eight finite mappings:

$\{red \to false, green \to false, blue \to false\}$ $\{red \to true, green \to false, blue \to false\}$
$\{red \to false, green \to false, blue \to true\}$ $\{red \to true, green \to false, blue \to true\}$
$\{red \to false, green \to true, blue \to false\}$ $\{red \to true, green \to true, blue \to false\}$
$\{red \to false, green \to true, blue \to true\}$ $\{red \to true, green \to true, blue \to true\}$

The following code illustrates array construction:

```
p: Pixel :=
      (red => true, green => false, blue => true);
```

or more concisely:

```
p: Pixel := (true, false, true);
```

The following code illustrates array indexing (using a Color variable c):

```
p(c) := not p(c);
```

Most programming languages support *multidimensional arrays*. A component of an *n*-dimensional array is accessed using *n* index values. We can think of an *n*-dimensional array as having a single index that happens to be an *n*-tuple.

EXAMPLE 2.9   ADA two-dimensional arrays

Consider the following ADA definitions:

```
type Xrange is range 0 .. 511;
type Yrange is range 0 .. 255;
type Window is array (YRange, XRange) of Pixel;
```

This two-dimensional array type has the following set of values:

$$\text{Window} = \text{Yrange} \times \text{Xrange} \to \text{Pixel} = \{0, \ldots, 255\} \times \{0, \ldots, 511\} \to \text{Pixel}$$

An array of this type is indexed by a pair of integers. Thus w(8,12) accesses that component of w whose index is the pair (8, 12).

Mappings occur in programming languages, not only as arrays, but also as *function procedures* (more usually called simply *functions*). We can implement a mapping in $S \to T$ by means of a function procedure, which takes a value in S (the **argument**) and computes its image in T (the **result**). Here the set S is not necessarily finite.

EXAMPLE 2.10   Functions implementing mappings

Consider the following C++ function:

```
bool isEven (int n) {
   return (n % 2 == 0);
}
```

This function implements one particular mapping in Integer → Boolean, namely:

$$\{\ldots, 0 \to \textit{true}, 1 \to \textit{false}, 2 \to \textit{true}, 3 \to \textit{false}, \ldots\}$$

We could employ a different algorithm:

```
bool isEven (int n) {
   int m = (n < 0 ? -n : n);
```

```
        while (m > 1) m -= 2;
        return (m == 0);
    }
```

but the function still implements the same mapping.

We can also write other functions that implement different mappings in Integer →
Boolean, such as:

```
    isOdd         {..., 0 → false, 1 → true, 2 → false, 3 → true, ...}
    isPositive    {..., −2 → false, −1 → false, 0 → false, 1 → true, 2 → true, ...}
    isPrime       {..., 0 → false, 1 → false, 2 → true, 3 → true, 4 → false, ...}
```

In most programming languages, a function may have multiple parameters. A
function with n parameters will have n arguments passed to it when called. We can
view such a function as receiving a single argument that happens to be an n-tuple.

EXAMPLE 2.11   Functions with multiple parameters

The following C or C++ function:

```
    float power (float b, int n) {
        ...
    }
```

implements a particular mapping in Float × Integer → Float. Presumably, it maps the pair
$(1.5, 2)$ to 2.25, the pair $(4.0, −2)$ to 0.0625, and so on.

It is noteworthy that mappings can be implemented by either arrays or
functions in programming languages (and that mappings from n-tuples can be
implemented by either n-dimensional arrays or n-parameter functions). Indeed,
we can sometimes use arrays and functions interchangeably – see Exercise 2.3.5.

It is important not to confuse function procedures with mathematical functions. A function procedure implements a mapping by means of a particular
algorithm, and thus has properties (such as efficiency) that are not shared by
mathematical functions. Furthermore, a function procedure that inspects or modifies global variables (for example a function procedure that returns the current
time of day, or one that computes and returns a random number) does not correspond to any mathematical function. For these reasons, when using the unqualified
term *function* in the context of programming languages, we must be very clear
whether we mean a mathematical function (mapping) or a function procedure.

2.3.3   Disjoint unions, discriminated records, and objects

Another kind of composite value is the ***disjoint union***, whereby a value is chosen
from one of several (usually different) sets.

We use the notation $S + T$ to stand for a set of disjoint-union values, each of which consists of a **tag** together with a **variant** chosen from either set S or set T. The tag indicates the set from which the variant was chosen. Formally:

$$S + T = \{left\ x \mid x \in S\} \cup \{right\ y \mid y \in T\} \tag{2.16}$$

Here *left x* stands for a disjoint-union value with tag *left* and variant *x* chosen from S, while *right x* stands for a disjoint-union value with tag *right* and variant *y* chosen from T. This is illustrated in Figure 2.4.

When we wish to make the tags explicit, we will use the notation *left S + right T*:

$$left\ S + right\ T = \{left\ x \mid x \in S\} \cup \{right\ y \mid y \in T\} \tag{2.17}$$

When the tags are irrelevant, we will still use the simpler notation $S + T$.

Note that the tags serve only to distinguish the variants. They must be distinct, but otherwise they may be chosen freely.

The basic operations on disjoint-union values in $S + T$ are:

- **construction** of a disjoint-union value, by taking a value in either S or T and tagging it accordingly;
- **tag test**, determining whether the variant was chosen from S or T;
- **projection** to recover the variant in S or the variant in T (as the case may be).

For example, a tag test on the value *right b* determines that the variant was chosen from T, so we can proceed to project it to recover the variant b.

We can easily infer the cardinality of a disjoint union:

$$\#(S + T) = \#S + \#T \tag{2.18}$$

This motivates the use of the notation "+" for disjoint union.

We can extend disjoint union to any number of sets. In general, the notation $S_1 + S_2 + \ldots + S_n$ stands for the set in which each value is chosen from one of $S_1, S_2, \ldots,$ or S_n.

The functional language HASKELL has **algebraic types**, which we can understand in terms of disjoint unions. In fact, the HASKELL notation is very close to our mathematical disjoint-union notation.

EXAMPLE 2.12   HASKELL algebraic types

Consider the HASKELL type definition:

```
data Number  = Exact Int | Inexact Float
```

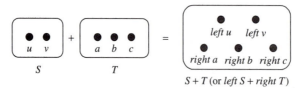

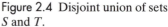

Figure 2.4 Disjoint union of sets S and T.

The set of values of this algebraic type is:

$$\text{Number} = \textit{Exact}\ \text{Integer} + \textit{Inexact}\ \text{Float}$$

The values of the type are therefore:

$$\{\dots, \textit{Exact}(-2), \textit{Exact}(-1), \textit{Exact}\ 0, \textit{Exact}(+1), \textit{Exact}(+2), \dots\}$$
$$\cup\ \{\dots, \textit{Inexact}(-1.0), \dots, \textit{Inexact}\ 0.0, \dots, \textit{Inexact}(+1.0), \dots\}$$

The following code illustrates construction of an algebraic value:

```
let pi = Inexact 3.1416
in ...
```

The following function illustrates tag test and projection:

```
rounded num =
-- Return the result of rounding the number num to the nearest integer.
    case num of
        Exact i -> i
        Inexact r -> round r
```

This uses pattern matching. If the value of num is *Inexact* 3.1416, the pattern "Inexact r" matches it, r is bound to 3.1416, and the subexpression "round r" is evaluated, yielding 3.

We can also understand the ***discriminated records*** of ADA in terms of disjoint unions.

EXAMPLE 2.13   ADA discriminated records (1)

Consider the following ADA definitions:

```
type Accuracy is (exact, inexact);
type Number (acc: Accuracy := exact) is
    record
        case acc of
            when exact =>
                ival: Integer;
            when inexact =>
                rval: Float;
        end case;
    end record;
```

This discriminated record type has the following set of values:

$$\text{Number} = \textit{exact}\ \text{Integer} + \textit{inexact}\ \text{Float}$$

Note that the values of type Accuracy serve as tags.

The following code illustrates construction of a discriminated record:

```
pi: constant Number :=
        (acc => inexact, rval => 3.1416);
```

The following function illustrates tag test and projection:

```
function rounded (num: Number) return Float is
-- Return the result of rounding the number num to the nearest integer.
    case num.acc is
        when exact =>
            return num.ival;
        when inexact =>
            return Integer(num.rval);
    end case;
end;
```

A discriminated record's tag and variant components are selected in the same way as ordinary record components. When a variant such as rval is selected, a run-time check is needed to ensure that the tag is currently inexact. The safest way to select from a discriminated record is by using a case command, as illustrated in Example 2.13.

In general, discriminated records may be more complicated. A given variant may have any number of components, not necessarily one. Moreover, there may be some components that are common to all variants.

EXAMPLE 2.14 Ada discriminated records (2)

Consider the following Ada definitions:

```
type Form is (pointy, circular, rectangular);
type Figure (f: Form) is
    record
        x, y: Float;
        case f is
          when pointy =>
            null;
          when circular =>
            r: Float;
          when rectangular =>
            w, h: Float;
        end case;
    end record;
```

This discriminated record type has the following set of values:

$$Figure = pointy(\text{Float} \times \text{Float})$$
$$+ circular(\text{Float} \times \text{Float} \times \text{Float})$$
$$+ rectangular(\text{Float} \times \text{Float} \times \text{Float} \times \text{Float})$$

Here are a few of these values:

pointy(1.0, 2.0)   – represents the point $(1, 2)$
circular(0.0, 0.0, 5.0)   – represents a circle of radius 5 centered at $(0, 0)$
rectangular(1.5, 2.0, 3.0, 4.0)   – represents a 3×4 box centered at $(1.5, 2)$

Each value in Figure is a tagged tuple. The first and second components of each tuple (named x and y) are common to all variants. The remaining components depend on the tag. When the tag is *pointy*, there are no other components. When the tag is *circular*, there is one other component (named r). When the tag is *rectangular*, there are two other components (named w and h).

How should we understand **objects**? Simplistically we could view each object of a particular class as a tuple of components. However, any object-oriented language allows objects of different classes to be used interchangeably (to a certain extent), and therefore provides an operation to test the class of a particular object. Thus each object must have a tag that identifies its class. So we shall view each object as a *tagged* tuple.

EXAMPLE 2.15   JAVA objects

Consider a JAVA program containing the following class declarations:

```
class Point {
   private float x, y;

   ...   // methods
}

class Circle extends Point {
   private float r;

   ...   // methods
}

class Rectangle extends Point {
   private float w, h;

   ...   // methods
}
```

Objects of these classes represent points, circles, and rectangles on the *xy* plane, respectively. The Circle class extends (is a subclass of) the Point class, so Circle objects inherit components x and y from Point, as well as having their own component r. The Rectangle class likewise extends the Point class, so Rectangle objects inherit components x and y from Point, as well as having their own components w and h.

The set of objects of this program is:

$$\begin{aligned} &Point(\text{Float} \times \text{Float}) \\ &+ Circle(\text{Float} \times \text{Float} \times \text{Float}) \\ &+ Rectangle(\text{Float} \times \text{Float} \times \text{Float} \times \text{Float}) \\ &+ \ldots \end{aligned}$$

Here "+..." reminds us that the set of objects is open-ended. The following class declaration:

```
class Date {
   private int m, d;
```

```
        public Date (int month, int day) {
            this.m = month;   this.d = day;
        }

        ...  // methods
    }
```

augments the set of objects in this program to:

$$Point(\text{Float} \times \text{Float})$$
$$+ \, Circle(\text{Float} \times \text{Float} \times \text{Float})$$
$$+ \, Rectangle(\text{Float} \times \text{Float} \times \text{Float} \times \text{Float})$$
$$+ \, Date(\text{Integer} \times \text{Integer})$$
$$+ \ldots$$

Compare Example 2.15 with Example 2.14. The important difference is that the set of objects in a program is *open-ended*, and can be augmented at any time simply by defining a new class (not necessarily related to existing classes). This open-endedness helps to explain the power of object-oriented programming.

It is important not to confuse disjoint union with ordinary set union. The tags in a disjoint union $S + T$ allow us to test whether the variant was chosen from S or T. This is not necessarily the case in the ordinary union $S \cup T$. In fact, if $T = \{a, b, c\}$, then:

$$T \cup T = \{a, b, c\} = T$$
$$T + T = \{\textit{left a, left b, left c, right a, right b, right c}\} \neq T$$

The **unions** of C and C++ are *not* disjoint unions, since they have no tags. This obviously makes tag test impossible, and makes projection unsafe. In practice, therefore, C programmers enclose each union within a structure that also contains a tag.

EXAMPLE 2.16   C unions

Consider the following C type definition:

```
union Untagged_Number {
    int ival;
    float rval;
};
```

The set of values of this union type is:

$$\text{Untagged-Number} = \text{Integer} \cup \text{Float}$$

Such a union type is useless on its own. Lacking a tag, we cannot perform a tag test, nor can we safely project a variant out of the union.

Now consider the following C type definitions:

```
enum Accuracy {exact, inexact};
struct Number{
```

```
         Accuracy acc;
         union {
           int ival;      /* used when acc contains exact */
           float rval;    /* used when acc contains inexact */
         } content;
      };
```

This structure crudely models a disjoint union, but it is very error-prone. The programmer's intentions are indicated by the comments, but only great care and self-discipline by the programmer can ensure that the structure is used in the way intended.

2.4   Recursive types

A *recursive type* is one defined in terms of itself. In this section we discuss two common recursive types, lists and strings, as well as recursive types in general.

2.4.1   Lists

A *list* is a sequence of values. A list may have any number of components, including none. The number of components is called the *length* of the list. The unique list with no components is called the *empty list*.

A list is *homogeneous* if all its components are of the same type; otherwise it is *heterogeneous*. Here we shall consider only homogeneous lists.

Typical list operations are:

- length

- emptiness test

- head selection (i.e., selection of the list's first component)

- tail selection (i.e., selection of the list consisting of all but the first component)

- concatenation.

Suppose that we wish to define a type of *integer-lists*, whose values are lists of integers. We may define an integer-list to be a value that is either empty or a pair consisting of an integer (its head) and a further integer-list (its tail). This definition is recursive. We may write this definition as a set equation:

$$\text{Integer-List} = nil\,\text{Unit} + cons(\text{Integer} \times \text{Integer-List}) \qquad (2.19)$$

or, in other words:

$$\text{Integer-List} = \{nil()\} \cup \{cons(i, l) \mid i \in \text{Integer}; l \in \text{Integer-List}\} \qquad (2.20)$$

where we have chosen the tags *nil* for an empty list and *cons* for a nonempty list. Henceforth we shall abbreviate *nil()* to *nil*.

Equations (2.19) and (2.20) are recursive, like our informal definition of integer-lists. But what exactly do these equations mean? Consider the following set of values:

$$\{nil\}$$
$$\cup \{cons(i, nil) \mid i \in \mathsf{Integer}\}$$
$$\cup \{cons(i, cons(j, nil)) \mid i, j \in \mathsf{Integer}\}$$
$$\cup \{cons(i, cons(j, cons(k, nil))) \mid i, j, k \in \mathsf{Integer}\}$$
$$\cup \ldots$$

i.e., the set:

$$\{cons(i_1, cons(\ldots, cons(i_n, nil)\ldots)) \mid n \geq 0; i_1, \ldots, i_n \in \mathsf{Integer}\} \qquad (2.21)$$

Set (2.21) corresponds to the set of all *finite* lists of integers, and is a solution of (2.20).

Set (2.21) is not, however, the only solution of (2.20). Another solution is the set of all *finite and infinite* lists of integers. This alternative solution is a superset of (2.21). It seems reasonable to discount this alternative solution, however, since we are really interested only in values that can be computed, and no infinite list can be computed in a finite amount of time.

Let us now generalize. The recursive set equation:

$$L = \mathsf{Unit} + (T \times L) \qquad (2.22)$$

has a *least solution* for L that corresponds to the set of all finite lists of values chosen from T. Every other solution is a superset of the least solution.

Lists (or sequences) are so ubiquitous that they deserve a notation of their own: T^* stands for the set of all finite lists of values chosen from T. Thus:

$$T^* = \mathsf{Unit} + (T \times T^*) \qquad (2.23)$$

In imperative languages (such as C, C++, and ADA), recursive types must be defined in terms of pointers, for reasons that will be explained in Section 3.6.1. In functional languages (such as HASKELL) and in some object-oriented languages (such as JAVA), recursive types can be defined directly.

EXAMPLE 2.17   JAVA lists

The following (unidiomatic) JAVA class declarations together define lists of integers:

```
class IntList {
    public IntNode first;

    public IntList (IntNode first) {
        this.first = first;
    }
}

class IntNode {
    public int elem;
    public IntNode succ;

    public IntNode (int elem, IntNode succ) {
```

```
        this.elem = elem;   this.succ = succ;
    }
}
```

The `IntNode` class is defined in terms of itself. So each `IntNode` object contains an `IntNode` component named `succ`. This might seem to imply that an `IntNode` object contains an `IntNode` object, which in turn contains another `IntNode` object, and so on forever; but sooner or later one of these objects will have its component `succ` set to **null**. The following code constructs an `IntList` object with four nodes:

```
IntList primes = new IntList(
    new IntNode(2, new IntNode(3,
        new IntNode(5, new IntNode(7, null)))));
```

EXAMPLE 2.18   HASKELL lists

We could define a type whose values are integer lists by writing the following HASKELL declaration:

```
data IntList = Nil | Cons Int IntList
```

This corresponds to equation (2.19). The following expressions construct values of type `IntList`:

```
Nil
Cons 13 Nil
Cons 2 (Cons 3 (Cons 5 (Cons 7 Nil)))
```

As it happens, HASKELL has *built-in* list types, such as:

`[Int]`   (whose values are integer lists)

`[String]`   (whose values are string lists)

`[[Int]]`   (whose values are integer-list lists)

We can construct the above integer lists more concisely as follows:

```
[]
[13]
[2, 3, 5, 7]
```

2.4.2 Strings

A *string* is a sequence of characters. A string may have any number of characters, including none. The number of characters is called the *length* of the string. The unique string with no characters is called the *empty string*.

Strings are supported by all modern programming languages. Typical string operations are:

- length
- equality comparison
- lexicographic comparison
- character selection

- substring selection

- concatenation.

How should we classify strings? No consensus has emerged among programming language designers.

One approach is to classify strings as *primitive values*. The basic string operations must then be built-in; they could not be defined in the language itself. The strings themselves may be of any length. ML adopts this approach.

Another approach is to treat strings as *arrays of characters*. This approach makes all the usual array operations automatically applicable to strings. In particular, character selection is just array indexing. A consequence of this approach is that a given string variable is restricted to strings of a fixed length. (This is because the length of an array is fixed once it is constructed. We will study the properties of array variables in Section 3.3.2.) Useful operations peculiar to strings, such as lexicographic comparison, must be provided in addition to the general array operations. ADA adopts this approach (but also supports bounded and unbounded string types using standard packages).

A slightly different and more flexible approach is to treat strings as *pointers to arrays of characters*. C and C++ adopt this approach.

In a programming language that supports lists, the most natural approach is to treat strings as *lists of characters*. This approach makes all the usual list operations automatically applicable to strings. In particular, the first character of a string can be selected immediately (by head selection), but the nth character cannot. Useful operations peculiar to strings must be provided in addition to the general list operations. HASKELL and PROLOG adopt this approach.

In an object-oriented language, the most natural approach is to treat strings as *objects*. This approach enables strings to be equipped with methods providing all the desired operations, and avoids the disadvantages of treating strings just as special cases of arrays or lists. JAVA adopts this approach.

2.4.3   Recursive types in general

As we have seen, a *recursive type* is one defined in terms of itself. Values of a recursive type are composed from values of the same type. List types, discussed in Section 2.4.1, are recursive types.

In general, the set of values of a recursive type, R, will be defined by a recursive set equation of the form:

$$R = \ldots + (\ldots R \ldots R \ldots) \qquad (2.24)$$

A recursive set equation may have many solutions. Fortunately, a recursive set equation always has a *least solution* that is a subset of every other solution. In computation, the least solution is the one in which we are interested.

The least solution to equation (2.24) can be determined iteratively as follows. Substitute the empty set for R in the right-hand side of (2.24), giving a first approximation for R. Then substitute this first approximation for R in the right-hand side of (2.24), giving a second and better approximation for R. Continue in this way, at each step substituting the latest approximation for R in the right-hand side of (2.24). The successive approximations are larger and larger subsets of the least solution.

The cardinality of a recursive type is infinite, even if every individual value of the type is finite. For example, the set of lists (2.21) is infinitely large, although every individual list in that set is finite.

EXAMPLE 2.19   HASKELL recursive types

The following HASKELL declaration defines a recursive type `IntTree`, whose values are binary trees containing integers at their leaves:

```
data IntTree = Leaf Int | Branch IntTree IntTree
```

The following expressions construct some values of type `IntTree`:

```
Leaf 11

Branch(Leaf 11)(Leaf 5)

Branch(Branch(Leaf 5)(Leaf 7))
      (Branch(Leaf 12)(Leaf 18))
```

The type definition corresponds to the following recursive set equation:

$$\text{Int-Tree} = Leaf\ \text{Integer} + Branch(\text{Int-Tree} \times \text{Int-Tree}) \tag{2.25}$$

Let us determine the least solution to (2.25) iteratively. Substituting the empty set for Int-Tree in (2.25), we get our first approximation:

$$Leaf\ \text{Integer} \tag{2.26}$$

which is in fact the set of all binary trees of depth 0. Substituting (2.26) for Int-Tree in (2.25), we get our second approximation:

$$Leaf\ \text{Integer}$$
$$+ Branch(Leaf\ \text{Integer} \times Leaf\ \text{Integer}) \tag{2.27}$$

which is in fact the set of all binary trees of depth 0 or 1. Substituting (2.27) for Int-Tree in (2.25), we get:

$$Leaf\ \text{Integer}$$
$$+ Branch(Leaf\ \text{Integer} \times Leaf\ \text{Integer})$$
$$+ Branch(Leaf\ \text{Integer} \times Branch(Leaf\ \text{Integer} \times Leaf\ \text{Integer}))$$
$$+ Branch(Branch(Leaf\ \text{Integer} \times Leaf\ \text{Integer}) \times Leaf\ \text{Integer})$$
$$+ Branch(Branch(Leaf\ \text{Integer} \times Leaf\ \text{Integer})$$
$$\times Branch(Leaf\ \text{Integer} \times Leaf\ \text{Integer})) \tag{2.28}$$

which is in fact the set of all binary trees of depth 0–2. Continuing in this way, we get closer and closer to the set of all finite binary trees.

2.5 Type systems

A programming language's *type system* groups values into types. This allows programmers to describe data effectively. It also helps prevent programs from performing nonsensical operations, such as multiplying a string by a boolean. Performing such a nonsensical operation is called a ***type error***.

Possession of a type system is one of the most important ways in which high-level languages differ from low-level languages. In a typical low-level language, the only "types" are bytes and words, so nonsensical operations cannot be prevented.

In this section we introduce some basic concepts in type systems: static vs dynamic typing, and type equivalence. In Chapter 8 we shall study more advanced concepts in type systems.

2.5.1   Static vs dynamic typing

Before any operation is to be performed, the types of its operands must be checked in order to prevent a type error. For example, before an integer multiplication is performed, both operands must be checked to ensure that they are integers. Similarly, before an *and* or *or* operation is performed, both operands must be checked to ensure that they are booleans. Before an array indexing operation is performed, the left operand must be checked to ensure that it is indeed an array (and not a primitive value or record). Such checks are called ***type checks***.

The type check must be performed before the operation itself is performed. However, there may still be some freedom in the timing: the type check could be performed either at compile-time or at run-time. This seemingly pragmatic issue in fact underlies an important classification of programming languages, into statically typed and dynamically typed languages.

In a ***statically typed*** language, each variable and each expression has a fixed type (which is either explicitly stated by the programmer or inferred by the compiler). Using this information, all operands can be type-checked *at compile-time*.

In a ***dynamically typed*** language, values have fixed types, but variables and expressions have no fixed types. Every time an operand is computed, it could yield a value of a different type. So operands must be type-checked after they are computed, but before performing the operation, *at run-time*.

Most high-level languages are statically typed. SMALLTALK, LISP, PROLOG, PERL, and PYTHON are examples of dynamically typed languages.

EXAMPLE 2.20   **C++ static typing**

Consider the following C++ function definition:

```
bool even (int n) {
    return (n % 2 == 0);
}
```

Although the compiler does not know the value of the parameter n, it does know that this value must be of type **int**, since that is stated in the declaration of n. From that knowledge the compiler can infer that both operands of "%" will be of type **int**, hence the result of "%" will also be of type **int**. Thus the compiler knows that both operands of "==" will be of type **int**. Finally, the compiler can infer that the returned value will be of type **bool**, which is consistent with the function's stated result type.

Now consider the function call "even(i+1)", where i is declared to be of type int. The compiler knows that both operands of "+" will be of type int, so its result will be of type int. Thus the type of the function's argument is known to be consistent with the type of the function's parameter.

Thus, even without knowledge of any of the values involved (other than the literals), the compiler can certify that no type errors are possible.

EXAMPLE 2.21   PYTHON dynamic typing

Now consider a function similar to that of Example 2.20, but this time expressed in the dynamically typed language PYTHON:

```python
def even (n):
    return (n % 2 == 0)
```

Here the type of n's value is *not* known in advance, so the operation "%" needs a run-time type check to ensure that its left operand is an integer.

This function could be called with arguments of different types, as in "even(i+1)", or "even("xyz")". However, no type error will be detected unless and until the left operand of "%" turns out not to be an integer.

The following function, also in PYTHON, illustrates that dynamic typing is sometimes genuinely useful:

```python
def respond (prompt):
    # Print prompt and return the user's response, as an integer if possible,
    # or as a string otherwise.
    try:
        response = raw_input(prompt)
        return int(response)
    except ValueError:
        return response
```

The following commands might be used to read a date into two variables:

```python
m = respond("Month? ")
d = respond("Day? ")
```

In the first command, the user's response (presumably a month name or number) is assigned to the variable m. In the second command, the user's response (presumably a day number) is assigned to the variable d.

The following commands might then be used to manipulate the date into a standard form, in which the values of both m and d are integers:

```python
if m == "Jan":
    m = 1
...
elif m == "Dec":
    m = 12
elif ! (isinstance(m, int) and 1 <= m <= 12):
    raise DateError,    \
        "month is not a valid string or integer"
if ! (isinstance(d, int) and 1 <= d <= 31):
    raise DateError, "day is not a valid integer"
```

The expression "m == "Jan"" will yield *true* only if *m*'s value is the string "Jan", *false* if it is any other string, and *false* if it is not a string at all. Note how the type of m's value influences the flow of control.

This example would be awkward to program in a statically typed language, where the type system tends to "get in the way".

The choice between static and dynamic typing is essentially pragmatic:

- Static typing is more efficient. Dynamic typing requires (possibly repeated) run-time type checks, which slow down the program's execution. Static typing requires only compile-time type checks, whose cost is minimal (and one-off). Moreover, dynamic typing forces all values to be tagged (in order to make run-time type checks possible), and these tags take up storage space. Static typing requires no such tagging.
- Static typing is more secure: the compiler can certify that the program contains no type errors. Dynamic typing provides no such security. (This point is important because type errors account for a significant proportion of programming errors.)
- Dynamic typing provides greater flexibility, which is needed by some applications where the types of the data are not known in advance.

In practice the greater security and efficiency of static typing outweigh the greater flexibility of dynamic typing in the vast majority of applications. It is no coincidence that most programming languages are statically typed.

2.5.2   Type equivalence

Consider some operation that expects an operand of type T_1. Suppose that it is given instead an operand whose type turns out to be T_2. Then we must check whether T_1 is **equivalent** to T_2, written $T_1 \equiv T_2$. What exactly this means depends on the programming language. (The following discussion assumes that the language is statically typed.)

One possible definition of type equivalence is **structural equivalence**: $T_1 \equiv T_2$ if and only if T_1 and T_2 have the same set of values.

Structural equivalence is so called because it may be checked by comparing the *structures* of the types T_1 and T_2. (It is unnecessary, and in general even impossible, to enumerate all values of these types.)

The following rules illustrate how we can decide whether types T_1 and T_2, defined in terms of Cartesian products, disjoint unions, and mappings, are structurally equivalent or not. (We could similarly phrase the rules in terms of the types of a specific programming language.)

- If T_1 and T_2 are both primitive, then $T_1 \equiv T_2$ if and only if T_1 and T_2 are identical. For example:

    Integer $\equiv$ Integer

    but   Integer $/\equiv$ Float

    (The symbol "$/\equiv$" means "is not equivalent to".)

- If $T_1 = A_1 \times B_1$ and $T_2 = A_2 \times B_2$, then $T_1 \equiv T_2$ if and only if $A_1 \equiv A_2$ and $B_1 \equiv B_2$. For example:

$$\text{Integer} \times \text{Float} \equiv \text{Integer} \times \text{Float}$$
$$\text{but} \quad \text{Integer} \times \text{Float} /\equiv \text{Float} \times \text{Integer}$$

- If $T = A_1 \rightarrow B_1$ and $T_2 = A_2 \rightarrow B_2$, then $T_1 \equiv T_2$ if and only if $A_1 \equiv A_2$ and $B_1 \equiv B_2$. For example:

$$\text{Integer} \rightarrow \text{Float} \equiv \text{Integer} \rightarrow \text{Float}$$
$$\text{but} \quad \text{Integer} \rightarrow \text{Float} /\equiv \text{Integer} \rightarrow \text{Boolean}$$

- If $T_1 = A_1 + B_1$ and $T_2 = A_2 + B_2$, then $T_1 \equiv T_2$ if and only if either $A_1 \equiv A_2$ and $B_1 \equiv B_2$, or $A_1 \equiv B_2$ and $B_1 \equiv A_2$. For example:

$$\text{Integer} + \text{Float} \equiv \text{Integer} + \text{Float}$$
$$\text{Integer} + \text{Float} \equiv \text{Float} + \text{Integer}$$
$$\text{but} \quad \text{Integer} + \text{Float} /\equiv \text{Integer} + \text{Boolean}$$

- Otherwise, $T_1 /\equiv T_2$.

Although these rules are simple, it is not easy to see whether two recursive types are structurally equivalent. Consider the following:

$$T_1 = \text{Unit} + (S \times T_1)$$
$$T_2 = \text{Unit} + (S \times T_2)$$
$$T_3 = \text{Unit} + (S \times T_2)$$

Intuitively, these three types are all structurally equivalent. However, the reasoning needed to decide whether two arbitrary recursive types are structurally equivalent makes type checking uncomfortably hard.

Another possible definition of type equivalence is ***name equivalence***: $T_1 \equiv T_2$ if and only if T_1 and T_2 were defined in the same place.

EXAMPLE 2.22   Structural vs name equivalence

Consider the following declarations in a hypothetical C-like language:

```
struct Position { int x, y; };
struct Position pos;
struct Date { int m, d; };
struct Date today;
void show (struct Date d);
```

Here the call "show(today);" would pass its type check, whether the language adopts structural or name equivalence. On the other hand, the call "show(pos);" would pass its type check only if the language adopts structural equivalence.

Now consider the following declarations (in a different part of the program):

```
struct OtherDate { int m, d; };
struct OtherDate tomorrow;
```

The call "show(tomorrow);" would pass its type check only if the language adopts structural equivalence. It would *fail* its type check if the language adopts name equivalence, since the type of tomorrow is *not* name-equivalent to the type of the parameter of show: the two types were defined in different places.

The following summarizes the advantages and disadvantages of structural and name equivalence:

- Name equivalence forces each distinct type to be defined in one and only one place. This is sometimes inconvenient, but it helps to make the program more maintainable. (If the same type is defined in several places, and subsequently it has to be changed, the change must be made consistently in several places.)

- Structural equivalence allows confusion between types that are only coincidentally similar (such as Position and Date in Example 2.22).

Structural equivalence is adopted by ALGOL68. Name equivalence is adopted by most programming languages, including C++ and ADA. Confusingly, name and structural equivalence are used for different types in C: a type definition introduced by **enum**, **struct**, or **union** defines a new type, while a type definition introduced by **typedef** simply introduces a synonym for an existing type.

2.5.3   The Type Completeness Principle

In Section 2.1 we listed the various types of values supported by various languages. Now consider PASCAL:

- PASCAL provides primitive values (booleans, characters, enumerands, integers, real numbers), composite values (records, arrays, sets, files), pointers, and procedures.

PASCAL procedures count as values because they can be passed as arguments to other procedures. However (unlike primitive and composite values), procedures cannot be assigned, nor used as components of composite values. We say that PASCAL procedures are **second-class values**, while PASCAL primitive values, composite values, and pointers are **first-class values**.

Even among PASCAL's first-class values there are finer class distinctions. For example, a function result must be a primitive value or pointer, but not a composite value. This restriction often makes coding awkward. For example, we might want to write a function with a record as its result; instead we are forced to write a proper procedure with a record variable parameter, which cannot be called from within an expression.

PASCAL's class distinctions are unusually fine, but class distinctions are found in nearly all the major programming languages including C, C++, JAVA, and ADA. On the other hand, the modern functional languages (such as ML and HASKELL) manage to avoid such class distinctions altogether: they allow *all* values, including functions, to be manipulated in similar ways.

We can characterize a language's class-consciousness in terms of its adherence to the ***Type Completeness Principle***:

No operation should be arbitrarily restricted in the types of its operands.

The word *arbitrarily* is important here. Insisting that the operands of the *and* operation are booleans is not an arbitrary restriction, since it is inherent in the nature of this operation. But insisting that only values of certain types can be assigned is an arbitrary restriction, as is insisting that only values of certain types can be passed as arguments or returned as function results.

The Type Completeness Principle is not meant to be dogma. It is merely a principle that language designers ought to bear in mind, because arbitrary restrictions tend to reduce the expressive power of a programming language. Sometimes restrictions are justified by other, conflicting, design considerations. For example, an imperative language's treatment of procedures as second-class values can be justified on the grounds that it avoids certain implementation problems. However, there is very little justification for PASCAL's restriction on function result types; more modern languages allow function results to be of any type.

2.6 Expressions

Having studied values and types, let us now examine the programming language constructs that compute values. An ***expression*** is a construct that will be ***evaluated*** to yield a value.

Expressions may be formed in various ways. In this section we shall survey the fundamental forms of expression:

- *literals*
- *constructions*
- *function calls*
- *conditional expressions*
- *iterative expressions*
- *constant and variable accesses*.

We will consider two other forms of expression in later chapters: *expressions with side effects* in Section 3.8, and *block expressions* in Section 4.4.2.

Here we are primarily interested in the concepts underlying expressions, not in their syntactic details. From the point of view of programming language design, what really matters is that the language provides all or most of the above forms of expression. A language that omits (or arbitrarily restricts) too many of them is likely to be impoverished. Conversely, a language that provides additional forms of expression is likely to be bloated: the additional forms are probably unnecessary accretions rather than genuine enhancements to the language's expressive power.

2.6.1 Literals

The simplest kind of expression is a ***literal***, which denotes a fixed value of some type.

EXAMPLE 2.23   Literals

Here are some typical examples of literals in programming languages:

365   3.1416   **false**   '%'   "What?"

These denote an integer, a real number, a boolean, a character, and a string, respectively.

2.6.2   Constructions

A *construction* is an expression that constructs a composite value from its component values. In some languages the component values must be literals; in others, the component values are computed by evaluating subexpressions.

EXAMPLE 2.24   C or C++ structure constructions

The following C or C++ structure construction:

```
{jan, 1}
```

constructs a value of the type Date (Example 2.6). The component values must be literals.

EXAMPLE 2.25   ADA record constructions

The following ADA record construction:

```
(m => today.m, d => today.d + 1)
```

constructs a value of the type Date (Example 2.5). The component values are computed.
        More concise notation is also supported, but only in a syntactic context where the type is apparent:

```
tomorrow: Date := (today.m, today.d + 1);
```

EXAMPLE 2.26   C++ array constructions

In the following C++ code:

```
int size[] =
    {31, 28, 31, 30, 31, 30, 31, 31, 30, 31, 30, 31};
...
if (is_leap(this_year))
    size[feb] = 29;
```

an array construction is used to initialize the variable size. The component values must be literals.

EXAMPLE 2.27 ADA array constructions

In the following ADA code:

```
size: array (Month) of Integer :=
    (31, 28, 31, 30, 31, 30, 31, 31, 30, 31, 30, 31);
...
if is_leap(this_year) then
    size(feb) := 29;
end if;
```

an array construction is used to initialize the variable size. In ADA constructions, component values may be computed, but in this example they are literals. (It would be nice to use a conditional expression to compute the feb component, instead of the literal 28, but ADA does not provide conditional expressions.)

The above array construction could also be expressed as:

```
size: array (Month) of Integer :=
    (feb => 28, apr|jun|sep|nov => 30, others => 31);
```

EXAMPLE 2.28 HASKELL list constructions

The following HASKELL list construction:

```
[31, if isLeap(thisYear) then 29 else 28,
 31, 30, 31, 30, 31, 31, 30, 31, 30, 31]
```

constructs a value of type [Int]. The component values are computed.

As illustrated by these examples, C++ and ADA provide constructions for structures (records) and arrays. C++ constructions are very restricted: they may occur only as initializers in variable declarations, and the component values must be literals. To construct a new structure or array value, we must assign to its components one by one. For example:

```
Date today, last_day;

today.m = ...;   today.d = ...;
last_day.m = today.m;   last_day.d = size(today.m);
```

which is both tedious and error-prone. In ADA we would write:

```
today := (m => ..., d => ...);
last_day := (m => today.m, d => size(today.m));
```

EXAMPLE 2.29 JAVA object constructions

The following JAVA object construction:

```
new Date(today.m, size(today.m))
```

constructs an object of class `Date` (Example 2.15). And the following:

```
new IntList(null)
```

constructs an object of class `IntList` (Example 2.17).

A JAVA construction is a call to an operation called a *constructor*. The effect of a constructor call is to construct a *new* object of a particular class, the constructor itself being defined as part of the class declaration. The constructor's parameters are typically used to initialize at least some of the new object's components; other components may be initialized to default values or computed in some way.

2.6.3   Function calls

A *function call* computes a result by applying a function procedure (or method) to one or more arguments. The function call typically has the form "$F(E)$", where F determines the function procedure to be applied, and the expression E is evaluated to determine the argument.

In most programming languages, F is just the identifier of a specific function. However, in those languages that treat functions as first-class values, F may be any expression yielding a function. For example, the HASKELL function call:

```
(if ... then sin else cos)(x)
```

applies either the sine function or the cosine function to the value of x.

In the case of a function of n parameters, the function call typically has the form "$F(E_1, \ldots, E_n)$". We can view this function call as passing n distinct arguments; or we can view it as passing a single argument that is an n-tuple. We may adopt whichever view is more convenient.

We shall study function procedures in greater detail in Section 5.1.1, and parameters in Section 5.2.

An *operator* may be thought of as denoting a function. Applying a unary or binary operator to its operand(s) is essentially equivalent to a function call with one or two argument(s):

$\oplus E$ is essentially equivalent to $\oplus(E)$ (where $\oplus$ is a unary operator)

$E_1 \otimes E_2$ is essentially equivalent to $\otimes(E_1, E_2)$ (where $\otimes$ is a binary operator)

For example, the conventional arithmetic expression:

```
a * b + c / d
```

is essentially equivalent to a composition of function calls:

```
+(*(a, b), /(c, d))
```

The convention whereby we write a binary operator between its two operands is called the *infix notation*, which is adopted by nearly all programming languages. The alternative convention whereby we write every operator before its operands is called the *prefix notation*, which is adopted only by LISP among the major programming languages.

Here are some examples of JAVA operators:

- The unary operator "!" denotes the function {*false* → *true, true* → *false*} in Boolean → Boolean.

- The binary operator "%" denotes the remainder function in Integer × Integer → Integer.

- The binary operator "+" denotes several functions at the same time: integer addition in Integer × Integer → Integer, real addition in Float × Float → Float, and concatenation in String × String → String. This is an example of *overloading* (see Section 8.3).

Several modern programming languages (such as C++, ADA, and HASKELL) explicitly recognize the analogy between operators and functions. "$E_1 \otimes E_2$" is then *exactly* equivalent to "$\otimes(E_1, E_2)$", and operators may be defined in exactly the same way as function procedures. Such languages are a bit easier to learn, because they do not have separate type rules for operators and functions. At the same time, such languages are notationally more convenient, since they allow us to define or redefine operators.

In other languages there is only a rough analogy between operators and functions. Each operator has its own type rules. For example, the JAVA binary operator "+" allows its operands to be a mixture of integers, real numbers, and strings. If one operand is a real number and the other is an integer, the integer is converted to a real number and real addition is performed. If one operand is a string and the other is a number, the number is converted to a string and concatenation is performed.

2.6.4 Conditional expressions

A **conditional expression** computes a value that depends on a condition. It has two or more subexpressions, from which exactly one is chosen to be evaluated.

Choice is of course fundamental in computation. All programming languages provide conditional expressions, or conditional commands, or both, and the underlying concepts are similar. Conditional commands will be discussed in Section 3.7.6.

C, C++, and JAVA provide *if-expressions*. HASKELL provides both if-expressions and *case expressions*.

EXAMPLE 2.30   C if-expression

The following C (or C++ or JAVA) if-expression yields the maximum of the values of x and y:

```
x>y ? x : y
```

The syntax is cryptic, but this expression may be read as "*if* x>y *then* x *else* y".

EXAMPLE 2.31   HASKELL conditional expressions

The following HASKELL case expression yields the number of days in thisMonth and thisYear:

```
case thisMonth of
    Feb -> if isLeap(thisYear) then 29 else 28
    Apr -> 30
    Jun -> 30
    Sep -> 30
    Nov -> 30
    _   -> 31
```

If the value of thisMonth is *Feb*, this yields the value of the if-expression "**if** ... **then** 29 **else** 28". If the value of thisMonth is *Apr* or *Jun* or *Sep* or *Nov*, this yields 30. Otherwise this yields 31. (The pattern "_" matches any value not already matched.)

2.6.5   Iterative expressions

An **iterative expression** is one that performs a computation over a series of values (typically the components of an array or list), yielding some result.

Iterative commands are commonplace in programming languages, and we shall study them in Section 3.7.7. Iterative expressions are rather more unusual, but they are a prominent feature of the functional language HASKELL, in the form of **list comprehensions**.

EXAMPLE 2.32   HASKELL list comprehensions

Given a list of characters cs, the following HASKELL list comprehension converts any lowercase letters to uppercase, yielding a modified list of characters:

```
[if isLowercase c then toUppercase c else c
   | c <- cs]
```

The *generator* "c <- cs" binds c to each component of s in turn. If the value of s is ['C', 'a', 'r', 'o', 'l'], this list comprehension will yield ['C', 'A', 'R', 'O', 'L'].

Given a list of integers ys, the following HASKELL list comprehension yields a list (in the same order) of those integers in ys that are multiples of 100:

```
[y | y <- ys, y 'mod' 100 = 0]
```

The generator "y <- ys" binds y to each component of ys in turn. The *filter* "y 'mod' 100 = 0" rejects any such component that is not a multiple of 100. If the value of ys is [1900, 1946, 2000, 2004], this list comprehension will yield [1900, 2000].

List comprehensions are inspired by the set comprehensions of mathematical notation. For example, given a set of integers *ys*, the following set comprehension:

$$\{y \mid y \in ys; y \bmod 100 = 0\}$$

denotes the set of those integers in the set *ys* that are multiples of 100.

2.6.6 Constant and variable accesses

A *constant access* is a reference to a named constant, and yields the value of that constant. A *variable access* is a reference to a named variable, and yields the *current* value of that variable.

EXAMPLE 2.33   ADA constant and variable accesses

Within the scope of the ADA declarations:

```
pi: constant Float := 3.1416;
r: Float;
```

consider the expression:

```
2.0 * pi * r
```

Here "pi" is a constant access, yielding the value 3.1416 to which pi is bound. On the other hand, "r" is a variable access, yielding the value currently contained in the variable named r.

The value of an expression containing constant and variable identifiers depends on how these identifiers were declared. In other words, it depends on the *environment* of the expression. (See Section 4.1.)

2.7 Implementation notes

In this section we briefly review how values of primitive, composite, and recursive types are represented in a computer. The purpose of this section is to reinforce conceptual understanding, so it ignores certain complications that arise in practice.

2.7.1 Representation of primitive types

The values of each primitive type T are typically represented by single or multiple bytes: 8-bit, 16-bit, 32-bit, and 64-bit representations are the most common.

The choice of representation is constrained by the type's cardinality #T. With n bits we can represent at most 2^n different values. Therefore the smallest possible representation is $\log_2(\#T)$ bits.

In principle, we could represent a boolean value by a single bit (0 for *false* and 1 for *true*). In practice the compiler will usually choose a whole byte, since most computers make access to individual bits awkward.

ASCII or ISO LATIN characters have 8-bit representations. UNICODE characters have 16-bit representations.

The representation of integers is related to the desired range. Assuming two's complement representation, in n bits we can represent integers in the range $\{-2^{n-1}, \ldots, 2^{n-1} - 1\}$. Typically it is the compiler that chooses n, and from that we can deduce the range of integers. On the other hand, if the programmer is able to define the range of integers, the compiler must use the defined range to determine the minimum n. In Example 2.2, the programmer has defined the range $\{0, \ldots, 10^{10}\}$; the two's complement representation must therefore have at least 35 bits, but in practice the compiler is likely to choose 64 bits.

The representation of real numbers is related to the desired range and precision. Nowadays most compilers adopt the IEEE floating-point standard (either 32 or 64 bits).

Enumerands are typically represented by unsigned integers starting from 0. In Example 2.3, the twelve enumerands of type Month would be represented by the integers $\{0, \ldots, 11\}$; the representation must have at least 4 bits, but in practice the compiler will choose a whole byte.

2.7.2   Representation of Cartesian products

The values of a Cartesian product type are represented simply by juxtaposing the components in a fixed order.

In Example 2.5, each value of the record type Date is represented by juxtaposing a component of type Month with a component of type Day_Number, as illustrated in Figure 2.5. The structure type of Example 2.6 is represented similarly.

Any record or structure component can be accessed efficiently, since the compiler can determine its offset relative to the start of the record or structure.

2.7.3   Representation of arrays

The values of an array type are represented by juxtaposing the components in ascending order of indices.

In Example 2.7, the variable p is an array of three boolean components, with indices $\{0, 1, 2\}$. The array is represented by juxtaposing the three components in ascending order of indices. This is illustrated in Figure 2.6(a), which also shows an array of five boolean components.

Figure 2.5 Representation of ADA records of type Date (Example 2.5), or C/C++ structures of type Date (Example 2.6).

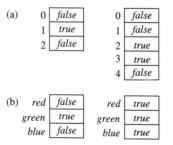

Figure 2.6 Representation of (a) C++ arrays of type **bool[]** (Example 2.7); (b) ADA arrays of type Pixel (Example 2.8).

In Example 2.8, each value of type `Pixel` is an array of three boolean components, with indices {*red*, *green*, *blue*}. Once again, the array is represented by juxtaposing the three components in ascending order of indices, as illustrated in Figure 2.6(b).

If *a* is an array, the component *a*[*i*] can be accessed by using *i* to compute the component's offset relative to the start of *a*, assuming that every component of *a* occupies the same fixed amount of space, say *s* bytes. If the lower bound of *a* is *l*, the component's offset is $s(i - l)$ bytes. If the lower bound *l* is 0 (as in C, C++, and JAVA), this simplifies to *si* bytes. This offset computation must be done at run-time, since the value of *i* is not known until run-time.

2.7.4 Representation of disjoint unions

Each value of a disjoint union type is represented by a *tag field* followed by one of several possible *variants*. The type (and therefore representation) of the variant depends on the *current* value of the tag field.

In Example 2.12, each value of the HASKELL algebraic type Number is represented by a tag field followed by either a variant of type `Int` (if the tag is *exact*) or a variant of type `Float` (if the tag is *inexact*). This is illustrated in Figure 2.7(a).

In Example 2.13, each value of the ADA discriminated record type Number is represented by a tag field of type `Accuracy` followed by either a component `ival` of type `Integer` (if the tag is *exact*) or a component `rval` of type `Float` (if the tag is *inexact*). This is illustrated in Figure 2.7(b). Note the similarity with Figure 2.7(a).

Both the tag field and the variants of a disjoint union can be accessed efficiently, since the compiler can determine their offsets relative to the start of the disjoint union.

A C or C++ union is represented like a disjoint union, but with no tag field.

The representation of objects is complicated by the possible existence of subclasses and superclasses. We defer discussion of that topic until Section 6.4.

2.7.5 Representation of recursive types

Consider the HASKELL recursive type definition of Example 2.18. An `IntList` value is represented by a *pointer* to a tag field, which is followed by one of two variants. If the tag is *cons*, the variant consists of an `Int` component and an `IntList` component. If the tag is *cons*, the variant is empty. This is illustrated in Figure 2.8.

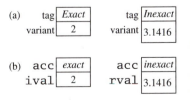

Figure 2.7 Representation of (a) HASKELL values of the algebraic type Number (Example 2.12); (b) ADA discriminated records of type Number (Example 2.13).

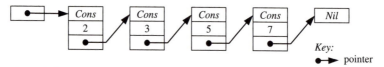

Figure 2.8 Representation of HASKELL lists of type IntList (Example 2.18).

The JAVA recursively defined class of Example 2.17 would be represented similarly. Recursively defined list types defined using explicit pointers in C++ or ADA would also be represented similarly. (See Exercise 2.7.2.)

Summary

In this chapter:

- We have studied values of primitive, composite, and recursive types supported by programming languages. In particular, we found that nearly all the composite types of programming languages can be understood in terms of Cartesian products, mappings, and disjoint unions.

- We have studied the basic concepts of type systems, in particular the distinction between static and dynamic typing, the issue of type equivalence, and the Type Completeness Principle.

- We have surveyed the forms of expressions found in programming languages: literals, constructions, function calls, conditional and iterative expressions, constant and variable accesses.

- We have seen how values of primitive, composite, and recursive types can be represented in computers.

Further reading

HOARE (1972, 1975) produced the first comprehensive and systematic treatment of composite types in terms of Cartesian products, disjoint unions, powersets, mappings, and recursive types. Hoare's treatment built on earlier work by McCARTHY (1965).

A detailed and technical treatment of types may be found in TENNENT (1981). Tennent shows that a simple treatment of types as sets of values needs to be refined when we consider recursive definitions involving function types.

Exercises

Exercises for Section 2.1

*2.1.1 Some programming languages have no concept of type. (a) Name at least one such language. (b) What are the advantages of types? (c) What are the disadvantages of types?

Exercises for Section 2.2

2.2.1 Write down the set of values of each primitive type in your favorite programming language.

2.2.2 Consider an application that processes amounts of money up to $100 000.00. Which primitive type would you use to represent such amounts: (a) in C or C++; (b) in JAVA; (c) in ADA?

2.2.3 Consider an application that processes certain economic data country by country. Which primitive type would you use to represent countries: (a) in C or C++; (b) in JAVA; (c) in ADA?

Exercises for Section 2.3

2.3.1 Using the notation of Cartesian products, mappings, and disjoint unions, write down (a) the set of values of each of the following C++ types:

```
enum Suit {club, diamond, heart, spade};
struct Card {Suit s; byte r;};
typedef Card[] Hand;
struct Turn { bool pass; Card play; };
```

and (b) the set of values of each of the following ADA types:

```
type Suit is (club, diamond, heart, spade);
type Rank is range 2 .. 14;
type Card is
    record
        s: Suit;
        r: Rank;
    end record;
type Hand is array (1 .. 7) of Card;
type Turn (pass: Boolean) is
    record
        case pass is
            when false => play: Card;
            when true  => null;
        end case;
    end record;
```

What is the cardinality of each type?

2.3.2 Explore the differences between C (or C++) arrays, JAVA arrays, and ADA arrays. Supposing that a1 and a2 are arrays with bounds 0 and 9, what is the effect in each language of (a) accessing a1[i] when i is out of range; (b) assigning a2 to a1?

2.3.3 JAVA arrays are classified as objects. How does this affect the use of arrays in JAVA programs?

2.3.4 Explore the relationship between $S \to (T \to U)$ and $(S \times T) \to U$. (*Hint:* Compare the types "**array** (S) **of array** (T) **of** U" and "**array** (S, T) **of** U" in ADA.)

2.3.5 Explore the relationship between arrays and function procedures. In your favorite programming language, implement each of the following using both an array and a function: (a) the mapping {*false* → *true, true* → *false*}; (b) the factorial function over the integers 0 through 10. In what ways are arrays and functions fundamentally different? Answer this question in terms of the *essential* properties of arrays and functions, neglecting any peculiarities that arrays or functions might have in your favorite language.

2.3.6 Using the notation of Cartesian products, mappings, disjoint unions, and lists, analyze the following bulk data types: (a) sequential files; (b) direct files; (c) relations (as in relational databases).

Exercises for Section 2.4

2.4.1 Write recursive types to represent integer lists of any length, (a) in C or C++, and (b) in ADA. (See also Exercise 2.7.2.)

2.4.2 Choose (a) a programming language in which strings are primitive values (such as ML); (b) a language in which strings are character arrays (such as C or ADA); (c) a language in which strings are character lists (such as HASKELL or PROLOG); and (d) a language in which strings are objects (such as JAVA). Make a table showing the string operations provided by each language. In language (b), which string operations are in fact available for *all* arrays? In language (c), which string operations are in fact available for *all* lists? In each language, are any of the operations identified in Section 2.4.2 missing, and could the missing operations be defined in the language itself?

2.4.3 Use the iterative method of Section 2.4.3 to determine the first four approximations to the least solution of the recursive set equation (2.22).

Exercises for Section 2.5

*2.5.1 Systematically analyze the type system of your favorite programming language, in the same way as various languages have been analyzed in this chapter. (a) What composite types are supported, and how is the set of values of each composite type defined in terms of its component types? (b) Can recursive types be defined, and if so how? (c) Is your language statically or dynamically typed? (d) How is type equivalence defined in your language?

*2.5.2 Which types of values in your favorite programming language may be (a) constants; (b) operands of operators; (c) results of operators; (d) arguments; (e) function results; (f) array/record/list components? How well does your language comply with the Type Completeness Principle?

2.5.3 (a) Find a program you have written in a *statically* typed language that would have been simpler to write in a dynamically typed language. (b) Find a program you have written in a *dynamically* typed language that could equally well have been written in a statically typed language.

*2.5.4 The experimental programming language AMBER (Cardelli 1986) is statically typed, but it has a special feature that supports a controlled form of dynamic typing. The type **dynamic** is equipped with the following operations: conversion of a given value of any type to **dynamic**; testing of a given **dynamic** value d to determine whether it was originally converted from type T; conversion of that **dynamic** value d back to type T. Show that the type **dynamic** can be understood in terms of disjoint unions.

2.5.5 Suppose that you are given a file of employee records (which has been generated by someone else's program). You are to write a program that reads and processes these records. Show that run-time type checks are inevitable, even if you choose to write your program in a statically typed language such as C, C++, or ADA.

Exercises for Section 2.6

2.6.1 Systematically analyze the forms of expression in your favorite programming language, comparing them with the forms of expression surveyed in Section 2.6. Are any relevant forms of expression missing? Are any exotic forms provided, and are they essential?

*2.6.2 Choose a programming language (such as ADA) that does not support conditional expressions. Design an extension to that language to allow conditional expressions.

**2.6.3 Choose a programming language (such as almost any imperative or object-oriented language) that does not support iterative expressions. Design an extension to that language to allow iterative expressions.

**2.6.4 Choose a programming language (such as C, C++, or JAVA) that does not support unrestricted structure/record and array constructions. Design an extension to that language to allow such constructions. Enable your constructions to have arbitrary subexpressions (not just literals) of the appropriate types. Enable your constructions to be used anywhere that expressions are allowed (not just in variable declarations). Look out for possible interactions between your extensions and other parts of the language.

Exercises for Section 2.7

2.7.1 Draw diagrams to show how the types of Exercise 2.3.1 would be represented in a computer.

2.7.2 Consider the recursive types you defined in answer to Exercise 2.4.1. Draw diagrams to show how these recursive types would be represented in a computer. Compare your answers with Figure 2.8.

Chapter 3

Variables and storage

"Once a programmer has understood the use of variables, he has understood the essence of programming." This remark of Edsger Dijkstra was actually about imperative programming, which is characterized by the use of variables and assignment. The remark might seem to be an exaggeration now that other programming paradigms have become popular, but imperative programming remains important in its own right and also underlies object-oriented and concurrent programming.

In this chapter we shall study:

- a simple model of *storage* that allows us to understand variables;
- *simple* and *composite variables*, and *total* and *selective updating* of composite variables;
- *static, dynamic,* and *flexible arrays*;
- the difference between *copy semantics* and *reference semantics*;
- lifetimes of *global, local, heap*, and *persistent variables*;
- *pointers*, which are references to variables;
- *commands*, which are program constructs that update variables;
- expressions with *side effects* on variables;
- how storage is allocated for global, local, and heap variables.

3.1 Variables and storage

In imperative (and object-oriented and concurrent) programming languages, a **variable** is a container for a value, and may be inspected and updated as often as desired. Variables are used to model real-world objects whose state changes over time, such as today's date, the current weather, the population of the world, or a country's economic performance.

The variables of imperative programs *do not* behave like mathematical variables. (A mathematical variable stands for a fixed but unknown value; there is no implication of change over time. The variables of functional and logic programs *do* behave like mathematical variables.)

To understand how the variables of imperative programs really do behave, we need some notion of **storage**. Now, real storage media (such as RAMs and disks) have many properties that are irrelevant for our purposes: word size, capacity, speed, and so on. Instead we shall use an abstract model of storage that is simple but adequate:

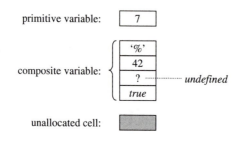

Figure 3.1 An abstract storage model.

- A store is a collection of **storage cells**, each of which has a unique *address*.
- Each storage cell has a current *status*, which is either *allocated* or *unallocated*. Each allocated storage cell has a current *content*, which is either a *storable value* or *undefined*.

We can picture each storage cell as a box, as shown in Figure 3.1.

In terms of this storage model, we can view a variable as a container consisting of one or more storage cells. More precisely:

- A *simple variable* occupies a single allocated storage cell.
- A *composite variable* occupies a group of contiguous allocated storage cells.

A **storable** value is one that can be stored in a single storage cell. Each programming language counts certain types of values as storable:

- C++'s storable values are primitive values and pointers. (Structures, arrays, unions, and objects are not storable, since none of these can be stored in a single storage cell. Functions also are not storable, since they cannot be stored at all. However, *pointers* to all of these things are storable.)
- JAVA's storable values are primitive values and pointers to objects. (Objects themselves are not storable, but every object is implicitly accessed through a pointer.)
- ADA's storable values are primitive values and pointers. (Records and arrays are not storable, since none of these can be stored in a single storage cell. Procedures also are not storable, since they cannot be stored at all. However, *pointers* to all of these things are storable.)

As a rule of thumb, most programming languages count primitive values and pointers as storable, but not composite values.

3.2 Simple variables

A **simple variable** is a variable that may contain a storable value. Each simple variable occupies a single storage cell.

The use of simple variables is such an elementary aspect of programming that we tend to take them for granted. However, it is worthwhile to reflect on exactly what happens when we declare, inspect, and update a simple variable.

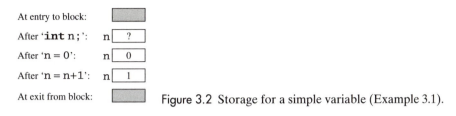

Figure 3.2 Storage for a simple variable (Example 3.1).

EXAMPLE 3.1   C simple variable

Consider the simple variable declared in the following C block:

```
{   int n;
    n = 0;
    n = n+1;
}
```

(1) The variable declaration "**int** n;" changes the status of some unallocated storage cell to allocated, but leaves its content *undefined*. Throughout the block, n denotes that cell.

(2) The assignment "n = 0" changes the content of that cell to zero.

(3) The expression "n+1" takes the content of that cell, and adds one. The assignment "n = n+1" (or "n++") adds one to the content of that cell.

(4) At the end of the block, the status of that cell reverts to unallocated.

Figure 3.2 shows the status and content of that cell at each step.

Strictly speaking, we should always say "the content of the storage cell denoted by n". We usually prefer to say more concisely "the value contained in n", or even "the value of n".

3.3   Composite variables

A *composite variable* is a variable of a composite type. Each composite variable occupies a group of contiguous storage cells.

A variable of a composite type has the same structure as a value of that type. For instance, a record variable is a tuple of component variables; and an array variable is a mapping from an index range to a group of component variables. The component variables can be inspected and updated selectively.

EXAMPLE 3.2   C++ record and array variables

Consider the following C++ (or C) declarations:

```
struct Date {
    int y, m, d;
};

Date today;
```

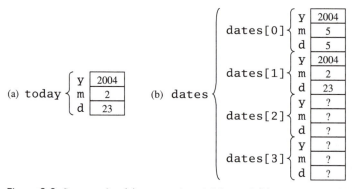

Figure 3.3 Storage for (a) a record variable, and (b) an array variable (Example 3.2).

Each Date value is a triple consisting of three **int** values. Correspondingly, a Date variable is a triple consisting of three **int** variables. Figure 3.3(a) shows the structure of the variable today, and the effect of the following assignments:

    today.m = 2;   today.d = 23;   today.y = 2004;

Now consider the array variable declared as follows:

    Date dates[4];

A value of this array type is a mapping from the index range 0–3 to four Date values. Correspondingly, a variable of this array type, such as dates, is a mapping from the index range 0–3 to four Date variables. Figure 3.3(b) shows the structure of the variable dates, and the effect of the following assignments:

    dates[0].y = 2004;   dates[0].m = 5;   dates[0].d = 5;
    dates[1] = today;

The last assignment copies the entire value of today. In other words, it updates the three storage cells of dates[1] with the contents of the three storage cells of today.

3.3.1   Total vs selective update

A composite variable may be updated either in a single step or in several steps, one component at a time. **Total update** of a composite variable means updating it with a new (composite) value in a single step. **Selective update** of a composite variable means updating a single component.

EXAMPLE 3.3   C++ total and selective updates

Consider the following declarations:

```
struct Date {
  int y, m, d;
};
Date today, tomorrow;
```

The following assignment:

```
tomorrow = today;
```

copies the entire value of `today` into the variable `tomorrow`. In other words, it copies the contents of the three storage cells of `today` into the three storage cells of `tomorrow`. This is an example of total update.

The following assignment:

```
tomorrow.d = today.d + 1;
```

updates a single component of `tomorrow`, leaving the other components undisturbed. This is an example of selective update.

3.3.2 Static vs dynamic vs flexible arrays

We can view an array variable as a mapping from an index range to a group of component variables. Let us examine how and when a given array variable's index range is determined. There are several possibilities: the index range might be fixed at compile-time, or it might be fixed at run-time when the array variable is created, or it might not be fixed at all.

A *static array* is an array variable whose index range is fixed at compile-time. In other words, the program code determines the index range.

C and C++ global and local arrays are static. An array's lower bound is always zero, but its length (and hence its upper bound) is fixed by the program code.

EXAMPLE 3.4   C++ static arrays

Consider the following C++ (or C) declarations:

```
float v1[] = {2.0, 3.0, 5.0, 7.0};
float v2[10];
```

The array variable `v1` has index range 0–3, which is determined by the array construction used to initialize it. The array variable `v2` has index range 0–9, which is determined by its declared length of 10. Both `v1` and `v2` have type **float**`[]`.

Now consider the following C++ function:

```
void print_vector (float v[], int n) {
// Print the array v[0],...,v[n-1] in the form "[...]".
   cout << '[' << v[0];
   for (int i = 1; i < n; i++)
     cout << ' ' << v[i];
   cout << ']';
}
```

This function's first parameter has type **float**`[]`, so its first argument could be either `v1` or `v2`:

```
print_vector(v1, 4);   print_vector(v2, 10);
```

A deficiency of C++ is that an array does not "know" its own length, hence the need for `print_vector`'s second parameter.

A **dynamic array** is an array variable whose index range is fixed at the time when the array variable is created.

In ADA, the definition of an array type must fix the type of the index range, but need not fix the lower and upper bounds. When an array variable is created, however, its bounds must be fixed. ADA arrays are therefore dynamic.

EXAMPLE 3.5   ADA dynamic arrays

Consider the following ADA type declaration:

```
type Vector is array (Integer range <>) of Float;
```

This type definition states only that `Vector`'s index range will be of type `Integer`; "`<>`" signifies that the lower and upper bounds are left open.

A `Vector` variable's bounds will be fixed only when the variable is created. Consider the following variable declarations:

```
v1: Vector(1 .. 4) := (2.0, 3.0, 5.0, 7.0);
v2: Vector(0 .. m) := (0 .. m => 0.0);
```

where m is a variable. The array variable `v1` has bounds 1–4, while the array variable `v2` has bounds 0–2 if m's current value happens to be 2.

A `Vector` value can be assigned to any `Vector` variable with the same length (not necessarily the same bounds). For example, the assignment "`v1 := v2;`" would succeed only if v2 happens to have exactly four components. An assignment to an ADA array variable never changes the array variable's index range.

Now consider the following ADA procedure:

```
procedure print_vector (v: in Vector) is
-- Print the array v in the form "[...]".
begin
   put('[');  put(v(v'first));
   for i in v'first + 1 .. v'last loop
     put(' ');  put(v(i));
   end loop;
   put(']');
end;
```

This procedure can be called with any `Vector` argument, regardless of its index range:

```
print_vector(v1);   print_vector(v2);
```

Within the body of `print_vector`, the lower and upper bounds of the parameter v are taken from the corresponding argument array, and can be accessed using the notation `v'first` and `v'last` (respectively).

A *flexible array* is an array variable whose index range is not fixed at all. A flexible array's index range may be changed when a new array value is assigned to it.

A JAVA array is actually a pointer to an object that contains the array's length as well as its components. When we assign an array object to a variable, the variable is made to point to that array object, whose length might be different from the previous array object. Thus JAVA arrays are flexible.

EXAMPLE 3.6   JAVA flexible arrays

Consider the following JAVA variable declarations:

```
float[] v1 = {2.0, 3.0, 5.0, 7.0};
float[] v2 = {0.0, 0.0, 0.0};
```

At this point the array variable v1 has index range 0–3, while v2 has index range 0–2.

However, after the following assignment:

```
v1 = v2;
```

v1 points to an array with index range 0–2. Thus v1's index range may vary during v1's lifetime.

Now consider the following JAVA function:

```
static void printVector (float[] v) {
// Print the array v in the form "[...]".
   System.out.print("[" + v[0]);
   for (int i = 1; i < v.length; i++)
      System.out.print(" " + v[i]);
   System.out.print("]");
}
```

This function can be called with any **float**[] argument, regardless of its index range:

```
printVector(v2);   printVector(v2);
```

Within the body of printVector, the length of the parameter v is taken from the corresponding argument array, and can be accessed using the notation v.length.

3.4   Copy semantics vs reference semantics

When a program assigns a composite value to a variable of the same type, what happens depends on the language. There are in fact two distinct possibilities:

* *Copy semantics.* The assignment *copies* all components of the composite value into the corresponding components of the composite variable.

* *Reference semantics.* The assignment makes the composite variable contain a *pointer* (or *reference*) to the composite value.

Copy semantics is adopted by C, C++, and ADA. However, programmers can also achieve the effect of reference semantics by using explicit pointers.

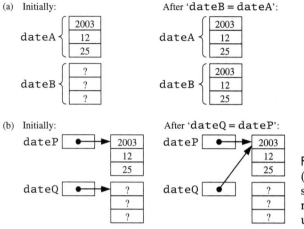

Figure 3.4 Assignment in C++ (Example 3.7): (a) copy semantics; (b) simulating reference semantics using pointers.

EXAMPLE 3.7 C++ copy semantics

The following C++ code illustrates copy semantics:

```
struct Date {
    int y, m, d;
};
Date dateA = {2003, 12, 25};
Date dateB;
dateB = dateA;
```

Figure 3.4(a) shows the effect of this assignment: dateB now contains a complete copy of dateA. Any subsequent update of dateA will have no effect on dateB, and *vice versa*.

This further C++ code achieves the effect of reference semantics:

```
Date* dateP = new Date;
Date* dateQ = new Date;
*dateP = dateA;
dateQ = dateP;
```

The variables dateP and dateQ contain *pointers* to Date variables. Figure 3.4(b) shows the effect of the assignment "dateQ = dateP": dateP and dateQ now point to the same variable. Any subsequent selective update of *dateP will also selectively update *dateQ, and *vice versa*.

JAVA adopts copy semantics for primitive values, and reference semantics for objects. However, programmers can achieve the effect of copy semantics even for objects by using the clone method.

EXAMPLE 3.8 JAVA reference semantics

Consider the following JAVA class declaration:

```
class Date {
    int y, m, d;
```

```
    public Date (int y, int m, int d) { ... }
}
```

The following JAVA code illustrates reference semantics:

```
Date dateR = new Date(2003, 12, 25);
Date dateS = new Date(2000, 1, 1);
dateS = dateR;
```

Figure 3.5(a) shows the effect of the assignment "dateS = dateR": dateR and dateS now point to the same variable. Any subsequent selective update of dateR will also selectively update dateS, and *vice versa*.

This further JAVA code achieves the effect of copy semantics:

```
Date dateT = new Date(2004, 1, 1);
dateT = dateR.clone();
```

Figure 3.5(b) shows the effect of the assignment "dateT = dateR.clone()". The method call "dateR.clone()" returns a pointer to a newly allocated object whose components are copies of dateR's components. The assignment makes dateT point to the newly allocated object.

The semantics of the *equality test* operation in any programming language should be consistent with the semantics of assignment. This enables the programmer to assume that, immediately after an assignment of V_1 to V_2, V_1 is equal to V_2, regardless of whether copy or reference semantics is used. It follows that the equality test operation should behave as follows:

- *Copy semantics.* The equality test operation should test whether corresponding components of the two composite values are equal.

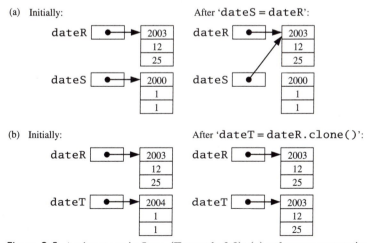

Figure 3.5 Assignment in JAVA (Example 3.8): (a) reference semantics; (b) effect of cloning. (Objects' tag fields are omitted here.)

- *Reference semantics*. The equality test operation should test whether the pointers to the two composite values are equal (i.e., whether they point to the same variable).

3.5   Lifetime

Every variable is **created** (or *allocated*) at some definite time, and **destroyed** (or *deallocated*) at some later time when it is no longer needed. The interval between creation and destruction of a variable is called its **lifetime**.

The concept of lifetime is pragmatically important. A variable needs to occupy storage cells only during its lifetime. When the variable is destroyed, the storage cells that it occupied may be deallocated, and may be subsequently allocated for some other purpose. Thus storage can be used economically.

We can classify variables according to their lifetimes:

- A *global variable*'s lifetime is the program's run-time.
- A *local variable*'s lifetime is an activation of a block.
- A *heap variable*'s lifetime is arbitrary, but is bounded by the program's run-time.
- A *persistent variable*'s lifetime is arbitrary, and may transcend the run-time of any particular program.

3.5.1   Global and local variables

A **global variable** is one that is declared for use throughout the program. A global variable's lifetime is the program's entire run-time: the variable is created when the program starts, and is destroyed when the program stops.

A **local variable** is one that is declared within a block, for use only within that block. A lifetime of a local variable is an activation of the block containing that variable's declaration: the variable is created on entry to the block, and is destroyed on exit from the block.

As we shall see in Section 4.4, a **block** is a program construct that includes local declarations. In all programming languages, the body of a procedure is a block. Some languages also have block commands, such as "{ ... }" in C, C++, or JAVA, or "**declare** ... **begin** ... **end**;" in ADA. An **activation** of a block is the time interval during which that block is being executed. In particular, an activation of a procedure is the time interval between call and return. During a single run of the program a block may be activated several times, and so a local variable may have several lifetimes.

EXAMPLE 3.9   Lifetimes of C++ global and local variables

Consider the following C++ (or C) program outline:

```
int g;

void main () {
```

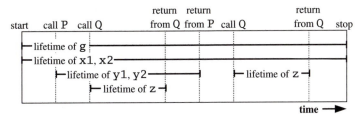

Figure 3.6 Lifetimes of local and global variables (Example 3.9).

```
    int x1; float x2;
    ... P(); ... Q(); ...
}

void P () {
    float y1; int y2;
    ... Q(); ...
}

void Q () {
    int z;
    ...
}
```

The blocks in this program are the bodies of procedures main, P, and Q. There is one global variable, g. There are several local variables: x1 and x2 (in main), y1 and y2 (in P), and z (in Q).

Notice that main calls P, which in turn calls Q; later main calls Q directly. Figure 3.6 shows the lifetimes of the global variable and local variables.

EXAMPLE 3.10   Lifetimes of C++ local variables of a recursive function

Consider the following C++ (or C) program outline:

```
void main () {
    int x;
    ... R(); ...
}

void R () {
    int w;
    ... R(); ...
}
```

Notice that main calls R, which in turn calls itself recursively. Figure 3.7 shows the lifetimes of the global variable g and the local variable w, on the assumption that R calls itself three times before the recursion unwinds.

These examples illustrate the general fact that the lifetimes of local variables are always nested, since the activations of blocks are themselves always nested. In

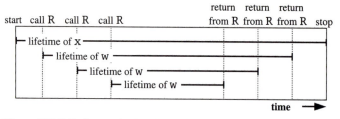

Figure 3.7 Lifetimes of a local variable of a recursive procedure (Example 3.10).

Figure 3.6, once P has called Q, the activation of Q must end before the activation of P can end.

A local variable will have several lifetimes if the block in which it is declared is activated several times. In Figure 3.6, since Q is activated on two separate occasions, the two lifetimes of z are disjoint.

In Figure 3.7, since R is called recursively, the lifetimes of w are nested. This makes sense only if we understand that each lifetime of w is really a lifetime of a distinct variable, which is created when R is called (more precisely, when the declaration of w is elaborated), and destroyed when R returns.

It follows that a local variable cannot retain its content over successive activations of the block in which it is declared. In some programming languages, a variable may be initialized as part of its declaration. But if a variable is not initialized, its content is *undefined, not* the value it might have contained in a previous activation of the block.

Some programming languages (such as C) allow a variable to be declared as a **static variable**, which defines its lifetime to be the program's entire run-time (even if the variable is declared inside a block). Thus static variables have the same lifetime as global variables. Although this feature addresses a genuine need, there are better ways to achieve the same effect, such as class variables in object-oriented languages.

3.5.2   Heap variables

The pattern of nested lifetimes characteristic of local and global variables is adequate for many purposes, but not all. We often need to create and destroy variables at will.

A **heap variable** is one that can be created, and destroyed, at any time during the program's run-time. A heap variable is created by an expression or command. It is anonymous, and is accessed through a *pointer*. (By contrast, a global or local variable is created by a declaration, and has an identifier.)

Pointers are first-class values, and thus may be stored, used as components of composite values, and so on. A program can build a complicated data structure (an arbitrary directed graph, in fact) in which connections between nodes are represented by pointers stored in the nodes. Such a structure can be selectively updated – to add a node, to remove a node, or to change a connection between nodes – by manipulation of pointers. This is more radical than selective update of a record or array variable, which affects the variable's content but not its structure.

EXAMPLE 3.11   ADA heap variables

The ADA program outlined here creates and manipulates lists whose elements are integers:

```
procedure main is

    type IntNode;
    type IntList is access IntNode;
    type IntNode is
        record
            elem: Integer;
            succ: IntList;
        end record;
    odds, primes: IntList := null;

    function cons (h: Integer; t: IntList)
            return IntList is
    -- Return a pointer to the list formed by prefixing element h to list t.
    begin
        return new IntNode'(h, t);
    end;

    procedure P is
    begin
        odds := cons(3, cons(5, cons(7, null)));
        primes := cons(2, odds);
    end;

    procedure Q is
    begin
        odds.succ := odds.succ.succ;
    end;

begin
    ... P; ... Q; ...
end;
```

Each value of type IntList is either a pointer to an IntNode record or the *null pointer*. We use a null pointer to represent the empty list or the end of a list.

Whenever the cons function is called, the expression "**new** IntNode'(h, t)" creates a heap variable of type IntNode, initializes it to contain the integer h and the pointer t, and yields a pointer to the newly created heap variable. The cons function simply returns that pointer.

The code in procedure P makes the variable odds contain a pointer to a list containing the integers 3, 5, and 7 (in that order), and makes the variable odds point to a list containing the integer 2 followed by the above three integers. Figure 3.8(a) shows the heap variables created by this code, together with the global variables odds and primes.

The code in procedure Q updates the pointer component of the first node of the odds list to point to the third node, in effect removing the second node from that list. This also removes the same node from the primes list. Figure 3.8(b) shows the new situation. The node containing 5 is now unreachable, so its lifetime is ended.

(a) Before removing the 5-node:

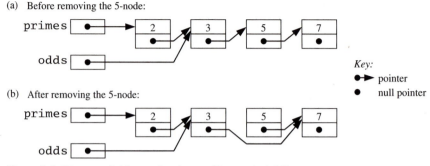

(b) After removing the 5-node:

Figure 3.8 Heap variables and pointers (Example 3.11).

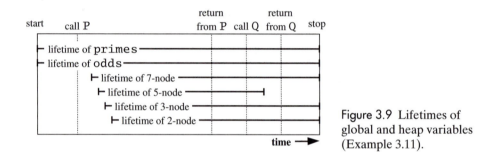

Figure 3.9 Lifetimes of global and heap variables (Example 3.11).

Figure 3.9 shows the lifetimes of the global and heap variables in this program.

But suppose, instead, that the assignment in procedure Q were "odds := odds.succ;", in effect removing the first node from the odds list. That node would still remain reachable in the primes list, so its lifetime would continue.

This example illustrates the general fact that the lifetimes of heap variables follow no particular pattern.

An **allocator** is an operation that creates a heap variable, yielding a pointer to that heap variable. In ADA, C++, and JAVA, an expression of the form "**new** …" is an allocator.

A **deallocator** is an operation that destroys a given heap variable. ADA's deallocator is a library procedure. C++'s deallocator is a command of the form "**delete** …". JAVA has no deallocator at all. Deallocators are unsafe, since any remaining pointers to a destroyed heap variable become *dangling pointers* (see Section 3.6.2).

A heap variable remains **reachable** as long as it can be accessed by following pointers from a global or local variable. A heap variable's lifetime extends from its creation until it is destroyed or it becomes unreachable.

3.5.3 Persistent variables

Files may be seen as composite variables. In particular, a *sequential file* is a sequence of components, and a *direct file* is (in effect) an array of components. A sequential file is read or written one component at a time, in serial order. A direct file is also read or written one component at a time, but in an arbitrary order, using each component's unique position number.

Usually files contain large bodies of long-lived data: they are persistent. A *persistent variable* is one whose lifetime transcends an activation of any particular program. By contrast, a *transient variable* is one whose lifetime is bounded by the activation of the program that created it. Global, local, and heap variables are transient.

Most programming languages including C, C++, JAVA, and ADA provide library procedures to create and destroy files. This allows a file to be created by a program at any time. It also allows the file to be destroyed at any later time, either during the same program activation or during a future activation of the same program or a different program.

There are certain analogies between persistent variables and transient variables. Persistent variables usually have arbitrary lifetimes, like heap variables; but some systems also allow persistent variables to have nested lifetimes, like local variables. Just as transient variables occupy primary storage, persistent variables occupy secondary storage. (Secondary storage has the same abstract properties as primary storage, see Section 3.1.)

Despite these analogies, most programming languages provide distinct types for persistent variables and transient variables. For example, ADA provides one family of types for sequential files, and another family of types for direct files, which are distinct from ordinary composite types.

Why not allow a persistent variable to be of any type? For instance, a persistent list variable would be a sequential file, and a persistent array variable would be a direct file.

The Type Completeness Principle suggests that all the types of the programming language should be available for both transient and persistent variables. A language applying this principle would be simplified by having no special file types, and no special commands or procedures for reading/writing data from/to files. The programmer would be spared the unprofitable effort of converting data from a persistent data type to a transient data type on input, and *vice versa* on output.

EXAMPLE 3.12 Persistent variable

Consider the following ADA type declarations:

```
type Country is (AT, BE, DE, DK, ES, FI, FR, GR,
    IE, IT, LU, NL, PT, SE, UK);
type Statistics is
    record
        population: Integer;
        area: Float;
```

```
            ...
         end record;
      type StatsTable is array (Country) of Statistics;
```

Let us suppose that a sequential file named stats.dat has components of type Statistics, one component for each value of type Country.

The following declaration instantiates the generic package Ada.Sequential_IO:

```
      package Stats_IO is new Ada.Sequential_IO(
          Element_Type => Statistics);
```

The resulting package Stats_IO provides a type File_Type, whose values are sequential files with Statistics components, together with procedures for opening, closing, reading, and writing such files.

The following application code calls these procedures. First it opens the file named stats.dat, placing a pointer to that file in statsFile. Then it reads the file's components and stores them in the transient array stats. Finally it closes the file.

```
      procedure loadStats (stats: out StatsTable) is
      -- Read into stats the contents of the file named stats.dat.
         statsFile: Stats_IO.File_Type;
      begin
         Stats_IO.open(statsFile, in_file, "stats.dat");
         for cy in Country loop
           Stats_IO.read(statsFile, stats(cy));
         end loop;
         Stats_IO.close(statsFile);
      end;
```

The following application code illustrates how the data stored in the transient array might be used:

```
      procedure analyzeStats (stats: in out StatsTable) is
      -- Print the population density of each country using the data in stats.
      begin
         for cy in Country loop
           put(Float(stats(cy).population)/stats(cy).area);
         end loop;
      end;

      procedure main is
         stats: StatsTable;
      begin
         loadStats(stats);
         analyzeStats(stats);
      end;
```

Now suppose, hypothetically, that ADA were extended with a new generic package, Ada.Persistence, that supports persistent variables of *any* type. The following declaration would instantiate this generic package:

```
      package Persistent_Stats is new Persistence(
          Data_Type => StatsTable);
```

The resulting package Persistent_Stats might provide a function procedure connect that enables a named file to be viewed as a persistent variable of type StatsTable.

The following hypothetical application code illustrates how the file named `stats.dat` would be viewed as a persistent variable, and how the data stored in it might be used:

```
procedure analyzeStats (stats: in out StatsTable) is
-- Print the population density of each country using the data in stats.
begin
   for cy in Country loop
      put(Float(stats(cy).population)/stats(cy).area);
   end loop;
end;

procedure main is
begin
   analyzeStats(
         Persistent_Stats.connect("stats.dat"));
end;
```

The program would no longer need to read data from the file into a transient variable, and consequently would be much more concise.

3.6 Pointers

A *pointer* is a reference to a particular variable. In fact, pointers are sometimes called *references*. The variable to which a pointer refers is called the pointer's *referent*.

A *null pointer* is a special pointer value that has no referent.

In terms of our abstract storage model (Section 3.1), a pointer is essentially the address of its referent in the store. However, each pointer also has a *type*, and the type of a pointer allows us to infer the type of its referent.

EXAMPLE 3.13 C++ pointers

In C++, each value of type "$T*$" is either a pointer to a variable of type T or a null pointer. Consider the following declarations:

```
struct IntNode {
   int elem;
   IntNode* succ;
}
IntNode* p;
```

Each value of type "IntNode*" is a pointer to a variable of type IntNode. If p is a pointer (but not null), the variable access "*p" yields the structure variable to which p points, and "(*p).elem" (or more concisely "p->elem") selects the component elem of that structure variable.

EXAMPLE 3.14 ADA pointers

In ADA, each value of type "**access** T" is either a pointer to a variable of type T or a null pointer.

Consider the following declarations:

```
type IntPointer is access IntNode;
type IntNode is
    record
        elem: Integer;
        succ: IntPointer;
    end record;
p: IntPointer;
```

Each value of type "**access** IntNode" is a pointer to a variable of type IntNode. If p is a pointer (but not null), the variable access "p.**all**" yields the record variable to which p points, and "p.**all**.elem" (or more concisely "p.elem") selects the component elem of that record variable.

3.6.1   Pointers and recursive types

Pointers and heap variables can be used to represent recursive values such as lists and trees, but the pointer itself is a low-level concept. Manipulation of pointers is notoriously error-prone and obscure in its effects, unless performed with care and discipline. For example, consider the C++ assignment "p->succ = q", in the context of the declarations of Example 3.13. Simple inspection of this pointer assignment suggests that a list is being manipulated, but we cannot tell *which* list is being manipulated. We cannot even tell whether the assignment deletes nodes from the list (q points to a later node of the same list), or stitches together parts of two different lists (q points to a node of a different list), or even introduces a cycle which changes the entire data structure (q points to an earlier node of the same list)!

Nevertheless, nearly all imperative languages provide pointers rather than supporting recursive types directly. The reasons for this lie in the semantics and implementation of assignment.

Given the C++ declarations:

```
IntNode* listA;   IntNode* listB;
```

the assignment "listA = listB" updates listA to contain the same pointer value as listB. In other words, listA now points to the same list as listB; the list is **shared** by the two pointer variables. Any selective update of the list pointed to by listA also selectively updates the list pointed to by listB, and *vice versa*, because they are one and the same list.

Suppose that C++ were extended to support list types directly, e.g.:

```
int list listA;   int list listB;
```

Now how should we expect the assignment "listA = listB" to be interpreted? There are two possible interpretations:

- *Copy semantics.* Store in listA a complete copy of the list contained in listB. Any subsequent update of either listA or listB would have no effect on the other. This would be consistent with assignment of structures in C++, and is arguably the most natural interpretation. However, copying of lists is expensive.

- *Reference semantics.* Store in listA a pointer to the list referred to by listB. This interpretation would involve sharing, and would amount to using pointers in disguise. It would be consistent with the assignment of arrays in C++. Another advantage of this interpretation would be ease of implementation.

A possible compromise would be to prohibit selective update of lists. Then assignment could be *implemented* by sharing. In the absence of selective updates, we cannot tell the difference between copy and reference semantics.

Similar points apply to other recursive types in imperative languages.

3.6.2 Dangling pointers

A **dangling pointer** is a pointer to a variable that has been destroyed. Dangling pointers arise from the following situations:

- A pointer to a heap variable still exists after the heap variable is destroyed.
- A pointer to a local variable still exists (e.g., it is stored in a global variable) at exit from the block in which the local variable was declared.

We have seen that some programming languages provide deallocators. Using a deallocator immediately destroys a heap variable; all existing pointers to that heap variable then become dangling pointers.

EXAMPLE 3.15   C++ dangling pointers to a heap variable

Consider the following C++ code:

```
struct Date {
    int y, m, d;
};
Date* dateP = new Date;
dateP->y = 2000;   dateP->m = 1;   dateP->d = 1;
Date* dateQ = dateP;
```

Both dateP and dateQ contain pointers to the same heap variable.

Now the following deallocator:

```
delete dateQ;
```

destroys that heap variable. The two pointers still exist, but they point to unallocated storage cells. Any attempt to inspect or update the dead heap variable:

```
cout << dateP->y;
dateP->y = 2003;
```

will then have unpredictable consequences.

Some programming languages, notably C and C++, allow us to obtain a pointer to a local variable. Such a pointer could still be in existence at exit from the block in which the local variable is declared.

EXAMPLE 3.16   C++ dangling pointer to a local variable

In C++ (or C), a pointer to a local variable can be obtained by using the "&" (address of) operator. The following function f returns a pointer to the local variable fv:

```
int* f () {
    int fv = 42;
    return &fv;
}
```

The following code calls f, which returns a pointer, and then attempts to update the pointer's referent:

```
int* p = f();
*p = 0;
```

But the pointer's referent is fv, and fv's lifetime ended on return from f! Once again, this code will have unpredictable consequences.

Attempting to access a destroyed variable is a serious fault, and one that is difficult to debug. Inspecting a destroyed variable has an unpredictable effect: it might simply inspect unallocated storage cells, or it might inspect storage cells that have since been reallocated to some new variable. (If that new variable has a different type from the destroyed variable, a type error then arises, even if the programming language is otherwise safe from run-time type errors.) Similarly, updating a destroyed variable has an unpredictable, possibly disastrous, effect.

Programming languages like C and C++ accept the risk of such faults as an occupational hazard, and the onus is on programmers to avoid them. Languages like ADA and JAVA, which are intended for highly robust applications, must eliminate or at least minimize the risk of such faults.

JAVA provides no deallocator, so the lifetime of a heap variable continues as long as it is reachable. Moreover, JAVA provides no means to obtain the address of a local variable. So dangling pointers cannot arise in JAVA.

ADA does provide a deallocator, which is a library procedure named Ada.Unchecked_Deallocation. Any compilation unit that uses the deallocator must be prefixed by the clause:

```
with Ada.Unchecked_Deallocation;
```

so at least the unsafe code is prominently flagged. ADA also provides means to obtain a pointer to a local variable, but such a pointer cannot be assigned to a variable with a longer lifetime, so this feature never gives rise to a dangling pointer.

3.7 Commands

Having considered variables and storage, let us now examine commands. A **command** is a program construct that will be **executed** in order to update variables.

Commands are a characteristic feature of imperative, object-oriented, and concurrent languages. Commands are often called *statements*, but we shall avoid using that term in this book because it means something entirely different in logic (and in English).

Commands may be formed in various ways. In this section we shall survey the following fundamental forms of commands. Some commands are primitive:

- *skips*
- *assignments*
- *proper procedure calls.*

Others are composed from simpler commands:

- *sequential commands*
- *collateral commands*
- *conditional commands*
- *iterative commands.*

We will also consider *block commands* in Section 4.4.1, and *exception-handling commands* in Section 9.4.

Here we are primarily interested in the concepts underlying commands, not in their syntactic details. A well-designed imperative, object-oriented, or concurrent language should provide all or most of the above forms of command; it is impoverished if it omits (or arbitrarily restricts) any important forms. Conversely, a language that provides additional forms of command is probably bloated; the additional ones are likely to be unnecessary accretions rather than genuine enhancements to the language's expressive power. For instance, special input/output commands (found in COBOL, FORTRAN, and PL/I) are unnecessary; input/output is better provided by library procedures (as in C, C++, JAVA, and ADA).

All the above commands exhibit *single-entry single-exit* control flow. This pattern of control flow is adequate for most practical purposes. But sometimes it is too restrictive, so modern imperative and object-oriented languages also provide *sequencers* (such as exits and exceptions) that allow us to program *single-entry multi-exit* control flows. We shall study sequencers in Chapter 9.

3.7.1 Skips

The simplest possible kind of command is the **skip** command, which has no effect whatsoever. In C, C++, and JAVA, the skip command is written simply "`;`".

Skips are useful mainly within conditional commands (Section 3.7.6).

3.7.2 Assignments

We have already encountered the concept of **assignment** in Sections 3.1–3.4. The assignment command typically has the form "$V = E$;" (or "$V := E$;" in

ADA). Here E is an expression which yields a value, and V is a variable access (Section 2.6.6) which yields a reference to a variable (i.e., its storage address). The variable is updated to contain the value. (If the variable is a component of a composite variable, the effect is selective update of that composite variable.)

More general kinds of assignment are possible. A **multiple assignment**, typically written in the form "$V_1 = \ldots = V_n = E;$", causes the same value to be assigned to several variables. For example, the following multiple assignment assigns zero to two variables, m and n:

```
m = n = 0;
```

Some programming languages (including C, C++, and JAVA) allow binary operators such as "+" to be combined with assignment. For example, the following command:

```
n += 1;
```

(which is equivalent to "n = n+1;") increments the value of the variable n. This kind of command can be traced back as far as COBOL, in which it is written less concisely as "ADD 1 TO n".

Before we leave assignments, let us study variable accesses in a little more detail. The following ADA commands contain four occurrences of the variable access n:

```
get(n);   n := n + 1;   put(n);
```

Two of these occurrences (underlined) yield the current content of the variable. The other two occurrences yield a reference to the variable, not the value contained in it.

What is the "meaning" of a variable access? We could think of a variable access as yielding a reference to a variable in some contexts, and the current content of that variable in other contexts. Alternatively, we could think of a variable access as always yielding a reference to a variable, but in certain contexts there is an implicit **dereferencing** operation that takes a reference to a variable and yields the current content of that variable. In the above commands, underlining shows where dereferencing takes place.

3.7.3   Proper procedure calls

A **proper procedure call** is a command that achieves its effect by applying a proper procedure (or method) to some arguments. The call typically has the form "$P(E_1, \ldots, E_n);$", where P determines the procedure to be applied, and the expressions $E_1, \ldots, E_n$ are evaluated to determine the arguments. Each argument may be a value or (if the corresponding expression is a variable access) a reference to a variable.

The net effect of a proper procedure call, like any command, is to update variables. The procedure can achieve this effect by updating variables passed as arguments, and/or by updating global variables. (Updating the procedure's local variables will have no net effect, because the lifetime of these variables is just the procedure's activation.)

Proper procedures and parameters will be discussed in greater detail in Sections 5.1.2 and 5.2, respectively.

3.7.4 Sequential commands

Since commands update variables, the order in which commands are executed is important. Much of the programming effort in an imperative language is concerned with control flow, i.e., ensuring that the commands will be executed in a suitable order. This and the following three subsections are concerned with ways of composing commands to achieve different control flows.

Sequential control flow is the most common. A *sequential command* specifies that two (or more) commands are to be executed in sequence. A sequential command might be written in the form:

$$C_1 ; C_2$$

meaning that command C_1 is executed before command C_2. Sequential control flow is available in every imperative language, and is so familiar that it needs no further discussion here.

3.7.5 Collateral commands

Less common is collateral control flow. A *collateral command* specifies that two (or more) commands may be executed in any order. A collateral command might be written in the form:

$$C_1 , C_2$$

where both C_1 and C_2 are to be executed, but in no particular order.

In the following collateral command:

```
m = 7 , n = n + 1;
```

the variables m and n are updated independently, and the order of execution is irrelevant.

An unwise collateral command would be:

```
n = 7 , n = n + 1;
```

The net effect of this collateral command depends on the order of execution. Let us suppose that n initially contains 0.

- If "n = 7" is executed first, n will end up containing 8.
- If "n = 7" is executed last, n will end up containing 7.
- If "n = 7" is executed between evaluation of "n + 1" and assignment of its value to n, n will end up containing 1.

Collateral commands are said to be nondeterministic. A computation is *deterministic* if the sequence of steps it will perform is entirely predictable; otherwise the computation is *nondeterministic*. If we perform a deterministic computation over and over again, with the same input, it will always produce the same output. (This is significant in software testing.) But if we perform a nondeterministic computation over and over again, with the same input, it might produce different output every time.

Although the sequence of steps performed by a nondeterministic computation is unpredictable, its output might happen to be predictable. We call such a computation ***effectively deterministic***. A collateral command is effectively deterministic if no subcommand inspects a variable updated by another subcommand.

3.7.6   Conditional commands

A ***conditional command*** has two or more subcommands, of which exactly one is chosen to be executed.

The most elementary form of conditional command is the ***if-command***, in which a choice between two subcommands is based on a boolean value. The if-command is found in every imperative language, and typically looks like this:

```
if (E) C₁
else C₂
```

If the boolean expression E yields *true*, C_1 is chosen; if it yields *false*, C_2 is chosen.

The if-command is typically abbreviated when the second subcommand is a skip:

```
if (E) C ≡      if (E) C
                else ;
```

The if-command can be generalized to allow choice among several subcommands:

```
if (E₁) C₁
else if (E₂) C₂
...
else if (Eₙ) Cₙ
else C₀
```

Here the boolean expressions $E_1, E_2, \ldots, E_n$ are evaluated *sequentially*, and the first E_i that yields *true* causes the corresponding subcommand C_i to be chosen. If no E_i yields true, C_0 is chosen instead.

The above conditional commands are deterministic: in each case we can predict which subcommand will be chosen. A *nondeterministic* conditional command is also sometimes useful, and might be written in the following notation:

```
if (E₁) C₁
or if (E₂) C₂
...
or if (Eₙ) Cₙ
```

Here the boolean expressions $E_1, E_2, \ldots, E_n$ would be evaluated *collaterally*, and any E_i that yields *true* would cause the corresponding subcommand C_i to be chosen. If no E_i yields *true*, the command would fail.

EXAMPLE 3.17 Nondeterministic if-command

Compare the following JAVA (or C or C++) if-command:

```
if (x >= y) max = x;
else max = y;
```

with the following hypothetical nondeterministic conditional command:

```
if (x >= y) max = x;
or if (x <= y) max = y;
```

The latter has the advantage of making explicit the condition under which "max = y;" may be executed; it also emphasizes that it does not matter which subcommand is chosen in the case that x and y have equal values. So this particular command is effectively deterministic.

Nondeterministic conditional commands tend to be available only in concurrent languages, where nondeterminism is present anyway, but their advantages are not restricted to such languages.

A more general form of conditional command is the **case command**, in which a choice between several subcommands is typically based on an integer (or other) value.

ADA's case command, in its simplest form, looks like this:

```
case E is
    when v₁ =>  C₁
    ...
    when vₙ =>  Cₙ
    when others => C₀
end case;
```

The expression E must yield a value of a discrete primitive type, such as a character, enumerand, or integer. If that value equals one of the values v_i, the corresponding subcommand C_i is chosen. If not, C_0 is chosen. (If "**when others**" is omitted, the compiler checks that $\{v_1, \ldots, v_n\}$ are *all* the possible values of E.) The values $v_1, \ldots, v_n$ must all be distinct, so the choice is deterministic.

EXAMPLE 3.18 ADA case command

In the following ADA case command, choice is based on a value of the enumeration type Month (Example 3.2):

```
today: Date;
name: String(1 .. 3);
...
case today.m is
    when jan =>  name := "JAN";
    when feb =>  name := "FEB";
    when mar =>  name := "MAR";
```

```
      ...
      when dec =>   name := "DEC";
end case;
```

The nearest equivalent to a case command in C, C++, and JAVA is the switch command. However, it has strange features, so we shall defer discussion until Section 11.3.2.

Programming languages vary in the types of values that may be used to control a case (or switch) command. C, C++, and JAVA allow integers only. ADA allows characters, enumerands, integers, or indeed values of any discrete primitive type. In principle, values of any type equipped with an equality test could be allowed. HASKELL does have this generality, allowing primitive values, strings, tuples, or disjoint unions (in fact any values except functions) to be used in case expressions.

3.7.7   Iterative commands

An *iterative command* (commonly known as a *loop*) has a subcommand that is executed repeatedly. The latter subcommand is called the loop *body*. Each execution of the loop body is called an *iteration*.

We can classify iterative commands according to when the number of iterations is fixed:

- *Indefinite iteration:* the number of iterations is not fixed in advance.
- *Definite iteration:* the number of iterations is fixed in advance.

Indefinite iteration is typically provided by the *while-command*, which consists of a loop body C and a boolean expression E (the *loop condition*) that controls whether iteration is to continue. The while-command typically looks like this:

```
while (E) C
```

The meaning of the while-command can be defined by the following equivalence:

```
while (E) C   ≡    if   (E) {
                         C
                         while (E) C
                  }
```

This definition makes clear that the loop condition in a while-command is tested *before* each iteration of the loop body.

Note that this definition of the while-command is recursive. In fact, iteration is just a special form of recursion.

C, C++, and JAVA also have a *do-while-command*, in which the loop condition is tested *after* each iteration:

```
do C while (E);   ≡    C
                       while (E) C
```

A form of loop that allows us to test the loop condition in the *middle* of an iteration has often been advocated. This might hypothetically be written:

$$\textbf{do}\ C_1\ \textbf{while}\ (E)\ C_2 \quad \equiv \quad \begin{array}{l} C_1 \\ \textbf{while}\ (E)\ \{ \\ \qquad C_2 \\ \qquad C_1 \\ \} \end{array}$$

This form subsumes both the while-command (if C_1 is a skip) and the do-while-command (if C_2 is a skip). The argument for including this form of loop in a programming language is undermined by experience, which suggests that this form is still not general enough! In practice, the while-command is perfectly adequate in the great majority of cases, but occasionally we need to write loops with *several* loop conditions in different parts of the loop body. That need is best served by some kind of escape sequencer (see Section 9.3).

EXAMPLE 3.19 Indefinite iteration

The following C while-command reads and prints all the characters in a file f (using a hypothetical function eof(f) that tests whether any characters remain to be read from file f):

```
char ch;
while (! eof(f)) {
    ch = getchar(f);
    putchar(ch);
}
```

The following code does the same thing, except that it assumes that getchar(f) returns NUL when no more characters remain to be read from f:

```
char ch = getchar(f);
while (ch != NUL) {
    putchar(ch);
    ch = getchar(f);
}
```

Note the duplication of the call "getchar(f)".

Hypothetically, we could avoid this duplication by testing the loop condition in the middle:

```
char ch;
do
    ch = getchar(f);
while (ch != NUL)
    putchar(ch);
```

Of course, every C programmer knows how to solve this problem concisely using an ordinary while-command:

```
while ((ch = getchar(f)) != NUL)
    putchar(ch);
```

However, this code uses a trick (incorporating the assignment into the loop condition) that is not available for arbitrary commands.

Now let us consider definite iteration, which concerns loops where the number of iterations is fixed in advance. Definite iteration is characterized by a **control sequence**, a predetermined sequence of values that are successively assigned (or bound) to a **control variable**.

The ADA **for-command** illustrates definite iteration. Its simplest form is:

```
for V in T loop
    C
end loop;
```

The control variable is V, and the control sequence consists of all the values of the type (or subtype) T, in ascending order. In the more explicit form:

```
for V in T range E₁ .. E₂ loop
    C
end loop;
```

the control sequence consists of consecutive values of type T from v_1 through v_2, where v_1 and v_2 are the values yielded by E_1 and E_2, respectively. In either form, T may be any discrete primitive type.

Some programming languages allow the control sequence to be an arbitrary arithmetic progression. This possibility is illustrated by ALGOL68:

```
for V := E₁ to E₂ by E₃ do C
```

Here the control sequence is the longest sequence $v_1, v_1 + v_3, v_1 + 2v_3, \ldots$ that does not properly encompass v_2, where v_1, v_2, and v_3 are the values yielded by E_1, E_2, and E_3, respectively.

The control sequence need not be restricted to an arithmetic progression, nor need it consist of primitive values. For instance, the control sequence could be the components of an array. This is now supported by JAVA.

EXAMPLE 3.20   Definite iteration over an array

Suppose that dates is an array of dates. The following JAVA for-command prints all these dates in order:

```
for (Date date : dates)
    System.out.println(date);
```

This is much more concise, more readable, and less error-prone than the old-style coding:

```
for (int i = 0; i < dates.length; i++)
    System.out.println(dates[i]);
```

In fact, JAVA now supports iteration over an arbitrary *collection*, such as an array, list, or set. This form of for-command is:

```
for (T V : E) C
```

Here V is the control variable, T is its type, and E yields a collection (whose components must be of type T). The control sequence consists of all components of the collection. Iteration over an array or list is deterministic, since the components are visited in order. Iteration over a set is nondeterministic, since the components are visited in no particular order.

The status of the control variable varies between programming languages. In some older languages (such as FORTRAN and PASCAL), it is an ordinary variable that must be declared in the usual way. This interpretation of a for-command with control variable V and loop body C is as follows:

```
determine the control sequence «v₁,...,vₙ»;
V = v₁;  C
...
V = vₙ;  C
```

But this interpretation leads to such awkward questions as the following:

(a) What is V's value after termination of the loop?

(b) What is V's value after a jump or escape out of the loop?

(c) What happens if C itself attempts to assign to V?

In other languages (such as ADA), the for-command itself constitutes a declaration of the control variable; moreover, its value is constant within the loop body. This interpretation of a for-command with control variable V and loop body C is as follows:

```
determine the control sequence «v₁,...,vₙ»;
{ constant V = v₁;  C }
...
{ constant V = vₙ;  C }
```

This makes the for-command completely self-contained, and neatly answers all the questions posed above:

(a) V has no value outside the loop: the scope of its declaration is the loop body only.

(b) Ditto.

(c) C cannot assign to V, since V is in fact a constant!

Finally, note that the for-command of C and C++ (and the old-style for-command of JAVA) is nothing more than syntactic shorthand for a while-command, and thus supports *indefinite* iteration:

```
for (C₁ E₁; E₂)   ≡   C₁
    C₂                while (E₁) {
                          C₂
                          E₂;
                      }
```

3.8 Expressions with side effects

The primary purpose of evaluating an expression is to yield a value. In some imperative and object-oriented languages, however, it is possible that evaluating an expression has the ***side effect*** of updating variables. Let us now consider expressions that have side effects.

3.8.1   Command expressions

Suppose that we are required to write an expression to evaluate the polynomial:

$$c_n x^n + \ldots + c_2 x^2 + c_1 x + c_0$$

given x, n, and an array of coefficients c_i. Any solution must be either recursive or iterative. A recursive solution would imply defining and calling a recursive function, which we might prefer to avoid. An iterative solution meets the problem that, while iterative *commands* are common, iterative *expressions* are not. So we need some kind of expression that contains a command: a ***command expression***.

EXAMPLE 3.21   Command expression

The following hypothetical command expression would evaluate our polynomial:

```
{
    float p = c[n];
    for (int i = n-1; n >= 0; n--)   p = p*x + c[i];
    p
}
```

Here we are assuming C-like notation. After elaborating the declarations and executing the commands after "{", the subexpression just before "}" would be evaluated to determine the value yielded by the command expression.

In ADA, the body of a function procedure is, in effect, a command expression. This allows assignments and iteration to be used in computing function results, but also makes it possible for a function call to have side effects (perhaps unintended).

In fact, any kind of command expression makes side effects possible. As it happens, the command expression of Example 3.21 updated only the local variables p and i, so it had no side effects. But now consider the following example.

EXAMPLE 3.22   Expressions with side effects

Consider the C function call "getchar(f)", which reads a character from file f and returns that character. This function call has a side effect on the file variable f. Consequently, the following code:

```
enum Gender {female, male};
Gender g;
if (getchar(f) == 'F')   g = female;
else if (getchar(f) == 'M')   g = male;
else ...
```

is misleading: *two different characters* are read and compared with 'F' and 'M'.

Side effects may introduce nondeterminism into expression evaluation. Consider any expression of the form "$E_1 \otimes E_2$", where $\otimes$ is a binary operator, and where E_1 has a side effect that affects the evaluation of E_2, or *vice versa*; the result of evaluating this expression depends on the order in which the subexpressions E_1 and E_2 are evaluated. Some programming languages allow subexpressions to be evaluated in any order, giving rise to nondeterminism. Other languages avoid such nondeterminism by insisting that subexpressions are evaluated from left to right.

In summary, side effects in expressions tend to make programs hard to understand. Undisciplined use of side effects is bad programming practice.

3.8.2   Expression-oriented languages

An ***expression-oriented*** language is an imperative or object-oriented language in which no distinction is made between expressions and commands. Evaluating any expression yields a value and may also have side effects. ALGOL68 and ML (and C-like languages, to some extent) are examples of expression-oriented languages.

One benefit of this design is to avoid duplication between expressions and commands. An expression-oriented language does not need both function procedures and proper procedures. Nor does it need both conditional expressions and conditional commands.

In an expression-oriented language the assignment "$V = E$" could be defined to yield the value of E, together with the side effect of storing that value in the variable yielded by V. Since the assignment is itself an expression, we can also write "$V_1 = (V_2 = E)$"; in other words, we get multiple assignment free. (However, some expression-oriented languages define their assignments differently. For example, an ML assignment expression actually yields the 0-tuple ().)

There is no obvious result for a skip or loop. Typically an expression-oriented language defines a skip or loop to yield a neutral value such as 0 or ().

Thus expression-oriented languages achieve a certain simplicity and uniformity by eliminating the distinction between expressions and commands. So why do conventional imperative languages still retain this distinction? The justification is an issue of programming style. Although expressions may have side effects in conventional languages, the use of side effects by programmers is informally deprecated. (Indeed the designers of ADA initially attempted, unsuccessfully, to prohibit side effects.) On the other hand, expression-oriented languages positively encourage the use of side effects, leading to a cryptic programming style that is well exemplified by the C-like languages:

```
while ((ch = getchar(f)) != NUL)
    putchar(ch);
```

3.9   Implementation notes

In this section we briefly examine how compilers allocate storage for global, local, and heap variables.

Each variable occupies storage space throughout its lifetime. That storage space must be allocated at the start of the variable's lifetime. The storage space may be deallocated at the end of the variable's lifetime, or at any time thereafter.

The amount of storage space occupied by each variable depends on its type (see Section 2.7). For this reason the compiler must know the type of each variable, because the compiler cannot predict the actual values it will contain. In most programming languages, each variable's type must be declared explicitly, or the compiler must be able to infer its type.

3.9.1   Storage for global and local variables

A *global variable*'s lifetime is the program's entire run-time. A fixed storage space can therefore be allocated to each global variable.

A *local variable*'s lifetime is an activation of the block in which the variable is declared. The lifetimes of local variables are nested, so storage space can be allocated to them in a *stack*, as we shall see shortly.

Recall the program outlined in Example 3.9. The variables x1 and x2 are local to main, so their lifetime is the program's entire run-time; in other words, x1 and x2 occupy storage throughout the program's run-time. The variables y1 and y2 are local to procedure P, so their lifetime is an activation of P; thus storage must be allocated for y1 and y2 when P is called, and deallocated when P returns. Similarly, storage must be allocated for the local variable z when procedure Q is called, and deallocated when Q returns. The net effect of all this is that storage space allocated to local variables expands and contracts stack-fashion. This is illustrated in Figure 3.10.

In general, storage for local variables is allocated on a stack of *activation frames*. Each activation frame contains enough space for the local variables of a particular procedure. An activation frame is pushed on to the stack when a procedure is called, and popped off the stack when the procedure returns.

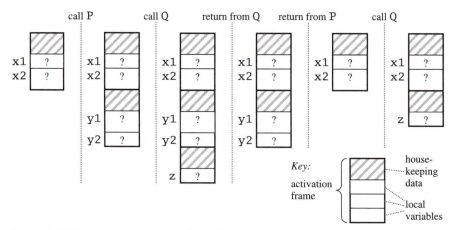

Figure 3.10 Storage for local variables (Example 3.9).

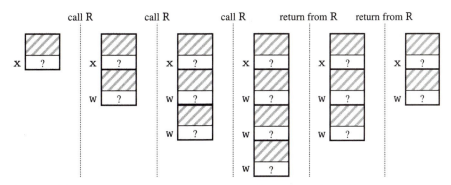

Figure 3.11 Storage for local variables of a recursive procedure (Example 3.10).

Storage allocation on a stack is economical: at any time, storage is allocated only to variables local to currently-active procedures. Moreover, storage can be allocated to local variables of recursive procedures in exactly the same way; this is illustrated in Figure 3.11 for the program outlined in Example 3.10.

3.9.2   Storage for heap variables

A *heap variable*'s lifetime starts when the heap variable is created and ends when it is destroyed or becomes unreachable. Since heap variables can be created and destroyed at arbitrary times, there is no pattern in their lifetimes analogous to the nested lifetimes of local variables.

Heap variables occupy a storage region called the *heap*. At any given time, the heap contains all currently-live heap variables (in no particular order) interspersed with unallocated storage space. When a new heap variable is to be created, some unallocated storage space is allocated to it. When a heap variable is to be destroyed, the storage space occupied by that heap variable reverts to being unallocated; in other words, that storage space is recycled. To keep track of the allocated and unallocated storage space we need a *heap manager*, part of the run-time system.

If the programming language has no deallocator, the heap manager must additionally be capable of finding and recycling unreachable heap variables. (Otherwise heap storage would eventually be exhausted.) This process is called *garbage collection*.

The effect of garbage collection is illustrated in Figure 3.12 for the program of Example 3.11. After the node containing 5 is removed from the odds and primes lists, the garbage collection algorithm will eventually discover that that node is unreachable, and will then recycle it as unallocated space.

The garbage collector must visit all heap variables in order to find all those that have become unreachable. In real applications there might be thousands or even millions of heap variables. Garbage collection is therefore time-consuming. However, garbage collection is far more reliable in practice than placing the onus on programmers to destroy their own unreachable heap variables. Programmers often forget to do so, resulting in uneconomical use of heap storage. Worse

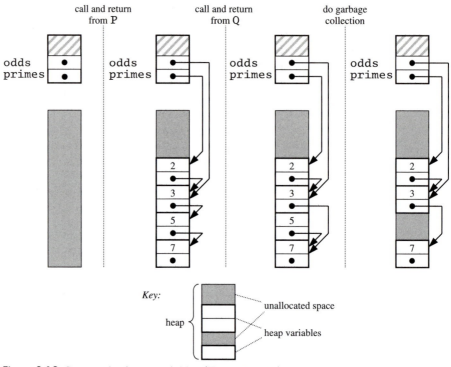

Figure 3.12 Storage for heap variables (Example 3.11).

still, programmers sometimes inadvertently destroy heap variables that are still reachable, a logical error that gives rise to dangling pointers.

3.9.3 Representation of dynamic and flexible arrays

An array indexing operation will have unpredictable consequences if the value used to index the array is out-of-range. To avoid this, in general, we need a run-time range check on the indexing value.

A *static array*'s index range is known at compile-time, so the compiler can easily generate object code to perform the necessary range check.

However, a *dynamic* or *flexible array*'s index range is known only at run-time. The array's index range must therefore be stored as part of the array's representation.

This is illustrated in Figure 3.13(a) for the ADA Vector type of Example 3.5. Each Vector array's representation includes its lower and upper bounds as well as its components.

If the programming language fixes all arrays' lower bounds at zero, it is sufficient for each array's representation to include its length as well as its components. This is illustrated in Figure 3.13(b) for the JAVA **float**[] type of Example 3.6.

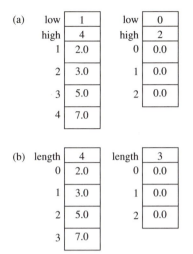

Figure 3.13 Representation of (a) ADA arrays of type Vector (Example 3.5); (b) JAVA arrays of type float[] (Example 3.6) (with tag fields omitted).

Summary

In this chapter:

- We have introduced a simple storage model that allows us to understand the behavior of variables.
- We have explored the behavior of simple and composite variables, in particular the difference between total and selective update of a composite variable, and the distinction between copy semantics and reference semantics.
- We have compared and contrasted the lifetimes of global, local, heap, and persistent variables.
- We have studied pointers, their use in representing recursive types, and the danger of dangling pointers.
- We have surveyed the forms of command found in programming languages, focusing on conceptual issues rather than syntactic differences.
- We have seen sources and consequences of side effects in expressions, and looked at expression-oriented languages that make no distinction between expressions and commands.
- We have seen how storage is allocated for global, local, and heap variables, and how dynamic and flexible arrays are represented.

Further reading

The notion that distinctions between persistent and transient data types should be avoided received much attention in the 1980s. For a survey of research on this topic, see ATKINSON and BUNEMAN (1987).

The nondeterministic conditional command discussed in Section 3.7.6, and a corresponding nondeterministic iterative command, were designed by DIJKSTRA (1976) to support the particular programming discipline that he advocated.

The design of loops with multiple exits attracted much attention in the 1970s. See, for example, ZAHN (1974).

Exercises

Exercises for Section 3.1

3.1.1 Which types of values are storable values in your favorite programming language?

Exercises for Section 3.2

3.2.1 Which types of variables are simple variables in your favorite programming language?

Exercises for Section 3.3

3.3.1 Systematically analyze the composite variables of your favorite programming language. Which types of variables are composite variables? How are they selectively updated? Can they also be totally updated? Are static, dynamic, and/or flexible arrays supported?

*3.3.2 In some programming languages (such as C, C++, and ADA), strings are treated as arrays of characters. Compare the consequences of this decision when a string variable is: (a) a static array; (b) a dynamic array; (c) a flexible array. In each case, can string operations such as comparison and concatenation be defined in the language itself?

Exercises for Section 3.4

3.4.1 Does your favorite programming language adopt copy semantics or reference semantics? If it adopts copy semantics, does it allow you to achieve the effect of reference semantics? If it adopts reference semantics, does it allow you to achieve the effect of copy semantics?

Exercises for Section 3.5

3.5.1 Systematically analyze the lifetimes of variables of your favorite programming language. Are global, local, and/or heap variables supported? What determines the lifetime of each variable?

3.5.2 Consider the following C program:

```
void main () {
    int f;
    f = fac(3);
}

int factorial (int n) {
    int p, i;
    p = 1;
    for (i = 2; i <= n; i++)
        p *= i;
    return p;
}
```

(a) Make a diagram, similar to Figure 3.6, showing the lifetimes of the local variables in this program. (Note that the formal parameter n is, in effect, a local variable of the `factorial` function.)

(b) Repeat with the above version of the factorial function replaced by the following recursive version:

```
int factorial (int n) {
    if (n > 1) return n * factorial(n-1);
    else return 1;
}
```

3.5.3 Complete the following ADA program (or rewrite it in your own favorite programming language):

```
procedure main is

    type IntNode;
    type IntList is access IntNode;
    type IntNode is
        record
            elem: Integer;
            succ: IntList;
        end record;

    IntList ints := null;

    procedure add (i: Integer) is
    -- Insert a node containing i into ints, keeping it sorted.
    begin
        ...
    end;

    procedure remove (i: Integer) is
    -- Remove the first node containing i from ints, or do nothing
    -- if there is no such node.
    begin
        ...
    end;

begin
    add(6);  add(2);  add(9);  add(5);
    remove(9);  remove(6);
end;
```

Make a diagram showing the lifetimes of the heap variables and of ints.

3.5.4 Summarize your favorite programming language's *transient* data types and *persistent* data types. Is there any overlap between them?

**3.5.5 Redesign your favorite programming language to eliminate all specific input/ output features. Instead, allow the programmer to create persistent variables (of any type) in much the same way as heap variables. What types would be suitable replacements for your language's existing persistent data types? Choose an existing program that contains a lot of (binary) input/output code, and rewrite it in your redesigned language.

Exercises for Section 3.6

3.6.1 Does your favorite programming language support pointers, either explicitly or implicitly? Can dangling pointers arise, and (if so) how?

**3.6.2 Choose an imperative language (such as C, C++, or ADA) that provides pointer types. Redesign that language to abolish pointer types, instead allowing programmers to define recursive types directly. Consider carefully the issue of copy semantics vs reference semantics.

Exercises for Section 3.7

3.7.1 Systematically analyze the forms of commands of your favorite programming language. Compare these with the forms discussed in Section 3.7. Are any relevant forms missing in your language? Are any exotic forms provided, and are they essential?

3.7.2 Design an extension to your favorite programming language that would add list types (allowing declarations such as "odds: **list of Integer;"). Lists are *not* to be selectively updatable. Provide suitable list constructions, including one for generating arithmetic progressions. Replace the existing for-command by one where the control sequence is specified by a list.

*3.7.3 We can gain insight into the nature of commands by stating equivalences between different commands. For example, if "C_1 ; C_2" is a sequential command and "C_1 , C_2" is a collateral command, we can state:

$$C \; ; \; \textbf{skip} \equiv C$$
$$C_1 \; , \; C_2 \quad \equiv \; C_2 , \; C_1$$

State as many other equivalences as you can discover. (Of course, "C_1 ; C_2" is *not* equivalent to "C_2 ; C_1".)

3.7.4 Recursively define the C command "**do** C **while** (E)", similarly to the way in which the while-command is recursively defined in Section 3.7.7.

*3.7.5 Consider the questions (a), (b), and (c), posed at the end of Section 3.7.7, concerning the interpretation of a for-command with control variable V and loop body C. How does your favorite programming language answer these questions?

Exercises for Section 3.8

*3.8.1 Some programmers assert that side effects in expressions are a useful feature of a programming language. Develop arguments both *for* and *against* this assertion.

*3.8.2 Non-void functions in C and C++, and ADA function procedures, not only return results but also may have side effects. Formulate restrictions on such functions that would eliminate side effects. Bear in mind that any such restrictions should, ideally, be enforceable by the compiler. Do your restrictions significantly reduce the language's expressive power?

Exercises for Section 3.9

3.9.1 Using diagrams similar to Figures 3.10 and 3.11, show the allocation of storage to the local variables of the programs in Exercise 3.5.2(a) and (b).

3.9.2 Using diagrams similar to Figures 3.10–3.12, show the allocation of storage to the local and heap variables of the program in Exercise 3.5.3.

Chapter 4

Bindings and scope

Every programming language enables programmers to write declarations that bind identifiers to entities such as values (constants), variables, and procedures. This concept is both fundamental and pragmatically important. Well-chosen identifiers help to make a program easy to understand. More importantly, binding an identifier to an entity in one place, and using that identifier to denote the entity in many other places, helps to make the program easy to modify: if the entity is to be changed, only its declaration must be modified, not the many parts of the code where the entity is used.

In this chapter we shall study:

- *bindings* and *environments*, which capture the associations between identifiers and the entities they denote;
- *scope, block structure*, and *visibility*, which are concerned with which parts of the program are affected by each declaration;
- *declarations*, which are program constructs that bind identifiers to entities;
- *blocks*, which are program constructs that delimit the scopes of declarations.

4.1 Bindings and environments

The expression "n+1" uses the identifier n; the expression "f(n)" uses the identifiers f and n. If identifiers occur in an expression, the expression cannot be understood in isolation; its meaning depends on the declarations of these identifiers elsewhere in the program. Similarly, the meaning of a command such as "m = n + 1;" or "print(m/2);" depends on the declarations of identifiers that occur in that command.

Many programming languages allow the same identifier to be declared in several parts of the program. The interpretation of an expression or command using that identifier then depends on where the expression or command appears in the program.

EXAMPLE 4.1   Effects of declarations

Consider the ADA expression "n+1", which uses the identifier n.

- If n is declared as follows:

```
n: constant Integer := 7;
```

then n denotes the integer seven, so the expression "n+1" is evaluated by adding one to seven.

- If n is declared as follows:

n: Integer;

then n denotes an integer variable, so the expression "n+1" is evaluated by adding one to the current value of that variable.

We can understand the effects of declarations by invoking the concepts of *bindings, environments* (explained in this section), and *scope* (explained in the next section).

A **binding** is a fixed association between an identifier and an entity such as a value, variable, or procedure. A declaration produces one or more bindings. The constant declaration in Example 4.1 binds n to the value 7. The variable declaration in Example 4.1 binds n to a newly created variable.

An **environment** (or *name space*) is a set of bindings. Each expression or command is interpreted in a particular environment, and all identifiers used in the expression or command must have bindings in that environment. It is possible that expressions and commands in different parts of the program will be interpreted in different environments.

Usually at most one binding per identifier is allowed in any environment. An environment is then a partial mapping from identifiers to entities.

| EXAMPLE 4.2 | Environments |

Consider the following ADA program skeleton:

```
procedure p is

    z: constant Integer := 0;
    c: Character;

    procedure q is
        c: constant Float := 3.0e6;
        b: Boolean;
    begin
(2)     ...
    end q;

    begin
(1)     ...
    end p;
```

The environment at point (1) is:

```
{   c → a character variable,
    p → a proper procedure,
    q → another proper procedure,
    z → the integer 0  }
```

The environment at point (2) is:

{   b → a boolean variable,
    c → the real number 3.0×10^6,
    p → a proper procedure,
    q → another proper procedure,
    z → the integer 0   }

A ***bindable*** entity is one that may be bound to an identifier. Programming languages vary in the kinds of entity that are bindable:

- C's bindable entities are types, variables, and function procedures.
- JAVA's bindable entities are values, local variables, instance and class variables, methods, classes, and packages.
- ADA's bindable entities include types, values, variables, procedures, exceptions, packages, and tasks.

4.2   Scope

The ***scope*** of a declaration is the portion of the program text over which the declaration is effective. Similarly, the ***scope*** of a binding is the portion of the program text over which the binding applies.

In some early programming languages, the scope of each declaration was the whole program. In modern languages, the scope of each declaration is influenced by the program's syntactic structure, in particular the arrangement of *blocks*.

4.2.1   Block structure

A ***block*** is a program construct that delimits the scope of any declarations within it. Each programming language has its own forms of blocks:

- The blocks of a C program are block commands ({ ... }), function bodies, compilation units (source files), and the program as a whole.
- The blocks of a JAVA program are block commands ({ ... }), method bodies, class declarations, packages, and the program as a whole.
- The blocks of an ADA program are block commands (**declare** ... **begin** ... **end;**), procedure bodies, packages, tasks, protected objects, and the program as a whole.

In Section 4.4 we shall look at the syntactic aspects of blocks. In this section we are concerned only with the language's ***block structure***, which is the arrangement of blocks in the program text. In particular, we are interested in whether blocks can be *nested* within one another.

Figures 4.1, 4.2, and 4.3 contrast three kinds of block structure. Each box represents a block. The scopes of some declarations are indicated by shading.

In a language with ***monolithic block structure*** (Figure 4.1), the only block is the whole program, so the scope of every declaration is the whole program. In other words, all declarations are global. This is exemplified by older versions of COBOL.

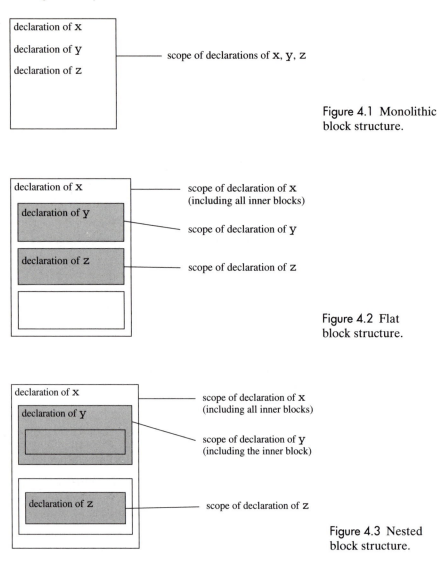

Figure 4.1 Monolithic block structure.

Figure 4.2 Flat block structure.

Figure 4.3 Nested block structure.

Monolithic block structure is the simplest possible block structure, but it is far too crude, particularly for writing large programs. Programmers must take care to ensure that all declarations have distinct identifiers. This is very awkward for large programs being developed by a team of programmers.

In a language with *flat block structure* (Figure 4.2), the program is partitioned into several non-overlapping blocks. This is exemplified by FORTRAN, in which procedure bodies may not overlap, but each procedure body acts as a block. A variable can be declared inside a particular procedure body, and its scope is that procedure body. The scope of each global variable (and the scope of each procedure itself) is the whole program.

Although flat block structure is an improvement on monolithic block structure, it still has disadvantages. One is that every procedure and every global variable must have a distinct identifier. Another is that any variable that cannot be local to a particular procedure is forced to be global, and thus have the whole program as its scope, even if it is accessed by only a couple of procedures.

In a language with ***nested block structure*** (Figure 4.3), blocks may be nested within other blocks. This is exemplified by the many ALGOL-like languages. C has a restrictive nested block structure, in which function bodies may not overlap, but block commands may be nested freely within function bodies. JAVA has a less restrictive nested block structure, in which method bodies and inner classes may be nested within a class. ADA has an unrestricted nested block structure, in which block commands, procedure bodies, packages, and so on may be freely nested one within another.

The advantage of nested block structure is that a block can be located anywhere an identifier has to be declared.

4.2.2 Scope and visibility

Consider all the occurrences of identifiers in a program. We must distinguish two different kinds of identifier occurrences:

- A ***binding occurrence*** of identifier I is an occurrence where I is bound to some entity X.

- An ***applied occurrence*** of I is an occurrence where use is made of the entity X to which I has been bound. At each such applied occurrence we say that I ***denotes*** X.

In a well-formed program, each applied occurrence of I corresponds to exactly one binding occurrence of I.

For example, the occurrence of the identifier n in the ADA declaration "n: **constant** Integer := 7;" is a binding occurrence, where n is bound to 7; thereafter, the two occurrences of n in the expression "n*(n-1)" are applied occurrences, at which n denotes 7.

When a program contains more than one block, it is possible for the same identifier I to be declared in different blocks. In general, I will denote a different entity in each block. This allows programmers to choose freely which identifiers to declare and use within a given block, without worrying about whether (by coincidence) the same identifiers might have been declared and used in other blocks.

But what happens if the same identifier is declared in two *nested* blocks? This possibility, which is illustrated in Figure 4.4, is a consequence of nested block structure.

Consider two nested blocks, such that the inner block lies within the scope of a declaration of identifier I in the outer block:

- If the inner block *does not* contain a declaration of I, then applied occurrences of I both inside and outside the inner block correspond to the same

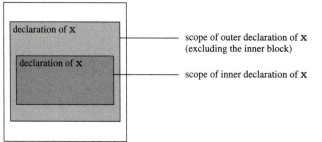

Figure 4.4 Hiding.

declaration of *I*. The declaration of *I* is then said to be **visible** throughout the outer and inner blocks.

- If the inner block *does* contain a declaration of *I* (as in Figure 4.4), then all applied occurrences of *I* inside the inner block correspond to the inner, not the outer, declaration of *I*. The outer declaration of *I* is then said to be **hidden** by the inner declaration of *I*.

Recall Example 4.2. The constant declaration of c inside procedure q hides the variable declaration of c inside procedure p. All the other declarations in the main program, however, are visible inside the procedure.

In this subsection we have made certain simplifying assumptions, which we shall later examine in detail:

- that the programming language is statically scoped (see Section 4.2.3);
- that the scope of each declaration is the entire enclosing block (see Section 4.3.8);
- that there is no overloading (see Section 8.3).

4.2.3   Static vs dynamic scoping

So far we have assumed that the programming language is *statically scoped*. In this subsection we explain what that means, and what is the alternative.

EXAMPLE 4.3   Static vs dynamic scoping

Consider the following outline of a program in a C-like language:

```
      const int s = 2;

      int f (int x) {
(1)       return s * x;
      }

      void p (int y) {
(2)       print(f(y));
      }
```

```
      void q (int z) {
          const int s = 3;
(3)       print(f(z));
      }
```

The result of the function call "f(...)" depends on how the language interprets the applied occurrence of s at point (1) in the body of function f:

- The body of function f could be executed in the environment of the *function definition*. In that environment s would denote 2, so "f(...)" would multiply the value of its argument by 2, regardless of where the function is called.

- The body of function f could be executed in the environment of the *function call*. Then the function call "f(y)" at point (2) would multiply the value of y by 2, since at that point s denotes 2. On the other hand, the function call "f(z)" at point (3) would multiply the value of z by 3, since at that point s denotes 3.

A language is **statically scoped** if the body of a procedure is executed in the environment of the procedure's definition. Thus we can decide at compile-time which binding occurrence of an identifier corresponds to a given applied occurrence.

A language is **dynamically scoped** if the body of a procedure is executed in the environment of the procedure call. That environment varies from one procedure call to another, so we cannot decide until run-time which binding occurrence of an identifier corresponds to a given applied occurrence.

With static scoping, we can determine the binding occurrence that corresponds to a given applied occurrence of identifier I, just by examining the program text. We find the smallest block containing the applied occurrence of I that also contains a binding occurrence of I; the latter is the binding occurrence we seek. The association between applied occurrences and binding occurrences is fixed. In Example 4.3, therefore, we could safely replace the applied occurrence of s in the body of function f by the literal 2.

With dynamic scoping, on the other hand, the binding occurrence that corresponds to a given applied occurrence of identifier I depends on the program's dynamic flow of control. Whenever the entity denoted by I is needed, we find the most recently elaborated declaration of I that is inside a currently active block.

There is a conflict between dynamic scoping and static typing. In Example 4.3, suppose that the global declaration of s were replaced by "char[] s = "...";". With static scoping, the type error in "return s*x;" would be detected by compile-time type checks. With dynamic scoping, the function call "f(z)" at point (3) would be unaffected, but the function call "f(y)" at point (2) would result in a type error. The compiler could predict that type error only if the program's flow of control were predictable – which is not the case, in general.

For this reason, dynamically scoped languages (such as SMALLTALK and early versions of LISP) are also dynamically typed. The conflict between dynamic scoping and static typing illustrates a more general problem with dynamic scoping, namely the fact that it tends to make code harder to understand. If a procedure P accesses a nonlocal constant or variable, or calls a nonlocal procedure, the effect will depend on where *P* was called. Indeed, *P* might be used in ways never anticipated by its programmer.

Nearly all programming languages (including C, C++, JAVA, and ADA) are statically scoped. In this book we shall generally assume static scoping, except in a few places where dynamic scoping is explicitly mentioned.

Let *X* be a program construct such as a command or expression. An applied occurrence of an identifier *I* is said to be *free* in *X* if there is no corresponding binding occurrence of *I* in *X*. In Example 4.3, the applied occurrences of s and x are free in "`return s*x;`"; but only the applied occurrence of s is free in the function definition as a whole, since the function definition contains a binding occurrence of x (as a formal parameter).

4.3 Declarations

Having considered bindings, environments, and scope, let us now examine the program constructs that produce bindings. A **declaration** is a construct that will be **elaborated** to produce bindings.

All declarations produce bindings; some have side effects such as creating variables. We shall use the term **definition** for a declaration whose *only* effect is to produce bindings.

Each programming language has several forms of simple declarations, covering all kinds of entities that are bindable in the language. Nearly all languages support the following:

- *type declarations*
- *constant declarations*
- *variable declarations*
- *procedure definitions.*

Some languages additionally support exception declarations, package declarations, class declarations, and so on.

Declarations may also be composed from simpler declarations:

- *collateral declarations*
- *sequential declarations*
- *recursive declarations.*

4.3.1   Type declarations

A **type declaration** binds an identifier to a type. We can distinguish two kinds of type declaration. A **type definition** binds an identifier to an existing type. A **new-type declaration** binds an identifier to a new type that is not equivalent to any existing type.

Type definitions fit with structural equivalence of types, while new-type declarations fit with name equivalence of types. (See Section 2.5.2.)

Some languages, such as C, C++, and HASKELL, support both type definitions and new-type declarations. These languages also adopt a mixture of structural and name equivalence.

EXAMPLE 4.4 C++ type declarations

In C++ (and C), **typedef** introduces a type definition that binds an identifier to an existing type. The following type definition:

```
typedef char* Alpha;
```

binds Alpha to the existing type whose values are pointers to characters. Thereafter Alpha is structurally equivalent to "**char***", so the types of the following variables are equivalent:

```
Alpha s1;
char* s2;
```

Thus we may assign s1 to s2, or *vice versa*.

On the other hand, the keywords **enum**, **struct**, and **union** all introduce type declarations that bind identifiers to new types. The following type declarations:

```
struct Book {Alpha title, int edn};
struct Author {Alpha name, int age};
```

bind Book and Author to two types that are not equivalent to each other (although their values happen to be structurally similar). Thus we may not assign a Book value to an Author variable, or *vice versa*.

ADA consistently adopts name equivalence, and every type declaration creates a new type.

EXAMPLE 4.5 ADA type declarations

The following ADA type declaration:

```
type Alpha is array (1 .. 32) of Character;
```

binds Alpha to a new array type. The following type declarations:

```
type Book is
    record
        title: Alpha;
        edn: Integer;
    end record;

type Author is
    record
        name: Alpha;
        age: Integer;
    end record;
```

bind Book and Author to two non-equivalent record types. Thus we may not assign a Book value to an Author variable, or *vice versa*.

4.3.2   Constant declarations

A **constant declaration** binds an identifier to a constant value.

A constant declaration typically has the form "**const** I = E;", and binds the identifier I to the value of the expression E; the constant's type is determined by the type of E. An alternative form is "**const** T I = E;", which states explicitly that the constant's type is T.

In some programming languages E must be an expression that can be evaluated at compile-time. E may be expressed in terms of literals, other constants, operators, and so on.

In the more modern languages (including C++, JAVA, and ADA), E is an arbitrary expression. In particular, E may access variables or parameters, in which case it must be evaluated at run-time.

EXAMPLE 4.6   ADA constant declarations

Consider the following ADA constant declarations:

```
pi: constant Float := 3.1416;
twice_pi: constant Float := 2.0 * pi;
```

The value bound to `pi` is given by a literal. The value bound to `twice_pi` is given by an expression that is evaluated at compile-time.

But now consider the constant declaration in the following function body:

```
function area (x, y, z: Float) return Float is
   s: constant Float := (x + y + z)/2.0;
begin
   return sqrt(s*(s-x)*(s-y)*(s-z));
end;
```

The value bound to `s` is given by an expression that can be evaluated only at run-time, since the values of the parameters x, y, and z are known only when the procedure is called.

4.3.3   Variable declarations

A **variable declaration**, in its simplest form, creates a single variable and binds an identifier to that variable. Most programming languages also allow a variable declaration to create several variables and bind them to different identifiers.

A **variable renaming definition** binds an identifier to an *existing* variable. In other words, it creates an *alias*. ADA supports variable renaming definitions, but few other languages do so.

EXAMPLE 4.7   ADA variable declarations

The following ADA variable declaration:

```
count: Integer;
```

creates an integer variable, and binds the identifier count to that variable. The following variable declaration:

```
count: Integer := 0;
```

does likewise, but also initializes the variable to zero.

The following ADA variable renaming definition:

```
pop: Integer renames population(state);
```

binds the identifier pop to an existing integer variable, namely a component of the array variable population. In other words, pop is now an alias for the component variable population(state). Subsequently, whenever desired, pop can be used to access this component variable concisely and efficiently:

```
pop := pop + 1;
```

4.3.4   Procedure definitions

A **_procedure definition_** binds an identifier to a _procedure_. In most programming languages, we can bind an identifier to either a function procedure or a proper procedure.

EXAMPLE 4.8   C++ procedure definitions

The following C++ procedure definition:

```
bool even (int n) {
    return (n % 2 == 0);
}
```

binds the identifier even to a function procedure that tests whether its integer argument is even.

The following C++ procedure definition:

```
void double (int& n) {
    n *= 2;
}
```

binds the identifier double to a proper procedure that doubles its argument, an integer variable.

4.3.5   Collateral declarations

We now consider how declarations may be composed. The choice is between _collateral_ composition, _sequential_ composition, and _recursive_ composition. Each of these has a different impact on the scope of bindings. We shall look at these forms of composition in this and the following two subsections.

A **_collateral declaration_** composes subdeclarations that are to be elaborated independently of each other. These subdeclarations may not use bindings produced by each other. The collateral declaration merges the bindings produced by its subdeclarations. Collateral declarations are uncommon in imperative and object-oriented languages, but they are common in functional and logic languages.

EXAMPLE 4.9   ML collateral declarations

The following ML collateral value definition:

```
val e  = 2.7183
and pi = 3.1416
```

combines independent subdeclarations of the identifiers e and pi. This collateral declaration produces the following bindings:

```
{   e → the real number 2.7183,
   pi → the real number 3.1416  }
```

The scope of these bindings starts at the *end* of the collateral declaration. Thus we could not extend the collateral declaration as follows:

```
val e  = 2.7183
and pi = 3.1416
and twicepi = 2 * pi   (* illegal! *)
```

Instead we would employ a sequential declaration:

```
val e  = 2.7183
and pi = 3.1416;
val twicepi = 2 * pi
```

4.3.6   Sequential declarations

A **sequential declaration** composes subdeclarations that are to be elaborated one after another. Each subdeclaration can use bindings produced by any *previous* subdeclarations, but not those produced by any *following* subdeclarations. The sequential declaration merges the bindings produced by its subdeclarations. Sequential declarations are supported by most imperative and object-oriented languages.

EXAMPLE 4.10   ADA sequential declarations

In the following ADA sequential declaration:

```
count: Integer := 0;

procedure bump is
begin
   count := count + 1;
end;
```

the identifier count is declared in the first subdeclaration and used in the second. The sequential declaration produces the following bindings:

{ count → a character variable,
  bump → a proper procedure }

ML has sequential declarations too. The problem noted in Example 4.9 was easily solved by a sequential declaration in which the collateral declaration of e and pi is followed by a declaration of twicepi.

4.3.7 Recursive declarations

A ***recursive declaration*** is one that uses the bindings that it produces itself. Such a construct is important because it enables us to define recursive types and procedures.

Some older languages (such as FORTRAN and COBOL) did not support recursion at all, seriously reducing their expressiveness. It was once commonly argued that recursion is inherently inefficient. This argument is no longer valid, since modern computer architectures support recursion easily. All modern programming languages do support recursion, although they usually restrict it to type and procedure definitions.

C, C++, and ADA are broadly similar in this respect. A single procedure definition may be recursive. A sequence of procedure definitions can be made mutually recursive, but this requires special means since a sequential declaration forces every identifier to be declared before it is used. Likewise, a single type declaration may be recursive, and a sequence of type declarations can be made mutually recursive.

EXAMPLE 4.11   ADA recursive type declarations

Consider the following ADA sequence of type declarations:

```
(1) type Int_Node;
(2) type Int_List is access Int_Node;
(3) type Int_Node is
          record
              elem: Integer;
              succ: Int_List;
          end record;
```

Declaration (1) is an *incomplete type declaration*: it binds Int_Node to an unknown type. Declaration (2) binds Int_List to a type whose values will be pointers to Int_Node variables. Declaration (3) completes the binding of Int_Node, here to a record type with an Int_List component. Thus the two types are mutually recursive.

An incompletely-declared type identifier such as Int_Node may be used *only* to declare a pointer type as in (2). This guarantees that every recursive type in ADA is defined in terms of pointers.

EXAMPLE 4.12   C recursive function definitions

The following C (or C++) function definition is recursive:

```
void print_decimal (int n) {
   if (n < 0) {
     print('-');
     print_decimal(-n);
   } else if (n >= 10) {
     print_decimal(n/10);
     print(n % 10 + '0');
   } else
     print(n + '0');
}
```

Now consider the following C (or C++) function definitions:

(1) `void parse_expression ();`

(2)
```
void parse_primary () {
     if (acceptable('(')) {
       parse_expression();
       accept(')');
     } else
       parse_variable();
}
```

(3)
```
void parse_expression () {
     parse_primary();
     while (acceptable('+'))
         parse_primary();
}
```

Declaration (1) binds `parse_expression` to an unknown function. Declaration (2) binds `parse_primary` to a function that calls `parse_expression`. Declaration (3) completes the binding of `parse_expression`, here to a function that calls `parse_primary`. Thus the two functions are mutually recursive.

4.3.8 Scopes of declarations

Collateral, sequential, and recursive declarations differ in their influence on scope:

- In a *collateral declaration*, the scope of each subdeclaration extends from the end of the collateral declaration to the end of the enclosing block.
- In a *sequential declaration*, the scope of each subdeclaration extends from the end of that subdeclaration to the end of the enclosing block.
- In a *recursive declaration*, the scope of every subdeclaration extends from the start of the recursive declaration to the end of the enclosing block.

These rules are illustrated most clearly by ML value declarations, which come in all these forms: see Figure 4.5.

4.4 Blocks

In Section 4.2.1 we defined a *block* to be a program construct that delimits the scope of any declarations within it. Let us now examine blocks in more detail.

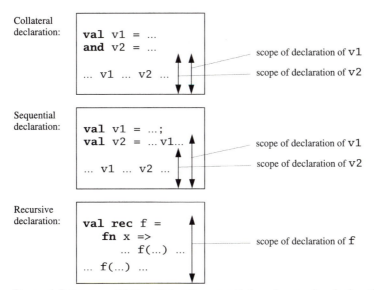

Figure 4.5 Scopes of ML collateral, sequential, and recursive declarations.

If we allow a command to contain a local declaration, we have a *block command*. If we allow an expression to contain a local declaration, we have a *block expression*. As we shall see, blocks can appear in other forms too.

4.4.1   Block commands

A ***block command*** is a form of command that contains a local declaration (or group of declarations) D and a subcommand C. The bindings produced by D are used only for executing C.

In C, C++, and JAVA, a block command has the form "{ D C }". In ADA, a block command has the form "**declare** D **begin** C **end**". In each case, the subcommand C is executed in an environment in which the bindings produced by D override the outside environment.

EXAMPLE 4.13   JAVA block command

Suppose that x and y are integer variables, and their contents are to be sorted such that x contains the smaller integer. We can easily implement this using an auxiliary variable, declared locally to a block command. In JAVA:

```
if (x > y) {
   int z = x;
   x = y;
   y = z;
}
```

The scope of z is just the block command, and the lifetime of the variable denoted by z is the activation of the block command.

4.4.2   Block expressions

A ***block expression*** is a form of expression that contains a local declaration (or group of declarations) *D* and a subexpression *C*. The bindings produced by *D* are used only for evaluating *E*.

In C, C++, and ADA, the body of a function procedure is, in effect, a block expression. The net effects of executing the function body are to yield a value (the function result), and possibly to cause side effects. This is just like evaluating an ordinary expression.

HASKELL has a block expression, of the form "**let** *D* **in** *E*", that may be placed wherever any other expression may be placed. The subexpression *E* is evaluated in an environment in which the bindings produced by *D* override the outside environment.

EXAMPLE 4.14   HASKELL and C++ block expressions

Suppose that variables a, b, and c contain the lengths of a triangle's three sides. The following HASKELL block expression yields the area of that triangle:

```
let
    s = (a + b + c)/2.0
in
    sqrt(s*(s-a)*(s-b)*(s-c))
```

To achieve the same effect in C++ (or ADA), we must first declare a function somewhere in the program:

```
float area (float x, y, z) {
    float s = (x + y + z)/2.0;
    return sqrt(s*(s-x)*(s-y)*(s-z));
}
```

and then call that function:

```
... area(a, b, c) ...
```

4.4.3   The Qualification Principle

We may summarize the preceding subsections as follows:

- A *block command* is a *command* containing a local declaration *D* and a *subcommand C*, the bindings produced by *D* being used only for *executing C*.

- A *block expression* is an *expression* containing a local declaration *D* and a *subexpression E*, the bindings produced by *D* being used only for *evaluating E*.

Note the analogy between block expressions and block commands. In principle, we can take this analogy further, by adding blocks to syntactic categories other than expressions and commands. The ***Qualification Principle*** states:

It is possible to include a block in any syntactic category, provided that the constructs in that syntactic category specify some kind of computation.

One very useful example of the Qualification Principle is this:

- A *block declaration* is a *declaration* containing a local declaration D and a *subdeclaration* D', the bindings produced by D being used only for *elaborating* D'.

Block declarations as such are unusual in programming languages. However, they do appear, in a disguised form, as packages and classes (Chapter 6). The essence of a block declaration is that it distinguishes between private (local) and public subdeclarations.

EXAMPLE 4.15   JAVA classes and ADA packages viewed as block declarations

Consider a large module that declares numerous entities (say A, B, C, X, Y, Z), but only a few of them (say A, B, C) are to be public, i.e., made visible outside the module, the remaining entities being auxiliary. Use of a block declaration allows the module's interface to be kept narrow by limiting the number of bindings visible outside the module.

This module could be implemented as a JAVA class:

```
class ... {
    ... //  public declarations of A, B, C
    ... //  private declarations of X, Y, Z
}
```

or as an ADA package:

```
package ... is
    ... -- public declarations of A, B, C
end;

package body ... is
    ... -- private declarations of X, Y, Z
end;
```

In each case, the bindings produced by the private declarations are used only for elaborating the public declarations. Only the bindings produced by the latter are available outside the class or package.

Summary

In this chapter:

- We have studied the concepts of bindings and environments.
- We have studied block structure, scope and visibility of bindings, and the difference between static and dynamic binding.
- We have surveyed various forms of declarations found in programming languages, and the scope of the bindings that they produce.

- We have surveyed various forms of blocks found in programming languages, in particular block expressions and block commands, and we have formulated the Qualification Principle.

Further reading

The Qualification Principle is stated and explained in TENNENT (1981).

Exercises

Exercises for Section 4.1

4.1.1 What is the environment at each numbered point in the following C (or C++) program?

```
    int n;

(1) void zero () {
(2)     n = 0;
    }

(3) void inc (int d) {
(4)     n += d;
    }

(5) void main (int argc, char** argv) {
(6)     ...
    }
```

4.1.2 What is the environment at each numbered point in the following ADA program?

```
    procedure main is

        max: constant Integer := 999;

(1)     type Nat is range 0 .. max;

(2)     m, n: Nat;

(3)     function func (n: Nat) return Nat is
        begin
(4)         ...
        end func;

(5)     procedure proc (m: Nat) is
(6)       n: constant Integer := 6;
        begin
(7)         ...
        end proc;

        begin
(8)         ...
        end main;
```

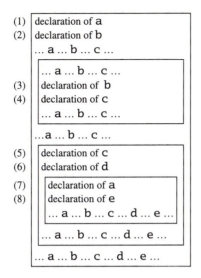

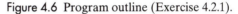

Figure 4.6 Program outline (Exercise 4.2.1).

Exercises for Section 4.2

4.2.1 Consider the program outline of Figure 4.6, which shows binding occurrences ("declaration of I") and applied occurrences ("... I ...") of some identifiers. What is the exact scope of each declaration? For each applied occurrence, state whether it is legal, and if so identify its associated binding occurrence. Assume that the programming language is: (a) ADA; (b) C (or C++); (c) your favorite language.

4.2.2 Consider the following outline of a program in a C-like language:

```
int add (int i) {
    return i + d;
}

void p () {
    const int d = 1;
(1)    print(add(20));
}

void q () {
    const int d = 2;
(2)    print(add(20));
}
```

(a) If the language is dynamically scoped, what would be printed at points (1) and (2)?

(b) If the language is statically scoped, what would happen?

Exercises for Section 4.3

4.3.1 In some languages all variables must be initialized in their declarations, perhaps using a default initial value for each type (such as *false* for booleans, 0 for integers, *null* for pointers). What are the advantages and disadvantages of compulsory initialization of variables?

4.3.2 List all the forms of type definition in C. Redesign this part of C's syntax so that there is only one form of type definition, say "**type** *I* = *T*;".

4.3.3 In HASKELL not only can we define a new function, such as:

```
cosine x = ...
```

we can also define a synonym for an existing function:

```
cos = cosine
```

How can we define a synonym for an existing function (a) in C (or C++); (b) in ADA? If necessary, suggest an extension to each language to make such synonyms easier to define.

Exercises for Section 4.4

*4.4.1 Systematically analyze the declarations and blocks of your favorite programming language. (a) What is the language's block structure? (b) Which entities are bindable? (c) What forms of declaration does the language provide? Compare these with the forms discussed in Section 4.3: are any relevant kinds missing? are any exotic kinds provided, and are they essential? (d) What are the language's scope and visibility rules? (e) What forms of blocks does it provide?

Chapter 5

Procedural abstraction

Abstraction is a mode of thought by which we concentrate on general ideas rather than on specific manifestations of these ideas. Abstraction is the whole basis of philosophy and mathematics, and is also fruitful in many other disciplines, including computer science.

In systems analysis, abstraction is the discipline by which we concentrate on essential aspects of the problem at hand, and ignore all inessential aspects. For example, in designing an air traffic control system we concentrate on details that are relevant to the working of the system (such as the aircraft's type and call sign), and ignore the numerous irrelevant details (such as the aircraft's color and external markings, the crew's names, and the passengers' names).

In programming, abstraction alludes to the distinction we make between *what* a program unit does and *how* that program unit works. This enables a separation of concerns between the programmers who use the program unit and the programmer who implements it. Furthermore, we can use low-level program units to implement higher-level program units, and in turn use these to implement still higher-level program units. In fact, we can introduce as many levels of abstraction as desired. Separation of concerns and multiple levels of abstraction are essential tools in building large software systems.

Procedural abstraction is concerned with the simplest program units, namely procedures. In this chapter we shall study:

- *proper procedures* and *function procedures*;
- *parameters* and *arguments*;
- how procedure calls and parameters are implemented.

In Chapter 6 we shall study methods, which are the counterparts of procedures in object-oriented languages.

5.1 Function procedures and proper procedures

A *procedure* is an entity that embodies a computation. In particular, a *function procedure* embodies an expression to be evaluated, and a *proper procedure* embodies a command to be executed. The embodied computation is to be performed whenever the procedure is called.

A procedure is often defined by one programmer (the *implementer*) and called by other programmers (the *application programmers*). These programmers have different viewpoints. The application programmers are concerned only with the procedure's *observable behavior*, in other words the outcome of calling the procedure. The implementer is concerned with how that outcome is to be achieved, in other words the choice of algorithm.

The effectiveness of procedural abstraction is enhanced by parameterization. We shall study parameter passing in detail in Section 5.2.

Note that the *methods* of object-oriented languages are essentially procedures by another name. The only difference is that every method is associated with a class or with a particular object. We shall consider methods in detail in Chapter 6.

5.1.1   Function procedures

A *function procedure* (or simply *function*) embodies an expression to be evaluated. When called, the function procedure will yield a value known as its *result*. The application programmer observes only this result, not the steps by which it was computed.

A C or C++ function definition has the form:

$$T\ I\ (FPD_1, \dots, FPD_n)\ B$$

where I is the function's identifier, the FPD_i are *formal parameter* declarations, T is the result type, and B is a block command called the function's **body**. B must contain at least one return of the form "**return** E;", where E is an expression of type T. The function procedure will be called by an expression of the form "$I(AP_1, \dots, AP_n)$", where the AP_i are *actual parameters*. This function call causes B to be executed, and the first return to be executed within B determines the result.

EXAMPLE 5.1   C++ function definition

The following C++ function definition:

```
float power (float x, int n) {
   float p = 1.0;
   for (int i = 1; i <= n; i++)
      p *= x;
   return p;
}
```

binds power to a function procedure with two formal parameters (x and n) and result type **float**. This computes the nth power of x, assuming that n is nonnegative. Note the use of local variables and iteration to compute the function's result.

The following C++ function definition uses recursion instead:

```
float power (float x, int n) {
   if (n == 0)
      return 1.0;
   else
      return x * power(x, n-1);
}
```

An ADA function definition has a slightly different form:

function *I* (*FPD*₁; ...; *FPD*ₙ) **return** *T* **is**
   D
begin
   C
end;

The function's body consists of the local declaration(s) *D* and the sequential command *C*. In effect, the function's body is a block command.

C, C++, and ADA function definitions are clumsy. The function's body is a block command, so programmers are almost encouraged to define functions with side effects. The function's result is determined by executing a return, but the end of the function's body could be reached without executing any return, in which case the function would fail. The fundamental problem is that the function's body must yield a value, like an expression, but syntactically it is a command.

A more natural design is for the function's body to be syntactically an expression. This is the case in functional languages such as ML and HASKELL.

EXAMPLE 5.2   HASKELL function definition

The following HASKELL function definition:

```
power (x: Float, n: Int) =
    if n = 0
    then 1.0
    else x * power(x, n-1)
```

binds power to a function procedure.

This HASKELL function returns the same result as the C++ functions of Example 5.1. However, its body is an expression.

Function definitions are easier to understand when the function's body is an expression. However, this benefit might be gained at the expense of efficiency or expressiveness. The first C++ function of Example 5.1 uses local variables and an iterative command; the second function instead uses recursion, but it might be less efficient in terms of storage space. For the HASKELL function of Example 5.2 there is no alternative to using recursion. (See Exercise 5.1.2.)

In general, a function call can be understood from two different points of view:

- The *application programmer's* view of the function call is that it will map the arguments to a result of the appropriate type. Only this mapping is of concern to the application programmer.

- The *implementer's* view of the function call is that it will evaluate or execute the function's body, using the function's formal parameters to access the corresponding arguments, and thus compute the function's result. Only the algorithm encoded in the function's body is the implementer's concern.

For example, consider the two C++ functions of Example 5.1. The application programmer's view of the first function is that it will map each pair (x, n) to the result x^n; the implementer's view is that it will compute its result by iteration. The application programmer's view of the second function is that it will map each pair (x, n) to the result x^n; the implementer's view is that it will compute its result by recursion. The application programmer's views of the two functions are the same; the implementer's views are different.

Function procedures are most commonly constructed in function definitions; indeed in most programming languages this is the only way to construct them. However, the functional languages such as ML and HASKELL separate the distinct concepts of function construction and binding. For instance, in HASKELL:

```
\(I: T) -> E
```

is an expression that yields a function procedure. Its formal parameter is I (of type T), and its body is E.

EXAMPLE 5.3   HASKELL function construction

The following HASKELL expression:

```
\(x: Float) -> x^3
```

yields a function that implements the cube function. The conventional function definition:

```
cube (x: Float) = x^3
```

is just an abbreviation for the value definition:

```
cube =
        \(x: Float) -> x^3
```

in which the value bound to cube happens to be a function.

Consider the following integration function, whose formal parameter f is the function to be integrated:

```
integral (a: Float, b: Float, f: Float->Float) = ...
```

This is supposed to compute the direct integral of f (x) over the interval [a..b]. When we call integral, the actual parameter corresponding to f can be any expression of type Float->Float, as in the following:

```
... integral(0.0, 1.0, cube) ...
... integral(0.0, 1.0, \(x:Float)->x*x) ...
```

5.1.2 Proper procedures

A **proper procedure** embodies a command to be executed, and when called will update variables. The application programmer observes only these updates, not the steps by which they were effected.

A C or C++ proper procedure definition has the form:

> **void** *I* (*FPD*₁, ..., *FPD*ₙ) *B*

where *I* is the function's identifier, the *FPD*ᵢ are the formal parameter declarations, and *B* is a block command called the procedure's **body**. The procedure will be called by a command of the form "*I*(*AP*₁, ..., *AP*ₙ);", where the *AP*ᵢ are actual parameters. This procedure call causes *B* to be executed.

Note that a C or C++ proper procedure definition is just a special case of a function definition, distinguished only by the fact that the result type is **void**.

EXAMPLE 5.4   **C++ proper procedure definition**

Consider the following C++ procedure definition:

```
void sort (int a[], int l, int r) {
  int minpos;   int min;
  for (int i = l; i < r; i++) {
    minpos = i;   min = a[minpos];
    for (int j = i+1; j <= r; j++) {
      if (a[j] < a[i]) {
        minpos = j;   min = a[minpos];
      }
    if (minpos != i) {
      a[minpos] = a[i];   a[i] = min;
    }
  }
}
```

This binds the identifier `sort` to a proper procedure. The application programmer's view is that the outcome of a procedure call like "`sort(nums, 0, n-1);`" will be to sort the values in `nums[0]`, ..., `nums[n-1]` into ascending order. The implementer's view is that the procedure's body employs the selection-sort algorithm.

The implementer might later substitute a more efficient algorithm, such as Quicksort:

```
void sort (int a[], int l, int r) {
  int p;
  if (r > l) {
    partition(a, l, r, p);
    sort(a, l, p-1);
    sort(a, p+1, r);
  }
}
```

However, the application programmer's view would be unchanged.

An ADA proper procedure definition has the form:

> **procedure** *I* (*FPD*₁; ...; *FPD*ₙ) **is**
>   *D*
> **begin**
>   *C*
> **end**;

The procedure's body consists of the local declaration(s) *D* and the sequential command *C*. In effect, the procedure's body is a block command.

EXAMPLE 5.5   ADA proper procedure definition

Consider the following ADA procedure definition:

```
procedure sort (a: in out Int_Array;
                l, r: in Integer) is
   p: Integer;
begin
   if r > l then
      partition(a, l, r, p);
      sort(a, l, p-1);
      sort(a, p+1, r);
   end if;
end;
```

In general, a procedure call can be understood from two different points of view:

- The *application programmer's* view of the procedure call is its final outcome, which is that certain variables are updated. Only this outcome is of concern to the application programmer.

- The *implementer's* view of the procedure call is that it will execute the procedure's body, using the procedure's formal parameters to access the corresponding arguments. Only the algorithm encoded in the procedure's body is the implementer's concern.

5.1.3   The Abstraction Principle

We may summarize the preceding subsections as follows:

- A *function procedure* abstracts over an *expression*. That is to say, a function procedure has a body that is an expression (at least in effect), and a function call is an expression that will yield a result by evaluating the function procedure's body.

- A *proper procedure* abstracts over a *command*. That is to say, a proper procedure has a body that is a command, and a procedure call is a command that will update variables by executing the proper procedure's body.

Thus there is a clear analogy between function and proper procedures. We can extend this analogy to construct other types of procedures. The ***Abstraction Principle*** states:

It is possible to design procedures that abstract over any syntactic category, provided only that the constructs in that syntactic category specify some kind of computation.

For instance, a variable access refers to a variable. We could imagine designing a new type of procedure that abstracts over variable accesses. Such a procedure, when called, would yield a variable. In fact, such procedures do exist, and are called ***selector procedures***:

- A *selector procedure* abstracts over a *variable access*. That is to say, a selector procedure has a body that is a variable access (in effect), and a selector call is a variable access that will yield a variable by evaluating the selector procedure's body.

Selector procedures are uncommon in programming languages, but they are supported by C++.

EXAMPLE 5.6   C++ selector procedure

Consider the following C++ function procedure:

```
typedef ... Queue;   // queues of integers

int first (Queue q);
    // Return the first element of q.
```

Using this function procedure, we can fetch the first element of a given queue, but we cannot *update* the first element:

```
int i = first(qA);   // fetches the first element of qA
first(qA) = 0;       // illegal!
```

Instead, we could make `first` a selector procedure:

```
int& first (Queue q);
    // Return a reference to the first element of q.
```

Now we could call this selector procedure as follows:

```
int i = first(qA);   // fetches the first element of qA
first(qA) = 0;       // updates the first element of qA
```

Because a selector call's result is a variable (as opposed to the variable's current value), the result variable can be either inspected or updated, as illustrated above.

Suppose that the implementer chooses to represent each queue by an array:

```
struct Queue {
  int elems[10];
  int front, rear, length;
};
```

Then the selector procedure would be implemented as follows:

```
int& first (Queue q) {
  return q.elems[q.front];
}
```

Here the variable access "`q.elems[q.front]`" determines the result variable. The selector call "`first(qA)`" therefore yields the variable `qA.elems[qA.front]`.

Suppose instead that the implementer chooses to represent queues by linked lists:

```
struct QNode {
    int elem;
    struct QNode * succ;
};
struct Queue {
    struct QNode * front;
    int length;
};
```

the selector procedure would be implemented as follows:

```
int& first (Queue q) {
    return q.front->elem;
}
```

Here the variable access "q.front->elem" determines the result variable. The selector call "first(qA)" therefore yields the variable qA.front->elem.

All programming languages provide not only a repertoire of built-in operators (such as "+" and "*"), but also a means (function definitions) to extend that repertoire. On the other hand, most programming languages provide only a fixed repertoire of built-in selectors (such as "$V.I$" for records and "$V[E]$" for arrays), with no means to extend that repertoire. This is an anomaly. The Abstraction Principle helps us to design programming languages that are both more regular and more expressive.

Another direction in which we might push the Abstraction Principle is to consider whether we can abstract over *declarations*. This is a much more radical idea, but it has been adopted in some modern languages such as C++, JAVA, and ADA. We get a construct called a ***generic unit***:

- A *generic unit* abstracts over a *declaration*. That is to say, a generic unit has a body that is a declaration, and a generic instantiation is a declaration that will produce bindings by elaborating the generic unit's body.

This is a very powerful concept, which we shall study in Chapter 7.

5.2 Parameters and arguments

If we simply make an expression into a function procedure, or make a command into a proper procedure, we generally end up with a procedure that will always perform the same computation whenever called. (But see Exercise 5.2.1.)

To realize the full power of the procedure concept, we need to *parameterize* procedures with respect to entities on which they operate.

EXAMPLE 5.7   Parameterizing a C++ function procedure

Throughout this example, assume the following type definition:

```
typedef float Vector[];
// A Vector value represents a vector in n-dimensional space.
```

Consider the following parameterless C++ function:

```
const int n = 3;
Vector v = {3.0, 4.0, 0.0};

float length () {
  float s = 0.0;
  for (int i = 0; i < n; i++)
     s += v[i]*v[i];
  return sqrt(s);
}
```

The function call "length()" always performs the same computation, computing the length of the particular vector v in three-dimensional space. Thus the function is almost useless at it stands.

We can make the function far more useful by parameterizing it with respect to v:

```
const int n = 3;

float length (Vector v) {
  float s = 0.0;
  for (int i = 0; i < n; i++)
     s += v[i]*v[i];
  return sqrt(s);
}
```

Now we can write function calls, such as "length(v1)" and "length(v2)", to compute the lengths of different vectors.

We can make the function still more useful by parameterizing it with respect to n:

```
float length (Vector v, int n) {
  float s = 0.0;
  for (int i = 0; i < n; i++)
     s += v[i]*v[i];
  return sqrt(s);
}
```

Now we can write function calls, such as "length(v1, 2)" and "length(v2, 3)", to compute the distances of different points from the origin in two-dimensional space, three-dimensional space, or indeed any-dimensional space.

An *argument* is a value or other entity that is passed to a procedure. An *actual parameter* is an expression (or other construct) that yields an argument. A *formal parameter* is an identifier through which a procedure can access an argument.

In all programming languages, first-class values may be passed as arguments. In most languages, either variables or pointers to variables may be passed as arguments. In some languages, either procedures or pointers to procedures may be passed as arguments. (In C, C++, and ADA, pointers to variables and pointers to procedures are themselves first-class values.)

When a procedure is called, each formal parameter will become associated, in some sense, with the corresponding argument. The nature of this association is called a *parameter mechanism*.

Different programming languages provide a bewildering variety of parameter mechanisms, e.g., value parameters, result parameters, value-result parameters, constant parameters, variable parameters, procedural parameters, and functional parameters. Fortunately, all these parameter mechanisms can be understood in terms of two basic concepts:

- A *copy parameter mechanism* binds the formal parameter to a local variable that contains a copy of the argument.
- A *reference parameter mechanism* binds the formal parameter directly to the argument itself.

In the following subsections we examine these two concepts.

5.2.1   Copy parameter mechanisms

A **copy parameter mechanism** allows for a value to be copied into and/or out of a procedure. The formal parameter *FP* denotes a local variable of the procedure. A value is copied into *FP* on calling the procedure, and/or is copied out of *FP* (to an argument variable) on return. The local variable is created on calling the procedure, and destroyed on return.

There are three possible copy parameter mechanisms:

- A **copy-in parameter** (also known as a *value parameter*) works as follows. When the procedure is called, a local variable is created and initialized with the argument value. Inside the procedure, that local variable may be inspected and even updated. (However, any updating of the local variable has no effect outside the procedure.)
- A **copy-out parameter** (also known as a *result parameter*) is a mirror-image of a copy-in parameter. In this case the argument must be a variable. When the procedure is called, a local variable is created but not initialized. When the procedure returns, that local variable's final value is assigned to the argument variable.
- A **copy-in-copy-out parameter** (also known as a *value-result parameter*) combines copy-in and copy-out parameters. In this case also, the argument must be a variable. When the procedure is called, a local variable is created and initialized with the argument variable's current value. When the procedure returns, that local variable's final value is assigned back to the argument variable.

C, C++, and JAVA support only copy-in parameters; ADA supports all three copy parameter mechanisms.

EXAMPLE 5.8   ADA copy parameter mechanisms

Consider the following ADA procedures:

```
type Vector is array (1 .. n) of Float;

procedure add  (v, w: in Vector;
                     sum: out Vector) is
```

```
(1) begin
      for i in 1 .. n loop
        sum(i) := v(i) + w(i);
      end loop;
(2) end;

    procedure normalize (u: in out Vector) is
(3)   s: Float := 0.0;
    begin
      for i in 1 .. n loop
        s := s + u(i)**2;
      end loop;
      s := sqrt(s);
      for i in 1 .. n loop
        u(i) := u(i)/s;
      end loop;
(4) end;
```

Also assume that the keyword **in** signifies a copy-in parameter, that **out** signifies a copy-out parameter, and that **in out** signifies a copy-in-copy-out parameter.

If a, b, and c are Vector variables, the procedure call "add(a, b, c);" works as follows. At point (1), local variables named v and w are created, and the values of a and b are assigned to v and w, respectively. Also at point (1), a local variable named sum is created but not initialized. The procedure's body then updates sum. At point (2), the final value of sum is assigned to c.

The procedure call "normalize(c);" works as follows. At point (3), local variable u is created, and the value of c is assigned to u. The body of normalize then updates u. At point (4), the final value of u is assigned to c.

The copy parameter mechanisms display a pleasing symmetry, as shown in Table 5.1. Since they are based on the concept of assignment, however, the copy parameter mechanisms are unsuitable for types that lack assignment (such as limited types in ADA). Another disadvantage is that copying of large composite values is expensive.

5.2.2   Reference parameter mechanisms

A *reference parameter mechanism* allows for the formal parameter *FP* to be bound directly to the argument itself. This gives rise to a simple uniform semantics of parameter passing, suitable for all types of values in the programming language

Table 5.1   Summary of copy parameter mechanisms (*FP* stands for the formal parameter).

Parameter mechanism	Argument	Effect at procedure call	Effect at return
Copy-in parameter	value	$FP := $ argument value;	–
Copy-out parameter	variable	–	argument variable $:= FP$;
Copy-in-copy-out parameter	variable	$FP := $ argument value;	argument variable $:= FP$;

(not just first-class values). Reference parameter mechanisms appear under several guises in programming languages:

- In the case of a ***constant parameter***, the argument must be a value. *FP* is bound to the argument value during the procedure's activation. Thus any inspection of *FP* is actually an indirect inspection of the argument value.

- In the case of a ***variable parameter***, the argument must be a variable. *FP* is bound to the argument variable during the procedure's activation. Thus any inspection (or updating) of *FP* is actually an indirect inspection (or updating) of the argument variable.

- In the case of a ***procedural parameter***, the argument must be a procedure. *FP* is bound to the argument procedure during the called procedure's activation. Thus any call to *FP* is actually an indirect call to the argument procedure.

These three parameter mechanisms are summarized in Table 5.2. Note how closely they resemble one another.

C does not support reference parameter mechanisms directly, but we can achieve the effect of variable parameters using pointers. If a C function has a parameter of type $T*$ (pointer to T), the corresponding argument must be a pointer to a variable of type T. The caller can obtain a pointer to any variable V by an expression of the form "$\&V$". Using such a pointer, the called function can inspect or update the variable V.

C++ does support variable parameters directly. If the type of a formal parameter is $T\&$ (reference to T), the corresponding argument must be a variable of type T.

ADA supports both constant and variable parameters.

EXAMPLE 5.9   ADA reference parameter mechanisms

Consider once more the ADA procedures of Example 5.8. But this time assume that the keyword **in** signifies a constant parameter, and that **out** or **in out** signifies a variable parameter.

Suppose that a, b, and c are Vector variables. The procedure call "add(a, b, c);" works as follows. At point (1), v and w are bound to the values of a and b, respectively; and sum is bound to the variable c. The body of add thus indirectly inspects a and b, and indirectly updates c.

Table 5.2   Summary of reference parameter mechanisms (*FP* stands for the formal parameter).

Parameter mechanism	Argument	Effect at procedure call	Effect at return
Constant parameter	value	bind *FP* to argument value	–
Variable parameter	variable	bind *FP* to argument variable	–
Procedural parameter	procedure	bind *FP* to argument procedure	–

The procedure call "`normalize(c);`" works as follows. At point (3), u is bound to the variable c. The body of `normalize` thus indirectly inspects and updates c.

Notice that nothing happens at points (2) and (4). Notice also that no copying takes place. The formal parameters v and w are treated as constants, so they cannot be updated; therefore the corresponding arguments a and b cannot be indirectly updated.

Examples 5.8 and 5.9 illustrate the fact that constant and variable parameters together provide similar expressive power to the copy parameter mechanisms, i.e., the ability to pass values into and out of a procedure. The choice between reference and copy parameter mechanisms is an important decision for the language designer.

Reference parameters have simpler semantics, and are suitable for all types of value (including procedures, which in most programming languages cannot be copied). Reference parameters rely on indirect access to argument data, so copy parameters are more efficient for primitive types, while reference parameters are usually more efficient for composite types. (In a distributed system, however, the procedure might be running on a processor remote from the argument data, in which case it may be more efficient to copy the data and then access it locally.)

ADA mandates copy parameter mechanisms for primitive types, but allows the compiler to choose between copy and reference parameter mechanisms for composite types. Since the type `Vector` of Examples 5.8 and 5.9 is composite, parameters of that type may be implemented either by copying or by reference. Either way, a procedure call such as "`add(a, b, c);`" will have the same effect, except possibly for a difference in efficiency.

A disadvantage of variable parameters is that aliasing becomes a hazard. *Aliasing* occurs when two or more identifiers are simultaneously bound to the same variable (or one identifier is bound to a composite variable and a second identifier to one of its components). Aliasing tends to make programs harder to understand and harder to reason about.

EXAMPLE 5.10   C++ aliasing

Consider the following C++ procedure with three variable parameters:

```
void pour (float& v1, float& v2, float& v) {
// Given two pots containing v1 and v2 liters of water, respectively,
// determine the effect of pouring v liters from the first pot into the second.
    v1 -= v;
    v2 += v;
}
```

Suppose that variables x, y, and z currently have values 4.0, 6.0, and 1.0, respectively. Then the call "`pour(x, y, z);`" would update x to 3.0 and y to 7.0, as we would expect. But now the call "`pour(x, y, x);`" would update x to 0.0 but leave y at 7.0, unexpectedly. To understand the behavior of the latter call, note that both v1 and v are aliases of x, and hence of each other.

Why is this behavior unexpected? When we read the procedure's body, we tend to assume that v1 and v denote distinct variables, so the assignment "v1 -= v;" updates only v1. Nearly always, the assumption that distinct identifiers denote distinct variables is justified. But very occasionally (in the presence of aliasing), this assumption is not justified, and then we are taken by surprise.

Aliasing most commonly arises from variable parameters, but can also arise from variable renaming definitions (Section 4.3.3). If a programming language has either of these constructs, the onus is on programmers to avoid harmful aliasing. (Note that the compiler cannot always detect aliasing. The aliasing in "pour(x, y, x);" is rather obvious. But in "pour(a[i], a[j], a[k]);", the compiler cannot know whether aliasing exists unless it can predict the values of i, j, and k.)

5.2.3   The Correspondence Principle

You might have noticed a correspondence between certain parameter mechanisms and certain forms of declaration. For example:

- A constant parameter corresponds to a constant definition. In each case, an identifier is bound to a first-class value.
- A variable parameter corresponds to a variable renaming definition. In each case, an identifier is bound to an existing variable.
- A copy-in parameter corresponds to an (initialized) variable declaration. In each case, a new variable is created and initialized, and an identifier is bound to that variable.

In the interests of simplicity and regularity, a language designer might wish to eliminate all inessential differences between declarations and parameter mechanisms. The **Correspondence Principle** states:

For each form of declaration there exists a corresponding parameter mechanism.

Note that the converse is not always true. For example, no programming language could reasonably have declarations that correspond to the copy-out and copy-in-copy-out parameter mechanisms.

If a programming language complies with the Correspondence Principle, programmers benefit for the following reason. Suppose that a program contains a procedure P, and a (nonlocal) declaration of an entity X on which P depends. Then we can parameterize P with respect to X, provided that the programming language supports the parameter mechanism that corresponds to the declaration of X. Since different calls to P can supply different arguments for X, the procedure is more flexible than it was originally.

HASKELL complies well with the Correspondence Principle, if we restrict our attention to first-class values. Its constant parameter mechanism corresponds directly to its value definition. (Recall that HASKELL functions are first-class values, and so need no special declarations or parameter mechanisms.)

C++ complies with the Correspondence Principle to a very limited extent. C++'s initialized variable declaration is shown beside the corresponding copy-in

Table 5.3   C++ declarations and parameter mechanisms (formal parameter declarations and actual parameters are underlined).

Declaration	Parameter mechanism

Initialized variable declaration:
 	
$T\ I = E\ ;$
	Copy-in parameter:
	
	void P ($\underline{T\ I}$) {
	
	. . .
	
	}
	Call:
	
	$P(\underline{E})\ ;$

(No equivalent)	Variable parameter:
	
	void P ($\underline{T\ \&\ I}$) {
	
	. . .
	
	}
	Call:
	
	$P(\underline{V})\ ;$

parameter mechanism in Table 5.3. In each case, the identifier I is bound to a newly-created variable initialized with the value of the expression E. In one case, E is provided by the variable declaration. In the other case, E is provided by the procedure call. A weakness of C++ is that it supports only two parameter mechanisms, copy-in and variable parameters.

Recall Example 5.7, where we started with an initialized variable declaration of v, a constant declaration of n, and a parameterless C++ function procedure. The copy-in parameter v corresponded exactly to the original initialized variable declaration. But the copy-in parameter n corresponded only approximately to the original constant declaration: n now denotes a variable that could be updated (which would have been a logical error in that application).

ADA complies with the Correspondence Principle to a greater extent. ADA's declarations are shown beside the corresponding parameter mechanisms in Table 5.4. A weakness of ADA is that it allows programmers little control over the choice between copy and reference parameter mechanisms.

If we wish to parameterize with respect to a procedure, both C++ and ADA depart from the Correspondence Principle. Neither language has a parameter mechanism that corresponds directly to a procedure definition. However, if we wish to pass a procedure P as an argument to another procedure, we can achieve essentially the same effect in C++ or ADA by passing a *pointer* to P.

5.3   Implementation notes

We have already seen, in Section 3.9.1, that a stack of activation frames is used to allocate storage to local variables of procedures. In fact, the stack is used to implement all aspects of procedure calls, including parameter passing.

Table 5.4 ADA declarations and parameter mechanisms (formal parameter declarations and actual parameters are underlined).

Declaration	Parameter mechanism

Initialized variable declaration:
 	
    I: T := E;
	Copy-in parameter:
	
	    procedure P ($\underline{I: \textbf{ in } T}$) **is**
	    begin
	        . . .
	    end;
	Call:
	    $P(\underline{E})$;

Constant definition:
 	
    I: **constant** T := E;
	Constant parameter:
	
	    procedure P ($\underline{I: \textbf{ in } T}$) **is**
	    begin
	        . . .
	    end;
	Call:
	    $P(\underline{E})$;

Variable renaming declaration:
 	
    I: T **renames** V;
	Variable parameter:
	
	    procedure P ($\underline{I: \textbf{ in out } T}$) **is**
	    begin
	        . . .
	    end;
	Call:
	    $P(\underline{V})$;

5.3.1 Implementation of procedure calls

When a procedure P is called, an activation frame is pushed on to the stack. That activation frame contains enough space for all of P's local variables, together with space for the return address and other housekeeping data. When P returns, that activation frame is popped off the stack.

At any given time, the stack contains activation frames for all currently-active procedures, in the order in which they were called (which is the reverse of the order in which they will return). (See Figure 3.10.)

Recursive procedures require no special treatment. During a recursive activation of a recursive procedure P, the stack contains several activation frames for P. (See Figure 3.11.)

5.3.2 Implementation of parameter mechanisms

To pass arguments between the calling procedure and the called procedure, we simply deposit them either in registers or in an activation frame. The various parameter mechanisms differ in the details.

Recall that the copy parameter mechanisms work in terms of a local variable denoted by the formal parameter. A *copy-in parameter* is implemented by passing in the argument value and using it to initialize the local variable. A *copy-out parameter* is implemented by passing out the local variable's final value, and using it to update the argument variable, on return from the called procedure. A *copy-in-copy-out parameter* is implemented by both passing in the argument variable's value and passing out the updated value.

A *reference parameter* is implemented by passing the *address* of the argument; the called procedure then uses this address to access the argument whenever required.

Summary

In this chapter:

- We have studied function procedures and proper procedures. We saw that a function procedure abstracts over an expression, and that a proper procedure abstracts over a command. We saw that the Abstraction Principle invites language designers to consider extending abstraction to other programming language constructs, such as a selector procedure which abstracts over a variable access.

- We have studied parameters and arguments. We saw that a programming language can choose between copy parameter mechanisms and reference parameter mechanisms. We saw that the Correspondence Principle exposes a duality between declarations and parameter mechanisms.

- We have briefly examined how procedures and parameters are implemented.

Further reading

The Abstraction and Correspondence Principles were formulated by TENNENT (1977, 1981). They were based on earlier work by LANDIN (1966) and STRACHEY (1967).

Exercises

Exercises for Section 5.1

5.1.1 Redesign the syntax of C or C++ function definitions and function calls to make a clear distinction between proper procedures and function procedures.

*5.1.2 Redesign the syntax of C, C++, or ADA function definitions so that a function's body is an expression (rather than a block command). Show that this change, in isolation, would reduce the expressive power of your language's functions. What other changes to your language would be needed to compensate? (*Hint:* Compare your language's expressions with the forms described in Sections 2.6, 3.8.1, and 4.4.2.)

*5.1.3 Redesign the syntax of C, C++, or ADA function definitions and function calls to allow a function to have multiple results.

5.1.4 Would it make sense to apply the Abstraction Principle to: (a) literals; (b) types?

Exercises for Section 5.2

5.2.1 Find at least one example of a parameterless procedure that does not perform exactly the same computation every time it is called. Under what circumstances, in general, will a parameterless procedure behave like this?

*5.2.2 Make a list of all entities that can be passed as arguments in your favorite programming language. Also make a list of any entities that *cannot* be passed as arguments. Why are the latter excluded?

5.2.3 Consider the following ADA procedure:

```
procedure multiply (m, n: in out Integer) is
begin
   m := m * n;
   put(m);   put(n);
end;
```

(a) Note that the copy-in-copy-out parameter mechanism is used here (since `Integer` is a primitive type). Suppose that i contains 2 and that j contains 3. Show what is written by the following procedure calls:

```
multiply(i, j);   multiply(i, i);
```

(b) Now suppose that the variable parameter mechanism were used instead. Show what would be written by each of the above procedure calls. Explain any difference.

5.2.4 Consider the procedure call "`add(a, b, c);`" of Examples 5.8 and 5.9. Show that the procedure call has the expected outcome, whether copy or reference parameter mechanisms are used. Repeat for the procedure call "`add(a, b, b);`". Show that (harmless) aliasing can arise in this case.

5.2.5 In C, C++, or ADA, would it make sense to apply the Correspondence Principle to: (a) types; (b) record or structure fields?

Exercises for Section 5.3

5.3.1 Consider the implementation of a procedure *P* with a formal parameter *FP* of type *T*.

(a) Assume that the copy-in-copy-out parameter mechanism is used. What exactly is passed to *P*, a value or an address? What happens when *P* is called? What happens inside *P* when it inspects *FP*? What happens inside *P* when it updates *FP*? What if anything happens when *P* returns?

(b) Repeat, this time assuming that the variable parameter mechanism is used instead.

PART III

ADVANCED CONCEPTS

Part III explains the more advanced programming language concepts, which are supported by the more modern programming languages:

- data abstraction (packages, abstract types, and classes);
- generic abstraction (generic units and type parameters);
- type systems (inclusion polymorphism, parametric polymorphism, overloading, and type conversions);
- control flow (jumps, escapes, and exceptions).

Chapter 6

Data abstraction

Software engineering depends on the decomposition of large programs into program units. The simplest program units are procedures, which we studied in Chapter 5. But the program units that make the best building blocks for large programs are packages, abstract types, and classes.

In this chapter we shall study:

- *packages*, which are program units that group together declarations of several (usually related) components;
- *encapsulation*, whereby components of a package may be either public or private;
- *abstract types*, which are types whose representations are private, but which are equipped with public operations;
- *classes*, which are program units that define the structure of families of objects, each object being a group of private variables equipped with public operations;
- *subclasses* and *inheritance*, which form the basis of object-oriented programming;
- how objects are represented, and how method calls are implemented.

We start with packages because they are simple and general, and because they clearly expose the concept of encapsulation. Abstract types are somewhat more specialized. Classes resemble abstract types in some respects, but are enriched by the concepts of subclasses and inheritance.

6.1 Program units, packages, and encapsulation

A ***program unit*** is any named part of a program that can be designed and implemented more-or-less independently. A well-designed program unit has a single purpose, and has a simple application program interface. If well designed, a program unit is likely to be *modifiable* (capable of being changed without forcing major changes to other program units), and is potentially *reusable* (capable of being used in many programs).

The ***application program interface*** (or ***API***) of a program unit is the minimum information that application programmers need to know in order to use the program unit successfully.

For instance, a procedure's API consists of its identifier, formal parameters, and result type if any (in order that application programmers can write well-formed procedure calls), together with a specification of its observable behavior (in order that application programmers can predict the outcome of these procedure calls). The procedure's API does *not* include the algorithm used in its definition.

135

A programming language whose only program units are procedures (such as PASCAL or C) is suitable only for small-scale program construction. For large-scale program construction, the language should support large-scale program units such as packages, abstract types, and classes.

6.1.1 Packages

A *package* is a group of several components declared for a common purpose. These components may be types, constants, variables, procedures, or indeed any entities that may be declared in the programming language.

Here we shall consider a simple package whose components are all public, i.e., visible to the application code that uses the package.

EXAMPLE 6.1   ADA simple package

The following ADA package groups declarations of types, constants, and variables:

```
package Earth is

    type Continent is (
            Africa, Antarctica, Asia, Australia,
            Europe, NAmerica, SAmerica);

    radius: constant Float := 6.4e3;    -- km

    area: constant array (Continent) of Float := (
            30.3e6, 13.0e6, 43.3e6, 7.7e6,
            10.4e6, 24.9e6, 17.8e6);        -- km²

    population: array (Continent) of Integer;

end Earth;
```

The Earth package produces the following set of bindings:

```
{ Continent    → the type Continent,
  radius       → the real number 6.4×10³,
  area         → the array value {Africa → 30.3×10⁶,...} ,
  population    → an array variable of type (Continent → Integer) }
```

where:

Continent = {*Africa, Antarctica, Asia, Australia, Europe, NAmerica, SAmerica*}

The following application code uses some components of the Earth package:

```
for cont in Earth.Continent loop
    put(Float(Earth.population(cont)
            / Earth.area(cont));
end loop;
```

Here Earth.Continent denotes a type component of the Earth package, Earth.population denotes a variable component, and Earth.area denotes a value component.

6.1.2   Encapsulation

In order to keep its API simple, a package typically makes only some of its components visible to the application code that uses the package; these components are said to be ***public***. Other components are visible only inside the package; these components are said to be ***private***, and serve only to support the implementation of the public components. A package with private components hides information that is irrelevant to the application code. This technique for making a simple API is called ***encapsulation***.

The concept of encapsulation is important, not only for packages, but also for other large-scale program units such as abstract types (Section 6.2) and classes (Section 6.3).

Consider the set of bindings produced by a package's component declarations. All these bindings are visible inside the package, but only the bindings of the public components are visible outside the package. Therefore we shall take the meaning of a package to be the set of bindings of its *public* components.

An ADA package with both public and private components is declared in two parts. The ***package specification*** declares only the public components, while the ***package body*** declares any private components. Moreover, if a public component is a procedure, the package specification only *declares* the procedure (providing its name, formal parameters, and result type if any), while the package body *defines* the procedure (providing its implementation). In other words, the package specification gives the package's interface, while the package body provides the implementation details.

EXAMPLE 6.2   ADA package with encapsulation

Consider a small trigonometric package, whose public components are to be the sine and cosine functions.

The following ADA package specification declares the package's public components, which are function procedures named `sin` and `cos`:

```
package Trig is

    function sin (x: Float) return Float;

    function cos (x: Float) return Float;

end Trig;
```

The corresponding package body defines both the public function procedures and the package's private components:

```
package body Trig is

    twice_pi: constant Float := 6.2832;

    function norm (x: Float) return Float is
    begin
        ...    -- code to compute x modulo twice_pi
    end;
```

```
function sin (x: Float) return Float is
begin
    ...  -- code to compute the sine of norm(x)
end;

function cos (x: Float) return Float is
begin
    ...  -- code to compute the cosine of norm(x)
end;

end Trig;
```

The package body declares a constant twice_pi and a function procedure norm, which are used to support the definitions of the sin and cos function procedures. Since twice_pi and norm are not declared in the package specification, they are taken to be private components.

The effect of elaborating the above package specification and body together is that the Trig package produces the following set of bindings:

$$\{ \text{ sin } \rightarrow \text{ function procedure that approximates the sine function,}$$

$$\text{cos } \rightarrow \text{ function procedure that approximates the cosine function} \}$$

The private components are excluded here, since they are not available to the application code. Thus the package has a simple API, which is desirable.

Application code can use the package's public components in the usual way, e.g.:

```
... Trig.cos(theta/2.0) ...
```

But the compiler would reject any attempt by the application code to access the private components directly:

```
... Trig.twicepi ...           -- illegal!
... Trig.norm(theta/2.0) ...   -- illegal!
```

Note that the package specification contains enough information for the application programmer to write legal calls to Trig.sin and Trig.cos, and for the compiler to type-check these calls.

A particularly important use of encapsulation is a package whose components include a private variable, together with one or more public procedures that access the private variable. The private variable cannot be accessed directly by the application code, but can be accessed by the public procedures.

The advantage of this encapsulation is that the private variable's representation can be changed (e.g., to make the procedures more efficient) without forcing any changes to the application code. Furthermore, the package could control the order of accesses to the private variable, e.g., to prevent inspection of the variable before it has been initialized.

EXAMPLE 6.3   ADA encapsulated variable

Consider a package whose components are a dictionary (set of words) together with procedures add and contains to operate on the dictionary. The dictionary itself is to be a private variable, but the procedures add and contains are to be public. Assume that each word is a value of type Word, declared elsewhere.

The following ADA package specification declares the public procedures:

```ada
package The_Dictionary is

   procedure add (wd: in Word);
   -- Add word wd to the dictionary if it is not already there.

   function contains (wd: Word) return Boolean;
   -- Return true if and only if word wd is in the dictionary.

end The_Dictionary;
```

The following package body provides all the implementation details, including declarations of private variables representing the dictionary. For the time being, suppose that we choose a naive representation for the dictionary:

```ada
package body The_Dictionary is
   maxsize: constant := 1000;

   size: Integer := 0;
   words: array (1 .. maxsize) of Word;
   -- The dictionary is represented as follows: size contains the number of
   -- words, and words(1..size) contains the words themselves, in no
   -- particular order.

   procedure add (wd: in Word) is
   begin
     if not contains(wd) then
        size := size + 1;
        words(size) := wd;
     end if;
   end;

   function contains (wd: Word) return Boolean is
   begin
     for i in 1 .. size loop
        if wd = words(i) then
           return true;
        end if;
     end loop;
     return false;
   end;

end The_Dictionary;
```

As well as declaring and initializing the private variables size and words, the package body defines the public procedures add and contains, which access the private variables.

The effect of elaborating the above package specification and body together is that the The_Dictionary package produces the following set of bindings:

{ add   → proper procedure that adds a word to the dictionary,
  contains   → function procedure that searches for a word in the dictionary }

Application code can call the public procedures:

```
if not The_Dictionary.contains(current_word) then
    ...
    The_Dictionary.add(current_word);
end if;
```

But the compiler would reject any attempt by the application code to access the private variables directly:

```
The_Dictionary.size := 0;    -- illegal!
```

Now suppose that we want to change to a more efficient representation for the dictionary (such as a search tree or hash table). We change the declarations of the private variables, and we change the definitions of the public procedures. All the necessary changes are localized in the package body. Since the dictionary representation is private, we can be sure that no changes are needed to the application code. Thus the package is inherently modifiable. This demonstrates clearly the benefits of encapsulation.

The variable components of a package have the same lifetimes as ordinary variables declared immediately outside that package. If the package of Example 6.3 was globally declared, the lifetime of its variable components (size and words) would be the program's entire run-time; if the package was declared inside a block, the lifetime of its variable components would be an activation of that block.

6.2 Abstract types

In Chapter 2 we viewed a type as a set of values equipped with suitable operations. When we wish to introduce a new type, it is good practice to define the new type and its operations in a single program unit. In defining the new type, we must choose a *representation* for the values of that type, and define the operations in terms of that representation. But sometimes even a well-chosen representation has unwanted properties, which the following example illustrates.

EXAMPLE 6.4   ADA public type

In Example 6.3 we saw an ADA package that grouped a private dictionary variable together with public procedures to operate on it.

Suppose now that we have an application that needs *several* dictionaries. An example of such an application would be a spellchecker that provides both a main dictionary and a user dictionary.

The following ADA package is a first attempt to solve this problem. Its components include a public Dictionary type, together with public procedures clear, add, and contains to operate on values and variables of that type. Each of these procedures has a parameter of type Dictionary. If we stick to our naive dictionary representation, the package specification looks like this:

```
package Dictionaries is
   maxsize: constant := 1000;
   type Dictionary is
         record
            size: Integer;
            words: array (1 .. maxsize) of Word;
         end record;
   procedure clear (dict: in out Dictionary);
   -- Make dictionary dict empty.
   procedure add (dict: in out Dictionary;
                       wd: in Word);
   -- Add word wd to dictionary dict if it is not already there.
   function contains (dict: Dictionary; wd: Word)
            return Boolean;
   -- Return true if and only if word wd is in dictionary dict.
end Dictionaries;
```

The type Dictionary is public, as is the constant maxsize. Note also that the public procedures add and contains now have parameters of type Dictionary, allowing these procedures to operate on any Dictionary variable created by the application code.

The corresponding package body implements the public procedures:

```
package body Dictionaries is
   procedure clear (dict: in out Dictionary) is
   begin
      dict.size := 0;
   end;
   procedure add (dict: in out Dictionary;
                       wd: in Word) is
   begin
      if not contains(dict, wd) then
         dict.size := dict.size + 1;
         dict.words(dict.size) := wd;
      end if;
   end;
   function contains (dict: Dictionary; wd: Word)
               return Boolean is
   begin
      for i in 1 .. dict.size loop
         if wd = dict.words(i) then
            return true;
         end if;
      end loop;
      return false;
   end;
end Dictionaries;
```

Using this package, the application code can declare as many variables of type Dictionary as it needs:

```
use Dictionaries;
main_dict, user_dict: Dictionary;
```

(The clause "use Dictionaries;" allows us to abbreviate Dictionaries. Dictionary to Dictionary, to abbreviate Dictionaries.add to add, and so on.)

The application code can operate on these variables by calling the public procedures:

```
if not contains(main_dict, current_word)
      and not contains(user_dict, current_word) then
   ...
   add(user_dict, current_word);
end if;
```

Unfortunately, making the type Dictionary public causes a number of difficulties. There is nothing to prevent application code from manipulating a Dictionary variable directly. For example, the code:

```
user_dict.size := 0;
```

is an attempted shortcut for "clear(user_dict);". But such code can be understood only by someone familiar with the chosen representation. Worse, such code must be located and modified whenever the representation is changed.

Another difficulty is that there is nothing to prevent application code from getting a Dictionary variable into an improper state. For example, the code:

```
user_dict.size := user_dict.size - 1;
```

is a crude attempt to remove the word most recently added to user_dict. But this code could make user_dict.size negative, which would be improper.

Yet another difficulty arises from the fact that the representation is non-unique: it allows the same set of words to be represented by different values of type Dictionary. This will happen if we add the same words in a different order:

```
dictA, dictB: Dictionary;
...
clear(dictA);   add(dictA, "bat");   add(dictA, "cat");
clear(dictB);   add(dictB, "cat");   add(dictB, "bat");
if dictA = dictB then ...
```

At this point the value of dictA is $(2, \{1 \to$ "bat", $2 \to$ "cat", $\ldots\})$, whereas the value of dictB is $(2, \{1 \to$ "cat", $2 \to$ "bat", $\ldots\}$. Both values represent the same set of words {"bat", "cat"}. Nevertheless, the above equality test yields the wrong result.

Here is a summary of the difficulties that can arise in practice when a package has a public type component:

- Application code can access the public type's representation directly. If we wish to change the representation (e.g., to make it more efficient), we have to modify not only the package but also any application code that accesses the representation directly. (Such code could be anywhere in the application program. Even if there turns out to be no such code, we have to read the whole program to be sure.)

- The public type's representation might have *improper* values that do not correspond to any values of the desired type. Even if the package's procedures are programmed correctly not to generate improper values, faulty application code might generate improper values.

- The public type's representation might be *non-unique*. A simple equality test might then yield the wrong result.

To avoid these problems we need an alternative way to define a new type. An ***abstract type*** is a type whose identifier is public but whose representation is private. An abstract type must be equipped with a group of ***operations*** to access its representation. The operations are typically procedures and constants. The values of the abstract type are defined to be just those values that can be generated by repeated use of the operations.

A few programming languages (such as ML) have a customized program unit that allows us to define an abstract type directly. In ADA, however, we define an abstract type by writing a package with a private or limited private type. A *private type* is equipped not only with the operations defined in the package but also with the built-in assignment and equality test operations. A *limited private type* is equipped *only* with the operations defined in the package.

| EXAMPLE 6.5 | ADA limited private type |

The following ADA package is similar to that of Example 6.4, except that the Dictionary type's representation is limited private. Since the type's identifier is public, the application can still declare variables of the Dictionary type. If we stick to our naive dictionary representation, the package specification looks like this:

```
package Dictionaries is

    type Dictionary is limited private;
    -- A Dictionary value represents a set of words.

    procedure clear (dict: in out Dictionary);
    -- Make dictionary dict empty.

    procedure add (dict: in out Dictionary;
                   wd: in Word);
    -- Add word wd to dictionary dict if it is not already there.

    function contains (dict: Dictionary; wd: Word)
            return Boolean;
    -- Return true if and only if word wd is in dictionary dict.

private

    maxsize: constant Integer := 1000;
    type Dictionary is
        record
            size: Integer;
```

```
                    words: array (1 .. maxsize) of Word;
                end record;

        end Dictionaries;
```

Here "**type** Dictionary **is limited private**;" declares the type, making its identifier public but hiding its representation. The representation is defined only in the **private** part of the package specification.

The corresponding package body is exactly the same as in Example 6.4.

Using this package, application code can declare as many variables of type Dictionary as it needs:

```
use Dictionaries;
main_dict, user_dict: Dictionary;
```

and can operate on these variables by calling the public procedures:

```
if not contains(main_dict, current_word)
        and not contains(user_dict, current_word) then
    ...
        add(user_dict, current_word);
end if;
```

However, application code cannot manipulate a Dictionary variable directly:

```
user_dict.size := 0;    -- illegal!
```

since the representation of type Dictionary is private. Thus we can be confident that a Dictionary variable will never have an improper value, since the package's procedures have been written carefully to generate only proper values, and there is no way for even faulty application code to generate improper values.

Since Dictionary is declared as a *limited* private type, variables of this type can be operated on *only* by the package's public procedures. Even the built-in assignment and equality test are forbidden. The reason for this decision is that an equality test such as:

```
dictA, dictB: Dictionary;
...
if dictA = dictB then ...
```

might still yield the wrong result, because dictA and dictB could contain the same set of words but differently represented.

In the unlikely event that we actually need an equality test for Dictionary values, the package must provide its own operation for this purpose. In the package specification we would declare this operation:

```
function "=" (dict1, dict2: Dictionary)
            return Boolean;
-- Return true if and only if dict1 and dict2 contain the same set of words.
```

And in the package body we would define this operation carefully to yield the correct result:

```
function "=" (dict1, dict2: Dictionary)
            return Boolean is
begin
    if dict1.size /= dict2.size then
        return false;
    end if;
```

```
      for i in 1 .. dict2.size loop
        if not contains(dict1, dict2.words(i)) then
          return false;
        end if;
      end loop;
      return true;
    end;
```

It does not matter whether an abstract type's representation is non-unique, because the representation is private. The key point is that only desired properties of the abstract type can actually be *observed* by application code using the operations with which the abstract type is equipped. In Example 6.5, the different representations of the same set of words are not observable, because the contains operation treats them all in the same way (and so too does the "=" operation, if provided).

We can easily change an abstract type's representation: we need change only the package body and the **private** part of the package specification. We can be sure that we need not change the application code, since the latter cannot access the representation directly.

(Note that it is anomalous that ADA requires the abstract type's representation to be defined in the **private** part of the package specification, rather than in the package body along with the other implementation details. The reason for this design anomaly will become clear in Section 11.4.5.)

Defining an abstract type does involve extra work: because its representation is private, we must equip it with sufficient operations to generate and process all desired values. We can classify operations on an abstract type T as follows. A *constructor* is an operation that computes a new value of type T, possibly using values of other types but not using an existing value of type T. A *transformer* is an operation that computes a new value of type T, using an existing value of type T. An *accessor* is an operation that computes a value of some other type, using an existing value of type T. In general, we must equip each abstract type with at least one constructor, at least one transformer, and at least one accessor. Between them, the constructors and transformers must be capable of generating all desired values of the abstract type.

In Example 6.5, clear is a constructor, add is a transformer, and contains is an accessor. Any set of words can be generated by first calling clear, and then calling add for each word in the set. Due to an implementation restriction, however, at most 1000 words can be added. Thus the set of values of this abstract type is:

$$\text{Dictionary} = \{s \mid s \text{ is a set of words}, \#s \leq 1000\}$$

6.3 Objects and classes

An ***object*** is a group of variable components, equipped with a group of operations that access these variables.

We can implement a single object by a package whose components are private variables and public operations, as in Example 6.3. In many applications, however, we need to create many similar objects. This leads naturally to the concept of a *class*.

6.3.1 Classes

A *class* is a set of similar objects. All the objects of a given class have the same variable components, and are equipped with the same operations.

Classes are, as we would expect, supported by all the object-oriented languages including C++ and JAVA (and somewhat indirectly by ADA95). In object-oriented terminology, an object's variable components are variously called *instance variables* or *member variables*, and its operations are usually called *constructors* and *methods*.

A *constructor* is an operation that creates (and typically initializes) a new object of the class. In both C++ and JAVA, a constructor is always named after the class to which it belongs.

A *method* is an operation that inspects and/or updates an existing object of the class.

EXAMPLE 6.6   JAVA class

For comparison with Examples 6.3 and 6.5, let us see how to implement dictionaries as objects.

Here is a possible JAVA class declaration (sticking to our naive dictionary representation):

```java
class Dictionary {

// A Dictionary object represents a set of words.

    private int size;
    private String[] words;
    // This dictionary is represented as follows: size contains the number
    // of words, and words[0],...,words[size-1] contain the words
    // themselves, in no particular order.

    public Dictionary (int maxsize) {
    // Construct an empty dictionary, with space for maxsize words.
        this.size = 0;
        this.words = new String[maxsize];
    }

    public void add (String wd) {
    // Add word wd to this dictionary if it is not already there.
        if (! contains(wd)) {
            this.words[this.size++] = wd;
        }
    }
```

```
public boolean contains (String wd) {
// Return true if and only if word wd is in this dictionary.
    for (int i = 0; i < this.size; i++) {
      if (wd.equals(this.words[i]))  return true;
    }
    return false;
  }

}
```

Each object of class Dictionary will have private variable components named size and words, and will be equipped with public methods named add and contains.

To create individual objects of the Dictionary class, we must call the constructor:

```
Dictionary mainDict = new Dictionary(10000);
Dictionary userDict = new Dictionary(1000);
```

The expression "new Dictionary(...)" creates and initializes a new object of class Dictionary, yielding a pointer to that object. So the above code creates two Dictionary objects, and makes the variables mainDict and userDict point to these objects. These two objects are similar but distinct.

We can operate on these objects by method calls:

```
if (! mainDict.contains(currentWord)
      && ! userDict.contains(currentWord)) {
    ...
    userDict.add(currentWord);
}
```

The method call "userDict.add(currentWord)" works as follows. First it takes the object to which userDict points, which is called the *target object*. Then it selects the method named add with which the target object is equipped. Then it calls that method with the value of currentWord as an argument.

Within the method body, **this** denotes the target object. Thus "**this**.size++" actually increments userDict.size, and "**this**.words" actually refers to userDict.words. (Actually, **this**.size and **this**.words may be abbreviated to size and words, respectively.)

Application code may not access the variable components size and words directly, since they are private:

```
userDict.size = 0;   // illegal!
```

Nor can application code make Dictionary objects contain improper values. Consequently, we can change the representation of Dictionary objects by modifying the Dictionary class alone; no modifications to the application code are needed.

JAVA adopts reference semantics for assignment and equality testing of objects. Thus the following equality test:

```
Dictionary dictA = ..., dictB = ...;
if (dictA == dictB)  ...
```

would actually compare *references* to two distinct Dictionary objects, wrongly yielding false even if the two dictionaries happen to contain the same words. If we want to support proper equality testing of Dictionary objects, the class must provide a method for this purpose:

```
class Dictionary {

    ...

    public boolean equals (Dictionary that) {
    //  Return true if and only if this dictionary and that contain the same set
    //  of words.
        if (this.size != that.size)  return false;
        for (int i = 0; i < that.size; i++) {
            if (! contains(that.words[i]))  return false;
        }
        return true;
    }

}
```

Application code would call that method as follows:

```
Dictionary dictA = ..., dictB = ...;
if (dictA.equals(dictB))  ...
```

A method call both names a method and identifies a ***target object***, which is the object on which the method will operate. In a JAVA method call "$O.M(E_1, \ldots, E_n)$", M is the method name, O identifies the target object, and the E_i are evaluated to yield the arguments. The target object must be equipped with a method named M, otherwise there is a type error. Inside the method's body, **this** denotes the target object.

EXAMPLE 6.7   C++ class

The following shows how we could declare a Dictionary class, analogous to that of Example 6.6, in C++:

```
class Dictionary {

//  A Dictionary object represents a set of words.

private:

    int size;
    String words[];
    //  This dictionary is represented as follows: size contains the number of
    //  words, and words[0],...,words[size-1] contain the words
    //  themselves, in no particular order.

public:

    Dictionary (int maxsize);
    //  Construct an empty dictionary, with space for maxsize words.

    void add (String wd);
    //  Add word wd to this dictionary if it is not already there.
```

```
boolean contains (String wd) const;
    // Return true if and only if word wd is in this dictionary.

}
```

In this class declaration, the variable components `size` and `words` are declared to be private, while the constructor and the methods `add` and `contains` are declared to be public.

This class declaration only *declares* the constructor and methods (providing their names, parameter types, and result types). We must therefore *define* these operations separately. For this purpose we use qualified names such as `Dictionary::add`, which denotes the add method of the `Dictionary` class:

```
Dictionary::Dictionary (int maxsize) {
    this->size = 0;
    this->words = new String[maxsize];
}
void Dictionary::add (String wd) {
    if (! contains(wd)) {
        this->words[this->size] = wd;
        this->size++;
    }
}
boolean Dictionary::contains (String wd) const {
    for (int i = 0; i < this->size; i++) {
        if (strcmp(wd, this->words[i]))  return true;
    }
    return false;
}
```

To create individual objects of the `Dictionary` class, we must call the constructor:

```
Dictionary* main_dict = new Dictionary(10000);
Dictionary* user_dict = new Dictionary(1000);
```

The expression "`new Dictionary(...)`" creates and initializes a new object of class `Dictionary`, yielding a pointer to that object. So the above code creates two `Dictionary` objects, and makes the variables `main_dict` and `user_dict` point to these objects. These objects are similar but distinct.

We can now access these objects by method calls:

```
if (! main_dict->contains(current_word)
    && ! user_dict->contains(current_word)) {
    ...
    user_dict->add(current_word);
}
```

The method call "`user_dict->add(...)`" is actually an abbreviation of "`(*user_dict).add(...)`". Thus the target object is `*user_dict`, i.e., the object to which `user_dict` points. Within the method body, **this** denotes a pointer to the target object. Thus `this->size` actually refers to `user_dict->size`, and so on. (Actually, we can abbreviate **this**`->size` to `size`.)

The following equality test:

```
Dictionary* dictA = ..., dictB = ...;
if (dictA == dictB)  ...
```

would compare *pointers* to the two Dictionary objects, wrongly yielding false even if the two dictionaries happen to contain the same words. No better is the following equality test:

```
Dictionary* dictA = ..., dictB = ...;
if (*dictA == *dictB) ...
```

which would actually compare the *representations* of the two Dictionary objects, wrongly yielding false if the same words have been added to the two dictionaries in different orders. If we need a correct equality test for Dictionary objects, the class must provide an operation for this purpose (overloading the "==" operator):

```
class Dictionary {

    ...

public:

    ...

    friend bool operator== (Dictionary* dict1,
        Dictionary* dict2);
    // Return true if and only if dictionaries dict1 and dict2 contain the
    // same set of words.

}
```

Here is a possible implementation:

```
bool Dictionary::operator== (Dictionary* dict1,
        Dictionary* dict2) {
    if (dict1->size != dict2->size)  return false;
    for (int i = 0; i < dict2->size; i++) {
        if (! dict1->contains(dict2->words[i]))
            return false;
    }
    return true;
}
```

In both JAVA and C++, the programmer is allowed to choose which components of an object are private and which are public. Constant components are often public, allowing them to be directly inspected (but not of course updated) by application code. Variable components should always be private, otherwise the benefits of encapsulation would be lost. Constructors and methods are usually public, unless they are auxiliary operations to be used only inside the class declaration.

The concepts of an abstract type (Section 6.2) and a class (this section) have much in common. Each allows application code to create several variables of a type whose representation is private, and to manipulate these variables only by operations provided for the purpose. However, there are differences between abstract types and classes.

We can clearly see a syntactic difference if we compare the application code in Examples 6.5 and 6.6:

- Refer to the ADA Dictionary abstract type of Example 6.5. To operate on a variable adict of this type, we write a call to the add procedure as follows:

```
add(adict, aword);
```

Here the variable adict is passed as an ordinary argument to the procedure, and is denoted by the formal parameter dict inside the procedure body.

- Refer to the JAVA Dictionary class of Example 6.5. To operate on an object adict of this class, we write a call to the add method as follows:

```
adict.add(aword);
```

Here adict is the method call's target object, and is denoted by the keyword **this** inside the method body.

A more important difference between the two concepts is that the class concept leads naturally to the concepts of *subclasses* and *inheritance*, which are fundamental to object-oriented programming.

6.3.2   Subclasses and inheritance

We have seen that a class C is a set of similar objects. Every object of class C has the same variable components, and is equipped with the same operations.

A *subclass* of C is a set of objects that are similar to one another but richer than the objects of class C. An object of the subclass has all the variable components of an object of class C, but may have extra variable components. Likewise, an object of the subclass is equipped with all the methods of class C, but may be equipped with extra methods.

If S is a subclass of C, we also say that C is a *superclass* of S.

A subclass is said to *inherit* its superclass's variable components and methods. In certain circumstances, however, a subclass may *override* some of its superclass's methods, by providing more specialized versions of these methods.

EXAMPLE 6.8   JAVA class and subclasses

Consider the following JAVA class declaration:

```
class Point {
    // A Point object represents a point in the xy plane.

    protected double x, y;
    // This point is represented by its Cartesian coordinates (x,y).

    public Point () {
    // Construct a point at (0, 0).
        x = 0.0;   y = 0.0;
    }
```

(1) **public double** distance () {
```
     //  Return the distance of this point from (0, 0).
         return Math.sqrt(x*x + y*y);
     }
```

(2) **public final void** move (**double** dx, **double** dy) {
```
     //  Move this point by dx in the x direction and by dy in the y direction.
         x += dx;   y += dy;
     }
```

(3) **public void** draw () {
```
     //  Draw this point on the screen.
         ...
     }
```
```
     }
```

Each `Point` object consists of variable components x and y, and is equipped with methods named `distance`, `move`, and `draw`.

Now consider the following class declaration:

```
     class Circle extends Point {

         //  A Circle object represents a circle in the xy plane.

         private double r;
         //  This circle is represented by the Cartesian coordinates of its center
         //  (x,y) together with its radius (r).

         public Circle (double radius) {
         //  Construct a circle of radius r centered at (0, 0).
             x = 0.0;   y = 0.0;   r = radius;
         }
```

(4) **public void** draw () {
```
     //  Draw this circle on the screen.
         ...
     }
```

(5) **public double** getDiam () {
```
     //  Return the diameter of this circle.
         return 2.0 * r;
     }
```
```
     }
```

The clause "**extends** Point" states that class `Circle` is a subclass of `Point` (and hence that `Point` is the superclass of `Circle`). Each `Circle` object consists of variable components x, y, and r, and is equipped with methods named `distance`, `move`, `draw`, and `getDiam`. Note that the extra variable component r is declared here, but not the variable components x and y that are inherited from the superclass. Likewise, the extra method `getDiam` is defined here, but not the methods `distance` and `move` that are inherited from the superclass. Also defined here is a new version of the `draw` method, which overrides the superclass's `draw` method.

Consider the following application code:

```
     Point p = new Point();          // p is at (0, 0)
     Circle c = new Circle(10.0);  // c is centered at (0, 0)
```

```
p.move(12.0, 5.0);          // now p is at (12, 5)
c.move(3.0, 4.0);           // now c is centered at (3, 4)
... p.distance() ...        // yields 13
... c.distance() ...        // yields 5
p.draw();                   // draws a point at (12, 5)
c.draw();                   // draws a circle centered at (3, 4)
... c.getDiam() ...         // yields 10
```

Note that it is perfectly safe to apply the inherited `distance` and `move` methods to `Circle` objects, since these methods access only the inherited `x` and `y` variable components, which are common to `Point` and `Circle` objects. The extra `getDiam` method accesses the extra variable component `r`, which is also safe because this method can be applied only to a `Circle` object (never to a `Point` object).

The `Circle` class's extra `getDiam` method and overriding `draw` method are permitted to access the extra variable component `r`, which is private but declared in the same class. They are also permitted to access the inherited variable components `x` and `y`, which are *protected* and declared in the superclass. (If `x` and `y` were private, on the other hand, we would be unable to implement the `Circle` class's `draw` method, unless we extended the `Point` class with `getX` and `getY` methods returning the values of `x` and `y`, respectively.)

Now consider the following variable:

```
Point p;
```

This variable can refer to any object whose class is *either* `Point` *or* `Circle` (or indeed any other subclass of `Point`). Consequently, the method call "`p.draw()`" will call either the `Point` class's `draw` method or the `Circle` class's `draw` method, depending on the class of object to which `p` *currently* refers. This is called *dynamic dispatch*.

Finally consider the following class declaration:

```
class Rectangle extends Point {

    // A Rectangle object represents a rectangle in the xy plane.

    private double w, h;
    // This rectangle is represented by the Cartesian coordinates of its
    // center (x,y) together with its width and height (w,h).

    public Rectangle (double width, double height) {
    // Construct a rectangle of width and height, centered at (0, 0).
        x = 0.0;   y = 0.0;   w = width;   h = height;
    }
```

(6)
```
    public void draw () {
    // Draw this rectangle on the screen.
        ...
    }
```

(7)
```
    public double getWidth () {
    // Return the width of this rectangle.
        return w;
    }
```

(8)
```
    public double getHeight () {
    // Return the height of this rectangle.
        return h;
    }

}
```

The clause "**extends** Point" states that class Rectangle is a subclass of Point (and hence that Point is the superclass of Rectangle). Each Rectangle object consists of variable components x, y, w, and h, and is equipped with methods named distance, move, draw, getWidth, and getHeight. Note that the extra variable components w and h are declared here, but not the variable components x and y that are inherited from the superclass. Likewise, the extra methods getWidth and getHeight are defined here, but not the methods distance and move that are inherited from the superclass. Also defined here is a new version of the draw method, which overrides the superclass's draw method.

A *private* component is visible only in its own class, while a *public* component is visible everywhere. A ***protected*** component is visible not only in its own class but also in any subclasses. Protected status is therefore intermediate between private status and public status.

A subclass may itself have subclasses. This gives rise to a *hierarchy* of classes.

Inheritance is important because it enables programmers to be more productive. Once a method has been implemented for a particular class *C*, that method is automatically applicable not only to objects of class *C* but also to objects of any subclasses that inherit the method from *C* (and *their* subclasses, and so on). In practice, this gain in programmer productivity is substantial.

Each method of a superclass may be either inherited or overridden by a subclass. A JAVA method is inherited by default; in that case objects of the superclass and the subclass share the same method. A JAVA method is overridden if the subclass provides a method with the same identifier, parameter types, and result type; in that case objects of the superclass are equipped with one version of the method, while objects of the subclass are equipped with another version.

A method is ***overridable*** if a subclass is allowed to override it. A JAVA method is overridable only if it is *not* declared as **final**. (For example, the methods distance and draw of the Point class in Example 6.8 are overridable, but not the method move.) A C++ method is overridable only if it is declared as **virtual**.

EXAMPLE 6.9   C++ class and subclasses

The C++ class and subclasses in this example correspond to the JAVA class and subclasses of Example 6.8.

Consider the following C++ class declaration:

```
class Point {
    // A Point object represents a point in the xy plane.

protected:
    double x, y;
    // This point is represented by its Cartesian coordinates (x,y).
```

```
public:

    Point ();
    // Construct a point at (0, 0).

    virtual double distance ();
    // Return the distance of this point from (0, 0).

    void move (double dx, double dy);
    // Move this point by dx in the x direction and by dy in the y direction.

    virtual void draw ();
    // Draw this point on the screen.

};
```

Each Point object consists of variable components x and y, and is equipped with methods named distance, move, and draw (of which only distance and draw are overridable). We have chosen not to define the methods and constructor in this class declaration, so we must define them elsewhere in the program.

Now consider the following class declaration:

```
class Circle : public Point {

    // A Circle object represents a circle in the xy plane.

private:

    double r;
    // This circle is represented by the Cartesian coordinates of its center (x,y)
    // together with its radius (r).

public:

    Circle (double radius);
    // Construct a circle of radius centered at (0, 0).

    void draw ();
    // Draw this circle on the screen.

    double getDiam ();
    // Return the diameter of this circle.

}
```

The clause ": public Point" states that class Circle is a subclass of Point (and that Point is the superclass of Circle). Each Circle object consists of variable components x, y, and r, and is equipped with methods named distance, move, draw, and getDiam.

The following is possible application code:

```
Point* p = new Point();        // p is at (0, 0)
Circle* c = new Circle(10.0);  // c is centered at (0, 0)
p->move(12.0, 5.0);            // now p is at (12, 5)
c->move(3.0, 4.0);             // now c is centered at (3, 4)
... p->distance() ...          // yields 13
... c->distance() ...          // yields 5
p->draw();                     // draws a point at (12, 5)
c->draw();                     // draws a circle centered at (3, 4)
... c->getDiam() ...           // yields 10.0
```

Finally consider the following class declaration:

```
class Rectangle : public Point {
```

> // A Rectangle object represents a rectangle in the *xy* plane.

```
private:
```

> ```
> double w, h;
> ```
> // This rectangle is represented by the Cartesian coordinates of its center
> // (x,y) together with its width and height (w,h).

```
public:
```

> ```
> Rectangle (double width, double height);
> ```
> // Construct a rectangle of width and height, centered at (0, 0).
>
> ```
> void draw ();
> ```
> // Draw this rectangle on the screen.
>
> ```
> double getWidth ();
> ```
> // Return the width of this rectangle.
>
> ```
> double getHeight ();
> ```
> // Return the height of this rectangle.

```
}
```

The clause ": public Point" states that class Rectangle is a subclass of Point. Each Rectangle object consists of variable components x, y, w, and h, and is equipped with methods named distance, move, draw, getWidth, and getHeight.

Dynamic dispatch occurs in a method call where it is impossible to determine at compile-time which version of the method is to be called. Dynamic dispatch entails a run-time determination of the target object's class followed by selecting the appropriate method for that class.

Dynamic dispatch is necessary only where the named method is overridable *and* the exact class of the target object is unknown at compile-time. (If the named method is not overridable, there can be only one version of it. If the exact class of the target object is known, the correct version of the method can be selected at compile-time.)

For instance, consider the JAVA method call "$O.M(E_1,\ldots,E_n)$" or the C++ method call "$O\text{->}M(E_1,\ldots,E_n)$", where M is an overridable method. The compiler will infer that the class of O is C (say), but the actual class of the target object could turn out to be either C or some subclass of C. The compiler will ensure that class C is equipped with a method named M, which guarantees that the target object (whatever its class) is indeed equipped with a method named M. But it might be the case that some subclasses inherit method M from class C, while other subclasses override method M, so the version to be called must be selected at run-time.

6.3.3   Abstract classes

An *abstract class* is a class in which no objects can be constructed. An abstract class may have variable components and methods, but it differs from ordinary classes in two respects:

- An abstract class has no constructor.
- Some of its methods may be undefined. (These are called *abstract methods*.)

The only purpose of an abstract class *A* is to serve as a superclass. Any subclasses of *A* inherit its variable components and methods in the usual way. If *A* has an abstract method, that method must be defined by all of *A*'s subclasses that are not themselves abstract.

EXAMPLE 6.10   JAVA abstract class and subclasses

Recall the Point class and the Circle and Rectangle subclasses of Example 6.8. There we treated circles and rectangles as special cases of points, which was rather artificial.

It is more natural to think of points, circles, and rectangles as special cases of *shapes*. While it makes sense to construct point, circle, and rectangle objects, however, it makes no sense to construct a shape object. The following JAVA abstract class captures the notion of a shape:

```java
abstract class Shape {

    // Shape objects represent different kinds of shapes in the xy plane.

    protected double x, y;
    // This shape's center is represented by its Cartesian coordinates (x,y).

    public double distance () {
    // Return the distance of this shape's center from (0, 0).
        return Math.sqrt(x*x + y*y);
    }

    public final void move (double dx, double dy) {
    // Move this shape by dx in the x direction and by dy in the y direction.
        x += dx;   y += dy;
    }

    public abstract void draw ();
    // Draw this shape on the screen.

}
```

Every Shape object will have variable components x and y, and will be equipped with methods named distance, move, and draw. The distance and move methods are defined here in the usual way, the former being overridable. However, the draw method cannot sensibly be defined here (what would it do?), so it is an abstract method.

Since Shape is an abstract class, it has no constructor, so we cannot construct any object of class Shape. So when we speak loosely of a "Shape object", we really mean an object of a *subclass* of Shape.

Now consider the following subclasses of Shape:

```
class Point extends Shape {

    // A Point object represents a point in the xy plane.

    public Point () {
    // Construct a point at (0, 0).
        x = 0.0;   y = 0.0;
    }

    public void draw () {
    // Draw this point on the screen.
        ...
    }

}
```

Each Point object consists of variable components x and y, and is equipped with methods named distance, move, and draw. All of these methods are inherited from the superclass Shape, except for the superclass's abstract draw method which is defined here.

```
class Circle extends Shape {

    // A Circle object represents a circle in the xy plane.

    private double r;
    // This circle is represented by the Cartesian coordinates of its center (x, y)
    // together with its radius (r).

    public Circle (double radius) {
    // Construct a circle of radius centered at (0, 0).
        x = 0.0;   y = 0.0;   r = radius;
    }

    public void draw () {
    // Draw this circle on the screen.
        ...
    }

    public double getDiam () {
    // Return the diameter of this circle.
        return 2.0 * r;
    }

}
```

Each Circle object consists of variable components x, y, and r, and is equipped with methods named distance, move, draw, and getDiam. Again the superclass's abstract draw method is defined here.

```
class Rectangle extends Shape {

    // A Rectangle object represents a rectangle in the xy plane.
```

```
private double w, h;
// This rectangle is represented by the Cartesian coordinates of its center
// (x,y) together with its width and height (w,h).

public Rectangle (double width, double height) {
// Construct a rectangle of width and height, centered at (0, 0).
    x = 0.0;   y = 0.0;   w = width;   h = height;
}

public void draw () {
// Draw this rectangle on the screen.
    ...
}

public double getWidth () {
// Return the width of this rectangle.
    return w;
}

public double getHeight () {
// Return the height of this rectangle.
    return h;
}

}
```

Each Rectangle object consists of variable components x, y, w, and h, and is equipped with methods named distance, move, draw, getWidth, and getHeight. Again the superclass's abstract draw method is defined here.

Figure 6.1 summarizes the relationships among these classes.

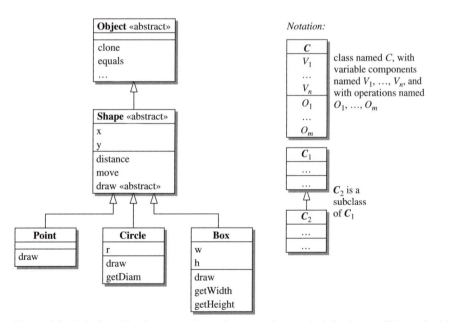

Figure 6.1 Relationships between JAVA classes under single inheritance (Example 6.10).

6.3.4   Single vs multiple inheritance

An object-oriented language supports ***single inheritance*** if it restricts each class to at most one superclass. Each subclass inherits the variable components and methods of its single superclass.

An object-oriented language supports ***multiple inheritance*** if it allows each class to have any number of superclasses. Each subclass inherits the variable components and methods of *all* its superclasses.

Single inheritance is supported by most object-oriented languages, including JAVA and ADA95. In JAVA each class's unique superclass is named in the class declaration's **extends** clause. If there is no such clause, the default superclass is Object. The Object class alone has no superclass. Thus all JAVA classes form a hierarchy with the Object class at the top, as illustrated in Figure 6.1.

Multiple inheritance is less usual, but it is supported by C++. A C++ class may be declared to have any number of superclasses (perhaps none). This gives rise to class relationships such as those illustrated in the following example and Figure 6.2.

EXAMPLE 6.11   C++ multiple inheritance

Consider the following C++ classes (in which methods are omitted for simplicity):

```
class Animal {
private:
    float weight;
    float speed;
public:
    ...
}
```

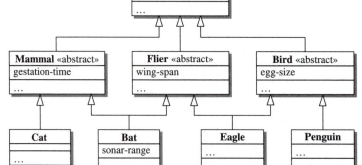

Figure 6.2 Relationships between C++ classes under multiple inheritance (Example 6.11).

```
class Mammal : public Animal {
private:
    float gestation_time;
public:
    ...
}

class Bird : public Animal {
private:
    float egg_size;
public:
    ...
}

class Flyer : public Animal {
private:
    float wing_span;
public:
    ...
}

class Cat : public Mammal {
public:
    ...
}

class Bat : public Mammal, public Flyer {
private:
    float sonar_range;
public:
    ...
}
```

In the declaration of the Mammal class, the clause ": **public** Animal" states that Mammal has one superclass, Animal. Thus a Mammal object has variable components weight and speed (inherited from Animal) and gestation_time. Similarly, the Bird and Flyer classes each have one superclass, Animal.

In the declaration of the Cat class, the clause ": **public** Mammal" states that Cat has one superclass, Mammal. Thus a Cat object has variable components weight and speed (inherited indirectly from Animal) and gestation_time (inherited from Mammal).

In the declaration of the Bat class, the clause ": **public** Mammal, **public** Flier" states that Bat has two superclasses, Mammal and Flyer. Thus a Bat object has variable components weight and speed (inherited indirectly from Animal), gestation_time (inherited from Mammal), wing_span (inherited from Flier), and sonar_range. A Bat object also inherits methods from both Mammal and Flyer as well as from Animal.

Figure 6.2 summarizes the relationships among these classes (and a few other possible classes).

Multiple inheritance is useful in some real applications (not just tongue-in-cheek applications like Example 6.11). However, multiple inheritance also gives rise to a conceptual difficulty (and to implementation difficulties, which will be explained in Section 6.4).

The conceptual difficulty is as follows. Suppose that the Animal class in Example 6.11 defines a method named M, which is overridden by both the Mammal and Flier subclasses. Then which version of method M is inherited by the Bat class? In other words, which version is called by the method call "$O\text{->}M$ (...)", where O identifies a Bat object? There are several possible answers to this question:

- Call the Mammal version of the method, on the grounds that Mammal is the first-named superclass of Bat.
- Force the programmer to state explicitly, in the Bat class declaration, whether the Mammal or the Flier version of the method is to be preferred.
- Force the programmer to state explicitly, in the method call, whether the Mammal or the Flier version of the method is to be preferred.
- Prohibit such a method call, on the grounds that it is ambiguous. This is C++'s answer.

None of these answers is entirely satisfactory. Consider an innocent application programmer who is expected to use a large class library. The programmer is broadly aware of the repertoire of classes but has only a partial understanding of their relationships, in particular the extent to which the library exploits multiple inheritance. Sooner or later the programmer will receive an unpleasant surprise, either because the compiler prohibits a desired method call, or because the compiler selects an unexpected version of the method.

6.3.5 Interfaces

In software engineering, the term *interface* is often used as a synonym for *application program interface*. In some programming languages, however, the term has a more specific meaning: an **interface** is a program unit that declares (but does not define) the operations that certain other program unit(s) must define.

An ADA package specification is a kind of interface: it declares all the operations that the corresponding package body must define. As we saw in Section 6.1, however, an ADA package specification has other roles such as defining the representation of a private type, so it is an impure kind of interface.

In JAVA, an interface serves mainly to declare abstract methods that certain other classes must define. We may declare any class as implementing a particular interface, in which case the class must define all the abstract methods declared in the interface. (A JAVA interface may define constants as well as declare abstract methods, but it may not do anything else.)

EXAMPLE 6.12   JAVA interfaces

Consider the following JAVA interface:

```
interface Comparable {
    // A Comparable object can be compared with another object to
```

```
    // determine whether it is equal to, less than, or greater than that other
    // object.

    public abstract int compareTo (Object other);

}
```

This interface declares one abstract method, compareTo. Any class that implements the Comparable interface must define a method named compareTo with the same parameter and result types.

Note that, when we speak loosely of a Comparable object, we really mean an object of a class that implements the Comparable interface.

Consider also the following interface:

```
interface Printable {

    // A Printable object can be rendered as a string.

    public abstract String toString ();

}
```

This interface also declares one abstract method, toString. (More generally, a JAVA interface may declare several abstract methods.)

Now consider the following JAVA class:

```
class Date implements Comparable, Printable {

    private int y, m, d;

    public Date (int year, int month, int day) {
        y = year;   m = month;   d = day;
    }

    public advance () {
        ...
    }

    public int compareTo (Object other) {
        Date that = (Date)other;
        return (this.y < that.y ? -1 :
                this.y > that.y ? +1 :
                this.m < that.m ? -1 :
                this.m > that.m ? +1 :
                this.d - that.d);
    }

    public String toString () {
        return (y + "-" + m + "-" + d);
    }

}
```

The Date class implements both the Comparable and Printable interfaces. As required, it defines a method named compareTo and a method named toString, as well as defining constructors and methods of its own.

Interfaces achieve some of the benefits of multiple inheritance, while avoiding the conceptual difficulty explained at the end of Section 6.3.4. In general, a JAVA class has exactly one superclass, but may implement any number of interfaces. The class can inherit method definitions from its superclass (and indirectly from its superclass's superclass, and so on), but it cannot inherit method definitions from the interfaces (since interfaces do not define anything). So there is never any confusion about which method is selected by a particular method call.

In Example 6.12, the Date class has one superclass (Object), and it implements two interfaces. The latter serve only to declare some methods with which the Date class must be equipped. In fact, the Date class defines both these methods itself. Alternatively, it would have been perfectly legal for the Date class to inherit its toString method from the Object class. (That would not have been sensible, however, since the specialized toString method defined in the Date class was more appropriate than the unspecialized toString method defined in the Object class.)

6.4   Implementation notes

Here we outline the implementation of objects and method calls in a language that supports only single inheritance. We also draw attention to the implementation difficulties of multiple inheritance.

6.4.1   Representation of objects

In general, each object of a given class is represented by a tag field (which indicates the class of the object) followed by the object's variable components.

Consider objects of the JAVA Point class and its subclasses in Example 6.8. Each Point object is represented by a tag field followed by two variable components (x and y) of type **double**. Each Circle object is represented by a tag field followed by three variable components (x, y, and r) of type **double**, and each Rectangle object is represented by a tag field followed by four variable components (x, y, w, and h) of type **double**. Objects of all three classes are illustrated in Figure 6.3.

Note that all JAVA objects are accessed through pointers, as shown in Figure 6.3. C++ and ADA95 objects, on the other hand, are accessed through pointers if and only if the programmer chooses to introduce pointers.

An object's tag field indicates its class. Tag fields are needed whenever objects of different classes can be used interchangeably. In particular, they are needed to implement dynamic dispatch (Section 6.4.2). In other circumstances (for example, when a class has no superclass or subclass), tag fields can be omitted.

The variable components of an object can be accessed efficiently, since the compiler can determine their offsets relative to the start of the object. This is true even when objects of a subclass can be used in place of objects of their superclass, assuming *single inheritance*, since inherited variable components are placed at the same offset in objects of the superclass and subclass. For example, the JAVA declaration "Point p;" allows p to refer to an object of class Point, Circle, or Rectangle, but p.x or p.y can be accessed efficiently without even bothering to test the object's class.

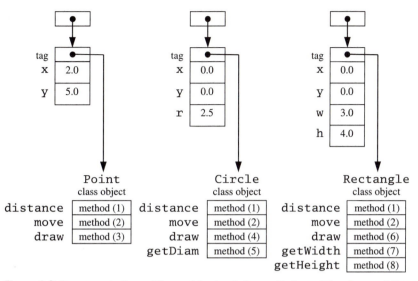

Figure 6.3 Representation of JAVA objects of classes Point, Circle, and Rectangle (Example 6.8).

In the presence of *multiple inheritance*, it is much more difficult to represent objects in such a way that variable components can be accessed efficiently. In Example 6.11, all objects have weight and speed components; so far so good. But a Cat object has a gestation_time component, a Bat object has gestation_time and wing_span components, an Eagle object has wing_span and egg_size components, and a Penguin object has an egg_size component. There is no simple way to represent objects of all these classes in such a way that a given component always has the same offset relative to the start of the object.

6.4.2   Implementation of method calls

In a method call, the target object's address is passed to the called method, whether it is an explicit parameter or not. For instance, in a JAVA method call of the form "$O.M(\dots)$", the address of the target object (determined by O) is passed to the method named M, enabling that method to inspect and/or update the target object. In effect, the target object is an implicit argument, and is denoted by **this** inside the method body.

If a particular method is never overridden, a call to that method can be implemented like an ordinary procedure call (see Section 5.3).

However, complications arise when a subclass overrides a method of its superclass. In Example 6.8, both the Circle and Rectangle subclasses override the Point class's draw method. When the method named draw is called with a target object whose class is not known at compile-time, dynamic dispatch is necessary to determine the correct method at run-time. Objects must be represented in such a way that dynamic dispatch is possible.

For each class *C* a *class object* is created, which contains a table of addresses of the methods with which class *C* is equipped. Figure 6.3 illustrates the `Point`, `Circle`, and `Rectangle` class objects. Note that they all share the same `distance` and `move` methods, but their `draw` methods are different. Moreover, the `Circle` class object alone contains the address of the method named `getDiam`, while the `Rectangle` class object alone contains the addresses of the methods named `getWidth` and `getHeight`.

An ordinary object's tag field contains a pointer to the appropriate class object. A method call "*O.M*(…)" is therefore implemented as follows:

(1) Determine the target object from *O*.

(2) Follow the pointer from the target object's tag field to the corresponding class object.

(3) Select the method named *M* in the class object.

(4) Call that method, passing the address of the target object.

The method named *M* can be accessed efficiently in step (3), since the compiler can determine its offset relative to the start of the class object, assuming *single inheritance*.

In the presence of *multiple inheritance*, it is much more difficult to implement dynamic dispatch efficiently. There is no simple way to represent class objects in such a way that a given method always has the same offset. This problem is analogous to the problem of representing the ordinary objects themselves (Section 6.4.1).

Summary

In this chapter:

- We have studied the concepts of packages, abstract types, and classes, which are program units well suited to be the building blocks of large programs.

- We have seen that a package consists of several (usually related) components, which may be any entities such as types, constants, variables, and procedures.

- We have seen that each component of a program unit may be either public or private, which is encapsulation. Encapsulation enables a program unit to have a simple application program interface.

- We have seen that an abstract type has a private representation and public operations (procedures). This encapsulation enables the abstract type's representation to be changed without affecting application code.

- We have seen that the objects of a class typically have private variable components and public operations. This encapsulation enables the objects' representation to be changed without affecting application code.

- We have seen that a class may have subclasses, which inherit some or all of the operations from their superclass.

- We have seen how objects are represented in a computer, and how method calls are implemented.

Further reading

The importance of encapsulation in the design of large programs was first clearly recognized by PARNAS (1972). He advocated a discipline whereby access to each global variable is restricted to procedures provided for the purpose, on the grounds that this discipline enables the variable's representation to be changed without forcing major changes to the rest of the program. A variable encapsulated in this way is just what we now call an object.

A discussion of encapsulation in general, and a rationale for the design of ADA packages in particular, may be found in Chapter 8 of ICHBIAH (1979).

The concept of abstract types was introduced by LISKOV and ZILLES (1974). This concept has proved to be extremely valuable for structuring large programs. Abstract types are amenable to formal specification, and much research has focused on the properties of such specifications, and in particular on exploring exactly what sets of values are defined by such a specification.

The concept of a class, and the idea that a class can inherit operations from another class, can be traced back to

SIMULA67, described in BIRTWHISTLE et al. (1979). However, SIMULA67 did not support encapsulation, so the variable components of an object could be accessed by application code. Furthermore, SIMULA67 confused the concept of object with the independent concepts of reference and coroutine.

The classification of operations into constructors, accessors, and transformers was first suggested by MEYER (1989). Meyer has been a major influence in the modern development of object-oriented programming, and he has designed his own object-oriented language EIFFEL, described in MEYER (1988).

In this chapter we have touched on software engineering. Programming is just one aspect of software engineering, and the programming language is just one of the tools in the software engineer's kit. A thorough exploration of the relationship between programming languages and the wider aspects of software engineering may be found in GHEZZI and JAZAYERI (1997).

Exercises

Exercises for Section 6.1

6.1.1   Choose a programming language (such as C or PASCAL) that does not support packages, abstract types, or classes. (a) How would the trigonometric package of Example 6.2 be programmed in your language? (b) What are the disadvantages of programming in this way?

*6.1.2   Choose a programming language (such as FORTRAN or PASCAL) that has built-in features for text input/output. Design (but do not implement) a package that provides equivalent functionality. The user of your package should be able to achieve all of your language's text input/output capabilities without using any of the language's built-in features.

Exercises for Section 6.2

6.2.1   (a) Design a Money abstract type, whose values are amounts of money expressed in your own currency. Equip your abstract type with operations such as addition and subtraction of amounts of money, and multiplication by a given integer. (b) Suggest an efficient representation for your abstract type. Use any suitable programming language.

6.2.2   (a) Design a Complex abstract type, whose values are complex numbers. Equip your abstract type with operations such as magnitude, complex addition, complex subtraction, and complex multiplication. (b) Suggest an efficient representation for your abstract type.

6.2.3   (a) Design a Date abstract type, whose values are calendar dates. Equip your abstract type with operations such as equality test, comparison ("is before"), adding or subtracting a given number of days, and conversion to ISO format "*yyyy-mm-dd*". (b) Suggest an efficient representation for your abstract type.

6.2.4 (a) Design a `Fuzzy` abstract type, whose values are *yes, no,* and *maybe.* Equip your abstract type with operations such as *and, or,* and *not.* (b) Suggest an efficient representation for your abstract type.

*6.2.5 (a) Design a `Rational` abstract type, whose values are rational numbers m/n. Equip your abstract type with operations such as construction from a given pair of integers m and n, addition, subtraction, multiplication, equality test, and comparison ("is less than"). (b) Implement your abstract type, representing each rational number by a pair of integers (m, n). (c) Modify your implementation, representing each rational number by a pair of integers *with no common factor.* What are the advantages and disadvantages of this modified representation?

Exercises for Section 6.3

6.3.1 (a) Design a `Counter` class, such that each `Counter` object is to be a counter (i.e., a nonnegative integer). Equip your class with operations to zero the counter, increment the counter, and inspect the counter. (b) Implement your class. Use any suitable object-oriented language.

6.3.2 Consider the class hierarchy in Figure 6.1. (a) Define classes for other useful shapes, such as straight lines, rectangles, etc., placing them in an appropriate hierarchy. Each of these classes must provide a `draw` operation. (b) Define a `Picture` class, such that each `Picture` object is to be a collection of shapes. Provide an operation that draws the whole picture, by drawing all of its component shapes.

*6.3.3 (a) Design a `Text` class, where each `Text` object is to be a text (i.e., a sequence of characters subdivided into paragraphs). Equip your class with operations to load a text from a given text-file, save a text to a text-file, insert a given sequence of characters at a selected position in a text, delete a selected sequence of characters, and display a text within a given line-width. (b) Implement your class.

6.3.4 Redesign and reimplement your `Rational` abstract type of Exercise 6.2.5 as a class.

6.3.5 A fictional bank offers the following types of customer accounts. A *basic account* has no frills at all. A *savings account* pays interest at the end of each day on the current balance. A *current account* provides the customer with an overdraft facility, a checkbook, an ATM card, and a PIN (personal identification number) to enable an ATM to verify his/her identity.

Suppose that the class hierarchy of Figure 6.4 has been designed for the software to maintain such accounts.

(a) Say which methods are inherited and which methods are overridden by each subclass.

(b) Outline how this class hierarchy would be expressed in C++, JAVA, or ADA95. Make reasonable assumptions about the parameters and result of each method. You need not define the methods in detail.

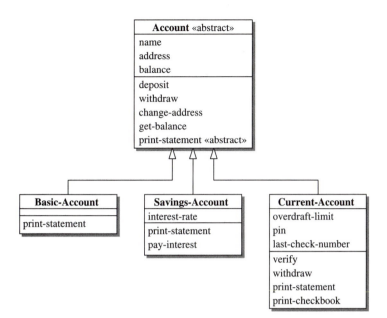

Figure 6.4 Class hierarchy (Exercise 6.3.5).

Exercises for Section 6.4

6.4.1 Draw diagrams showing the representation of objects of the classes you designed in Exercises 6.3.1–6.3.4.

Chapter 7

Generic abstraction

Cost-effective software engineering demands reuse of previously-implemented program units. To be reusable, a program unit must be capable of being used in a variety of applications. Typical examples of reusable program units are stack, queue, list, and set classes (or abstract types). It turns out that these and many other reusable program units are intrinsically *generic*, i.e., capable of being parameterized with respect to the type of data on which they operate. Thus the concept of a generic unit is important in practice. Unfortunately, generic units are supported only by a few of the major programming languages, and this has tended to inhibit software reuse.

In this chapter we shall study:

- *generic units*, and how they may be *instantiated* to generate ordinary program units;
- generic units with *type parameters*;
- implementation of generic units.

7.1 Generic units and instantiation

In the last chapter we studied program units like packages, abstract types, and classes. Such program units may depend on entities (such as values and types) that are defined elsewhere in the program, but then they are not reusable. The key to reuse is to parameterize such program units.

A ***generic unit*** is a program unit that is parameterized with respect to entities on which it depends. ***Instantiation*** of a generic unit generates an ordinary program unit, in which each of the generic unit's formal parameters is replaced by an argument.

A generic unit can be instantiated as often as required, thus generating on demand a family of similar program units. This concept places a very powerful tool into programmers' hands. A single generic unit can be instantiated several times in the same program, thus avoiding duplication of program code. It can also be instantiated in many different programs, thus facilitating reuse.

Let us note, in passing, that generic units are predicted by the Abstraction Principle. In Section 5.1.3 we saw that a function procedure is an abstraction over an expression, and that a proper procedure is an abstraction over a command. Likewise:

- A *generic unit* is an abstraction over a *declaration*. That is to say, a generic unit has a body that is a declaration, and a generic instantiation is a declaration that will produce bindings by elaborating the generic unit's body.

Generic units are in fact supported by ADA, C++, and (since 2004) JAVA. These three languages have approached the design of generics from three different angles, and a comparison is instructive.

In this section we study ADA and C++ generic units parameterized with respect to *values* on which they depend. (JAVA does not support such generic units.) In Section 7.2 we shall study ADA, C++, and JAVA generic units parameterized with respect to *types* (or *classes*) on which they depend, an even more powerful concept.

7.1.1 Generic packages in ADA

ADA supports both generic procedures and generic packages. Here we shall focus on generic packages.

EXAMPLE 7.1   ADA generic package

The following ADA generic package encapsulates an abstract type whose values are bounded queues of characters. The package is parameterized with respect to the capacity of the queue.

```
generic
   capacity: Positive;
package Queues is

   type Queue is limited private;
   -- A Queue value represents a queue whose elements are characters and
   -- whose maximum length is capacity.

   procedure clear (q: out Queue);
   -- Make queue q empty.

   procedure add (q: in out Queue;
                  e: in Character);
   -- Add element e to the rear of queue q.

   procedure remove (q: in out Queue;
                     e: out Character);
   -- Remove element e from the front of queue q.

private

   type Queue is
      record
         length: Integer range 0 .. capacity;
         front, rear: Integer range 0 .. capacity-1;
         elems: array (0 .. capacity-1) of Character;
      end record;
   -- A queue is represented by a cyclic array, with the queued elements
   -- stored either in elems(front..rear-1) or in
   -- elems(front..capacity-1) and elems(0..rear-1).

end Queues;
```

The clause "`capacity: Positive;`" between the keywords **generic** and **package** states that `capacity` is a formal parameter of the generic package, and that it denotes an unknown positive integer value. This formal parameter is used both in the generic package specification above (in the definition of type `Queue`) and in the package body below.

The package body would be as follows (for simplicity neglecting checks for underflow and overflow):

```
package body Queues is

   procedure clear (q: out Queue) is
   begin
     q.front := 0;  q.rear := 0;  q.length := 0;
   end;

   procedure add (q: in out Queue;
                  e: in Character) is
   begin
     q.elems(q.rear) := e;
     q.rear := (q.rear + 1) mod capacity;
     q.length := q.length + 1;
   end;

   procedure remove (q: in out Queue;
                     e: out Character) is
   begin
     e := q.elems(q.front);
     q.front := (q.front + 1) mod capacity;
     q.length := q.length - 1;
   end;

end Queues;
```

We must instantiate this generic package by a special form of declaration called an *instantiation*:

```
package Line_Buffers is new Queues(120);
```

This instantiation of `Queues` is elaborated as follows. First, the formal parameter `capacity` is bound to 120 (the argument of the instantiation). Next, the specification and body of `Queues` are elaborated, generating a package that encapsulates queues with space for up to 120 characters. That package is named `Line_Buffers`.

Here is another instantiation:

```
package Input_Buffers is new Queues(80);
```

This instantiation generates a package that encapsulates queues with space for up to 80 characters. That package is named `Input_Buffers`.

The result of an instantiation is an ordinary package, which can be used like any other package:

```
inbuf: Input_Buffers.Queue;
...
Input_Buffers.add(inbuf, '*');
```

7.1.2   Generic classes in C++

C++ supports both generic functions (called *function templates*) and generic classes (called *class templates*). Here we shall focus on generic classes.

EXAMPLE 7.2   C++ generic class

The following C++ generic class is similar to Example 7.1, encapsulating an abstract type whose values are bounded queues of characters. The class is parameterized with respect to the capacity of the queue.

```
template
  <int capacity>
class Queue {

// A Queue object represents a queue whose elements are characters and
// whose maximum length is capacity.

private:

  char elems[capacity];
  int front, rear, length;
  // The queue is represented by a cyclic array, with the queued elements
  // stored either in elems[front..rear-1] or in
  // elems[front..capacity-1] and elems[0..rear-1].

public:

  Queue ();
  // Construct an empty queue.

  void add (char e);
  // Add element e to the rear of this queue.

  char remove ();
  // Remove and return the front element of this queue.

}
```

The clause "**int capacity**" between angle brackets states that capacity is a formal parameter of the generic class, and that it denotes an unknown integer value. This formal parameter is used in the class's component declarations.

We can define the generic class's constructor and methods separately, as follows:

```
template
  <int capacity>
Queue<capacity>::Queue () {
  front = rear = length = 0;
}

template
  <int capacity>
void Queue<capacity>::add (char e) {
  elems[rear] = e;
  rear = (rear + 1) % capacity;
  length++;
}
```

```
template
  <int capacity>
char Queue<capacity>::remove () {
  char e = elems[front];
  front = (front + 1) % capacity;
  length--;
  return e;
}
```

Note that every constructor and method definition must be prefixed by "`template <int capacity>`". This notation is cumbersome and error-prone.

We can instantiate this generic class as follows:

```
typedef Queue<80> Input_Buffer;
typedef Queue<120> Line_Buffer;
```

The instantiation Queue<80> generates an instance of the Queue generic class in which each occurrence of the formal parameter capacity is replaced by the value 80; the generated class is named Input_Buffer. The instantiation "Queue<120>" generates another instance of Queue in which each occurrence of capacity is replaced by 120; the generated class is named Line_Buffer.

We can now declare variables of type Input_Buffer and Line_Buffer in the usual way:

```
Input_Buffer inbuf;
Line_Buffer outbuf;
Line_Buffer errbuf;
```

Alternatively, we can instantiate the generic class and use the generated class directly:

```
Queue<80> inbuf;
Queue<120> outbuf;
Queue<120> errbuf;
```

A C++ generic class can be instantiated "on the fly", as we have just seen. This gives rise to a conceptual problem and a related pragmatic problem:

- The conceptual problem is concerned with type equivalence. If the two variables outbuf and errbuf are separately declared with types Queue<120> and Queue<120>, C++ deems the types of these variables to be equivalent, since both types were obtained by instantiating the same generic class with the same argument. But if two variables were declared to be of types Queue<m> and Queue<n-1>, the compiler could not decide whether their types were equivalent unless it could predict the values of the variables m and n. For this reason, C++ instantiations are restricted: it must be possible to evaluate their arguments at compile-time.

- The pragmatic problem is that programmers lose control over code expansion. For example, if "Queue<120>" occurs in several places in the program, a simple-minded C++ compiler might generate several instances of Queue, while a smart compiler should create only one instance.

(ADA avoids these problems by insisting that generic units are instantiated before being used. If we instantiated the same ADA generic package twice with the same arguments, the generated packages would be distinct, and any type components of these generated packages would be distinct. This is consistent with ADA's usual name equivalence rule for types. So ADA allows arguments in instantiations to be evaluated at run-time.)

7.2   Type and class parameters

We have seen that, if a program unit uses a *value* defined elsewhere, the program unit can be made generic and parameterized with respect to that value.

If a program unit uses a *type* (or class) defined elsewhere, the Correspondence Principle (see Section 5.2.3) suggests that we should be able to make the program unit generic and parameterize it with respect to that type. Thus we have a completely new kind of parameter, a *type parameter*.

ADA, C++, and JAVA generic units may have type parameters. In this section we use similar examples to compare generic units with type parameters in these languages.

7.2.1   Type parameters in ADA

An ADA generic unit may be parameterized with respect to any type on which it depends.

EXAMPLE 7.3   ADA generic package with a type parameter

The following ADA generic package encapsulates an abstract type whose values are homogeneous lists. The package is parameterized with respect to the type of the list elements.

```
generic
  type Element is private;
package Lists is

  type List is limited private;
  -- A List value represents a list whose elements are of type Element.

  procedure clear (l: out List);
  -- Make list l empty.

  procedure add (l: in out List; e: in Element);
  -- Add element e to the end of list l.

  ... -- other operations

private

  capacity: constant Integer := ...;

  type List is
      record
          length: Integer range 0 .. capacity;
```

```
        elems: array (1 .. capacity) of Element;
      end record;

end Lists;
```

The clause "**type** Element **is private**;" between the keywords **generic** and **package** states that Element is a formal parameter of the generic package, and that it denotes an unknown type. This formal parameter is used both in the package specification and in the package body:

```
package body Lists is

  procedure clear (l: out List) is
  begin
    l.length := 0;
  end;

  procedure add (l: in out List; e: in Element) is
  begin
    l.length := l.length + 1;
    l.elems(l.length) := e;
  end;

  ... -- other operations

end Lists;
```

The following instantiation of Lists:

```
package Phrases is new Lists(Character);
```

is elaborated as follows. First, the formal parameter Element is bound to the Character type (the argument in the instantiation). Then the specification and body of Lists are elaborated, generating a package that encapsulates lists with elements of type Character. That package is named Phrases, and can be used like any ordinary package:

```
sentence: Phrases.List;
...
Phrases.add(sentence, '.');
```

Now consider the following application code:

```
type Transaction is record ... end record;
package Transaction_Lists is new Lists(Transaction);
```

This instantiation of Lists is elaborated similarly. The generated package named Transaction_Lists encapsulates lists with elements of type Transaction.

If a generic unit is parameterized with respect to a *value*, it can use the corresponding argument value, although it does not know what that value is. By the same reasoning, if a generic unit is parameterized with respect to a *type*, it should be able to use the corresponding argument type, although it does not know what that type is. But there is a paradox here: if the generic unit knows nothing about the argument type, it can declare variables of the type, but it cannot apply any operations to these variables! So the generic unit *must* know at least some of the operations with which the type is equipped.

In Example 7.3, the clause "**type** Element **is private**;" between the keywords **generic** and **package** is ADA's way of stating that the argument type is equipped with (at least) the assignment and equality test operations. Inside the generic package, therefore, values of type Element can be assigned by commands like "l.elems(l.length) := e;". The compiler does not know the actual type of these values, but at least it does know that the type is equipped with the assignment operation.

Often a type parameter must be assumed to be equipped with a more specialized operation. The following example illustrates such a situation.

EXAMPLE 7.4   ADA generic package with a type parameter and a function parameter

The following ADA generic package encapsulates sequences, i.e., sortable lists. The generic package is parameterized with respect to the type Element of the sequence elements. Since one of its operations is to sort a sequence of elements, the generic package is also parameterized with respect to a function precedes that tests whether one value of type Element should precede another in a sorted sequence.

```
generic
  type Element is private;
  with function precedes (x, y: Element) return Boolean;
package Sequences is

  type Sequence is limited private;
  -- A Sequence value represents a sequence whose elements are of
  -- type Element.

  procedure clear (s: out Sequence);
  -- Make sequence s empty.

  procedure append (s: in out Sequence;
                    e: in Element);
  -- Add element e to the end of sequence s.

  procedure sort (s: in out Sequence);
  -- Sort sequence s with respect to the function precedes.

private

  capacity: constant Integer := ...;

  type Sequence is
      record
        length: Integer range 0 .. capacity;
        elems: array (1 .. capacity) of Element;
      end record;

end Sequences;
```

The clause "**type** Element **is private**;" states that Element is a formal parameter of the generic package, and that it denotes an unknown type equipped with the assignment and equality test operations. The clause "**with function** `precedes (x, y: Element)` **return** `Boolean;`" states that `precedes` is also a formal parameter, and that it denotes an unknown function that takes two arguments of the type denoted by `Element` and returns a result of type `Boolean`. Between them, these two clauses say that the unknown type denoted by `Element` is equipped with a boolean function named `precedes` as well as the assignment and equality test operations.

The package body uses both the `Element` type and the `precedes` function:

```
package body Sequences is

   ...

   procedure sort (s: in out Sequence) is
      e: Element;
   begin
      ...
      if precedes(e, s.elems(i)) then ...
      ...
   end;

end Sequences;
```

Here is a possible instantiation of `Sequences`:

```
type Transaction is record ... end record;

function earlier (t1, t2: Transaction) return Boolean;
-- Return true if and only if t1 has an earlier timestamp than t2.

package Transaction_Sequences is
        new Sequences(Transaction, earlier);
```

This instantiation is elaborated as follows. First, the formal parameter `Element` is bound to the `Transaction` type (the first argument), and the formal parameter `precedes` is bound to the `earlier` function (the second argument). Then the specification and body of `Sequences` are elaborated, generating a package encapsulating sequences of `Transaction` records that can be sorted into order by timestamp. The generated package is named `Transaction_Sequences`, and can be used like any ordinary package:

```
audit_trail: Transaction_Sequences.Sequence;
...
Transaction_Sequences.sort(audit_trail);
```

Here are two further instantiations:

```
package Ascending_Sequences is
        new Sequences(Float, "<");

package Descending_Sequences is
        new Sequences(Float, ">");

readings: Ascending_Sequences.Sequence;
...
Ascending_Sequences.sort(readings);
```

The first instantiation generates a package encapsulating sequences of real numbers that can be sorted into *ascending* order. This is so because "<" denotes a function that takes two arguments of type `Float` and returns a result of type `Boolean`. The second instantiation generates a package encapsulating sequences of real numbers that can be sorted into *descending* order. This is so because ">" also denotes a function that takes two arguments of type `Float` and returns a result of type `Boolean`, but of course the result is true if and only if its first argument is numerically *greater* than its second argument.

In general, if an ADA generic unit is to have a type parameter T, we specify it by a clause of the form:

type T **is** specification of operations with which T is equipped ;

The compiler checks the generic unit itself to ensure that:

$$\text{operations used for } T \text{ in the generic unit}$$
$$\subseteq \text{operations with which } T \text{ is equipped} \qquad (7.1)$$

The compiler separately checks every instantiation of the generic unit to ensure that:

$$\text{operations with which } T \text{ is equipped}$$
$$\subseteq \text{operations with which the argument type is equipped} \qquad (7.2)$$

Together, (7.1) and (7.2) guarantee that the argument type is indeed equipped with all operations used for T in the generic unit.

Summarizing, the design of ADA generic units enables the compiler to type-check the declaration of each generic unit, and separately to type-check every instantiation of the generic unit. Thus, once implemented, ADA generic units can be safely reused.

7.2.2   Type parameters in C++

A C++ generic unit may be parameterized with respect to any type or class on which it depends.

EXAMPLE 7.5   C++ generic class with a type parameter (1)

The following C++ generic class encapsulates homogeneous lists. It is parameterized with respect to the type `Element` of the list elements.

```
template
  <class Element>
class List is

    // A List object represents a list whose elements are of type Element.

private:

    const int capacity = ...;
    int length;
    Element elems[capacity];
```

```
public:

    List ();
    // Construct an empty list.

    void append (Element e);
    // Add element e to the end of this list.

    ... // other methods

}
```

The clause "**class** Element" between angle brackets states that Element is a formal parameter of the generic class, and that it denotes an unknown type. (Do not be misled by C++'s syntax: the unknown type may be *any* type, not necessarily a class type.)

As usual, we define the generic class's constructor and methods separately:

```
template
  <class Element>
List<Element>::List () {
  length = 0;
}

template
  <class Element>
void List<Element>::append (Element e) {
  elems[length++] = e;
}

... // other methods
```

Consider the following instantiation:

```
typedef List<char> Phrase;
```

This instantiation List<**char**> is elaborated as follows. First, the formal parameter Element is bound to the **char** type. Then the generic class and the corresponding constructor and method definitions are elaborated, generating a class that encapsulates lists with elements of type **char**. The generated class can be used like any other class:

```
Phrase sentence;
...
sentence.add('.');
```

Finally, consider the following application code:

```
struct Transaction { ... };

typedef List<Transaction> Transaction_List;
```

This instantiation is elaborated similarly. The generated class encapsulates lists with elements of type Transaction.

EXAMPLE 7.6 C++ generic class with a type parameter (2)

The following C++ generic class encapsulates sequences, i.e., sortable lists. It is parameterized with respect to the type Element of the sequence elements.

```
template
  <class Element>
class Sequence is
```

// A Sequence object represents a sequence whose elements are of
// type Element.

private:

```
const int capacity = ...;
int length;
Element elems[capacity];
```

public:

```
Sequence ();
```
// Construct an empty sequence.

```
void append (Element e);
```
// Add element e to the end of this sequence.

```
void sort ();
```
// Sort this sequence into ascending order.

```
}
```

As usual, we define the constructor and methods separately, for example:

```
template
  <class Element>
void Sequence<Element>::sort () {
  Element e;
  ...
  if (e < elems[i])  ...
  ...
}
```

Note the use of the "<" operation in the definition of the sort method. This code is perfectly legal, although it assumes without proper justification that the argument type denoted by Element is indeed equipped with a "<" operation.

Here is a possible instantiation:

```
typedef Sequence<float> Number_Sequence;
Number_Sequence readings;
...
readings.sort();
```

This instantiation Sequence<**float**> is elaborated as follows. First, the formal parameter Element is bound to the **float** type. Then the generic class and corresponding method definitions are elaborated, generating a class encapsulating sequences of **float** values that can be sorted into ascending order.

Now consider the following instantiation:

```
typedef char* String;
typedef Sequence<String> String_Sequence;
```

The instantiation Sequence<String> generates a class String_Sequence encapsulating sequences of String values (where a String value is a pointer to an array of characters). Unfortunately, this class's `sort` operation does not behave as we might expect: the "<" operation when applied to operands of type **char*** merely compares pointers; it does *not* compare the two strings lexicographically!

Finally consider the following instantiation:

```
struct Transaction { ... };
typedef Sequence<Transaction> Transaction_Sequence;
```

The compiler will reject the instantiation `Sequence<Transaction>`, because the `Transaction` type is not equipped with a "<" operation.

The problem with the above generic class is that one of its methods is defined in terms of the "<" operation, but some types are equipped with an unsuitable "<" operation, and other types are equipped with no "<" operation at all.

The problem illustrated in Example 7.6 exposes a weakness in C++ generics. Various workarounds are possible, such as passing a comparison function to the `sort` method, but none is entirely satisfactory.

In general, if a C++ generic unit is to have a type parameter T, we specify it simply by enclosing in angle brackets a clause of the form:

```
class T
```

This clause reveals nothing about the operations with which T is supposed to be equipped. When the compiler checks the generic unit, all it can do is to note which operations are used for T. The compiler must then check every instantiation of the generic unit to ensure that:

$$\text{operations used for } T \text{ in the generic unit}$$
$$\subseteq \text{ operations with which the argument type is equipped} \qquad (7.3)$$

C++ generic units are not a secure foundation for software reuse. The compiler cannot completely type-check the definition of a generic unit; it can only type-check individual instantiations. Thus future reuse of a generic unit might result in unexpected type errors.

7.2.3   Class parameters in JAVA

Until 2004, JAVA did not support any form of generic abstraction. However, JAVA now supports *generic classes*, which are classes parameterized with respect to other classes.

EXAMPLE 7.7   JAVA generic class with a class parameter

The following JAVA generic class encapsulates homogeneous lists. The class is parameterized with respect to the class of the elements of the list.

```
class List <Element> {
    // A List object represents a list whose elements are of class Element.
```

```
        private length;
        private Element[] elems;

        public List () {
        // Construct an empty list.
            ...
        }

        public void append (Element e) {
        // Add element e to the end of this list.
            ...
        }

        ... // other methods

    }
```

The class declaration's heading states that Element is a formal parameter of the List generic class, and that it denotes an unknown class.

This generic class can be instantiated as follows:

```
List<Character> sentence;
List<Transaction> transactions;
```

Here sentence refers to a list whose elements are objects of class Character, and transactions refers to a list whose elements are objects of class Transaction.

The argument in an instantiation must be a class, not a primitive type:

```
List<char> sentence;   // illegal!
```

If a JAVA generic class must assume that a class parameter is equipped with particular operations, the class parameter must be specified as implementing a suitable interface (see Section 6.3.5). Such a class parameter is said to be ***bounded*** by the interface.

EXAMPLE 7.8   JAVA generic class with a bounded class parameter

Consider the following JAVA generic interface:

```
interface Comparable <Item> {

    // A Comparable<Item> object can be compared with an object of
    // class Item to determine whether the first object is equal to, less than,
    // or greater than the second object.

    public abstract int compareTo (Item that);
    // Return 0 if this object is equal to that, or
    // a negative integer if this object is less than that, or
    // a positive integer if this object is greater than that.

}
```

If a class *C* is declared as implementing the interface Comparable<*C*>, *C* must be equipped with a compareTo operation that compares the target object (of class *C*) with another object of class *C*.

The following JAVA generic class encapsulates sequences, i.e., sortable lists, equipped with a sort operation:

```
class Sequence
        <Element implements Comparable<Element>> {

    // A Sequence object represents a sequence whose elements are of
    // type Element.

    private length;
    private Element[] elems;

    public Sequence () {
    // Construct an empty sequence.
        ...
    }

    public void append (Element e) {
    // Add element e to the end of this sequence.
        ...
    }

    public void sort () {
    // Sort this sequence into ascending order.
        Element e;
        ...
        if (e.compareTo(elems[i]) < 0)   ...
        ...
    }

}
```

The clause "Element **implements** Comparable<Element>" between angle brackets states that Element is a formal parameter of the generic class, and that it denotes an unknown class equipped with a compareTo operation.

Here is a possible instantiation of the Sequence class:

```
Sequence<Transaction> auditTrail;
...
auditTrail.sort();
```

where we are assuming that the Transaction class is declared as follows:

```
class Transaction implements Comparable<Transaction> {

    private ...;   // representation

    public int compareTo (Transaction that) {
    // Return 0 if this transaction has the same timestamp as that, or
    // negative if this transaction has an earlier timestamp than that, or
    // positive if this transaction has a later timestamp than that.
        ...
    }

    ... // other methods

}
```

On the other hand, the instantiation Sequence<Point> would be illegal: the Point class (Example 6.8) is not declared as implementing the Comparable<Point> interface.

In general, if a JAVA generic unit is to have a class parameter *C*, we specify it by a clause of the form:

    class *C* **implements** *Int*

where *Int* is an interface. (If "**implements** *Int*" is omitted, an empty interface is assumed.) The compiler checks the generic unit itself to ensure that:

$$\text{operations used for } C \text{ in the generic unit}$$
$$\subseteq \text{operations declared in } Int \qquad (7.4)$$

The compiler separately checks every instantiation of the generic unit to ensure that:

$$\text{operations declared in } Int$$
$$\subseteq \text{operations with which the argument class is equipped} \qquad (7.5)$$

Together, (7.4) and (7.5) guarantee that the argument class is indeed equipped with all operations used for *C* in the generic unit.

The design of JAVA generic units (unlike those of C++) is based on type theory. The practical significance of this is that the compiler can type-check the declaration of each generic unit, and separately type-check every instantiation. Thus JAVA generic units can be safely reused.

The weakness of JAVA generic classes is that they can be parameterized only with respect to classes. They cannot be parameterized with respect to primitive types such as **char**, **int**, and **float** (a consequence of JAVA's lack of type completeness), nor can they be parameterized with respect to *values* on which they depend.

7.3 Implementation notes

Generic units with type parameters pose interesting implementation problems. Since a type parameter denotes an unknown type, the compiler cannot determine from the generic unit itself how values of that type will be represented. (In particular, the compiler cannot determine how much storage space variables of that unknown type will occupy.) Only when the generic unit is instantiated does the compiler have all that information.

7.3.1 Implementation of ADA generic units

Recall the Lists generic package of Example 7.3. The type parameter Element denotes an unknown type, so the compiler does not yet know how values of type Element will be represented. Moreover, the compiler does not yet know how values of type List will be represented, since that type is defined in terms of Element.

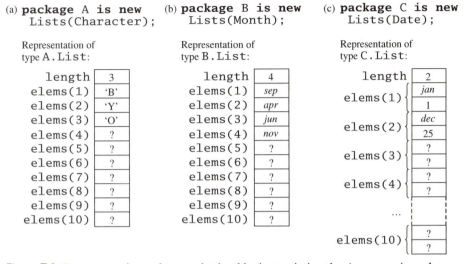

Figure 7.1 Representations of types obtained by instantiating the ADA generic package Lists (Example 7.3).

When the generic package is instantiated, however, the type parameter Element is replaced by a known type. Figure 7.1(a) illustrates an instantiation in which Element is replaced by Character. Similarly, Figure 7.1(b) and (c) illustrate instantiations in which Element is replaced by an enumeration type Month and by a record type Date, respectively. These three instantiations define three distinct types (A.List, B.List, and C.List), and the compiler knows the representation of each type.

In general, each instantiation of an ADA generic package is compiled by generating object code specialized for that instantiation.

In some cases, however, different instantiations can share the same object code if the types involved have similar representations. In Figure 7.1(a) and (b), the representations of the types A.List and B.List are similar enough to make shared object code feasible.

7.3.2 Implementation of C++ generic units

Implementation of C++ generic classes is broadly similar to the implementation outlined in Section 7.3.1, but is slightly complicated by the fact that C++ generic classes can be instantiated "on the fly".

Recall the List generic class of Example 7.5. The application code could be peppered with declarations of variables of type List<**float**> (say). In C++'s type system all these types are regarded as equivalent, so all these variables are equipped with the same operations. If a generic class is instantiated in different places with the same arguments, the compiler must make all these instantiations share the same object code.

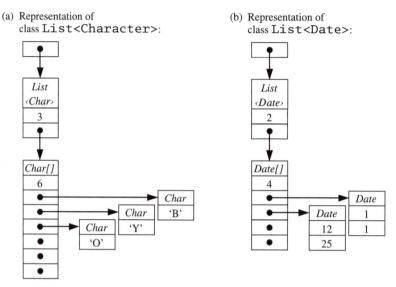

(a) Representation of
    class List<Character>:

(b) Representation of
    class List<Date>:

Figure 7.2 Representations of classes obtained by instantiating the JAVA generic class
List (Example 7.7).

7.3.3 Implementation of JAVA generic units

Implementation of JAVA generic classes is greatly simplified by the fact that
they can be parameterized with respect to classes only (not values or primitive
types), together with the fact that objects of all classes are accessed through
pointers.

Recall the List generic class of Example 7.7. All objects of class
List<Element> have similar representations, as illustrated in Figure 7.2,
regardless of the actual class denoted by Element. Therefore, all instantiations
of the List generic class can share the same object code.

Summary

In this chapter:

- We have seen the importance of generic abstraction for software reuse.
- We have studied generic units, and seen how they may be instantiated to generate
  ordinary program units. We have seen that procedures, packages, and classes can
  all be made generic.
- We have seen how generic units may be parameterized with respect to values.
- We have seen how generic units may be parameterized with respect to types,
  including types equipped with specific operations.
- We have seen how generic units can be implemented, paying particular attention to
  the problems caused by type parameters.

Further reading

A rationale for the design of ADA generic units may be found in Chapter 8 of ICHBIAH (1979).

Likewise, a rationale for the design of C++ generic units may be found in Chapter 15 of STROUSTRUP (1994). Chapter 8 of STROUSTRUP (1997) gives many examples of C++ generic units, including several possible workarounds for the problem identified in Example 7.6.

JAVA generic classes were based on a proposal by BRACHA et al. (1998). The paper lucidly explains the design of generic classes, showing how it is solidly founded on type theory. The paper also shows in detail how generic classes can be implemented easily and efficiently.

Exercises

Exercises for Section 7.1

7.1.1 Consider the ADA generic package of Example 7.1 and the C++ generic class of Example 7.2.

(a) Instantiate each of these generic units to declare a queue `line` with space for up to 72 characters. Write code to read a line of characters, adding each character to the queue `line` (which is initially empty).

(b) Modify each of these generic units to provide an operation that tests whether a queue is empty. Write code to remove all characters from the queue `line`, and print them one by one.

Exercises for Section 7.2

7.2.1 Consider the ADA generic package of Example 7.3, the C++ generic class of Example 7.5, and the JAVA generic class of Example 7.7. Instantiate each of these so that you can declare a variable `itinerary` to contain a list of airports. Assume that you are given a suitable type or class `Airport`.

7.2.2 Consider the ADA generic package of Example 7.4, the C++ generic class of Example 7.6, and the JAVA generic class of Example 7.8. Instantiate each of these so that you can declare a sequence of words, where a word is a string of letters. Do this in such a way that the `sort` operation will sort the words into alphabetical order.

7.2.3 Consider the ADA generic package of Example 7.1 and the C++ generic class of Example 7.2.

(a) Modify each of these generic units so that it is parameterized with respect to the type of the queue elements as well as the capacity of the queue.

(b) Why cannot we declare a JAVA generic class whose parameters are the type of the queue elements and the capacity of the queue?

(c) Declare a JAVA generic class whose parameter is the class of the queue elements, such that the capacity of the queue is a parameter of the *constructor*.

*7.2.4 Design a generic unit that implements sets. A *set* is an unordered collection of values in which no value is duplicated. Parameterize your generic unit with respect to the type of the values in the set. Provide an operation that constructs an empty set, an operation that adds a given value to a set, an operation that unites two sets, and an operation that tests whether a given value is contained in a set. Implement your generic unit in either ADA, C++, or JAVA.

Assume as little as possible about the type of the values in the set. What assumption(s) are you absolutely forced to make about that type?

*7.2.5 Design a generic unit that implements maps. A *map* is an unordered collection of (key, value) entries in which no key is duplicated. Parameterize your generic unit with respect to the type of the keys and the type of the values. Provide an operation that constructs an empty map, an operation that adds a given (key, value) entry to a map, an operation that tests whether a map contains an entry with a given key, and an operation that retrieves the value in the entry with a given key. Implement your generic unit in either ADA, C++, or JAVA.

Assume as little as possible about the type of the keys and the type of the values. What assumption(s) are you absolutely forced to make about these types?

Chapter 8

Type systems

Older programming languages had very simple type systems in which every variable and parameter had to be declared with a specific type. However, experience shows that their type systems are inadequate for large-scale software development. For instance, C's type system is too weak, allowing a variety of type errors to go undetected, while on the other hand, PASCAL's type system is too rigid, with the consequence that many useful (and reusable) program units, such as generic sorting procedures and parameterized types, cannot be expressed at all.

These and other problems prompted development of more powerful type systems, which were adopted by the more modern programming languages such as ADA, C++, JAVA, and HASKELL.

In this chapter we shall study:

- *inclusion polymorphism*, which is concerned with subtypes and subclasses, and their ability to inherit operations from their parent types and superclasses;
- *parametric polymorphism*, which is concerned with procedures that operate uniformly on arguments of a whole family of types;
- *parameterized types*, which are types that take other types as parameters;
- *overloading*, whereby the same identifier can denote several distinct procedures in the same scope;
- *type conversions*, including casts and coercions.

8.1 Inclusion polymorphism

Inclusion polymorphism is a type system in which a type may have subtypes, which inherit operations from that type. In particular, inclusion polymorphism is a key concept of object-oriented languages, in which a class may have subclasses, which inherit methods from that class.

8.1.1 Types and subtypes

Recall that a type T is a set of values, equipped with some operations. A ***subtype*** of T is a subset of the values of T, equipped with the same operations as T. Every value of the subtype is also a value of type T, and therefore may be used in a context where a value of type T is expected.

The concept of subtypes is a fruitful and pervasive notion in programming. A common situation is that we declare a variable (or parameter) of type T, but know that the variable will range over only a subset of the values of type *T*. It is better if the programming language allows us to declare the variable's *subtype*, and thus declare more accurately what values it might take. This makes the program easier to understand, and possibly more efficient.

The older programming languages support subtypes in only a rudimentary form. For example, C has several integer types, of which **char** and **int** may be seen as subtypes of **long**, and two floating-point types, of which **float** may be seen as a subtype of **double**. PASCAL supports *subrange types*, a subrange type being a programmer-defined range of values of a discrete primitive type.

ADA supports subtypes much more systematically. We can define a subtype of any primitive type (including a floating-point type) by defining a subrange of that primitive type's values. We can define a subtype of any array type by fixing its index bounds. We can define a subtype of any discriminated record type by fixing the tag.

EXAMPLE 8.1   ADA primitive types and subtypes

The following ADA declarations define some subtypes of Integer:

```
subtype Natural is Integer range 0 .. Integer'last;
subtype Small is Integer range -3 .. +3;
```

These subtypes, which are illustrated in Figure 8.1, have the following sets of values:

$$Natural = \{0, 1, 2, 3, 4, 5, 6, \ldots\}$$
$$Small = \{-3, -2, -1, 0, +1, +2, +3\}$$

We can declare variables of these subtypes:

```
i: Integer;
n: Natural;
s: Small;
```

Now an assignment like "i := n;" or "i := s;" can always be performed, since the assigned value, although unknown, is certainly in the type of the variable i. On the other hand, an assignment like "n := i;", "n := s;", "s := i;", or "s := n;" requires a run-time range check, to ensure that the assigned value is actually in the subtype of the variable being assigned to.

The following ADA declaration defines a subtype of Float:

```
subtype Probability is Float range 0.0 .. 1.0;
```

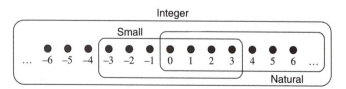

Figure 8.1 Integer subtypes in ADA.

EXAMPLE 8.2   ADA array type and subtypes

The following ADA declarations define an array type and some of its subtypes:

```
type String is array (Integer range <>) of Character;

subtype String1 is String(1 .. 1);
subtype String5 is String(1 .. 5);
subtype String7 is String(1 .. 7);
```

The values of type String are strings (character arrays) of any length. The values of subtypes String1, String5, and String7 are strings of length 1, 5, and 7, respectively. These subtypes are illustrated in Figure 8.2.

EXAMPLE 8.3   ADA discriminated record type and subtypes

The following ADA declarations define a discriminated record (disjoint union) type and all of its subtypes:

```
type Form is (pointy, circular, rectangular);
type Figure (f: Form := pointy) is
    record
        x, y: Float;
        case f is
            when pointy =>
                null;
            when circular =>
                r: Float;
            when rectangular =>
                h, w: Float;
        end case;
    end record;

subtype Point is Figure(pointy);
subtype Circle is Figure(circular);
subtype Rectangle is Figure(rectangular);
```

The values of type Figure are tagged tuples, in which the tags are values of the type Form = {*pointy*, *circular*, *rectangular*}:

$$
\begin{aligned}
\text{Figure} = {} & pointy(\text{Float} \times \text{Float}) \\
& + circular(\text{Float} \times \text{Float} \times \text{Float}) \\
& + rectangular(\text{Float} \times \text{Float} \times \text{Float} \times \text{Float})
\end{aligned}
$$

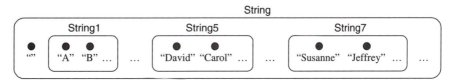

Figure 8.2   Array subtypes in ADA.

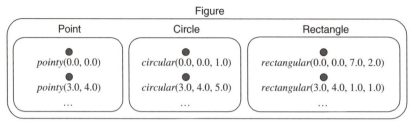

Figure 8.3 Discriminated record subtypes in ADA.

The values of subtype Point are those in which the tag is fixed as *pointy*, the values of subtype Circle are those in which the tag is fixed as *circular*, and the values of subtype Rectangle are those in which the tag is fixed as *rectangular*:

$$Point = pointy(\text{Float} \times \text{Float})$$
$$Circle = circular(\text{Float} \times \text{Float} \times \text{Float})$$
$$Rectangle = rectangular(\text{Float} \times \text{Float} \times \text{Float} \times \text{Float})$$

These subtypes are illustrated in Figure 8.3.

Here are some possible variable declarations, using the type and some of its subtypes:

```
diagram: array (...) of Figure;
frame: Rectangle;
cursor: Point;
```

Each component of the array `diagram` can contain any value of type Figure. However, the variable `frame` can contain only a value of the subtype Rectangle, and the variable `cursor` can contain only a value of the subtype Point.

If the programming language supports subtypes, we cannot uniquely state the subtype of a *value*. For example, Figure 8.1 shows that the value 2 is not only in the type Integer but also in the subtypes Natural and Small, and indeed in numerous other subtypes of Integer. However, the language should allow the subtype of each *variable* to be declared explicitly.

Let us now examine the general properties of subtypes. A necessary condition for S to be a subtype of T is that every value of S is also a value of T, in other words $S \subseteq T$. A value known to be in subtype S can then safely be used wherever a value of type T is expected.

The type T is equipped with operations that are applicable to all values of type T. Each of these operations will also be applicable to values of the subtype S. We say that S **inherits** these operations. For example, any function of type Integer $\rightarrow$ Boolean can safely be inherited by all the subtypes of Integer, such as Natural and Small in Figure 8.1, so the same function may be viewed as being of type Natural $\rightarrow$ Boolean or Small $\rightarrow$ Boolean. No run-time check is needed to ensure that the function's argument is of type Integer.

Suppose that a value known to be of type T_1 is computed in a context where a value of type T_2 is expected. This happens, for example, when an expression E

of type T_1 occurs in an assignment "$V := E$" where the variable V is of type T_2, or in a function call "$F(E)$" where F's formal parameter is of type T_2. In such a context we have insisted until now that T_1 must be equivalent to T_2 (Section 2.5.2). In the presence of subtypes, however, we can allow a looser compatibility between types T_1 and T_2.

T_1 is **compatible** with T_2 if and only if T_1 and T_2 have values in common. This implies that T_1 is a subtype of T_2, or T_2 is a subtype of T_1, or both T_1 and T_2 are subtypes of some other type.

If T_1 is indeed compatible with T_2, there are two possible cases of interest:

- T_1 is a subtype of T_2, so all values of type T_1 are values of type T_2. In this case, the value of type T_1 can be used safely in a context where a value of type T_2 is expected; no run-time check is necessary.

- T_1 is not a subtype of T_2, so some (but not all) values of type T_1 are values of type T_2. In this case, the value of type T_1 can be used only after a run-time check to determine whether it is also a value of type T_2. This is a kind of run-time type check, but much simpler and more efficient than the full run-time type checks needed by a dynamically typed language.

8.1.2 Classes and subclasses

In Section 6.3 we saw that a class C is a set of objects, equipped with some operations (constructors and methods). These methods may be inherited by the subclasses of C. Any object of a subclass may be used in a context where an object of class C is expected.

Consider a class C and a subclass S. Each object of class C has one or more variable components, and is equipped with methods that access the variable components. Each object of class S inherits all the variable components of objects of class C, and may have additional variable components. Each object of class S potentially inherits all the methods of objects of class C, and may be equipped with additional methods that access the additional variable components.

Subclasses are not exactly analogous to subtypes. The objects of the subclass S may be used wherever objects of class C are expected, but the former objects have additional components, so the set of objects of subclass S is not a subset of the objects of C. Nevertheless, the subclass concept is closely related to the subtype concept. The following example shows how.

EXAMPLE 8.4   JAVA subclasses as subtypes

Consider the JAVA class Point of Example 6.8:

```java
class Point {
    protected double x, y;
    public void draw () {...}   // Draw this point.
    ... // other methods
}
```

and its subclasses `Circle` and `Rectangle`:

```
class Circle extends Point {
    private double r;

    public void draw () {...}   // Draw this circle.

    ... // other methods
}
class Rectangle extends Point {
    private double w, h;

    public void draw () {...}   // Draw this rectangle.

    ... // other methods
}
```

These classes model points, circles, and rectangles (respectively) on the *xy* plane. For a circle or rectangle, x and y are the coordinates of its center.

The methods of class `Point` are inherited by the subclasses `Circle` and `Rectangle`. This is safe because the methods of class `Point` can access only the x and y components, and these components are inherited by the subclasses.

Now let us consider the types Point, Circle, and Rectangle, whose values are `Point` objects, `Circle` objects, and `Rectangle` objects, respectively. We view objects as tagged tuples:

$$Point = Point(\text{Double} \times \text{Double})$$
$$Circle = Circle(\text{Double} \times \text{Double} \times \text{Double})$$
$$Rectangle = Rectangle(\text{Double} \times \text{Double} \times \text{Double} \times \text{Double})$$

Clearly, Circle and Rectangle are *not* subtypes of Point.

However, let Point‡ be the type whose values are objects of class `Point` or any subclass of `Point`:

$$Point‡ = Point(\text{Double} \times \text{Double})$$
$$+ Circle(\text{Double} \times \text{Double} \times \text{Double})$$
$$+ Rectangle(\text{Double} \times \text{Double} \times \text{Double} \times \text{Double})$$

Clearly, Circle and Rectangle (and indeed Point) are subtypes of Point‡. The relationship between these types is illustrated in Figure 8.4.

JAVA allows objects of any subclass to be treated like objects of the superclass. Consider the following variable:

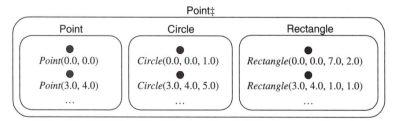

Figure 8.4 Object subtypes in JAVA.

```
Point p;
...
p = new Point(3.0, 4.0);
...
p = new Circle(3.0, 4.0, 5.0);
```

This variable may refer to an object of class `Point` or any subclass of `Point`. In other words, this variable may refer to any value of type Point‡.

In general, if *C* is a class, then *C*‡ includes not only objects of class *C* but also objects of every subclass of *C*. Following ADA95 terminology, we shall call *C*‡ a ***class-wide type***.

Comparing Figures 8.3 and 8.4, we see that discriminated record types and classes have similar roles in data modeling; in fact they can both be understood in terms of disjoint unions (Section 2.3.3). The major difference is that classes are superior in terms of extensibility. Each subclass declaration, as well as defining the set of objects of the new subclass, at the same time extends the set of objects of the superclass's class-wide type. The methods of the superclass remain applicable to objects of the subclass, although they can be overridden (specialized) to the subclass if necessary. This extensibility is unique to object-oriented programming, and accounts for much of its success.

EXAMPLE 8.5   JAVA extensibility

Consider once again the `Point` class and its `Circle` and `Rectangle` subclasses of Example 8.4. Suppose that we now declare further subclasses:

```
class Line extends Point {
    private double length, orientation;

    public void draw () { ... }   // Draw this line.
}

class Textbox extends Rectangle {
    private String text;

    public void draw () { ... }   // Draw this text.
}
```

These subclass declarations not only define the set of objects of the two new subclasses:

$$\text{Line} = \textit{Line}(\text{Double} \times \text{Double} \times \text{Double})$$
$$\text{Textbox} = \textit{Textbox}(\text{Double} \times \text{Double} \times \text{String})$$

but also extend their superclasses' class-wide types:

$$\text{Point‡} = \textit{Point}(\text{Double} \times \text{Double})$$
$$+ \textit{Circle}(\text{Double} \times \text{Double} \times \text{Double})$$
$$+ \textit{Rectangle}(\text{Double} \times \text{Double} \times \text{Double} \times \text{Double})$$
$$+ \textit{Line}(\text{Double} \times \text{Double} \times \text{Double})$$
$$+ \textit{Textbox}(\text{Double} \times \text{Double} \times \text{String})$$

$$\text{Rectangle‡} = Rectangle(\text{Double} \times \text{Double} \times \text{Double} \times \text{Double})$$
$$+ \; Textbox(\text{Double} \times \text{Double} \times \text{String})$$

The `draw` methods of the `Point`, `Circle`, and `Rectangle` classes are unaffected by this change. Only the overriding `draw` methods of the `Line` and `Textbox` classes have to be defined.

See also Exercise 8.1.3.

8.2 Parametric polymorphism

In this section we shall study a type system that enables us to write what are known as polymorphic procedures.

Consider, for example, a function procedure to compute the length of a list. An ordinary function could operate on (say) lists of characters, but could not also operate on lists of other types. A polymorphic function, on the other hand, could operate on lists of any type, exploiting the fact that the algorithm required to implement the function (counting the list elements) does not depend on the type of the list elements.

A ***monomorphic*** ("single-shaped") procedure can operate only on arguments of a fixed type. A ***polymorphic*** ("many-shaped") procedure can operate uniformly on arguments of a whole family of types.

Parametric polymorphism is a type system in which we can write polymorphic procedures. The functional languages ML and HASKELL are prominent examples of languages that exhibit parametric polymorphism. We shall use HASKELL to illustrate this important concept.

In passing, note that some of the benefits of parametric polymorphism can also be achieved using C++ or JAVA generic classes, which we covered in Chapter 7. (See also Exercise 8.2.7.)

8.2.1 Polymorphic procedures

In HASKELL it is a simple matter to declare a polymorphic function. The key is to define the function's type using type variables, rather than specific types. We shall introduce this idea by a series of examples.

A ***type variable*** is an identifier that stands for any one of a family of types. In this section we shall write type variables as Greek letters (α, β, γ, ...), partly for historical reasons and partly because they are easily recognized. In HASKELL type variables are conventionally written as lowercase Roman letters (a, b, c, ...), which is unfortunate because they can easily be confused with ordinary variables.

EXAMPLE 8.6   HASKELL polymorphic function (1)

The following HASKELL monomorphic function accepts a pair of integers and returns the second of these integers:

```
second (x: Int, y: Int) = y
```

This monomorphic function is of type Integer × Integer → Integer. The function call "second(13, 21)" will yield 21. However, the function call "second(13, true)" would be *illegal*, because the argument pair does not consist of two integers.

But why should this function be restricted to accepting a pair of integers? There is no integer operation in the function definition, so the function's argument could in principle be any pair of values whatsoever. It is in fact possible to define the function in this way:

```
second (x: σ, y: τ) = y
```

This polymorphic function is of type $\sigma \times \tau \rightarrow \tau$. Here σ and τ are type variables, each standing for an arbitrary type.

Now the function call "second(13, true)" is legal. Its type is determined as follows. The argument is a pair of type Integer × Boolean. If we systematically substitute Integer for σ and Boolean for τ in the function type $\sigma \times \tau \rightarrow \tau$, we obtain Integer × Boolean → Boolean, which matches the argument type. Therefore the result type is Boolean.

Consider also the function call "second(name)", where the argument name is of type String × String. This function call is also legal. If we systematically substitute String for σ and String for τ in the function type $\sigma \times \tau \rightarrow \tau$, we obtain String × String → String, which matches the argument type. Therefore the result type is String.

This polymorphic function therefore accepts arguments of many types. However, it does not accept just any argument. A function call like "second(13)" or "second(1978, 5, 5)" is still illegal, because the argument type cannot be matched to the function type $\sigma \times \tau \rightarrow \tau$. The allowable arguments are just those values that have types of the form $\sigma \times \tau$, i.e., pairs.

A *polytype* derives a family of similar types. Two examples of polytypes are $\sigma \times \tau$ and $\sigma \times \tau \rightarrow \tau$. A polytype always includes one or more type variables.

The family of types derived by a polytype is obtained by making all possible *systematic* substitutions of types for type variables. The family of types derived by $\sigma \times \tau \rightarrow \tau$ includes Integer × Boolean → Boolean and String × String → String. It does *not* include Integer × Boolean → Integer, or Integer → Integer, or Integer × Integer × Integer → Integer. In other words, each type in the family derived by $\sigma \times \tau \rightarrow \tau$ is the type of a function that accepts a pair of values and returns a result of the same type as the second component of the pair.

EXAMPLE 8.7   HASKELL polymorphic function (2)

Consider the following HASKELL monomorphic function:

```
either (b: Bool) (x1: Char) (x2: Char) =
    if b then x1 else x2
```

The type of this monomorphic function is Boolean → Character → Character → Character. The following code contains a call to the either function:

```
translate (x: Char) =
    either (isspace x) x '*'
```

The either function's first parameter clearly must be of type Boolean, since it is tested by an if-expression. But the second and third parameters need not be of type Character, since no character operations are applied to them.

Here now is a polymorphic version of the either function:

```
either (b: Bool) (x1: τ) (x2: τ) =
    if b then x1 else x2
```

The type of this function is Boolean → τ → τ → τ. Thus the first argument must be a boolean, and the other two arguments must be values of the same type as each other. The following code illustrates what we can do with the polymorphic either function:

```
translate (x: Char) =
    either (isspace x) x '*'

max (m: Int, n: Int) =
    either (m > n) m n
```

The latter call would be illegal with the original monomorphic either function.

The polytype Boolean → τ → τ → τ derives a family of types that includes Boolean → Character → Character → Character, Boolean → Integer → Integer → Integer, and many others.

EXAMPLE 8.8   HASKELL polymorphic function (3)

The following defines the integer identity function in HASKELL:

```
idInt (x: Int) = x
```

This monomorphic function is of type Integer → Integer, and maps any integer to itself.

The following defines the polymorphic identity function:

```
id (x: τ) = x
```

This polymorphic function is of type τ → τ, and maps any value to itself. In other words, it represents the following mapping:

$$id = \{false \to false, true \to true,$$
$$\ldots, -2 \to -2, -1 \to -1, 0 \to 0, 1 \to 1, 2 \to 2, \ldots,$$
$$\text{``''} \to \text{``''}, \text{``}a\text{''} \to \text{``}a\text{''}, \text{``}ab\text{''} \to \text{``}ab\text{''}, \ldots,$$
$$\ldots\}$$

8.2.2 Parameterized types

A *parameterized type* is a type that takes other type(s) as parameters. For instance, consider array types in C. We can think of τ[] as a parameterized type, which can be specialized to an ordinary type (such as **char**[], or **float**[], or **float**[][]) by substituting an actual type for the type variable τ.

All programming languages have built-in parameterized types. For instance, C and C++ have τ[] and τ*, while ADA has "**array** (σ) **of** τ" and "**access** τ". But only a few programming languages, notably ML and HASKELL, allow programmers to define their own parameterized types. The following examples illustrate the possibilities.

EXAMPLE 8.9   HASKELL **parameterized type (1)**

Consider the following HASKELL parameterized type definition:

> **type** Pair τ = (τ, τ)

In this definition τ is a type parameter, denoting an unknown type. The definition makes "Pair τ" a parameterized type whose values are homogeneous pairs.

An example of specializing this parameterized type would be "Pair Int". By substituting Int for τ, we see that the resulting type is "(Int, Int)", whose values are pairs of integers. Another example would be "Pair Float", a type whose values are pairs of real numbers.

EXAMPLE 8.10   HASKELL **parameterized type (2)**

The following HASKELL (recursive) parameterized type definition defines homogeneous lists with elements of type τ:

> **data** List τ = Nil | Cons (τ, List τ)

Now "List Int" is a type whose values are lists of integers.

We can go on to define some polymorphic functions on lists:

```
head (l: List τ) =
    case l of
        Nil          -> ... -- error
        Cons(x,xs) -> x
tail (l: List τ) =
    case l of
        Nil          -> ... -- error
        Cons(x,xs) -> xs
length (l: List τ) =
    case l of
        Nil          -> 0
        Cons(x,xs) -> 1 + length(xs)
```

As a matter of fact, HASKELL has a built-in parameterized list type, written [τ], equipped with head, tail, and length functions.

Rather than using the notation of any particular programming language, we shall henceforth use mathematical notation like Pair<τ> and List<τ> for parameterized types. Thus we can rewrite the type definitions of Examples 8.9 and 8.10 as equations:

$$\text{Pair}<\tau> = \tau \times \tau \tag{8.1}$$

$$\text{List}<\tau> = \text{Unit} + (\tau \times \text{List}<\tau>) \tag{8.2}$$

Using this notation, the types of the functions defined in Example 8.10 are as follows:

$$head : \text{List} <\tau> \rightarrow \tau$$
$$tail : \text{List} <\tau> \rightarrow \text{List} <\tau>$$
$$length : \text{List} <\tau> \rightarrow \text{Integer}$$

8.2.3   Type inference

Most statically typed programming languages insist that we explicitly declare the type of every entity declared in our programs. This is illustrated clearly by ADA constant, variable, and function declarations:

```
I: constant T := E;
I: T;
function I (I': T') return T;
```

in which the type of each constant, variable, parameter, and function result is declared explicitly.

By contrast, consider the HASKELL constant definition:

```
I = E
```

The type of the declared constant is not stated explicitly, but is *inferred* from the type of the expression E.

Type inference is a process by which the type of a declared entity is inferred, where it is not explicitly stated. Some functional programming languages such as HASKELL and ML rely heavily on type inference, to the extent that we rarely need to state types explicitly.

So far we have been writing HASKELL function definitions in the form:

```
I (I': T') = E
```

Here the type of the formal parameter I' is explicitly declared to be T'. On the other hand, the function result type must be inferred from the function body E. In fact, we need not declare the parameter type either; instead we can write more concisely:

```
I I' = E
```

The type of I' is then inferred from its applied occurrences in the function's body E.

EXAMPLE 8.11   HASKELL type inference (1)

Consider the following HASKELL function definition:

```
even n = (n 'mod' 2 = 0)
```

The operator mod has type Integer $\rightarrow$ Integer $\rightarrow$ Integer. From the subexpression "n 'mod' 2" we can infer that n must be of type Integer (otherwise the subexpression would be ill-typed). Then we can infer that the function body is of type Boolean. So the function even is of type Integer $\rightarrow$ Boolean.

Type inference sometimes yields a monotype, but only where the available clues are strong enough. In Example 8.11, the function's body contained a monomorphic operator, mod, and two integer literals. These clues were enough to allow us to infer a monotype for the function.

The available clues are not always so strong: the function body might be written entirely in terms of polymorphic functions. Indeed, it is conceivable that the function body might provide no clues at all. In these circumstances, type inference will yield a polytype.

EXAMPLE 8.12 HASKELL type inference (2)

Consider the following HASKELL function definition:

```
id x = x
```

Let τ be the type of x. The function body yields no clue as to what τ is; all we can infer is that the function result will also be of type τ. Therefore the type of id is $\tau \rightarrow \tau$. This function is, in fact, the polymorphic identity function of Example 8.8.

EXAMPLE 8.13 HASKELL type inference (3)

Consider the following definition of an operator " . ":

```
f . g =
    \x -> f(g(x))
```

We can see that both f and g are functions, from the way they are used. Moreover, we can see that the result type of g must be the same as the parameter type of f. Let the types of f and g be $\beta \rightarrow \gamma$ and $\alpha \rightarrow \beta$, respectively. The type of x must be α, since it is passed as an argument to g. Therefore, the subexpression "f(g(x))" is of type γ, and the expression "\x -> f(g(x))" is of type $\alpha \rightarrow \gamma$. Therefore, " . " is of type $(\beta \rightarrow \gamma) \rightarrow (\alpha \rightarrow \beta) \rightarrow (\alpha \rightarrow \gamma)$.

In fact, " . " is HASKELL's built-in operator that composes two given functions.

EXAMPLE 8.14 HASKELL type inference (4)

Recall the following HASKELL parameterized type definition from Example 8.10:

```
data List τ = Nil | Cons (τ, τ list)
```

The following function definition does not state the type of the function's parameter or result, but relies on type inference:

```
length l =
    case l of
        Nil        -> 0
        Cons(x,xs) -> 1 + length(xs)
```

The result type of length is clearly Integer, since one limb of the case expression is an integer literal (and the other is an application of the operator "+" to an integer literal). The case expression also tells us that the value of l is either Nil or of the form "Cons(x,xs)". This allows us to infer that l is of type List<τ>. We cannot be more specific, since the function body contains no clue as to what τ is. Thus length is of type List<τ> → Integer.

HASKELL adopts a *laissez-faire* attitude to typing. The programmer may declare the type of an entity voluntarily, or may leave the compiler to infer its type.

Excessive reliance on type inference, however, tends to make large programs difficult to understand. A reader might have to study the whole of a program in order to discover the types of its individual functions. Even the implementer of the program could have trouble understanding it: a slight programming error might cause the compiler to infer different types from the ones intended by the implementer, resulting in obscure error messages. So explicitly declaring types, even if redundant, is good programming practice.

8.3 Overloading

In discussing issues of scope and visibility, in Section 4.2.2, we assumed that each identifier denotes at most one entity in a particular scope. Now we relax that assumption.

An identifier is said to be **overloaded** if it denotes two or more distinct procedures in the same scope. Such overloading is acceptable only if every procedure call is unambiguous, i.e., the compiler can uniquely identify the procedure to be called using only type information.

In older programming languages such as C, identifiers and operators denoting certain built-in functions are overloaded. (Recall, from Section 2.6.3, that we may view an operator application like "n + 1" as a function call, where the operator "+" denotes a function. From this point of view, an operator acts as an identifier.)

| EXAMPLE 8.15 | C overloaded functions |

The C "−" operator simultaneously denotes four distinct built-in functions:

- integer negation (a function of type Integer → Integer)
- floating-point negation (a function of type Float → Float)
- integer subtraction (a function of type Integer × Integer → Integer)
- floating-point subtraction (a function of type Float × Float → Float).

No ambiguity can arise. In function calls such as "−y" and "x−y", the number of operands and their types uniquely determine which function is being called.

In more modern languages such as ADA, C++, and JAVA, overloading is not restricted to built-in procedures. Programmers are at liberty to overload previously-defined identifiers and operators.

EXAMPLE 8.16   ADA overloaded functions

The ADA "/" operator simultaneously denotes two distinct built-in functions:

- integer division (a function of type Integer × Integer → Integer)
- floating-point division (a function of type Float × Float → Float).

For example, the function call "7/2" yields the Integer value 3, while "7.0/2.0" yields the Float value 3.5.

The following function declaration further overloads the "/" operator:

```
function "/" (m, n: Integer) return Float;
-- Return the quotient of m and n as a real number.
```

Now "/" denotes three distinct functions:

- integer division (a function of type Integer × Integer → Integer)
- floating-point division (a function of type Float × Float → Float)
- floating-point division of integers (a function of type Integer × Integer → Float).

Now the function call "7/2" yields either the Integer value 3 or the Float value 3.5, depending on its context.

Because the functions for integer division and floating-point division of integers differ only in their result types, in general the identification of "/" in a function call will depend on the context as well as the number and types of actual parameters. The following function calls illustrate the resulting complexities. (In the right-hand column, subscripting is used to distinguish the three functions: "$/_{\text{ii}}$" is integer division, "$/_{\text{ff}}$" is floating-point division, and "$/_{\text{if}}$" is floating-point division of integers.)

```
n: Integer;  x: Float;
...
x := 7.0/2.0;          - computes 7.0/ff2.0 = 3.5
x := 7/2;              - computes 7/if2 = 3.5
n := 7/2;              - computes 7/ii2 = 3
n := (7/2)/(5/2);      - computes (7/ii2)/ii(5/ii2) = 3/ii2 = 1
```

Some function calls are ambiguous, even taking context into account:

```
x := (7/2)/(5/2);      - computes
                         either (7/ii2)/if(5/ii2) = 3/if 2 = 1.5
                         or     (7/if2)/ff(5/if2) = 3.5/ff 2.5 = 1.4
```

We can characterize overloading in terms of the types of the overloaded functions. Suppose that an identifier F denotes both a function f_1 of type $S_1 \to T_1$ and a function f_2 of type $S_2 \to T_2$. (Recall that this covers functions with multiple arguments, since S_1 or S_2 could be a Cartesian product.) The overloading may be either context-independent or context-dependent.

Context-independent overloading requires that S_1 and S_2 are non-equivalent. Consider the function call "$F(E)$". If the actual parameter E is of type S_1, then F here denotes f_1 and the result is of type T_1. If E is of type S_2, then F here denotes f_2 and the result is of type T_2. With context-independent overloading, the function to be called is always uniquely identified by the type of the actual parameter.

Context-dependent overloading requires only that S_1 and S_2 are non-equivalent or that T_1 and T_2 are non-equivalent. If S_1 and S_2 are non-equivalent, the function to be called can be identified as above. If S_1 and S_2 are equivalent but T_1 and T_2 are non-equivalent, context must be taken into account to identify the function to be called. Consider the function call "$F(E)$", where E is of type S_1 (equivalent to S_2). If the function call occurs in a context where an expression of type T_1 is expected, then F must denote f_1; if the function call occurs in a context where an expression of type T_2 is expected, then F must denote f_2.

With context-dependent overloading, it is possible to formulate expressions in which the function to be called cannot be identified uniquely, as we saw in Example 8.16. The programming language must prohibit such ambiguous expressions.

C exhibits context-independent overloading: the parameter types of the overloaded functions are always non-equivalent. ADA exhibits context-dependent overloading: either the parameter types or the result types of the overloaded functions may be non-equivalent.

Not only function procedures but also proper procedures and even literals can be overloaded, as the following example illustrates. (See also Exercises 8.3.2 and 8.3.3.)

EXAMPLE 8.17   ADA overloaded proper procedures

The ADA `Text_IO` package overloads the identifier "`put`" to denote two distinct built-in proper procedures:

> **procedure** put (item: Character);
> -- Write item to standard output.

> **procedure** put (item: String);
> -- Write all characters of item to standard output.

For example, the procedure call "`put('!');`" writes a single character, while "`put("hello");`" writes a string of characters.

The following is a legal ADA procedure declaration:

> **procedure** put (item: Integer);
> -- Convert item to a signed integer literal and write it to standard output.

Now the procedure call "`put(13);`" would write "`+13`".

We must be careful not to confuse the distinct concepts of overloading (which is sometimes called *ad hoc polymorphism*) and parametric polymorphism. Overloading means that a small number of separately-defined procedures happen to have the same identifier; these procedures do not necessarily have related types, nor do they necessarily perform similar operations on their arguments.

Polymorphism is a property of a single procedure that accepts arguments of a large family of related types; the parametric procedure is defined once and operates uniformly on its arguments, whatever their type.

Overloading does not actually increase the programming language's expressive power, as it could easily be eliminated by renaming the overloaded procedures. Thus the ADA procedures of Example 8.17 could be renamed putChar, putStr, and putInt, with no consequence other than a modest loss of notational convenience. On the other hand, parametric polymorphism genuinely increases the language's expressive power, since a polymorphic procedure may take arguments of an *unlimited* variety of types.

8.4   Type conversions

A *type conversion* is a mapping from the values of one type to corresponding values of a different type. A familiar example of a type conversion is the natural mapping from integers to real numbers:

$$\{\ldots, -2 \to -2.0, -1 \to -1.0, 0 \to 0.0, +1 \to +1.0, +2 \to +2.0, \ldots\}$$

There are many possible type conversions from real numbers to integers, including truncation and rounding. Other examples of type conversions are the mapping from characters to the corresponding strings of length 1, the mapping from characters to the corresponding character-codes (small integers), and the mapping from character-codes to the corresponding characters.

Type conversions are not easily characterized mathematically. Some type conversions map values to mathematically-equal values (e.g., integers to real numbers), but others do not (e.g., truncation and rounding). Some type conversions are one-to-one mappings (e.g., the mapping from characters to strings of length 1), but most are not. Some type conversions are total mappings (e.g., the mapping from characters to character-codes), but others are partial mappings (e.g., the mapping from character-codes to characters). Where a type conversion is a partial mapping, there is a significant practical consequence: it could cause the program to fail.

Programming languages vary, not only in which type conversions they define, but also in whether these type conversions are explicit or implicit.

A *cast* is an explicit type conversion. In C, C++, and JAVA, a cast has the form "$(T)E$". In ADA, a cast has the form "$T(E)$". If the subexpression E is of type S (not equivalent to T), and if the programming language defines a type conversion from S to T, then the cast maps the value of E to the corresponding value of type T.

A *coercion* is an implicit type conversion, and is performed automatically wherever the syntactic context demands it. Consider an expression E in a context where a value of type T is expected. If E is of type S (not equivalent to T), and if the programming language allows a coercion from S to T in this context, then the coercion maps the value of E to the corresponding value of type T. A typical example of such a syntactic context is an assignment "$V := E$", where V is of type T.

EXAMPLE 8.18   PASCAL coercions and ADA casts

PASCAL provides a coercion from Integer to Float, using the natural mapping from integers to real numbers shown above. On the other hand, PASCAL provides no coercion from Float to Integer, but forces the programmer to choose an explicit type conversion function (trunc or round) to make clear which mapping is desired.

```
var n: Integer;  x: Real;
...
x := n;            -- converts the value of n to a real number
n := x;            -- illegal!
n := round(x);     -- converts the value of x to an integer by rounding
```

ADA does not provide any coercions at all. But it does support all possible casts between numeric types:

```
n: Integer;  x: Float;
...
x := n;              -- illegal!
n := x;              -- illegal!
x := Float(n);       -- converts the value of n to a real number
n := Integer(x);     -- converts the value of x to an integer by rounding
```

Note that ADA chooses rounding as its mapping from real numbers to integers. This choice is arbitrary, and programmers have no choice but to memorize it.

Some programming languages are very permissive in respect of coercions. For instance, C allows coercions from integers to real numbers, from narrow-range to wide-range integers, from low-precision to high-precision real numbers, and from values of any type to the unique value of type **void**. To these JAVA adds coercions from every type to String, from a subclass to its superclass, from a primitive type to the corresponding wrapper class and *vice versa*, and so on.

The general trend in modern programming languages is to minimize or even eliminate coercions altogether, while retaining casts. At first sight this might appear to be a retrograde step. However, coercions fit badly with parametric polymorphism (Section 8.2) and overloading (Section 8.3), concepts that are certainly more useful than coercions. Casts fit well with any type system, and anyway are more general than coercions (not being dependent on the syntactic context).

8.5   Implementation notes

This chapter is largely theoretical, but it raises one practical issue not considered elsewhere in this book: how can we implement parametric polymorphism efficiently?

8.5.1   Implementation of parametric polymorphism

Polymorphic procedures operate uniformly on arguments of a variety of types. An argument passed to a polymorphic procedure might be an integer in one call, a real number in a second call, a tuple in a third call, and a list in a fourth call.

One way to implement a polymorphic procedure would be to generate a separate instance of the procedure for each distinct argument type. However, such an implementation would be unsuitable for a functional programming language such as ML or HASKELL, in which programs tend to include a large proportion of polymorphic procedures.

A better way is to represent values of all types in such a way that they look similar to a polymorphic procedure. We can achieve this effect by representing every value by a pointer to a heap object, as shown in Figure 8.5. Consider the following polymorphic functions:

- The polymorphic either function of Example 8.7 has type Boolean → τ → τ → τ. Its second and third arguments are of type τ, i.e., they could be values of *any* type. The function can only copy the values, and this is implemented by copying the pointers to the values.

- The second function of Example 8.6 has type σ × τ → τ. Its argument is of type σ × τ, so it must be a pair, but the components of that pair could

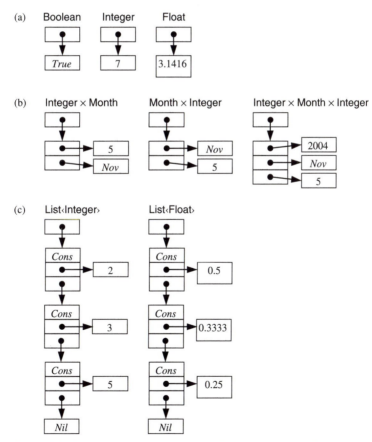

Figure 8.5 Representation of values of different types in the presence of parametric polymorphism: (a) primitive values; (b) tuples; (c) lists.

be values of *any* type. The function could select either component of the argument pair, so all pairs must have similar representations. Compare the pairs of type Integer × Month and Month × Integer in Figure 8.5(b).

- The head, tail, and length functions of Example 8.10 have types List<τ> → τ, List<τ> → List<τ>, and List<τ> → Integer, respectively. Each function's argument is of type List<τ>, so it must be a list, but the components of that list could be values of *any* type. The function could test whether the argument list is empty or not, or select the argument list's head or tail, so all lists must have similar representations. Compare the lists of type List<Integer> and List<Float> in Figure 8.5(c).

When a polymorphic procedure operates on values of unknown type, it cannot know the operations with which that type is equipped, so it is restricted to copying these values. That can be implemented safely and uniformly by copying the *pointers* to these values.

This implementation of parametric polymorphism is simple and uniform, but it is also costly. All values (even primitive values) must be stored in the heap; space must be allocated for them when they are first needed, and deallocated by a garbage collector when they are no longer needed.

Summary

In this chapter:

- We have studied inclusion polymorphism, which enables a subtype or subclass to inherit operations from its parent type or class.
- We have studied parametric polymorphism, which enables a procedure to operate uniformly on arguments of a whole family of types, and the related concept of parameterized types.
- We have studied type inference, whereby the types of declared entities are not stated explicitly in the program but are left to be inferred by the compiler.
- We have studied overloading, whereby several procedures may have the same identifier in the same scope, provided that these procedures have non-equivalent parameter types and/or result types.
- We have studied type conversions, both explicit (casts) and implicit (coercions).
- We have seen how parametric polymorphism influences the representation of values of different types.

Further reading

Much of the material in this chapter is based on an illuminating survey paper by CARDELLI and WEGNER (1985). The authors propose a uniform framework for understanding parametric polymorphism, abstract types, subtypes, and inheritance. Then they use this framework to explore the consequences of combining some or all of these concepts in a single programming language. (However, no major language has yet attempted to combine them all.)

For another survey of type systems see REYNOLDS (1985). Unlike Cardelli and Wegner, Reynolds adopts the point of view that the concepts of coercion and subtype are essentially the same. For example, if a language is to provide a coercion from Integer to Float, then Integer should be defined as a subtype of Float. From this point of view, subtypes are not necessarily subsets.

The system of polymorphic type inference used in languages like ML and HASKELL is based on a type inference algorithm independently discovered by HINDLEY (1969) and MILNER (1978). ML's type system is described in detail in WIKSTRÖM (1987), and HASKELL's type system in THOMPSON (1999). For a detailed discussion of overloading in ADA, see ICHBIAH (1979).

Exercises

Exercises for Section 8.1

8.1.1 Show that two different subtypes of an ADA primitive type may overlap, but two different subtypes of an ADA array or record type are always disjoint.

8.1.2 Consider the class hierarchy of Figure 6.4. Write down equations (similar to those at the end of Example 8.4) defining the set of values of each of the types Account, Basic-Account, Savings-Account, Current-Account, and Account‡.

8.1.3 Compare ADA discriminated record types with JAVA classes and subclasses, in terms of extensibility.

(a) Define the following ADA function, where `Figure` is the discriminated record type of Example 8.3:

```
function area (fig: Figure) return Float;
```

(b) Now suppose that straight lines and text boxes are to be handled as well as points, circles, and rectangles. Modify the ADA code (type and function definitions) accordingly.

(c) Add definitions of the following JAVA method to each of the classes of Example 8.4:

```
float area ();
```

(d) Now suppose that straight lines and text boxes are to be handled as well. Modify the JAVA code accordingly.

Exercises for Section 8.2

8.2.1 Consider the HASKELL list functions defined in Example 8.10. Similarly define: (a) a function to reverse a given list; (b) a function to concatenate two given lists; (c) a function to return the kth element of a given list. State the type of each function, using the notation defined at the end of Section 8.2.2.

8.2.2 Define the following polymorphic functions in HASKELL: (a) "map f xs" returns a list in which each element is obtained by applying the function f to the corresponding element of list xs; (b) "filter f xs" returns a list consisting of every element x of list xs such that f x yields *true*. State the types of map and filter.

*8.2.3 Define a parameterized type Set<τ> in HASKELL. Equip it with operations similar to those in Exercise 7.2.4, and state the type of each operation.

8.2.4 Write a HASKELL function `twice`, whose argument is a function f and whose result is the function h defined by $h(x) = f(f(x))$. What is the type of `twice` ? Given that the following function returns the second power of a given integer:

```
sqr (i: Int) = i * i
```

use `twice` to define a function that returns the fourth power of a given integer.

8.2.5 Infer the types of the following HASKELL functions, given that the type of `not` is Boolean → Boolean:

```
negation p = not . p;

cond b f g =
     \ x -> if b x then f x else g x
```

8.2.6 Infer the types of the following HASKELL list functions, given that the type of "+" is Integer → Integer → Integer:

```
sum1 []       = 0
sum1 (n:ns) = n + sum1 ns

insert z f []       = z
insert z f (x:xs) = f x (insert z f xs)

sum2 xs = insert 0 (+) xs
```

Compare the functions `sum1` and `sum2`.

*8.2.7 Investigate the extent to which the benefits of parametric polymorphism can be achieved, in either C++ or JAVA, using generic classes and generic functions (methods). In your chosen language, attempt to code (a) the `second` polymorphic function of Example 8.6; (b) the `id` polymorphic function of Example 8.8; (c) the `Pair` parameterized type of Example 8.9; (d) the `List` parameterized type and the `head`, `tail`, and `length` polymorphic functions of Example 8.10.

Exercises for Section 8.3

8.3.1 Suppose that the operator "++" (denoting concatenation) is overloaded, with types Character × Character → String, Character × String → String, String × Character → String, and String × String → String. Is this overloading context-dependent or context-independent? Identify each occurrence of "++" in the following expressions:

```
c ++ s
(s ++ c) ++ c
s ++ (c ++ c)
```

where c is a Character variable and s is a String variable.

8.3.2 Adapt the characterization of overloading in Section 8.3 to cover *proper procedures*. Is the overloading of proper procedures context-dependent or context-independent?

Consider a language in which the operator "/" is overloaded, with types that include Integer × Integer → Integer and Integer × Integer → Float. The language also has an overloaded proper procedure `write` whose argument may be either Integer or Float. Find examples of procedure calls in which the procedure to be called cannot be identified uniquely.

8.3.3 Adapt the characterization of overloading in Section 8.3 to cover *literals*. Is the overloading of literals context-dependent or context-independent?

Consider a language in which arithmetic operators such as "+" and "−" are overloaded, with types Integer × Integer → Integer and Float × Float → Float. It is now proposed to treat the literals 1, 2, 3, etc., as overloaded, with types Integer and Float, in order to allow expressions like "x+1", where x is of type Float. Examine the implications of this proposal. (Assume that the language has no coercion that maps Integer to Float.)

Exercises for Section 8.4

8.4.1 What type conversions are allowed in your favorite language? What is the mapping performed by each type conversion? Separately consider (a) casts and (b) coercions.

Chapter 9

Control flow

Using sequential, conditional, and iterative commands (Section 3.7) we can implement a variety of control flows, each of which has a single entry and a single exit. These control flows are adequate for many purposes, but not all.

In this chapter we study constructs that enable us to implement a greater variety of control flows:

- *sequencers*, which are constructs that influence the flow of control;
- *jumps*, which are low-level sequencers that can transfer control almost anywhere;
- *escapes*, which are sequencers that transfer control out of textually enclosing commands or procedures;
- *exceptions*, which are sequencers that can be used to signal abnormal situations.

9.1 Sequencers

Figure 9.1 shows four flowcharts: a simple command, a sequential subcommand, an if-command, and a while-command. Each of these flowcharts has a single entry and a single exit. The same is true for other conditional commands, such as case commands, and other iterative commands, such as for-commands. (See Exercise 9.1.1.) It follows that *any* command formed by composing simple, sequential, conditional, and iterative commands has a single-entry single-exit control flow.

Sometimes we need to implement more general control flows. In particular, single-entry multi-exit control flows are often desirable.

A **sequencer** is a construct that transfers control to some other point in the program, which is called the sequencer's **destination**. Using sequencers we can implement a variety of control flows, with multiple entries and/or multiple exits. In this chapter we shall examine several kinds of sequencers: jumps, escapes, and exceptions. This order of presentation follows the trend in language design from low-level sequencers (jumps) towards higher-level sequencers (escapes and exceptions).

The mere existence of sequencers in a programming language radically affects its semantics. For instance, we have hitherto asserted that the sequential command "C_1; C_2" is executed by first executing C_1 and then executing C_2. This is true only if C_1 **terminates normally**. But if C_1 executes a sequencer, C_1 **terminates abruptly**, which might cause C_2 to be skipped (depending on the sequencer's destination).

215

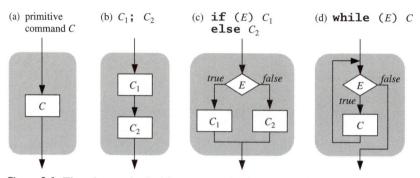

Figure 9.1 Flowcharts of primitive, sequential, if-, and while-commands.

Some kinds of sequencers are able to *carry* values. Such values are computed at the place where the sequencer is executed, and are available for use at the sequencer's destination.

9.2 Jumps

A *jump* is a sequencer that transfers control to a specified program point. A jump typically has the form "**goto** L;", and this transfers control directly to the program point denoted by L, which is a *label*.

EXAMPLE 9.1   Jumps

The following program fragment (in a C-like language) contains a jump:

```
if (E₁)
    C₁
else {
    C₂
    goto X;
}
C₃
while (E₂) {
       C₄
   X: C₅
}
```

Here the label X denotes a particular program point, namely the start of command C_5. Thus the jump "**goto** X;" transfers control to the start of C_5.

Figure 9.2 shows the flowchart corresponding to this program fragment. Note that the if-command and while-command have identifiable subcharts, which are highlighted. The program fragment as a whole has a single entry and a single exit, but the if-command has two exits, and the while-command has two entries.

Unrestricted jumps allow any command to have multiple entries and multiple exits. They tend to give rise to "spaghetti" code, so called because its flowchart is tangled.

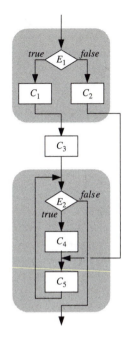

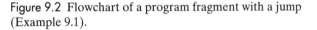

Figure 9.2 Flowchart of a program fragment with a jump (Example 9.1).

"Spaghetti" code tends to be hard to understand. It is worth reflecting on why this is so. Simple commands like assignments, and even composite single-entry single-exit commands, are largely self-explanatory. But jumps are not self-explanatory at all. For example, what effect does the jump "**goto** Z;" have on the program's behavior? It might be a forward jump that causes commands to be skipped, or a backward jump that causes commands to be repeated. We cannot tell until we locate the label Z, which might be many pages away.

Most major programming languages support jumps, but they are really obsolete in the modern languages. JAVA refuses to support jumps, on the grounds that the higher-level escapes and exceptions are sufficient in practice.

Even in programming languages that do support jumps, their use is constrained by the simple expedient of restricting the scope of each label: the jump "**goto** L;" is legal only within the scope of L. In C, for example, the scope of each label is the smallest enclosing block command ("{ ... }"). It is therefore possible to jump within a block command, or from one block command out to an enclosing block command; but it is *not* possible to jump into a block command from outside, nor from one function's body to another. The jump in Example 9.1 would in fact be illegal in C.

The last point does not imply that the flowchart of Figure 9.2 cannot be programmed in C. We simply rewrite the while-command in terms of equivalent conditional and unconditional jumps:

```
while (E₂) {    ≡    goto Y;
       C₄                W: C₄
    X: C₅                X: C₅
    }                    Y: if (E₂) goto W;
```

The resulting code is even less readable, however. C's jumps are not restricted enough to prevent "spaghetti" coding.

A jump within a block command is relatively simple, but a jump out of a block command is more complicated. Such a jump must destroy the block's local variables before transferring control to its destination.

EXAMPLE 9.2   Jump out of a block command

Consider the following (artificial) C code:

```
char stop;
stop = '.';
do {
  char ch;
  ch = getchar();
  if (ch == EOT)   goto X;
  putchar(ch);
} while (ch != stop);
printf("done");
X: ;
```

The jump "**goto** X;" transfers control out of the block command {…}. Therefore it also destroys the block command's local variable ch.

A jump out of a procedure's body is still more complicated. Such a jump must destroy the procedure's local variables and terminate the procedure's activation before transferring control to its destination. Even greater complications arise when a jump's destination is inside the body of a *recursive* procedure: which recursive activations are terminated when the jump is performed? To deal with this possibility, we have to make a label denote not simply a program point, but a program point within a particular procedure activation.

Thus jumps, superficially very simple, in fact introduce unwanted complexity into the semantics of a high-level programming language. Moreover, this complexity is unwarranted, since wise programmers in practice avoid using jumps in complicated ways. In the rest of this chapter, we study sequencers that are both higher-level than jumps and more useful in practice.

9.3 Escapes

An *escape* is a sequencer that terminates execution of a textually enclosing command or procedure. In terms of a flowchart, the destination of an escape is always the exit point of an enclosing subchart. With escapes we can program single-entry multi-exit control flows.

ADA's *exit sequencer* terminates an enclosing loop, which may be a while-command, a for-command, or a basic loop ("**loop** C **end loop**;" simply causes the loop body C to be executed repeatedly). An exit sequencer within a loop body terminates the loop.

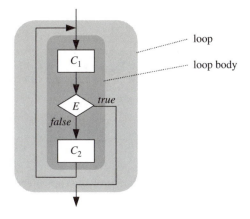

Figure 9.3 Flowchart of a loop with an escape.

In the following basic loop, there is a single (conditional) exit sequencer:

```
loop
    C₁
    exit when E;
    C₂
end loop;
```

The corresponding flowchart is shown in Figure 9.3, in which both the loop body and the basic loop itself are highlighted. Note that the loop has a single exit, but the loop body has two exits. The normal exit from the loop body follows execution of C_2, after which the loop body is repeated. The other exit from the loop body is caused by the exit sequencer, which immediately terminates the loop.

It is also possible for an exit sequencer to terminate an *outer* loop. An ADA exit sequencer may refer to any named enclosing loop. The following example illustrates this possibility.

EXAMPLE 9.3   ADA exit sequencer

The following type represents a diary for a complete year:

```
type Year_Diary is array (Month_Number, Day_Number)
     of Diary_Entry;
```

Consider the following procedure:

```
function search (diary: Year_Diary;
                 this_year: Year_Number;
                 key_word: String)
     return Date is
-- Search diary for the first date whose entry matches key_word.
-- Return the matching date, or January 1 if there is no match.
     match_date: Date := (this_year, 1, 1);
```

```
    begin
       search:
(1)     for m in Month_Number loop
(2)        for d in Day_Number loop
              if matches(diary(m,d), key_word) then
                 match_date := (this_year, m, d);
(3)              exit search;
              end if;
           end loop;
        end loop;
      return match_date;
    end;
```

Here the outer loop starting at (1) is named search. Thus the sequencer "**exit** search;" at (3) terminates that outer loop.

On the other hand, a simple "**exit**;" at (3) would terminate only the inner loop (2).

The ***break sequencer*** of C, C++, and JAVA allows any composite command (typically a loop or switch command) to be terminated immediately.

EXAMPLE 9.4   JAVA break sequencers

The following JAVA method corresponds to Example 9.3:

```
static Date search (DiaryEntry[][] diary;
                    int thisYear;
                    String keyWord) {
   Date matchDate = new Date(thisyear, 1, 1);
   search:
      for (int m = 1; m <= 12; m++) {
         for (int d = 1; d <= 31; d++) {
            if (diary[m][d].matches(keyWord)) {
               matchDate = new Date(thisYear, m, d);
               break search;
            }
         }
      }
   return matchDate;
}
```

A particularly important kind of escape is the ***return sequencer***. This may occur anywhere in a procedure's body, and its destination is the end of the procedure's body. A return sequencer in a function's body must also carry the function's result. Return sequencers are supported by C, C++, JAVA, and ADA.

EXAMPLE 9.5   C++ return sequencer

Consider the following C++ function:

```
int gcd (int m, n) {
// Return the greatest common divisor of positive integers m and n.
    int p = m, q = n;
    for (;;) {
        int r = p % q;
        if (r == 0) return q;
        p = q;   q = r;
    }
}
```

The sequencer "**return** q;" escapes from the function's body, carrying the value of q as the function's result.

Escapes are usually restricted so that they cannot transfer control out of procedures. For example, a return sequencer always terminates the immediately enclosing procedure body, and an exit sequencer inside a procedure's body can never terminate a loop enclosing that procedure. Without such restrictions, escapes would be capable of terminating procedure activations, causing undue complications (similar to those caused by jumps out of procedures, explained at the end of Section 9.3).

The only escape that can terminate procedure activations without undue complications is the **halt sequencer**, which terminates the whole program. In some programming languages this is provided as an explicit sequencer (such as **STOP** in FORTRAN); in others it is lightly disguised as a built-in procedure (such as exit() in C). A halt sequencer may carry a value (typically an integer or string), representing the reason for terminating the program, that will be reported to the user of the program.

9.4   Exceptions

An *abnormal situation* is one in which a program cannot continue normally. Typical examples are the situations that arise when an arithmetic operation overflows, or an input/output operation cannot be completed. Some abnormal situations are specific to particular applications, for example ill-conditioned data in mathematical software, or syntactically ill-formed source code in a compiler.

What should happen when such an abnormal situation arises? Too often, the program simply halts with a diagnostic message. It is much better if the program transfers control to a *handler*, a piece of code that enables the program to *recover* from the situation. A program that recovers reasonably from such situations is said to be *robust*.

Typically, an abnormal situation is detected in some low-level program unit, but a handler is more naturally located in a high-level program unit. For example, suppose that an application program attempts to read a nonexistent record from a file. This abnormal situation would be detected in the input/output subsystem, but any handler should be located in the application code where a suitable recovery action can be programmed. Furthermore, the program might contain several calls to the input/output subsystem, reading records for different purposes. The most appropriate recovery action will depend on the purpose for which the record was read. Thus the program might need several handlers specifying different recoveries from the same kind of abnormal situation. For all these reasons, neither jumps nor escapes are powerful enough to transfer control from the point where the abnormal situation is detected to a suitable handler.

A common technique for handling abnormal situations is to make each procedure pass back a suitable *status flag*. (In the case of a function procedure, the status flag can be the function result, which is the C convention. In the case of a proper procedure, the status flag must be passed back through a parameter.) The procedure sets its status flag to indicate which if any abnormal situation it has detected. On return, the application code can test the status flag. This technique has the advantage of requiring no special programming language construct, but it also has serious disadvantages. One is that the application code tends to get cluttered by tests of status flags. Another is that the programmer might forgetfully or lazily omit to test a status flag. In fact, abnormal situations represented by status flags are by default ignored!

Exceptions are a superior technique for handling abnormal situations. An *exception* is an entity that represents an abnormal situation (or a family of abnormal situations). Any code that detects an abnormal situation can *throw* (or *raise*) an appropriate exception. That exception may subsequently be *caught* in another part of the program, where a construct called an *exception handler* (or just *handler*) recovers from the abnormal situation. Every exception can be caught and handled, and the programmer has complete control over where and how each exception is handled. Exceptions cannot be ignored: if an exception is thrown, the program will halt unless it catches the exception.

The first major programming language with a general form of exception handling was PL/I. An *on-command* associates a handler with a given exception *e*. Thereafter, if any operation throws exception *e*, the associated handler is executed, then the offending operation may be resumed. The handler associated with a given exception may be updated at any time. The dynamic nature of the exception–handler association and the fact that the offending operation may be resumed make the PL/I exception concept problematic, and we shall not consider it further here.

A better exception concept has been designed into more modern languages such as ADA, C++, and JAVA. A handler for any exception may be attached to any command. If that command (or any procedure called by it) throws the exception, execution of that command is terminated and control is transferred to the handler. The command that threw the exception is never resumed.

Let us first consider ADA exceptions, which are the simplest. The sequencer "**raise** *e*;" throws exception *e*. ADA has an *exception-handling command* of the form:

```
begin
   C₀
exception
   when e₁  => C₁
   ...
   when eₙ  => Cₙ
end;
```

This is able to catch any of the exceptions $e_1, \ldots, e_n$. There are three possibilities:

- If the subcommand C_0 terminates normally, then the exception-handling command as a whole terminates normally. (None of the handlers is executed.)
- If the command C_0 throws one of the named exceptions e_i, then execution of C_0 is terminated abruptly, the handler C_i is executed, and then the exception-handling command as a whole terminates normally.
- If the command C_0 throws any other exception, then the exception-handling command itself is terminated abruptly, and throws that same exception.

EXAMPLE 9.6   ADA exceptions

Consider an ADA program that is to read and process rainfall data for each month of the year. Assume the following type definition:

```
type Annual_Rainfall is array (Month_Number) of Float;
```

The following procedure reads the annual rainfall data:

```
      procedure get_annual (input: in out File_Type;
                            rainfall: out Annual_Rainfall) is
         r: Float;
      begin
         for m in Month_Number loop
(1)         begin
(2)            get(input, r);
(3)            rainfall(m) := r;
            exception
               when data_error =>
(4)               put("Bad data for "); put(m);
                  skip_bad_data(input);
                  rainfall(m) := 0.0;
            end;
         end loop;
      end;
```

This illustrates how the program can recover from reading ill-formed data. The command (2) calls the library procedure `get` to read a numeric literal. That procedure will throw the `end_error` exception if no more data remain to be read, or the `data_error` exception if the numeric literal is ill-formed. The enclosing exception-handling command starting at (1) is able to catch a `data_error` exception. If the command (2) does indeed throw `data_error`, the sequential command (2,3) is terminated abruptly, and the exception handler starting at (4) is executed instead; this prints a warning message, skips the ill-formed data, and substitutes zero for the missing number. Now the exception-handling command terminates normally, and execution of the enclosing loop then continues. Thus the procedure will continue reading the data even after encountering ill-formed data.

The following main program calls `get_annual`:

```
      procedure main is
        rainfall: Annual_Rainfall;
        input: File_Type;
(5)   begin
          open(input, ...);
(6)       get_annual(input, rainfall);
(7)       ...  // process the data in rainfall
      exception
        when end_error =>
(8)        put("Annual rainfall data is incomplete");
      end;
```

This illustrates how the program can respond to incomplete input data. As mentioned above, the library procedure `get` will throw `end_error` if no more data remain to be read. If indeed this happens, the procedure `get_annual` does not catch `end_error`, so that exception will be thrown by the command (6) that calls `get_annual`. Here the exception will be caught, with the exception handler being the command (8), which simply prints a message to the user. In consequence, the command (7) will be skipped.

Although not illustrated by Example 9.6, we can attach different handlers for the same exception to different commands in the program. We can also attach handlers for several different exceptions to the same command.

Note the following important properties of exceptions:

- If a subcommand throws an exception, the enclosing command also throws that exception, unless it is an exception-handling command able to catch that particular exception. If a procedure's body throws an exception, the corresponding procedure call also throws that exception.

- A command that throws an exception is terminated abruptly (and will never be resumed).

- Certain exceptions are built-in, and may be thrown by built-in operations. Examples are arithmetic overflow and out-of-range array indexing.

- Further exceptions can be declared by the programmer, and can be thrown explicitly when the program itself detects an abnormal situation.

C++ and JAVA, being object-oriented languages, treat exceptions as objects. JAVA, for instance, has a built-in `Exception` class, and every exception is an object of a subclass of `Exception`. Each subclass of `Exception` represents a different abnormal situation. An exception object contains an explanatory message (and possibly other values), which will be carried to the handler. Being first-class values, exceptions can be stored and passed as parameters as well as being thrown and caught.

The JAVA sequencer "**throw** E;" throws the exception yielded by expression E. The JAVA exception-handling command has the form:

```
try
    C₀
catch (T₁ I₁) C₁
...
catch (Tₙ Iₙ) Cₙ
finally C_f
```

this is able to catch any exception of class T_1 or ... or T_n. If the subcommand C_0 throws an exception of type T_i, then the exception handler C_i is executed with the identifier I_i bound to that exception. Just before the exception-handling command terminates (whether normally or abruptly), the subcommand C_f is executed unconditionally. (The **finally** clause is optional.)

An important feature of JAVA is that every method must specify the exceptions that it might throw. A method's heading may include an *exception specification* of the form "**throws** T_1, ... , T_n", where $T_1, ..., T_n$ are the classes of exceptions that could be thrown. In the absence of an exception specification, the method is assumed never to throw an exception. (Actually, this is an over-simplification: see Section 12.4.2.)

| EXAMPLE 9.7 | JAVA exceptions |

Consider a JAVA program that is to read and process rainfall data for each month of the year (as in Example 9.6).

The following method attempts to read a numeric literal:

```
static float readFloat (BufferedReader input)
        throws IOException, NumberFormatException {
    ...  // skip space characters
    if (...)  // end of input reached
(1)    throw new IOException("end of input");
    String literal = ...;  // read non-space characters
(2) float f = Float.parseFloat(literal);
    return f;
}
```

This method specifies that it might throw an exception of class IOException or NumberFormatException (but no other). If the end of input is reached (so that no literal can be read), the sequencer at (1) constructs an exception of class IOException (containing an explanatory message) and throws that exception. If a literal is read but turns out not to be a well-formed numeric literal, the library method Float.parseFloat called at (2) constructs an exception of class NumberFormatException (containing the ill-formed literal) and throws that exception.

The following method reads the annual rainfall data:

```
static float[] readAnnual (BufferedReader input)
        throws IOException {
    float[] rainfall = new float[12];
    for (int m = 0; m < 12; m++) {
```

```
(3)     try {
(4)         float r = readFloat(input);
(5)         rainfall[m] = r;
        }
        catch (NumberFormatException e) {
(6)         System.out.println(e.getMessage()
                + " is bad data for " + m);
            rainfall[m] = 0.0;
        }
    }
    return rainfall;
}
```

This illustrates how the program can recover from reading ill-formed data. Consider the call to `readFloat` at (4). The enclosing exception-handling command, which starts at (3), is able to catch a `NumberFormatException`. Thus if `readFloat` throws a `NumberFormatException`, the code (4,5) is terminated abruptly, and the exception handler starting at (6) is executed instead; this prints a warning message incorporating the ill-formed literal carried by the exception (extracted by "`e.getMessage()`"), and substitutes zero for the missing number. Now the exception-handling command terminates normally, and the enclosing loop continues. Thus the remaining rainfall data will be read normally.

The following main program calls `readAnnual`:

```
static void main () {
    float[] rainfall;
(7) try {
(8)     rainfall = readAnnual();
(9)     ...  // process the data in rainfall
    }
    catch (IOException e) {
(10)        System.out.println(
                "Annual rainfall data is incomplete");
    }
}
```

This illustrates how the program can respond to incomplete input data. If `readFloat` throws an `IOException`, the method `readAnnual` does not catch it, so it will be thrown by the method call at (8). The enclosing exception-handling command, starting at (7), does catch the exception, the handler being the command (10), which simply prints a warning message to the user. In consequence, the command (9) will be skipped.

9.5   Implementation notes

9.5.1   Implementation of jumps and escapes

Most jumps and escapes are simple transfers of control, easily implemented in object code. However, a jump or escape out of a block is more complicated: variables local to that block must be destroyed before control is transferred. A jump or escape out of a procedure is still more complicated: the procedure's stack frame must be popped off the stack before control is transferred.

9.5.2   Implementation of exceptions

The implementation of exceptions is interesting because it entails a trade-off. The issue is how efficiently control is transferred to the appropriate exception handler when an exception is thrown, bearing in mind that the exception handler is typically not in the procedure that throws the exception but in a calling procedure. The best implementation depends on how frequently exceptions are thrown.

If we assume that exceptions are *infrequently* thrown, the program should be executed at close to full speed as long as it does not throw an exception, but transfer of control to an exception handler need not be particularly fast when (and if) the program does throw an exception. In this case an efficient implementation is as follows:

(a) At a procedure call, mark the calling procedure's activation frame to indicate whether the procedure call is inside an exception-handling command.

(b) When exception e is thrown, pop unmarked activation frames off the stack one by one. Then transfer control to the appropriate exception-handling command. If the latter contains a handler for exception e, execute that handler. If not, throw exception e again.

If we assume that exceptions are *frequently* thrown, transfer of control to the exception handler should be reasonably fast, even if extra instructions are needed to anticipate this eventuality. In this case, an efficient implementation is as follows:

(a) At the start of an exception-handling command, push the address of the exception-handling code and the address of the topmost activation frame on to a separate *exception stack*.

(b) At the end of an exception-handling command, pop a pair of addresses off the exception stack.

(c) When exception e is thrown, note the exception-handling code and activation frame addresses at the top of the exception stack. Pop all activation frames above the noted activation frame. Then transfer control to the noted exception-handling code. If the latter contains a handler for exception e, execute that handler. If not, throw exception e again.

Summary

In this chapter:

- We have studied the effect of sequencers on the program's control flow.
- We have studied jumps, seeing how they result in "spaghetti" code, and how jumps out of procedures cause undue complications.
- We have studied escapes, including exits and returns, which support flexible single-entry multi-exit control flows.
- We have studied exceptions, which are an effective technique for robust handling of abnormal situations.
- We have seen how jumps, escapes, and exceptions can be implemented efficiently.

Further reading

BÖHM and JACOPINI (1966) proved that every flowchart can be programmed entirely in terms of sequential commands, if-commands, and while-commands. Their theorem is only of theoretical interest, however, since the elimination of multi-entry and multi-exit control flows requires us to introduce auxiliary boolean variables and/or to duplicate commands. Since that is unnatural, the existence of sequencers in programming languages is justified.

The dangers of jumps were exposed in a famous letter by DIJKSTRA (1968b). An extended discussion of the use and abuse of jumps may be found in KNUTH (1974).

A variety of loops with multiple exits were proposed by ZAHN (1974).

The term *sequencer* was introduced by TENNENT (1981). Tennent discusses the semantics of sequencers in terms of continuations, a very powerful semantic concept beyond the scope of this book. Tennent also proposed a sequencer abstraction – an application of the Abstraction Principle – but this proposal has not been taken up by any major programming language.

A discussion of exceptions may be found in Chapter 12 of ICHBIAH (1979). This includes a demonstration that exception handling can be implemented efficiently – with negligible overheads on any program unless it actually throws an exception.

Which (if any) exceptions a procedure might throw is an important part of its observable behavior. JAVA methods must have exception specifications, but in C++ function definitions they are optional. A critique of C++ exception specifications may be found in SUTTER (2002).

Exercises

Exercises for Section 9.1

9.1.1 Extend Figure 9.1 by drawing the flowcharts of: (a) a C, C++, or JAVA do-while command; (b) a C, C++, or JAVA for-command; (c) a C, C++, or JAVA switch command; (d) an ADA case command.

Exercises for Section 9.2

9.2.1 Consider the following code fragment (in C, C++, or JAVA):

```
p = 1;   m = n;   a = b;
while (m > 0) {
    if (m % 2 != 0) p *= a;
    m /= 2;
    a *= a;
}
```

(a) Draw the corresponding flowchart. Outline the subcharts corresponding to the while-command, the if-command, and the bracketed sequential command. Note that these subcharts are properly nested.

(b) Rewrite the code fragment entirely in terms of conditional and unconditional jumps. Explain why this makes the code fragment harder to read.

*9.2.2 Some programming languages count labels as values.

(a) ALGOL60 allows labels to be passed as arguments. Explain why use of this feature can make a program hard to understand.

(b) PL/I counts labels as first-class values, which can be stored as well as passed as arguments. Explain why use of this feature can make a program even harder to understand.

(c) Show that the effect of passing a label as an argument can be achieved (indirectly) in C.

Exercises for Section 9.3

9.3.1 Consider the hypothetical form of loop, "**do** C_1 **while** (E) C_2", which was mentioned in Section 3.7.7.

(a) Draw the hypothetical loop's flowchart. Compare it with the ADA loop whose flowchart is in Figure 9.3.

(b) We would classify the hypothetical loop as a single-entry single-exit control flow, but the ADA loop as a single-entry multi-exit control flow. What is the distinction?

9.3.2 Modify the ADA code of Example 9.3 and the JAVA code of Example 9.4 to avoid using any sequencer. You will need to replace the for-loops by while-loops. Is your code more or less readable than the original code?

9.3.3 Modify the ADA code of Example 9.3 and the JAVA code of Example 9.4 to construct the default date (January 1) only if the search fails.

9.3.4 C, C++, and JAVA have a *continue sequencer*, which terminates the current iteration of the enclosing loop, thus causing the next iteration (if any) to be started immediately. Show that the continue sequencer can be understood in terms of an all-purpose escape.

Exercises for Section 9.4

9.4.1 Rewrite the ADA program of Example 9.6 or the JAVA program of Example 9.7 using status flags rather than exceptions. Each status flag is to be a copy-out parameter or function result of type {*ok, end-error, data-error*}. Compare and contrast the status-flag and exception-handling versions of the program.

9.4.2 Consider the ADA package `The_Dictionary` of Example 6.3. Make this package declare an exception, which is to be thrown on attempting to add a word to a full dictionary.

9.4.3 Consider your text input/output package of Exercise 6.1.2. Make your package declare suitable exceptions, which are to be thrown on attempting to read past end-of-file, to read ill-formed input data, etc.

*9.4.4 C++'s input/output library classes use status flags. Redesign them to use exceptions instead.

Chapter 10

Concurrency

The constructs introduced in the preceding chapters are sufficient to write *sequential programs* in which no more than one thing happens at any time. This property is inherent in the way control passes in sequence from command to command, each completing before the next one starts. *Concurrent programs* are able to carry out more than one operation at a time. Concurrent programming in high-level languages dates back to PL/1 and ALGOL68, but did not become commonplace until relatively recently, with languages such as ADA and JAVA.

This chapter removes our former restriction to sequential program structures and considers the language design concepts needed for concurrent programming. In particular, we shall study:

- the semantic differences between sequential and concurrent programming;
- the problematic ways in which basic programming constructs interact with each other in the presence of concurrency;
- low-level primitives that introduce and control concurrency;
- high-level control abstractions in modern, concurrent languages.

10.1 Why concurrency?

To be honest, concurrency is a nuisance. It makes program design more difficult, and it greatly reduces the effectiveness of testing. Nevertheless, there are important reasons for including concurrency in our repertoire of programming language design concepts.

The first of these reasons, and historically the most important one, is the quest for speed. An early milestone in computer architecture was the provision of hardware to let a computer execute input/output operations and CPU operations simultaneously. This immediately introduced concurrent programming. For best performance, computation had to be optimally overlapped with input and output. This was far from easy. So computer manufacturers introduced operating systems to automate the handling of concurrency. Operating systems are the archetypal concurrent programs, and the need to overlap computation with input/output still offers an important motivation for concurrent programming.

By running two or more jobs concurrently, *multiprogramming* systems try to make good use of resources that would otherwise be left idle. When a job is held up, waiting for the end of an input/output operation that cannot be fully overlapped, a multiprogramming system passes control of the CPU to a lower-priority job that is ready to run. At the end of the awaited input/output operation, the low-priority job is interrupted and the high-priority job is resumed. If the speed of the high-priority job is limited by input/output and the speed of the low-priority job is limited by the CPU, they run synergistically, using both input/output devices and CPU to good effect.

Multiaccess, or *server*, systems extend this principle, allowing many jobs to be run, each on behalf of a remote user. The demand from many concurrent users may easily exceed the capacity of one CPU. *Multiprocessor* systems deal with this by providing two or more CPUs, operating simultaneously on a common workload in shared storage.

Distributed systems consist of several computers that not only operate independently but can also intercommunicate efficiently. These have the potential for both higher (aggregate) performance and greater reliability than centralized systems based on similar hardware.

As CPU speeds begin to approach basic technological limits, further gains in performance can be looked for only in the better exploitation of concurrency. In that sense, concurrent programming is the future of all programming.

The second reason for including concurrency in programming languages is the need to write programs that faithfully model concurrent aspects of the real world. For example, *simulation* is a field in which concurrent programming has a long history. This takes concurrency out of the narrow domain of operating systems and makes it an important topic for many application programmers.

The third reason for interest in concurrency is the development of new, and more highly concurrent, computer architectures.

The least radical of these ideas gives a single CPU the ability to run more than one program at a time. It switches from one program to another (under hardware control) when it would otherwise be held up, waiting for access to main storage. (Main storage access is typically much slower than the execution time of a typical instruction.) In effect, this simulates a multiprocessor computer in a single CPU.

Many other architectures inspired by concurrency have been tried, but none of them has had enough success to enter the mainstream. They may yet have their day.

- *Array processors* provide many processing elements that operate simultaneously on different parts of the same data structure. By this means high performance can be achieved on suitable tasks – essentially, those for which the data fall naturally into rectangular arrays. Problems in linear algebra, which arise in science, engineering, and economics, are well suited to array processors.

- *Dataflow* computers embody an approach in which operations wait until their operands (perhaps the results of earlier operations) become available. They are aimed at extracting the maximum concurrency from the evaluation of expressions and may be especially suitable for functional programming languages.

- *Connectionism*, also known as *parallel distributed processing*, is a fundamentally different approach based on the modeling of neural networks in living brains. Some think that this is the way to realize the dream of artificial intelligence.

The study of concurrent programming aims to provide a framework that would unify all of these developments. It must be admitted that this goal is still remote.

Well-designed sequential programs are reasonably understandable; their complexity grows in proportion to their size. This is possible because sequential programs have important properties that make them, more or less, intellectually manageable. As we shall see, concurrent programs do not generally share these properties.

10.2 Programs and processes

A *sequential process* is a totally ordered set of steps, each step being a *change of state* in some component of a computing system. Their total ordering is defined in the sense that, given any two steps, it is always possible to say which is the earlier. A *sequential program* specifies the possible state changes of a sequential process, which take place in an order determined by the program's control structures. A *concurrent program* specifies the possible state changes of two or more sequential processes. No ordering is naturally defined between the state changes of one of these processes and the state changes of any of the others. Therefore, they are said to execute *concurrently*, and they may even execute *simultaneously*.

An example of a sequential process is the execution of a program written in a simple language such as C. The state changes constituting such a process are the results of executing assignment and input/output commands that update the variables of the program. These actions are ordered by the sequencing rules of the language, which define how control flows from command to command. Note that, because of the total ordering, we can associate the state changes of a sequential process with the passage of real (physical) time, although no specific rate of progress is implied.

If we consider the execution of a machine-code program the same holds good, except that the sequencing rules are defined by the computer architecture, and that not only storage but also registers (such as the program counter) are variables of the state.

To be completely honest, state changes at the most basic level might not be totally ordered in time. For example, during a `store` instruction, the bits of the source operand may be copied concurrently into the destination operand. However, it is not possible to examine the bits of the destination operand independently, to monitor the order in which they change. As far as the programmer is concerned, they all change at once. This departure from strict sequentiality is therefore irrelevant, because it is not observable.

For the sake of speed, some realizations of a computer architecture may allow even greater departures from strictly sequential execution. For example, a CPU may be able to overlap three instructions, one in the instruction-fetch phase, one in the instruction-decode phase, and one in the instruction-execute phase. If this has no observable side effects, the departure from sequentiality again is irrelevant to the programmer. Computer architects include *interlocks* in the hardware to ensure that overlapped execution does not affect the outcome. For example, if two instructions are in progress at the same time, and the second depends on a result of the first, the computer will delay the second instruction to ensure that the result becomes available before any attempt is made to use it.

Similarly, a high-level programming language might allow some freedom as to the ordering of operations within a program. In a language where expressions have no side effects, for example, two subexpressions may be evaluated in either order, or collaterally, or even concurrently. We can preserve the notion of a sequential process by looking at a large enough unit of action, such as the evaluation of a complete expression, or the execution of a complete command.

10.3   Problems with concurrency

We now look at ways in which concurrent programs differ from sequential programs.

10.3.1   Nondeterminism

Correct sequential programs are *deterministic*. A deterministic program (see Section 3.7.5) follows a sequence of steps that is completely reproducible in multiple executions with the same input. Determinism is a very important property, since it makes it feasible to verify programs by testing.

A few constructs, such as collateral commands (Section 3.7.5) and nondeterministic conditional commands (Section 3.7.6), introduce some unpredictability into sequential programs – we cannot tell in advance exactly which sequence of steps they will take. The compiler is free to decide the order of execution, so a given program might behave differently under different compilers. In practice, however, a particular compiler will fix the order of execution. The program's behavior is still reproducible, even if not portable.

A concurrent program, on the other hand, is likely to be genuinely *nondeterministic*, even under a specific compiler. That is to say, we cannot predict either the sequence of steps that it takes or its final outcome.

Usually we attempt to write programs that are *effectively deterministic* (Section 3.7.5), so that their outcomes are predictable. But an incorrect concurrent program may behave as expected most of the time, deviating from its normal behavior intermittently and irreproducibly. Such concurrent programming errors are among the most difficult to diagnose. The search for ways to prevent them motivates much of what follows.

10.3.2   Speed dependence

A sequential program is ***speed-independent*** because its correctness does not depend on the rate at which it is executed. This is a property so basic that we tend to take it for granted. Among other benefits, it allows computer manufacturers to produce a range of architecturally compatible machines that differ in speed and cost. The same software runs correctly on all models in the range, thanks to speed independence.

The outcome of a concurrent program is ***speed-dependent***, in general, as it may depend on the *relative* speeds at which its constituent sequential processes run.

Consequently, small random fluctuations in the speeds of CPUs and input/output devices may lead to nondeterminism.

Where *absolute* speeds must be taken into account – where the computer must synchronize its behavior with external physical equipment such as sensors and servomechanisms – we have a ***real-time*** program.

When outcomes are speed-dependent, a ***race*** condition is said to exist.

EXAMPLE 10.1 Race conditions

Suppose that two processes, P and Q, update the same `String` variable s, as follows:

```
In P:   s := "ABCD";
In Q:   s := "EFGH";
```

The programmer reasons as follows. One outcome is that P completes its assignment to s before Q starts on its assignment, so that the final value of s is "EFGH". If things happen the other way about, the outcome is that s takes the value "ABCD".

But other outcomes are possible. Suppose that P and Q update s one character at a time. Then s could end up with any of the sixteen values "ABCD", "ABCH", ..., "EFGD", "EFGH"; and there could be a different outcome each time P races Q in this way!

Example 10.1 shows that just two processes sharing access to a single variable can produce many different outcomes, and that the outcome on any one occasion is not predictable. Think of the chaos that could result from multiple uncontrolled accesses by dozens of processes to hundreds of variables! This is the nightmare that the discipline of concurrent programming aims to prevent.

Some help is provided in cases like this by the ability to declare that a variable is ***atomic***; i.e., that it must be inspected and updated as a whole, and not piecemeal. In Java, object references and variables of primitive types other than **long** and **double** are always atomic. In Ada, any variable v can be declared atomic by "**pragma** atomic(v);", although the compiler is free to reject such a declaration if it cannot be feasibly implemented on the target architecture. The *components* of an Ada array a can be made atomic by: "**pragma** atomic_components(a);".

If the declaration "**pragma** atomic(s);" for the variable in Example 10.1 were accepted, that would reduce the number of outcomes from sixteen to just two: a final value of "ABCD" and a final value of "EFGH".

However, this is far from a complete solution to the general problem.

EXAMPLE 10.2 A race condition despite atomicity

Suppose that two processes, P and Q, update the same `Integer` variable i, which is declared to be atomic and to have initial value 0, thus:

```
In P:   i := i + 1;
In Q:   i := 2 * i;
```

The programmer reasons as follows. One outcome is that *P* gains access to i before *Q*, so that i is first incremented, then multiplied, with result 2. Another outcome is that *Q* gains access to i before *P*, so that i is first multiplied, then incremented, with result 1. Therefore i must finally contain either 1 or 2.

But there is a third possible outcome. Bear in mind that most computer architectures implement an assignment by firstly evaluating the expression in a CPU register, and then copying the result from the register into the destination cell. Now consider this train of events: *P* loads i into a register; *Q* loads i into a register; *P* adds 1 and yields 1; *Q* multiplies by 2 and yields 0; *P* stores its register into i; *Q* stores its register into i. The result of this interleaving of *P* and *Q* is to leave i with the value 0!

10.3.3   Deadlock

Deadlock is a situation in which two or more processes are unable to make any further progress because of their mutually incompatible demands for resources. Deadlock can occur if, and only if, the following conditions all hold.

- *Mutual exclusion*: A process may be given *exclusive* access to resources.

  For example, if a process were reading data from a keyboard, it would make no sense to allow another process to use the keyboard at the same time.

- *Incremental acquisition*: A process continues to hold previously acquired resources while waiting for a new resource demand to be satisfied.

  For example, if a process must wait for a DVD drive to be allocated, it would be senseless to take away a scanner that had previously been acquired in order to copy data from it on to the DVD.

- *No preemption*: Resources cannot be removed from a process until it voluntarily relinquishes them.

  For example, if a process has opened a file for writing, it must be allowed to keep it until it has completed. Forcibly removing the file would be tantamount to killing the process, and might leave the contents of the file in a corrupted state.

- *Circular waiting*: There may be a cycle of resources and processes in which each process is awaiting resources that are held by the next process in the cycle.

  For example, process *P* holds a DVD drive; the DVD drive is needed by process *Q*; *Q* holds a scanner; and the scanner is needed by process *P*.

  So: *P* cannot proceed until it gets the scanner; the scanner will not become available until *Q* completes and frees it; *Q* will not complete until after it gets the DVD; the DVD will not become available until *P* completes and frees it; *P* will not complete until after it gets the scanner; and so on *ad infinitum*.

There are several approaches to the problem of deadlock.

The simplest approach is to *ignore* it and hope that it will not happen often enough to have a serious effect on reliability. When deadlock does strike, the system's users must deal with it as best they can (probably by restarting the whole system).

A more principled approach is to allow deadlocks to take place, but undertake to *detect* them and to *recover* from them automatically, so that the system as a whole keeps running. This involves killing some of the processes involved, and should be done in such a way as to minimize the cost of the work lost. In an embedded system, especially, this might not be a feasible strategy, for the processes to be killed might be critical to its mission. An alternative is to *roll back* the execution of some processes to a point before the problem arose. This is done by restoring the processes to the state they were in when it was recorded at an earlier *checkpoint*. Execution can then be resumed, but this time suspending the rolled-back processes until the danger has passed. Again, this strategy is not always workable.

A third approach is to *prevent* deadlocks by removing one or more of the preconditions. As we have seen, some resources must be granted for exclusive use, and since forcible removal of resources may be equivalent to killing the process involved, just two possibilities remain:

(a) Eliminate the incremental acquisition condition by requiring every process to request, at once, all the resources it will need.

(b) Eliminate the circular waiting condition by imposing a total ordering on resources and insisting that they be requested in that order.

Method (a) can lead to poor utilization of resources if processes are forced to acquire them prematurely. Method (b) may be better in this respect, if the total ordering is well chosen, but it requires considerable programming discipline, and cannot be appropriate for good utilization in all cases.

A fourth possible approach is to make the schedulers of the system actively *avoid* deadlock by timing the allocation of requested resources, in such a way that deadlock cannot occur. The maximum resource requirement must be declared to the schedulers in advance, but need not be reserved at once. The *banker's algorithm* (to be discussed in Section 13.3.4) is such a scheduler.

10.3.4 Starvation

A concurrent program has the **liveness** property if it is guaranteed that every process will make some progress over a sufficiently long (but finite) span of time. To meet this condition the system must be (a) free of deadlock, and (b) scheduled fairly.

Scheduling is the allocation of resources to processes over time, aiming to further some objective, such as good response time or high CPU utilization. **Fair scheduling** ensures that no process needing a resource is indefinitely prevented from obtaining it by the demands of competing processes.

An example of a fair scheduling rule is to make the processes that need a resource *queue* for it, in first-come first-served order. This guarantees that, if the resource becomes available often enough, a process needing it will eventually make its way to the head of the queue and so gain access. An example of an unfair rule is one that gives preferential access to high-priority processes, for it might indefinitely delay a low-priority process should there always be a high-priority demand waiting to be serviced. The term **starvation** is used when a process is indefinitely prevented from running by unfair scheduling.

10.4   Process interactions

Section 3.7.4 introduced the notation "$B;C$" for the sequential composition of commands B and C, and Section 3.7.5 gave the notation "B, C" for their collateral composition. The difference is that in sequential composition all of the steps of B must be completed before any of the steps of C are begun; whereas, in collateral composition, the steps of B and C may be interleaved arbitrarily.

However, neither notation admits the possibility that the commands B and C may be executed *simultaneously*. A **parallel command** specifies that two (or more) commands may be executed concurrently. We write "$B \parallel C$" to mean that B and C may be executed simultaneously or interleaved arbitrarily. (The symbol "$\parallel$" is used to suggest parallelism.) Note that "$B \parallel C$" does not *require* simultaneity, but does permit it. Concurrent composition also permits collateral execution and sequential execution, each a special case of reduced concurrency.

Concurrent programs are distinguished from sequential programs, not only by the presence of concurrent composition, but also by the presence of operations that cause interactions between processes. We now consider the kinds of interaction that may take place between commands that are composed concurrently.

10.4.1   Independent processes

Commands B and C are **independent** if no step of B can affect the behavior of any component step of C, and *vice versa*. If B and C are independent, it follows that any step of B may be executed either before, or after, or at the same time as, any step of C. In particular, all the steps of B can be executed either before or after all the steps of C, so "$B;C$" and "$C;B$" are both equivalent to "$B \parallel C$" (and so is "B, C"). It follows that the concurrent composition of independent processes is deterministic.

This is an important result, because it provides the basis for multiaccess server systems that run many jobs by multiprogramming one or more processors. Provided only that the jobs *are* independent, the users of such a system need take no special precautions arising from the concurrency.

Unfortunately, it is undecidable, in general, whether commands B and C actually are independent. However, a *sufficient* condition is that neither command can update a variable that the other inspects or updates. This criterion has the advantage that it can be (at least partially) checked at compile-time, so long as there is no aliasing. However, we have to define *variable* in its widest sense, as any component of the system whose state may be changed.

10.4.2   Competing processes

Commands B and C **compete** if each needs exclusive access to the same resource r for some of its steps. Let B be the sequence "$B_1; B_2; B_3$", and let C be the sequence "$C_1; C_2; C_3$". We assume that B_1, C_1, B_3, and C_3 are independent, none of them accessing r. However, B_2 and C_2 must not take place simultaneously nor overlap in time, for both require exclusive access to r. They are called ***critical sections*** with respect to r.

"$B \parallel C$" may be executed in either of the following ways:

$$\ldots; \quad B_2; \quad \ldots; \quad C_2; \quad \ldots$$

or:

$$\ldots; \quad C_2; \quad \ldots; \quad B_2; \quad \ldots$$

but not:

$$\ldots; \quad B_2 \parallel C_2; \quad \ldots$$

So "$B \parallel C$" has two possible outcomes, which are exactly the outcomes of the sequences "$B; C$" and "$C; B$" respectively. If the effects of the critical sections depend on the state of r when it is acquired, and if they change that state, then "$B \parallel C$" is nondeterministic in general – its outcome depends on the relative speeds at which B and C are executed.

A concurrent program is said to have the ***safety*** property if its critical sections never overlap in time. (It is *safe* in the sense that all of the commands it applies to a resource will have their normal, sequential, effect.)

EXAMPLE 10.3   Nondeterminism despite mutual exclusion

Suppose that two processes, P and Q, update the same `Integer` variable i, assumed to be atomic and to have initial value 0. Assume also that arrangements have been made for P and Q to mutually exclude each other's assignment command in its entirety:

```
In P:   i := i + 1;

In Q:   i := 2 * i;
```

If P executes its assignment before Q, the final value of i is 2. If Q executes its assignment before P, the final value of i is 1. There is a race between P and Q, but these are its only possible outcomes.

Example 10.3 illustrates ***bounded nondeterminism***: the outcome is not predictable, but belongs to a known, fixed set of outcomes, all of which may be equally acceptable.

10.4.3   Communicating processes

Again, let B be the sequence "$B_1; B_2; B_3$", and let C be the sequence "$C_1; C_2; C_3$". There is ***communication*** from B to C if B_2 produces data that C_2 consumes, so that B_2 must complete before C_2 starts. In this situation, "$B \parallel C$" has the same outcome as "$B; C$".

It is useful to extend this to a cascade of processes, each consuming the output of the preceding process and producing input for the next. In software, as in hardware, such a cascade is commonly known as a *pipeline*.

EXAMPLE 10.4   Unix and MS-DOS pipelines

The Unix operating system's command language provides the notation "$B \mid C$". This means that the commands B and C are executed concurrently, with the output from command B becoming the input to C. The notation can easily be extended to a longer pipeline, "$A \mid \ldots \mid Z$". In this way, commands that were written independently may be composed, contributing much to the power of the command language.

The MS-DOS operating system's command language also provided this notation, but did not support concurrent execution. It therefore implemented the command "$B \mid C$" as if the user had issued the sequence of two commands "$B > f; C < f$", where B writes its output (in its entirety) to a temporary file f, then C runs and reads its input from that temporary file.

Processes B and C **intercommunicate** if there is communication in both directions. This makes the possible outcomes of "$B \parallel C$" very much more numerous. We are therefore forced to impose a severe discipline on the forms of intercommunication permitted, if we want to preserve the intellectual manageability of our programs.

The designers of concurrent programming languages have invented many concepts and notations for concurrency. The choice of concurrent control structures is therefore somewhat controversial. The remainder of this chapter focuses on concepts in the mainstream of concurrent programming, including both concurrency primitives (Section 10.5) and high-level constructs (Section 10.6).

10.5 Concurrency primitives

In this section we consider a set of low-level operations that affect concurrency, by creating it, by destroying it, or by controlling it. An understanding of these operations is valuable because it provides a basis for understanding the higher-level constructs of concurrent programming languages, and because it shows how these higher-level constructs might be implemented.

But first, a clarification about our use of the term *process*. Up to now, we have used it to mean nothing more specific than a flow of control through a program, but the word carries more baggage than that. Let us now unpack it.

A conventional, *heavyweight*, process is the execution of a program. To support that execution, an operating system normally provides an address space, an allocation of main storage, and a share of the CPU time, as well as access to files, input/output devices, networks, and so on. This amounts to a substantial overhead, so that the creation of a process takes a non-trivial amount of the computer's resources, and *context switching* the computer from one process to another takes a significant time. Implementing a concurrent system by means of many processes therefore incurs a penalty: poor execution efficiency.

A ***thread*** is a lightweight alternative. Like a heavyweight process, a thread is a flow of control through a program, but it does not possess independent computational resources. Instead, a thread exists within a process and depends on the resources of the process. Switching the computer from thread to thread is a matter of swapping the contents of its working registers. The rest of the execution environment remains the same, so thread-to-thread context switching can be very rapid. (The thread concept originated in the real-time world, where the term ***task*** is more often used. True to their origins, ADA uses "task" terminology while JAVA goes with "thread".)

In what follows we are interested primarily in the semantics of concurrent programming concepts, and only secondarily in their pragmatic qualities (such as efficiency). For that reason, we will use the term ***process*** neutrally to mean a flow of control, when what is being said applies equally well to heavyweight processes and to lightweight threads (as it usually does).

10.5.1 Process creation and control

The primitive operations on processes are the following:

- `create` a new, dormant, *child* process;
- `load` the program code to be executed by a process;
- `start` the execution of a process;
- `suspend` the execution of a process (temporarily);
- `resume` the execution of a (suspended) process;
- let a process `stop` itself at the end of its execution;
- let its creator `wait` for the process to stop;
- `destroy` a stopped process, freeing any resources allocated to it.

It is often convenient to combine `create`, `load`, and `start` into one operation, usually called `fork`. When this is done, `wait` and `destroy` may be combined into a single operation, `join`. The `fork` operation is often defined so that the child process's program is an exact copy of its parent's. There must be a means by which the parent process and its child can subsequently be made to follow different paths through this program. One method is to give a code address as a parameter to `fork`, so that the parent continues at the instruction following the `fork`, whereas the child continues at the given address. An alternative method that is more convenient for use in a high-level language is employed in the UNIX operating system. The UNIX `fork` operation is a parameterless function that returns an integer. In the parent process this integer is an identification number for the newly created child process, but in the child process it is zero.

These primitives are quite general, letting us create any desired system of concurrently active processes. In this they resemble jumps, which allow us to set up any sequential control flow. They have a similar disadvantage: a scan of the static program text does not easily reveal the control flow, which develops dynamically.

EXAMPLE 10.5   Forking a new process in UNIX

A common fragment of a UNIX concurrent program is the following:

```
child_id := fork;
if child_id = 0 then
    perform the child process's program code ;
else
    continue with the parent process's program code ;
end if;
```

Here fork is a parameterless function that returns either the child process's identification number or zero.

So much for process creation and termination. We also need operations to enable orderly competition and communication. Initially we will present these in rather an abstract manner; later we will describe various alternative realizations.

To make the critical sections of competing processes disjoint in time, we need primitive operations for mutual exclusion. These are:

- acquire(r), to gain exclusive access to resource r;

- relinquish(r), to give up exclusive access to resource r.

If resource r is already allocated, acquire(r) **blocks** the process that calls it, i.e., holds it up so that (for the time being) the acquire operation makes no progress. When relinquish(r) is called, r is made free for reallocation. Processes waiting to gain control of r are **unblocked** and rescheduled. One of them will be able to complete the call of its acquire(r) operation and so get exclusive access to r.

A similar pair of operations provides inter-process communication. The most basic communication operation sends the smallest possible amount of information – the fact that some condition c now exists. Typical conditions that a receiver might be interested in are, for instance "an input/output operation has completed", or "CPU 2 has rebooted". We can view conditions as values of an abstract type, in which each value represents a different condition to be communicated. The primitive operations for communication are:

- transmit(c), called by a sender to notify an occurrence of the condition c;

- receive(c), called by a receiver to wait for an occurrence of c.

An important issue in the design of communication primitives is how selective the transmission is. Some implementations of transmit communicate with a specific receiving process. Others are "broadcast" operations that make the transmission available to any interested receiver. Another issue concerns what is to happen when no process is waiting to receive at the time of transmission. In some designs the transmission is lost. In others the transmission is stored until a receive operation is performed.

10.5.2 Interrupts

The end of a concurrent input/output operation is a relatively infrequent condition to which the CPU should respond quickly. It would not normally be efficient to test repeatedly for this, so, when parallel input/output transfers were introduced, the end of each input/output operation was made to cause an *interrupt*. That is to say, a signal from the input/output hardware forces an asynchronous call to a routine that will deal with the new situation. So an interrupt is, in effect, an invisible procedure call inserted at a random point in the program!

If we view the activity of an input/output device as an *external process*, we can treat the interrupt as a mechanism for inter-process communication. This is extended, in many operating systems, to a facility whereby one (internal) process can interrupt another, a well-known example being the UNIX `kill` system call. Using this mechanism for reliable inter-process communication is every bit as tricky as the idea of an invisible, random, procedure call might suggest. Unfortunately, it is one of the most-used mechanisms for communication between application code and graphical user interfaces.

In many computer systems there is only one CPU, and concurrency is supported by switching the CPU rapidly from one process to another (*context switching*). This happens whenever a blocked process, of higher priority than the process currently running, becomes unblocked and ready to run. A process can therefore give itself exclusive use of the CPU by ensuring that no context switch is possible. Since context switches are driven by interrupts, it suffices to ensure that no interrupt can occur. How this is done depends on the computer architecture, but it is usually possible to defer acting on interrupt requests until a later time. A process that gains exclusive control of the CPU, by this means, prevents every other process from accessing any resource whatever. This gives it exclusive access to the whole system, including the one resource it actually needs. So, deferring interrupts implements the `acquire` operation for any resource, and restoring them implements `relinquish`.

Acquiring all resources in order to use just one of them is a heavy-handed way of gaining exclusivity, and has disadvantages. If a computer inhibits interrupts too often, or for too long, it will be unresponsive. Many computer architectures classify interrupts into several priority levels, depending on the urgency of communication with the external device. This makes it possible to inhibit only those interrupts that may lead to conflict over a particular resource. Designing software to exploit such an interrupt system effectively requires considerable expertise and finesse.

10.5.3 Spin locks and wait-free algorithms

On a multiprocessor, several processes may be executing simultaneously. Manipulating the interrupt system of such a machine does not provide a means of mutual exclusion, for preventing one CPU from responding to interrupts does nothing to exclude access to a shared resource by processes running on the other CPUs.

In these circumstances a different mechanism must be used. A *spin lock* is a "busy-waiting loop", in which a process waits for access to a shared resource by repeatedly testing a flag that indicates whether the resource is free.

Spin-lock algorithms depend upon the fair serialization of concurrent load and store operations by the CPU/store interface. That is, they assume that accesses to the same storage location initiated concurrently are performed sequentially, and that no process is starved of storage cycles. Given these properties it is possible to program fair spin locks – algorithms that implement `acquire(r)` and `relinquish(r)` operations without starving any competing process of access to resource *r*.

This is no small feat, as we shall see. It was first achieved in *Dekker's algorithm*, and presented by Dijkstra (1968a) with an illuminating preamble, in the form of a series of incorrect attempts that illustrate the subtle problems that arise. Here we shall follow that development. We assume that there are two processes, numbered 1 and 2, and that each is executing a program of the following form, with a cyclic pattern of accesses to resource *r* (*self* is the number of the executing process):

```
loop
    noncritical code for process self;
    acquire(r);
    critical section for process self;
    relinquish(r);
    exit when process self is finished;
end loop;
```

The `acquire(r)` operation, although stated as an action on *r*, actually focuses on locking out the competing process.

The first idea is to use a variable `turn`, initialized to either 1 or 2, that indicates which of the two processes has permission to enter its critical section. Each process implements the exclusion primitives as follows, where *other* is 1 when *self* is 2, and *vice versa*:

```
acquire(r) ≡
    while turn = other loop null; end loop;

relinquish(r) ≡
    turn := other;
```

This certainly guarantees that only one of the processes can enter its critical section. However, it is too rigid, because they are forced to enter their critical sections alternately. Should either be held up, or stop, the other will be locked out of its critical section after at most one more cycle.

A second attempt uses an array `claimed`, with one boolean component for each process, indicating whether that process has claimed the right to enter its critical section. Both components of `claimed` are initialized to false. Each process *self* implements the exclusion primitives as follows:

```
acquire(r) ≡
    while claimed(other) loop null; end loop;
    claimed(self) := true;

relinquish(r) ≡
    claimed(self) := false;
```

This fails if process 1 (say) is held up between finding `claimed(2)` to be false and setting `claimed(1)` to true. A "window of opportunity" then opens for process

2 to enter its loop and discover `claimed(1)` to be still false. Both processes will now set their components of `claimed` to true and go on to enter their critical sections concurrently. Thus mutual exclusion is not guaranteed.

We might attempt to rectify this fault as follows:

```
acquire(r) ≡
  claimed(self) := true;
  while claimed(other) loop null; end loop;
```

But now a problem arises if process 1 (say) is held up after setting `claimed(1)` to true, but before entering the loop. This allows process 2 to do the same. Now both processes will discover that the other is claiming the shared resource. Consequently both must loop indefinitely and neither can ever enter its critical section.

To correct this fault we allow each process, while looping, to withdraw its claim temporarily. This gives the other process an opportunity to go ahead:

```
acquire(r) ≡
  claimed(self) := true;
  while claimed(other) loop
    claimed(self) := false;
    while claimed(other) loop null; end loop;
    claimed(self) := true;
  end loop;
```

This idea works (albeit rather inefficiently) in most circumstances, but it has one fatal flaw. If both processes run at exactly the same speed, and perfectly in phase, they may execute the code in lock step, in which case neither will ever discover that the other process has offered it a chance to proceed. This attempt fails, by being speed-dependent.

Dekker's algorithm combines the best features of these four failed attempts. It uses both `turn` and `claimed`, initialized as before:

```
acquire(r) ≡
  claimed(self) := true;
  while claimed(other) loop
    if turn = other then
      claimed(self) := false;
      while turn = other loop null; end loop;
      claimed(self) := true;
    end if;
  end loop;

relinquish(r) ≡
  turn := other;
  claimed(self) := false;
```

This overcomes the previous objection: the if-command uses `turn` as a tie-breaker, forcing the processes out of phase, so that one of them must find itself able to proceed.

Dekker's algorithm is rather complex, and is hard to generalize to more than two processes while preserving fairness. *Peterson's algorithm* is free of these defects:

```
acquire(r) ≡
  claimed(self) := true;
  turn := other;
  while claimed(other) and (turn = other)
    loop null; end loop;

relinquish(r) ≡
  claimed(self) := false;
```

That it took almost twenty years to discover so simple an algorithm speaks volumes about the difficulty we find in understanding concurrent systems.

There is a serious problem with all of the spin-lock code above. Many compilers optimize accesses to a variable inside a loop by pre-loading the variable into a register, and accessing the register instead of the variable (because a register can be accessed much faster than a storage cell). If turn in Dekker's algorithm is treated in this way, the innermost loop would never exit, because a relinquishing process would update the storage cell, while the acquiring process uselessly re-examined an unchanging value in a register!

To prevent this, it is necessary to tell the compiler that a variable may be updated by more than one process. This is done by declaring it to be *volatile*. The compiler then ensures that inspections and updates are always directed to its storage cell. In C, C++, and JAVA, the **volatile** qualifier may be included in a type. In JAVA, **long** and **double** variables declared volatile are also thereby made atomic (variables of other types are always atomic, whether volatile or not). However, the volatility of a pointer to an object does not extend to the object itself. If variable components of the object need to be volatile, they must themselves be declared as such. Similarly, the volatility of an array does not extend to the array's components, and there is no way in JAVA to make them volatile. In ADA, a variable declared to be atomic is automatically volatile. A variable *v* that cannot be atomic can be made volatile by "**pragma** volatile(*v*);". The components of an array *a* can be made volatile by "**pragma** volatile_components(*a*);".

Spin locks are wasteful of CPU time. Unless the waiting time is short, it would be better for an acquiring process to give up the CPU each time around the loop, and wait until there is a better chance of being able to continue. But this is not always possible. Consider the CPU scheduler's own data structures, which must be modified under mutual exclusion. To avoid an infinite regress, spin locks used by the scheduler cannot contain calls on scheduler operations (such as those a process uses to make itself wait). These non-blocking spin locks may be significant bottlenecks, limiting the performance of a highly concurrent system.

A way of reducing this overhead is to use *wait-free algorithms*, which have been proven correct, despite the fact that they apply no locking. Some of these algorithms need hardware support, in the form of special instructions that atomically update more than one storage cell. But *Simpson's algorithm* (1990) creates an atomic shared variable of type *T* (in effect), using just four atomic flag variables and an array of four volatile components of type *T*. The remarkable thing about Simpson's algorithm is that it neither blocks nor spins.

EXAMPLE 10.6 Simpson's algorithm

The following code implements an atomic shared variable of arbitrary type T, equipped with update and inspect operations, using a wait-free algorithm.

```
data_bank : array (Boolean, Boolean) of T;
pragma volatile_components(data_bank);

data_col : array (Boolean) of Boolean
     := (false, false);
pragma atomic_components(data_col);

last_row_inspected : Boolean := false;
pragma atomic(last_row_inspected);

last_row_updated : Boolean := false;
pragma atomic(last_row_updated);

procedure update (item : in T) is
   row : constant Boolean := not last_row_inspected;
   col : constant Boolean := not last_row_updated;
begin
   data_bank(row, col) := item;
   data_col(row) := col;
   last_row_updated := row;
end update;

function inspect return T is
   row : constant Boolean := last_row_updated;
   col : Boolean;
begin
   last_row_inspected := row;
   col := data_col(row);
   return data_bank(row, col);
end inspect;
```

Now for the skeleton in the closet! A basic assumption of most shared-variable algorithms is that an update to a variable v by one process is immediately observable by any other process that uses v. A necessary condition for this is that v be declared volatile, so that each access goes to v's storage cell, and not a copy in an internal CPU register. But that is *not* sufficient. The great disparity in speed between CPU and storage means that many computer designs rely on complicated buffering schemes to reduce the delay on access to storage. These schemes keep copies of data in transit between a CPU and storage. For example, it is common to keep a per-CPU copy of recently accessed data in a *cache*. Caching is normally transparent to a single process, but can cause major difficulties with variables shared between two or more processes.

Consider a multiprocessor computer that uses *write-back caches*, so that an update to v in one CPU's cache does not reach v's cell in common storage until its cache entry is re-allocated to another variable. An update to v by CPU A need not be observable to CPU B until some time after it is observable to all processes running on A. So A can see data inconsistent with that seen by B. To prevent this,

A must flush *v* from its cache, so that its storage cell is updated; and *B* must also flush *v* from its cache, so that the next inspection by *B* fetches the updated value from *v*'s storage cell.

Ensuring that this will happen is error-prone, inefficient, and non-portable. No major programming language provides operations to flush buffered copies of shared variables. So programs using shared variables, on such computers, must use machine-dependent and extra-linguistic means to coordinate their accesses properly. This creates yet another obstacle to correct and reusable programming with shared variables. Bear this in mind throughout the following discussion of low-level concurrency primitives. A huge advantage of supporting concurrency in a programming language is that it enables the compiler to handle these difficult implementation issues transparently and portably, with little or no explicit programming effort.

10.5.4   Events

An *event* is an entity that represents a category of state changes. We can view events *e* as values of an abstract type that is equipped with operations event_wait(*e*) and event_signal(*e*), where:

- event_wait(*e*) *always* blocks, and unblocks only when the next signaled occurrence of an event of category *e* occurs;

- event_signal(*e*) unblocks *all* processes that are waiting for *e*.

The operations event_wait and event_signal provide implementations of the transmit and receive primitives, where we make a unique event represent each condition.

EXAMPLE 10.7   A blocking spin lock

Events can be used to program a blocking version of the spin-lock operation acquire(*r*). With each resource *r* we associate an event r_freed that is signaled by every process relinquishing *r*. Then (using Peterson's algorithm) we have:

```
acquire(r) ≡
  claimed(self) := true;
  turn := other;
  while claimed(other) and (turn = other) loop
    event_wait(r_freed);
  end loop;
```

Considered as communication primitives, events have important drawbacks.

Firstly, the net effect of a pair of wait and signal operations depends on the order in which they execute, so they are not *commutative*. For example, the sequence:

(1) process Q waits for e

(2) process P signals e

unblocks Q, as intended, whereas the sequence:

(1) process P signals e

(2) process Q waits for e

leaves Q waiting for a signal that has come and gone. If the signaling of e is not repeated, Q gets stuck. This makes code that uses events liable to be speed-dependent.

Secondly, `event_signal(e)` awakens *all* processes blocked on event e, so this implementation of the `transmit` operation is interpreted as "broadcast". One-to-one transmission requires auxiliary data to identify the intended recipient. All awakened processes must test this data, note whether the signal is for them, and repeat the wait if it is not. Selective waiting therefore suffers significant context-switching overhead.

Thirdly, events are not useful for mutual exclusion, so separate provision must be made for that (such as spin locks or interrupt management).

Despite their various disadvantages, it is worth noting that the combination of interrupt management and events provided the original basis for process management in the very successful UNIX family of operating systems.

10.5.5 Semaphores

The abstract type *semaphore* has the three operations: `sema_initialize(s, n)`, `sema_wait(s)`, and `sema_signal(s)`, where:

- `sema_initialize(s, n)` must be called to initialize the semaphore s with the integer n, before any other operation is applied to s;
- `sema_wait(s)` may either block or complete, depending on the state of s;
- `sema_signal(s)` unblocks *at most one* process that is waiting on s.

To be more specific, these operations are defined in terms of their effects on three integer values associated with s: $s.waits$ is the number of completed calls to `sema_wait(s)`; $s.signals$ is the number of completed calls to `sema_signal(s)`; and $s.initial$ is the value of n in the single allowed call to `sema_initialize(s, n)`. The integer n is the number of calls by which `sema_wait` can lead `sema_signal`. For example, if n is 0, the first call to `sema_wait` is forced to block until there has been a call to `sema_signal`; whereas if n is 1, the first call to `sema_wait` will complete without blocking.

Any sequence of `sema_wait` and `sema_signal` operations on s must leave invariant the relation:

$$0 \leq s.waits \leq s.signals + s.initial \qquad (10.1)$$

To achieve this, a process is blocked within a wait operation until it can complete without violating (10.1). So, if a process calls `sema_wait(s)` when $s.waits = s.signals + s.initial$, then it will be blocked. It will not resume until some other process completes a call to `sema_signal(s)`, increasing the value of *s.signals*.

If several processes are waiting on the semaphore *s*, it is not defined which of them will be resumed by a signal operation on *s*. This provides a degree of freedom that can be exploited to implement an appropriate scheduling criterion for the application. We require only that this be fair. (This is the usual *strong semaphore*. Some researchers have described a *weak semaphore* that does not guarantee fairness.)

By contrast with events, semaphore operations *are* commutative, because unawaited signals are remembered by virtue of the semaphore invariant. If a process *P* signals *s* when no process *Q* is waiting on *s*, the occurrence of the signals is noted in *s.signals*, and is taken into account if *Q* later waits on *s*. Semaphore-based synchronization is therefore much less susceptible to speed-dependent programming errors than the use of events.

Again unlike events, the semaphore signal operation awakens only one process, so that this version of `transmit` is more like "send a telegram" than "broadcast". Highly selective and efficient communication is therefore possible. (Admittedly, it is less easy to broadcast using semaphores, if that is what is required.)

A further major advantage of semaphores is that they can be used both for mutual exclusion and for communication.

To program mutual exclusion we associate with each shared resource *r* a semaphore `r_mutex`. Every process using *r* must bracket its critical sections with calls to `sema_wait(r_mutex)` and `sema_signal(r_mutex)`, doing duty for `acquire(r)` and `relinquish(r)`, respectively.

Simple communication is effected in the same way. We associate a semaphore `c_sem` with each condition *c* to be transmitted. The `transmit` and `receive` operations become `sema_signal(c_sem)` and `sema_wait(c_sem)`, respectively. This reveals a deep connection between mutual exclusion and communication that was not apparent with events, because event operations are not commutative.

EXAMPLE 10.8　A shared buffer

Using semaphores, it is easy to write code that efficiently communicates an arbitrary amount of data, by means of a *buffer* variable shared between the sending and receiving processes. Here we show a simple protocol that ensures (a) that a receiver never tries to take old data from an empty buffer, and (b) that a sender never tries to overwrite a full buffer with new data. The semaphores `full` and `empty` are used to transmit the information that the buffer has been filled or emptied, respectively.

In their parent process:

```
sema_initialize(full, 0);
sema_initialize(empty, 1);
```

In a sender:

```
loop
   sema_wait(empty);
   place data in the buffer;
   sema_signal(full);
end loop;
```

In a receiver:

```
loop
   sema_wait(full);
   take data from the buffer;
   sema_signal(empty);
end loop;
```

When the buffer is empty, as initially, a receiver blocks at its wait operation, because $full.waits = full.signals + full.initial$ (the latter being 0). The receiver does not resume, nor access the buffer, until a sender has placed data there and signaled $full$. Conversely, because $empty.waits < empty.signals + empty.initial$, a sender does not wait, but immediately places data in the buffer, signals $full$, and loops round.

When the buffer is full, after a sender has signaled $full$, a receiver does not wait, but immediately takes data from the buffer, signals $empty$, and loops round. A sender is then symmetrically forced to wait for the receiver.

Note that this works for any number of concurrent sending and receiving processes.

Semaphores do have a serious disadvantage, which is shared by events and indeed by all of the low-level primitives we have discussed. This disadvantage is that the connection between any given resource or condition and the associated semaphore operations is merely conventional. The convention works only if the programmer remembers to call these operations at all necessary points, but this cannot be ensured by compile-time checking. It is too easy to forget a wait or signal operation, with disastrous results.

The problem is that all these primitives are at a very low level of abstraction, and allow a badly structured program to be written as easily as a well-structured one. Semaphores are appropriately treated as machine-level operations, and indeed some computer architectures have included semaphore instructions that were competitive with interrupts for communication with input/output devices. Semaphores implemented in software (e.g., using spin locks) incur a greater cost, perhaps much greater, depending on whether operating system intervention is required.

10.5.6 Messages

In a distributed system, processes run on a network of computers that do not share primary storage, so that spin locks, events, and semaphores cease to be appropriate. Instead, the network provides a data communication service that supports process interaction by the exchange of **messages**. Message passing can be the basis for communication in shared-storage systems as well, and this is attractive because it simplifies later porting to a distributed system. Indeed, the first known message-based operating system was for a single-CPU computer, described in Brinch Hansen (1973). But message passing does involve greater overheads than (say) the use of semaphores, and this can be a deciding factor when shared-storage interaction is an option.

Message passing requires a *channel* that can carry a message from process to process. Such a channel may either be explicitly identified, or implied by the identities of the sender and receiver processes. An explicitly identified channel may be known as a *message queue*, a *buffer*, or the like; such a channel may allow communication between an arbitrary number of senders and receivers. An implicitly identified channel can support only one-to-one communication. There is also a question of whether the channel supports communication in one direction only (*simplex*), or in both directions (*duplex*).

The lifetime of a channel may be bounded by the activation of the communication procedure (local), by the lifetime of the communicating processes (global), or by operations outside these processes (persistent).

The primitive operations on a channel include:

- `connect` a process to a channel;
- `disconnect` a process from a channel;
- `send` a message on a channel;
- `receive` a message from a channel, or wait for its arrival;
- `test` for the existence of an incoming message on a channel.

A message may contain either a copy of data belonging to the sender, or a pointer to shared data. The former is more common in distributed systems and the latter in shared storage systems. Messages may be fixed or variable in length, and channels may have a fixed capacity or be able to expand and contract to meet demand. When a sender has dispatched a message, it may be blocked pending a reply, so that communication proceeds synchronously. Alternatively, a sender may be free to continue after a send operation, so that communication is asynchronous.

The designer of a message-based system thus has a great number of alternatives to explore, and such systems have indeed been very diverse.

10.5.7   Remote procedure calls

A disadvantage of basing a design on message passing is that the division of the system into processes is strongly reflected in the program text. Operations within the same process are invoked by procedure calls, and operations in other processes by message passing. This poses a maintenance problem when the distribution of functions among processes is changed.

It is possible to avoid this, and retain the advantages of procedural notation, by exploiting the **remote procedure call**. The run-time environment determines the site where a procedure is located, and communicates with that site to invoke it.

The site that provides the procedure, on receiving a remote call, may create a process to implement the operation. Alternatively, a server process at the remote site may receive all calls for a procedure and provide that service to each caller in turn. If more concurrency would be beneficial, the server may fork threads to serve concurrent callers. The choice is determined by the relative costs of process or thread creation as against communication, and by the degree of concurrency desired. These are pragmatic issues, rather than questions of principle.

10.6 Concurrent control abstractions

Good programmers make great efforts to ensure that a program expresses clearly what it means. The concern is to make obvious in its source code the essential relationships between the parts of a program. These include data flow relationships, and the properties of types, as well as control flow relationships. We also observe the principle that *simple* relationships are both technically sufficient and psychologically preferable.

Programming language designers have largely succeeded in creating abstractions that facilitate sequential programming of this quality. Attention has increasingly turned to the problems raised by concurrency and distribution. This section presents some of the more significant language design concepts in mainstream concurrent programming.

10.6.1 Conditional critical regions

The **conditional critical region** is a composite command that provides both mutual exclusion and communication. The key idea is that every variable shared between processes must be declared as such. A variable not so declared is local to one process, and a compiler can easily check that no such variable is accessed by any other process. At a stroke this removes one of the main sources of error in concurrent programming.

The conditional critical region takes the form (in pseudo-ADA syntax):

```
region v do
    C
end region;
```

The subcommand C is a critical section with respect to the shared variable v. A shared variable may be accessed *only* within such a conditional critical region, which again is easy for the compiler to check. At most one process at a time is allowed to execute in a particular conditional critical region, this being readily implemented with a semaphore. So mutually exclusive access to all shared variables is automatic.

Within the conditional critical region, the **await command** "await E" blocks until the expression E (which accesses the shared variable v) yields the value true. While waiting, a process relinquishes its exclusive use of the shared variable. When it resumes, its exclusivity is reacquired.

EXAMPLE 10.9 Conditional critical regions

The following pseudo-ADA code illustrates a bounded buffer type:

```
type Message_Buffer is
    shared record
        size : Integer range 0 .. capacity;
        front, rear : Integer range 1 .. capacity;
        items : array (1 .. capacity) of Message;
    end record;
procedure send_message (item : in Message;
                buffer : in out Message_Buffer) is
begin
  region buffer do
    await buffer.size < capacity;
    buffer.size := buffer.size + 1;
    buffer.rear := buffer.rear mod capacity + 1;
    buffer.items(buffer.rear) := item;
  end region;
end send_message;

procedure receive_message (item : out Message;
                buffer : in out Message_Buffer) is
begin
  region buffer do
    await buffer.size > 0;
    buffer.size := buffer.size - 1;
    item := buffer.items(buffer.front);
    buffer.front := buffer.front mod capacity + 1;
  end region;
end receive_message;
```

As Example 10.9 shows, the conditional critical region highlights the points of interaction between processes, with a minimum of conceptual and notational clutter:

- Both mutual exclusion and communication are provided in full generality, with no need for auxiliary flags or variables.
- Mutual exclusion is guaranteed at compile-time.
- Transmission of conditions is automatic and implicit. A process that establishes a condition need not be aware that it is of interest to any other process.
- Reception is simple, explicit, and commutes with transmission.

These properties lend clarity to programs written in terms of conditional critical regions. But they come at the cost of some busy waiting: the command "**await** E;" must be implemented in terms of a loop that re-evaluates E at least as often as any process leaves a critical section that updates the variables accessed by E.

10.6.2   Monitors

Despite their advantages, conditional critical regions were trumped by another notation that quickly became a standard feature of concurrent programming languages.

The argument is simple: processes should be coupled as loosely as possible to any variables they share. Chapter 6 showed how we can achieve loose coupling by encapsulating each shared variable in a package equipped with suitable operations to access it. We can go further and arrange for automatic mutual exclusion on calls to these operations.

The *monitor* is a kind of package, combining encapsulation with mutual exclusion and communication. CONCURRENT PASCAL, described in Brinch Hansen (1977), and MODULA, described in Wirth (1977), were two influential PASCAL-like languages that promoted monitors as the way to structure concurrency.

MODULA monitors ensure mutual exclusion for the operations of an abstract type. However, unlike conditional critical regions, they do not support automatic signaling. Instead, a predefined type `signal` is provided with `send` and `wait` operations. A `signal` is implemented as a queue of processes waiting to proceed within the monitor. The `wait` operation blocks the running process and places it on the nominated signal's queue. While waiting on a signal, a process gives up its exclusive use of the monitor. The `send` operation unblocks the process at the head of the nominated signal's queue. When the latter process resumes, it regains its exclusive use of the monitor.

EXAMPLE 10.10   A MODULA monitor

The following monitor, coded in MODULA, implements a bounded buffer object. For all its rather dated appearance, it exemplifies important techniques that some more modern languages, such as JAVA, fail to exploit effectively.

```
INTERFACE MODULE BufferMonitor;

DEFINE sendMessage, receiveMessage;   (* public *)

TYPE MessageBuffer =
    RECORD
        size : 0 .. capacity;
        front, rear : 1 .. capacity;
        items : ARRAY 1 .. capacity OF Message
    END;

VAR
  buffer : MessageBuffer;
  nonfull, nonempty : signal;

PROCEDURE sendMessage (item : Message);
  BEGIN
  IF buffer.size = capacity THEN wait(nonfull);
  buffer.size := buffer.size + 1;
  buffer.rear := buffer.rear MOD capacity + 1;
```

```
            buffer.items[buffer.rear] := item;
            send(nonempty)
        END;

    PROCEDURE receiveMessage (VAR item : Message);
        BEGIN
        IF buffer.size = 0 THEN wait(nonempty);
        buffer.size := buffer.size - 1;
        item := buffer.items[buffer.front];
        buffer.front := buffer.front MOD capacity + 1;
        send(nonfull)
        END;

    BEGIN (* initialization of buffer *)
    buffer.size := 0;
    buffer.front := 1;
    buffer.rear := 0
    END BufferMonitor;
```

Like semaphores and events, signals are associated with conditions only by a convention that must be respected in the logic of the monitor. Signals allow a more efficient implementation of inter-process communication than is possible with the conditional critical region, but at the cost of more work for the programmer and more opportunity for error. For example, one danger is this: the programmer might assume that a pre-condition established before waiting still holds true after resuming. That will be the case if, and only if, *all* other processes that call operations of the monitor take care to re-establish that pre-condition. This couples the logic of those processes very tightly indeed, and in that sense is a serious failure of modularity.

By contrast, the conditional critical region await command specifies an arbitrary predicate, and the programmer can be confident that the process will not continue until that predicate is fully satisfied. The result is much greater logical clarity.

10.6.3 Rendezvous

The difficulties associated with shared variables have led many researchers to concentrate on well-structured message passing as an alternative. Hoare (1978) proposed the notation that has come to be called CSP (Communicating Sequential Processes). The essential feature of CSP is that processes interact only by means of unbuffered (synchronous) communication, or **rendezvous**. In order to rendezvous, each process executes a command indicating its willingness to communicate with the other. This is, in effect, a kind of input command in the receiver, and a kind of output command in the sender. Each process blocks if the other one has not yet reached its rendezvous point. When both processes are ready, a message is copied from the sender to the receiver; then both are unblocked and continue independently.

CSP was more of a thought experiment than a practical tool, but it inspired many later developments, including the languages OCCAM and ADA.

ADA was the first major programming language to incorporate high-level concurrent programming features. A *task module* is in some ways similar to a package, but its body is executed as a new process. Global variables are accessible by a task body, as a normal consequence of ADA's scope rules, so tasks may interact by their effect on shared variables. However, ADA provides little support for this, and the programmer is responsible for ensuring that sharing global variables has no harmful effects.

Instead, the preferred mode of communication between tasks is the rendezvous, which is encouraged by a rich set of language features. A task module may declare public *entries*, which resemble procedures. (In fact, entries are the *only* public components of a task module.) A calling task communicates by means of an *entry call*, which is syntactically similar to a procedure call, and may pass parameters to the entry. A called task communicates by means of an *accept command*, a composite command that has access to the arguments of an entry call. A caller blocks until its entry call is served, and waits in a queue. A called task blocks at an accept command for an entry with no queued calls. Additional language features allow for bounded nondeterminism in accepting calls, and offer the option not to wait if no rendezvous can be achieved (either immediately, or after a specified time limit).

Since rendezvous takes place only when it suits the called task, it is possible to ensure that communication always follows a strict protocol. An entry call can have no effect on a task until the latter chooses to respond to it. This is a big advantage of rendezvous over both messages and remote procedure calls, which may arrive in an uncontrolled order that the server process must always be ready to cope with.

Like a package, an ADA task module has both a specification and a body. The specification declares the entries it makes public. The body contains private declarations, and the implementation of the public entries in terms of accept commands. Unlike a package, a task module can be either a *single task* or a *task type* that can be used to create many tasks with the same interface.

EXAMPLE 10.11   Rendezvous in ADA

The following ADA task type implements a single-slot buffer abstract type:

```
task type Message_Buffer is
  entry send_message (item : in Message);
  entry receive_message (item : out Message);
end Message_Buffer;

task body Message_Buffer is
  buffer : Message;
begin
  loop
    accept send_message (item : in Message) do
      buffer := item;
    end;
    accept receive_message (item : out Message) do
```

```
                    item := buffer;
            end;
        end loop;
    end Message_Buffer;
```

The variable declaration:

```
urgent, pending : Message_Buffer;
```

creates two tasks of type `Message_Buffer`. Each of these tasks runs concurrently with the process that elaborated the declaration. They can now be called independently to store and fetch messages:

```
msg : Message;
...
pending.send_message(msg);
pending.receive_message(msg);
urgent.send_message(msg);
```

where, for example, "pending.send_message(msg);" is a call to the entry send_message in the task `pending`, passing the value of `msg` as an argument.

Note how the control structure of `Message_Buffer` ensures that messages are alternately stored and fetched, so that any attempt by a caller to fetch when the buffer is empty is automatically forced to wait until the buffer is refilled.

Note also the absence of explicit signaling and mutual exclusion constructs. The latter are not needed, because variables local to a task body (such as `buffer`) can be accessed only by that task, which therefore does so safely.

Summary

Sequential programs do one thing at a time, but concurrent programs can do many things at a time. This provides performance and flexibility, but at the cost of greatly increased logical complexity. In this chapter:

- We have seen how concurrency leads to problems of *determinism*, *liveness* (*starvation* and *deadlock*), and *safety* (*mutual exclusion*) that do not exist in sequential programs.

- We have seen how concurrency is created, destroyed and controlled at the most primitive level encountered in a modern programming language.

- We have seen how concurrency can be managed using high-level control abstractions.

Further reading

The theory of communicating processes was given a firm foundation by HOARE (1986). There is a wide-ranging anthology of original papers on concurrent programming in GEHANI and McGETTRICK (1988). An extended introduction to concurrency in ADA95 is given in COHEN (1995). A full treatment is given in BURNS and WELLINGS (1998), and a similar depth of coverage for concurrency in JAVA can be found in LEA (2000). Distributed systems are treated in depth by COULOURIS et al. (2000).

Exercises

Exercises for Section 10.3

10.3.1 Despite what is said in Section 10.3.1, most programmers have seen sequential programs behave unpredictably, test runs with the same input data giving different results. Explain why this happens, and why it does not contradict Section 10.3.1.

Exercises for Section 10.4

10.4.1 Processes that share variables must (normally) arrange for time-wise disjoint access to them.

(a) Give a simple example of what can go wrong without mutual exclusion.

(b) Show a problem that cannot be corrected by using the `atomic` qualifier in ADA or the **volatile** qualifier in JAVA.

(c) Give a *simple* example of concurrent operation on an atomic shared variable that does *not* require mutual exclusion.

Exercises for Section 10.5

10.5.1 Consider the variable `claimed`, used in Dekker's and Peterson's algorithms.

(a) Should it, or its components, be atomic and/or volatile? Write any necessary declarations in ADA.

(b) What problem arises in JAVA?

*10.5.2 This exercise looks at Simpson's algorithm more closely (see Example 10.6).

(a) Explain why the local variables `row` and `col` in `update` need not be declared atomic.

(b) Explain why the local variable `col` in `inspect` need not be declared atomic.

(c) Give an argument for the correctness of Simpson's algorithm.

10.5.3 In Example 10.7, what would happen if a process that relinquished resource r failed to signal the event `r_freed`?

10.5.4 Sketch code, along the lines of Example 10.9, to implement a buffer with capacity for n data items, using the semaphores `mutex`, `free_slots`, and `full_slots`, initialized as follows:

```
sema_initialize(mutex, 1);
sema_initialize(free_slots, n);
sema_initialize(full_slots, 0);
```

10.5.5 A program contains many shared variables of the type T:

```
type T is
    record
        initialized : Boolean := false;
        ...
    end record;
```

The programmer, worried about the inefficiency of semaphore operations, tries to initialize these variables safely, *without mutual exclusion*, as follows:

```
procedure initialize (v : in out T) is
begin
    if not v.initialized then
        ... ;    -- give v its initial value
        v.initialized := true;
    end if;
end initialize;
```

(a) Explain the race condition that prevents it from working reliably.

(b) Recognizing the mistake, the programmer does some research and learns about *double-checked locking*, a technique that uses mutual exclusion only when necessary, and rewrites `initialize` as follows:

```
sema_initialize(mutex, 1);
...
procedure initialize (v : in out T) is
begin
    if not v.initialized then
        sema_wait(mutex);
        if not v.initialized then
            ... ;    -- give v its initial value
            v.initialized := true;
        end if;
        sema_signal(mutex);
    end if;
end initialize;
```

Explain the programmer's reasoning in thinking that this solves the mutual exclusion problem efficiently.

(c) Unfortunately, it actually fails to be safe. Explain why. What can be done to make it work reliably?

*10.5.6 The hypothetical primitive "**start** *C*" (*not* part of ADA) causes the subcommand *C* to be executed in a new thread, concurrent with the one that executes the start primitive. The new thread shares all presently existing variables with its parent, but subsequently created variables are not shared.

(a) Using the **start** primitive, modify the following sequential procedure so that as many components as possible of sum are computed concurrently:

```
type Matrix is array (1 .. n, 1 .. n) of Float;
procedure add (a, b : in Matrix;
                    sum : out Matrix) is
begin
    for i in 1 .. n loop
        for j in 1 .. n loop
            sum(i,j) := a(i,j) + b(i,j);
        end loop;
    end loop;
end add;
```

How many processes can be active concurrently in your version? Assume that starting a process takes time T, and that executing the assignment takes time t. In what circumstances would the concurrent version be faster?

(b) Using the **start** primitive, modify the following procedure so that as many as possible of the nodes of the tree `atree` are visited concurrently.

```
type TreeNode;
type Tree is access TreeNode;
type TreeNode is
    record
        datum : T; left, right : Tree;
    end record;

procedure traverse (atree : Tree; ...) is
begin
   if atree.left /= null then
      traverse(atree.left, ...);
   end if;
   if atree.right /= null then
      traverse(atree.right, ...);
   end if;
   ...   -- process atree.datum here
end traverse;
```

What kinds of processing operations could be performed in the sequential version that could *not* be performed in the concurrent version?

Exercises for Section 10.6

10.6.1 How do the `wait` and `send` operations of MODULA compare with event operations, and with semaphore operations? What does that say about the liability of MODULA-like monitors to speed-dependent faults?

10.6.2 Show that it is not possible, in Example 10.11, for more than one caller to obtain a copy of any one message.

PART IV

PARADIGMS

Part IV surveys the major programming paradigms:

- imperative programming
- object-oriented programming
- concurrent programming
- functional programming
- logic programming
- scripting.

Each chapter identifies the key concepts that characterize a particular paradigm, discusses the pragmatics of programming in that paradigm, and illustrates that paradigm by case studies of major languages.

Chapter 11

Imperative programming

In this chapter we shall study:

- the key concepts that characterize imperative programming languages;
- the pragmatics of imperative programming;
- the design of two major imperative languages, C and ADA.

11.1 Key concepts

Imperative programming is so called because it is based on commands that update variables held in storage. (The Latin verb *imperare* means "to command".) In the 1950s, the first programming language designers recognized that variables and assignment commands constitute a simple but useful abstraction from the memory fetch and update of computers' instruction sets. This close relationship with computer architecture enables imperative programs to be implemented very efficiently, at least in principle.

Imperative programming remained the dominant paradigm until the 1990s, when it was challenged by object-oriented programming. The vast majority of commercial software currently in use was written in imperative languages, as is much of the software currently being developed. Most of today's professional programmers are skilled largely or exclusively in imperative programming.

The key concepts of imperative programming are classically:

- variables
- commands
- procedures

and, more recently:

- data abstraction.

Variables and *commands* are key concepts of imperative programming for the following reason. Many programs are written to model real-world processes affecting real-world entities, and a real-world entity often possesses a state that varies with time. So real-world entities can be modeled naturally by variables, and real-world processes by commands that inspect and update these variables.

For example, consider an aircraft flight control program. The aircraft has a state consisting of its position, altitude, speed, payload, fuel load, and so on. In order to perform its function, the flight control program must model the aircraft's state. Since the state changes with time, it is most naturally modeled by a group of variables.

Variables are also used in imperative programming to hold intermediate results of computations. However, variables used in this way are *not* central to imperative programming, and indeed they can often be eliminated by reprogramming.

For example, we could write both iterative and recursive versions of a procedure to compute b^n. The iterative version needs local variables to control the iteration and to accumulate the product. The recursive version needs no local variables at all. (See Exercise 11.1.1.)

Ideally, variables would be used *only* to model states of real-world entities. However, to avoid any need for variables to hold intermediate results, the imperative language must have a rich repertoire of expressions, including block expressions, conditional expressions, and iterative expressions, as well as recursive functions. In practice, the major imperative languages (such as C and ADA) are not sufficiently rich in this respect.

Procedures are a key concept of imperative programming because they abstract over commands. We can distinguish between a procedure's observable behavior and the algorithm (commands) by which the procedure achieves its behavior, a useful separation of concerns between the procedure's users and its implementer.

Data abstraction is not strictly essential in imperative programming, and indeed it is not supported by classical imperative languages such as C and PASCAL, but it has become a key concept in the more modern imperative languages such as ADA. We can distinguish between an abstract type's properties and its representation, between the observable behavior of the abstract type's operations and the algorithms by which these operations achieve their behavior, again a useful separation of concerns between the abstract type's users and its implementer.

11.2 Pragmatics

The key concepts of imperative programming influence the architecture as well as the coding of imperative programs. By the **architecture** of a program we mean the way in which it is decomposed into program units, together with the relationships between these units.

The quality of a program's architecture is important to software engineers because it directly affects the cost of implementing and later maintaining the program. One important measure of quality is **coupling**, which means the extent to which program units are sensitive to changes in one another. A group of program units are *tightly coupled* if modifications to one are likely to force major modifications to the others, while they are *loosely coupled* if modifications to one are likely to force at most minor modifications to the others. Ideally, all program units of a program should be loosely coupled. A program with this quality is likely to be easier (and less costly) to maintain in the long run, since an individual program unit can be modified when required without forcing major modifications to other program units.

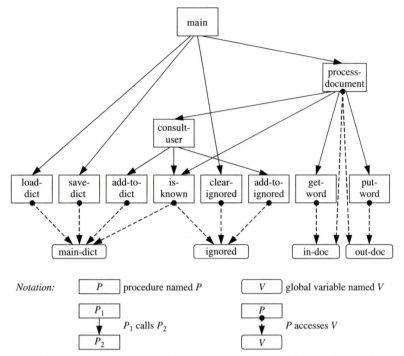

Figure 11.1 Architecture of an imperative program with global variables.

A traditional imperative program consists of procedures and global variables. Figure 11.1 shows the architecture of such a program, which consists of several procedures, and several global variables that are accessed by these procedures. The procedures call one another, but this creates only loose coupling: a modification to the implementation of one procedure is unlikely to affect its callers. However, access to the global variables creates tight coupling: any modification to a global variable's representation is likely to force modifications to all the procedures that access it; moreover, each procedure is sensitive to the way that the global variable is initialized, inspected, and updated by other procedures.

Larger programs with architectures similar to that of Figure 11.1 will be difficult and costly to maintain. The maintenance programmer will be unable to understand any individual procedure without also understanding the role of each global variable that it accesses, and the roles of other procedures that access the same global variable. Any modification to a procedure could trigger a cascade of modifications to other procedures.

Problems such as these explain why data abstraction has become a key concept in the more modern imperative languages (and, indeed, why object-oriented programming has become important in its own right). The program units of a well-designed imperative program are now procedures and *packages* (or *abstract types*).

Figure 11.2 illustrates the architecture of such a program. There are no global variables, only local variables and parameters (not shown). Two abstract types

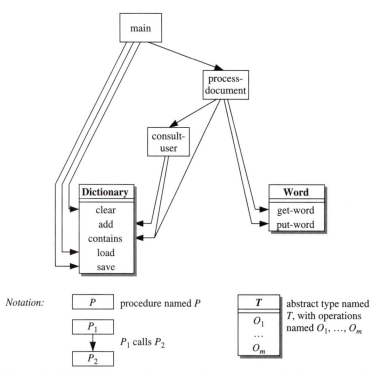

Figure 11.2 Architecture of an imperative program with data abstraction.

have been designed, each equipped with operations sufficient for this application. Now all the program units are loosely coupled to one another. The maintenance programmer will be able to understand each unit individually, and can modify it without fearing a cascade of modifications to other units. In particular, since the representation of each abstract type is private, the maintenance programmer can safely modify the representation without forcing modifications to other units.

11.2.1 A simple spellchecker

In order to illustrate imperative programming in this chapter (and other paradigms in later chapters), we shall use a simple spellchecker as a running example.

The spellchecker uses a *dictionary* of known words, which will be loaded from a file into main storage when the program is run. The spellchecker is required to copy words and punctuation from an *input document* to an *output document*, interactively consulting the user about each unknown word. If the user chooses to *accept* the unknown word, the word must be added to the dictionary. If the user chooses to *ignore* the unknown word, this and all subsequent occurrences of the same word must be ignored. If the user chooses to *replace* the unknown word, a new word entered by the user must replace the unknown word in the output document.

Figure 11.1 in fact shows a possible architecture for the spellchecker. The global variable "main-dict" contains the dictionary that has been loaded from its file (and which will later be saved to the same file). The global variable "ignored" contains a temporary dictionary of words that the user has chosen to ignore. The global variables "in-doc" and "out-doc" refer to the input and output documents. The lowest-level procedures ("load-dict", ... , "put-word") operate on the global variables. The higher-level procedures ("consult-user", "process-document", "main") work largely by calling the lower-level procedures.

Figure 11.2 shows an alternative architecture for the spellchecker, based on abstract types. The abstract type **Word** is equipped with operations for reading and writing words from and to documents. The abstract type **Dictionary** is equipped with operations for loading, saving, clearing, adding to, and searching dictionaries. The two dictionaries "main-dict" and "ignored" are now local variables of "main", and are passed as parameters to "process-document" and "consult-user".

11.3   Case study: C

C was originally designed in the early 1970s by Dennis Ritchie, primarily for writing the UNIX operating system and its associated compilers and utilities. An internationally-recognized standard was developed in the 1980s; this smoothed off some (but by no means all) of the original language's many rough edges. The latest (1999) C standard includes many new features, but has not yet been widely adopted; these new features are not considered here.

C is characterized by the presence of low-level operations and weak type checking. It also lacks modern concepts such as data abstraction, generic abstraction, or exceptions. Nevertheless, expert C programmers can use it to write very efficient systems software, the continuing success of the UNIX family of operating systems being testimony to that fact.

C is popular in its own right, and it is an ancestor of two other popular languages (C++ and JAVA). It makes an instructive case study, illustrating both good and bad design.

11.3.1   Values and types

C has a limited repertoire of primitive types: enumeration types, integer types (with various ranges, both signed and unsigned), and floating point types (with single- or double-precision). There is no specific boolean type: *false* and *true* are conventionally represented by zero and nonzero integers. There is also no specific character type: characters are conventionally represented by values of type **char** but, despite the type's name, these values are just small integers.

C has a reasonable repertoire of composite types: array types, structure types, and union types. Unions are untagged; thus the onus is on the programmer to add an explicit tag field if it is necessary to know the current state of a union. (See Example 2.15.)

C does not support recursive types directly. Instead, programmers must declare recursive types using pointers.

EXAMPLE 11.1   C linked list

Consider the following C type definitions:

```
struct IntNode;
typedef IntNode* IntPtr;
struct IntNode {
    int elem;
    IntPtr succ;
};
```

The values of type IntPtr are pointers to nodes of a linked list. Each node will contain an integer elem and a pointer succ to the node's successor, except the last node, which will contain a null pointer (conventionally represented by 0).

C complies poorly with the Type Completeness Principle. Only primitive values, pointers, and structures are first-class values: they may be assigned, passed as arguments, and returned as function results. Arrays are not first-class values: only *pointers* to arrays can be assigned, passed as arguments, and returned as function results. Similarly, strings (which are represented by character arrays) are not first-class values.

C's expression repertoire includes function calls and conditional expressions, but not iterative expressions. Array and structure constructions (whose components must all be literals) may be used to initialize global variables, but not in any other syntactic context.

A C assignment "$V = E$" is actually an expression, yielding the value of E as well as assigning that value to the variable V. C also allows ordinary binary operators to be combined with assignment: if $\otimes$ is a binary operator, then "$V \otimes= E$" is a concise alternative to "$V = V \otimes E$". Still more concise are C's pre- and post-increment operators, both named "++": if V is an integer or pointer variable, "++V" increments V and yields its *new* value, while "V++" increments V and yields its *original* value. C similarly provides pre- and post-decrement operators named "--".

C's type system is extremely weak. A pointer can be cast to an integer, an integer can be cast to a pointer, and a pointer of one type can be cast to a different pointer type; in effect, integers and pointers of different types can be used interchangeably. Another serious weakness is that certain function calls are not type-checked, as we shall see in Section 11.3.5.

If p is a pointer, "*p" denotes the variable to which p points. Conversely, if v is a global or local variable, "&v" yields a pointer to that variable. If v is a local variable, that pointer will become a dangling pointer on exit from the block in which v was declared.

If p is a pointer to a structure or union variable that has a field named f, we can access that field using the notation "p->f", which is just an abbreviation for "(*p).f".

C allows pointer arithmetic, even without resort to casts. If p is a pointer and i is an integer, "p+i" and "p-i" are legal expressions, yielding pointers (which, however, are not necessarily meaningful). The array-indexing notation "$a[i]$" is just an abbreviation for "$*(a+i)$", since a is interpreted as a pointer to the array component with index 0.

EXAMPLE 11.2   Concise programming in C (1)

The following code copies all characters from standard input to standard output, stopping when a NUL character (0) is read:

```
char ch;
while ((ch = getchar()) != 0)
   putchar(ch);
```

The expression "ch = getchar()" reads a character (by calling the library function getchar), assigns that character to ch, and yields that character. The enclosing expression "(...) != 0" compares that character with the NUL character. Note how using an assignment as a subexpression enables us to write very concise code.

The following alternative code takes advantage of the fact that C's while-command treats any nonzero integer as *true*:

```
char ch;
while (ch = getchar())
   putchar(ch);
```

This version is even more concise, but also extremely cryptic. (Moreover, it is very confusing for programmers more familiar with programming languages in which "=" is the equality test operator, not the assignment operator!)

EXAMPLE 11.3   Concise programming in C (2)

Consider the following C function:

```
int palindromic (char s[], int n) {
/*  Return nonzero if and only if the sequence of characters in s[0],...,
 *  s[n-1] is a palindrome.
 */
   int l, r;
   l = 0;   r = n-1;
   while (l < r) {
      if (s[l++] != s[r--])
         return 0;
   }
   return 1;
}
```

Note that the result type is **int**, although the result is logically a boolean. Note also the use of post-increment and post-decrement operators to make the loop body concise and efficient.

Now consider the following alternative version:

```
int palindromic (char s[], int n) {
   char* lp, rp;
```

```
        lp = &a[0];   rp = &a[n-1];
        while (lp < rp) {
           if (*lp++ != *rp--)
              return 0;
        }
        return 1;
     }
```

This replaces the integer variables l and r (which were used to index the array s) by pointer variables lp and rp (which point to components of the array s). The expression "*lp++" yields the character that lp points to, and then increments lp (making it point to the next component of s). The expression "*rp--" likewise yields the character that rp points to, and then decrements rp (making it point to the previous component of s). The expression "lp < rp" tests whether the component that lp points to precedes (is leftwards of) the component that rp points to.

This second version is perfectly legal, but much more difficult to understand than the first version. However, it illustrates a programming idiom that experienced C programmers learn to recognize.

Examples 11.2 and 11.3 capture much of the essence of C programming. Its many critics cite such examples as proof of C's awfulness; its many fanatics cite the same examples as proof of C's power! A more measured judgment would be that C is a powerful tool in the hands of an expert programmer, but a dangerous weapon in the hands of a novice.

11.3.2   Variables, storage, and control

C supports global and local variables. It also supports heap variables in a low-level manner. Its allocator is a function malloc whose argument is the *size* of the heap variable to be allocated:

```
IntNode* ptr;
ptr = malloc(sizeof IntNode);
```

The expression "sizeof *T*" yields the size (in bytes) of a value of type *T*.

C has some of the characteristics of an expression language. As we have seen, an assignment is an expression. A function call is also an expression (even if the result type is **void**). Given any expression *E*, we can write a command "*E*;"; its effect is to evaluate *E* and then discard its value, leaving only its side effects. Thus "*V* = *E*;" is effectively an assignment command, and "*F*(…);" is effectively a proper procedure call.

The fact that C assignments are expressions, and that all C procedures are functions, actually forces programmers to write expressions with side effects. C programmers must exercise considerable self-discipline to avoid writing unreadable code.

Apart from those already mentioned, C's repertoire of commands includes a skip command, sequential commands, conditional commands (if- and switch commands), iterative commands (while-, do-while-, and for-commands), and block commands. If- and loop conditions are actually integer expressions; zero is interpreted as *false*, and any other integer as *true*.

C's break, continue, and return sequencers allow single-entry multi-exit control flows to be programmed as easily as single-entry single-exit control flows. C also supports jumps, but they are essentially redundant because the other sequencers are sufficient for all practical purposes. C does not support exceptions.

C's switch command usually has the form:

```
switch (E) {
   case v₁: C₁
   ...
   case vₙ: Cₙ
   default: C₀
}
```

The expression E must yield an integer value. If that value equals one of the values v_i, the corresponding subcommand C_i is chosen. If not, C_0 is chosen. (If "**default**: C_0" is omitted, C_0 is taken to be a skip.) If the values v_i are not all distinct, the first match is chosen, so the choice is deterministic.

A bizarre feature of C's switch command is that control flows from the chosen subcommand C_i to the following subcommands $C_{i+1}, \ldots, C_n$, and C_0. Nearly always, however, we want control to flow from C_i to the end of the switch command. To make that happen, each subcommand (except the last) must include a break sequencer.

EXAMPLE 11.4   **C switch command**

In the following C switch command, choice is based on a value of the enumeration type Month (Example 3.2):

```
Month m;
...
switch (m) {
   case jan:  printf("JAN");  break;
   case feb:  printf("FEB");  break;
   case mar:  printf("MAR");  break;
   ...
   case dec:  printf("DEC");
}
```

C's for-command is actually syntactic shorthand for a while-command, conveniently gathering the loop initialization code (C_1), loop condition (E_1), and loop continuation code (E_2) together in one place:

```
for (C₁ E₁; E₂) C₂   ≡   C₁
                          while (E₁) {
                             C₂
                             E₂;
                          }
```

Thus C's for-command supports *indefinite* iteration. (In most imperative languages, the for-command supports definite iteration.)

EXAMPLE 11.5   C for-command

Recall the type `IntPtr` defined in Example 11.1. Values of type `IntPtr` are pointers to nodes of a linked list whose elements are integers.

The following C function uses a for-command to iterate over all the nodes of such a linked list:

```
int list_sum (IntPtr first) {
/* Sum the elements of the linked list to which first points. */
    int sum;   IntPtr p;
    for (p = first; p != 0; p = p->succ)
        sum += p->elem;
    return sum;
}
```

The expression "p != 0" is legal here because 0 is a valid literal in all pointer types; it denotes the null pointer.

11.3.3   Bindings and scope

A C program consists of global type definitions, global variable declarations, and function definitions. One of these functions must be named `main`, and that is the main program.

Inside a function or block command, we may declare local types, local variables, and static variables. Local variables have shorter lifetimes than global variables, and unlike global variables are not a cause of tight coupling between functions.

A *static variable* is global in the sense that its lifetime is the program's entire run-time, but local in the sense that its scope is the function or block command within which it is declared.

11.3.4   Procedural abstraction

C supports function procedures only. However, we can achieve the effect of a proper procedure by writing a function whose result type is **void**.

C supports only one parameter mechanism, the copy-in parameter. That is to say, each formal parameter behaves like a local variable that is initialized to the corresponding argument value. However, we can achieve the effect of a reference parameter by passing a *pointer* to a variable as an argument.

EXAMPLE 11.6   C function with pointer arguments

Consider the following C function:

```
void minimax (int[] a, int n, int* min, int* max) {
/* Set *min to the minimum, and *max to the maximum, of the integers in
```

```
 *  a[0],...,a[n-1].
 */
    *min = *max = a[0];
    int i;
    for (i = 1; i < n; i++) {
      int elem = a[i];
      if (elem < *min)   *min = elem;
      else if (elem > *max)   *max = elem;
    }
}
```

Here is a possible call to the function:

```
int[] temps = {13, 15, 20, 18, 21, 14, 12};
int low, high;
...
minimax(temps, 7, &low, &high);
```

The formal parameters min and max are in effect reference parameters. The corresponding arguments are *pointers* to variables.

C functions are not first-class values. In particular, a function F_1 cannot be passed as an argument to another function F_2. However, we can achieve the same effect by passing a *pointer* to F_1 as an argument to F_2.

11.3.5 Independent compilation

Independent compilation means that a large program is broken into several distinct parts, called *compilation units*, which are compiled (and recompiled) independently of one another. After all compilation units have been compiled, they must be *linked* together to build a single executable program.

A C compilation unit is a group of type definitions, global variable declarations, function specifications, and function definitions.

A *function specification* states only the function's identifier, result type, and formal parameter types. A *function definition* states the function's identifier, result type, formal parameter types and identifiers, and body. Function specifications are important in the context of independent compilation.

A C compilation unit U must be self-contained, in the following sense:

- U must not refer to any global variable declared in another compilation unit, unless that variable's declaration (with the keyword **extern**) is reproduced in U.

- U must not refer to any type defined in another compilation unit, unless that type's definition is reproduced in U.

- U must not refer to any function defined in another compilation unit, unless that function's specification is reproduced in U. The presence of that function specification allows the compiler to type-check calls to that function.

Independent compilation facilitates development of a large program: its compilation units can be developed separately. It also facilitates maintenance: only modified compilation units need be recompiled.

A serious weakness of independent compilation is that type checking across compilation units is compromised. In C, if several compilation units are meant to use the same type T, the definition of T must be included in each of these compilation units; but there is no check that these definitions are equivalent. Similarly, if several compilation units are meant to call the same function F, the specification of F must be included in each of these compilation units; but there is no check that these specifications are equivalent. We could start a programming project by pasting common type definitions and function specifications into each of the compilation units; however, the programmer developing one compilation unit might find some reason to modify the common code, but forget to ensure that the code is modified consistently in all the other compilation units. A partial solution to this problem will be mentioned in Section 11.3.6.

EXAMPLE 11.7   C independent compilation

Consider a program consisting of two compilation units. The first defines a function:

```
/*  Compilation unit 1  */

int funk (int a, float b, float c) {
    ...
}
```

The second defines the main program, which calls funk:

```
/*  Compilation unit 2  */

int funk (int, float, float);

void main () {
    int n;
    float p, q;
    ...
... funk(n, p, q);
    ...
}
```

Note the specification of funk, which is needed to make the second compilation unit self-contained. The compiler type-checks each call to funk against that function specification.

But now suppose that the programmer responsible for compilation unit 1 changes funk's type (i.e., changes its result type, changes a parameter type, removes a parameter, or adds a new parameter), and then recompiles compilation unit 1; but forgets to ensure that the function specification and calls in compilation unit 2 are modified consistently. The C compiler will not detect the inconsistency, because it compiles each compilation unit independently of all the others. The linker will not detect the inconsistency, because it does not have the necessary type information. So the program will run, but will fail in some unpredictable manner when it first calls funk.

11.3.6 Preprocessor directives

A characteristic feature of C is its *preprocessor*. This is a special language processor that supports text inclusion, text expansion, and conditional compilation.

The preprocessor is driven by *preprocessor directives*, which are lines starting with "#".

EXAMPLE 11.8   C preprocessor directives

The following directive:

```
#include "common.h"
```

includes the whole text contained in file common.h, at this point in the code.

The following directives:

```
#define FALSE 0
#define TRUE  1
```

cause all subsequent occurrences of FALSE to be replaced by 0, and all subsequent occurrences of TRUE to be replaced by 1. These directives are the nearest equivalent of constant definitions in C.

The following directive:

```
#define UNTIL(COND)  while (!(COND))
```

causes a subsequent occurrence of the code "UNTIL(i >= n)" (say) to be replaced by the code "**while** (!(i >= n)". This directive defines a text expansion.

The following directives:

```
#ifdef X
... /* version 1 code */
#endif

#ifndef X
... /* version 2 code */
#endif
```

include the version 1 code only if the symbol X has been defined by a previous #define directive, or the version 2 code only if X has *not* been so defined. These directives achieve the effect of conditional compilation: they allow us to maintain two versions of a piece of code (which might be quite lengthy) within the same source text.

The #include directive helps to address the problem of reproducing common code in several compilation units. We place the common code in a *header file* named common.h (say), and place "#include common.h" in each compilation unit. Any change to the header file will then affect all these compilation units. This is only a partial solution, however, since the C compiler cannot enforce systematic and consistent use of header files.

11.3.7 Function library

The C programming language comes with a modest function library, including character handling functions, string handling functions, mathematical functions, date and time functions, storage allocation functions, signal handling functions, input/output functions, and so on. For each group of functions there is a header file that contains the relevant function specifications together with related type definitions. In particular, for the input/output functions there is a header file named stdio.h.

The C function library is pre-compiled. The application program's compilation units must be linked with the library functions needed by the application.

11.3.8   A simple spellchecker

To conclude this overview of imperative programming in C, let us examine a C implementation of the simple spellchecker specified in Section 11.2.1. The program's architecture is shown in Figure 11.1. The program consists of several compilation units, and is shown in Programs 11.1–11.4.

```c
#include <stdio.h>

typedef ... Word;

typedef ... Dictionary;

extern Dictionary main_dict;
extern Dictionary ignored;

extern FILE* in_doc;
extern FILE* out_doc;

int get_word (Word*);
/* Read the next word from in_doc, copying any preceding punctuation to
   out_doc. Return nonzero if there is no next word to be read. */

void put_word (Word);
/* Write the given word to out_doc. */

void load_dict (char*);
/* Load main_dict from the named file. */

void save_dict (char*);
/* Save main_dict to the named file. */

void add_to_dict (Word);
/* Make the given word a member of main_dict. */

int is_known (Word);
/* Return nonzero if and only if the given word is a member of either main_dict or
   ignored. */

void clear_ignored ();
/* Make ignored empty. */

void add_to_ignored (Word);
/* Make the given word a member of ignored. */
```

Program 11.1 Header file in C (spellchecker.h).

```
#include <stdio.h>
#include "spellchecker.h"

FILE* in_doc;
FILE* out_doc;

int get_word (Word* wd) {
  ...
}

void put_word (Word wd) {
  ...
}
```

Program 11.2 Declarations of file variables and definitions of word functions in C (in outline).

```
#include "spellchecker.h"

Dictionary main_dict, ignored;

...   /* auxiliary functions */

void load_dict (char* filename) {
  ...
}

void save_dict (char* filename) {
  ...
}

void add_to_dict (Word wd) {
  ...
}

int is_known (Word wd) {
  ...
}

void clear_ignored () {
  ...
}

void add_to_ignored (Word wd) {
  ...
}
```

Program 11.3 Declarations of dictionary variables and definitions of dictionary functions in C (in outline).

Program 11.1 gathers together all the type definitions, global variable declarations, and function specifications that will be needed in this program. This code is placed in a header file named spellchecker.h, and that header file is included in each compilation unit that refers to any of these types, variables, or functions.

Program 11.2 shows declarations of the global variables in_doc and out_doc, and outlines definitions of the get_word and put_word functions that access these variables. The standard input/output library is needed here, so its header file stdio.h is included. Note that the get_word function returns a status flag to indicate whether it has read a word or reached the end of the input document.

Program 11.3 shows declarations of the global variables main_dict and ignored, and outlines definitions of the functions that access these variables.

Program 11.4 outlines definitions of the high-level functions consult_user, process_document, and main. Note that process_document repeatedly calls get_word within a loop, each time testing its status flag; if that flag indicates that the end of the document has been reached, the loop is terminated.

```c
#include <stdio.h>
#include "spellchecker.h"

void consult_user(Word* wd) {
/*  Ask the user what to do with the word, which is unknown.
    If the user chooses to accept the word, make it a member of main_dict.
    If the user chooses to ignore the word, make it a member of ignored.
    If the user chooses to replace the word, get the user to enter a replacement word,
    and update the word.  */
  ...
}

void process_document () {
/*  Copy all words and punctuation from the input document to the output document,
    but ask the user what to do with any words that are unknown (i.e., not in
    main_dict or ignored).  */
  Word current_word;
  in_doc = fopen("indoc.txt", "r");
  out_doc = fopen("outdoc.txt", "w");
  for (;;) {
    if (get_word(&current_word) != 0)
      break;
    if (! is_known(current_word))
      consult_user(&current_word);
    put_word(current_word);
  }
  fclose(in_doc);  fclose(out_doc);
}

int main () {
  load_dict("dict.txt");
  clear_ignored();
  process_document();
  save_dict("dict.txt");
}
```

Program 11.4 Definitions of the consult_user, process_document, and main functions in C (in outline).

11.4   Case study: ADA

ADA was designed in the late 1970s to be a general-purpose imperative and concurrent programming language, suitable in particular for implementation of large-scale and embedded systems. The ADA design team was large, and received inputs from a still larger number of interested persons, but the design effort was dominated by Jean Ichbiah. (Too many programming languages bear the hallmarks of design by committee: a proliferation of badly-integrated features, attempting to satisfy the conflicting demands of all the committee members. Ichbiah's firm control ensured that ADA largely avoided that fate.)

As a consequence of the way it was developed, ADA is a large but reasonably coherent language. It supports nearly all the concepts described in this book. In particular, unlike classical imperative languages such as C and PASCAL, ADA supports data abstraction, generic abstraction, and exceptions.

ADA was extended in the early 1990s, primarily to support object-oriented programming. Where necessary to distinguish between the two versions of the language, we refer to them as ADA83 and ADA95, respectively.

This section is an overview of the imperative parts of ADA. We shall turn to the object-oriented and concurrent parts of ADA in Chapters 12 and 13, respectively.

11.4.1   Values and types

ADA has a full repertoire of primitive types: `Boolean`, `Character`, enumeration types, and numeric types (integer, floating-point, and fixed-point). Unusually, ADA allows programmers to declare their own numeric types, which is good for portability.

ADA has an adequate repertoire of composite types: array types, record types, and discriminated record types (disjoint unions).

ADA does not support recursive types directly. Instead, programmers must declare recursive types using pointers.

ADA complies well with the Type Completeness Principle. Constants, variables, parameters, and function results can be of any type. The equality-test operations "=" and "/=", and the assignment operation ":=", can be applied to operands of any type (unless the programmer chooses otherwise by declaring a type to be *limited*).

ADA supports subtypes systematically in the sense that all types can have subtypes (see Section 8.1.1). However, an ADA subtype is not itself a type. In particular, an ADA type declaration creates a new and distinct type, but an ADA subtype declaration merely names a subtype of an existing type. A type is compatible with any of its subtypes.

EXAMPLE 11.9   ADA types and subtypes

`Natural` is a subtype of `Integer`:

```
subtype Natural is Integer range 0 .. Integer'last;
```

The following function's second parameter is of subtype `Natural`:

```
function power (b: Float; n: Natural) return Float;
```

In a function call to `power`, the compiler merely checks that the second argument's type is compatible with `Natural` (i.e., its type is `Integer` or a subtype of `Integer`). However, a run-time check may be needed to ensure that the argument's *value* is in the subtype `Natural`.

Finally, consider the following proper procedure:

```
procedure inc (i: in out Integer);
```

In a procedure call to `inc`, the compiler merely checks that the argument's type is compatible with `Integer` (i.e., its type is `Integer` or a subtype of `Integer`). No run-time check is needed.

ADA's expression repertoire includes record and array constructions and function calls. It does not include conditional expressions, iterative expressions, or block expressions. Thus programmers are forced to use function calls for computations that are too complicated for this rather limited expression repertoire. The point is that an ADA function's body is syntactically a command, and so may contain loops, exception handlers, and so on. By the same token, however, function calls potentially have side effects.

11.4.2   Variables, storage, and control

ADA supports global, local, and heap variables. A heap variable of type T is allocated by an expression of the form "**new** T", or alternatively "**new** T' (…)" which also initializes the heap variable.

ADA's repertoire of commands is conventional for a modern imperative language: a skip command, assignment commands, procedure calls, sequential commands, conditional commands (if- and case commands), iterative commands (while- and for-commands, and basic loops), block commands, and exception-handling commands.

ADA's exit and return sequencers allow single-entry multi-exit control flows to be programmed as easily as single-entry single-exit control flows. ADA also supports jumps, although they are redundant.

ADA was the first major language to provide a secure form of exception handling. An ADA83 exception could not carry a value. An ADA95 exception can carry a string, enabling the handler to receive additional information about the abnormal situation represented by the exception (but that information has to be encoded as a string before the exception is thrown, and decoded by the handler after it is caught).

11.4.3   Bindings and scope

An ADA program consists of program units: procedures, packages, and generic units. The programmer specifies which of these procedures is to be treated as the main program.

Within a program unit or block command we declare anything: types and subtypes, constants and variables, exceptions, tasks, and even other program units.

Procedures, packages, and generic units are major program units and are normally declared either globally or inside other program units. Although it is legal in ADA to declare a program unit inside an inner block, that would allow the program unit to access variables declared in outer blocks, giving rise to tight coupling.

11.4.4   Procedural abstraction

ADA supports both proper procedures and function procedures.

ADA supports three parameter *modes*, which emphasize the direction of data flow (into and/or out of the procedure) rather than the underlying parameter mechanisms.

- ***In-parameter***: the formal parameter is a constant, and is bound to the argument (a first-class value).
- ***In-out-parameter***: the formal parameter is a variable, and permits both inspection and updating of the argument (also a variable).
- ***Out-parameter***: the formal parameter is a variable, and permits only updating of the argument (also a variable).

For primitive types, ADA insists that the above effects are achieved by copy-in, copy-in-copy-out, and copy-out mechanisms, respectively (Section 5.2.1).

For composite types, ADA allows the compiler to choose whether the above effects are achieved by copy or reference mechanisms. Reference mechanisms (Section 5.2.2) introduce the risk of aliasing, but are usually more efficient than copy mechanisms for large records and arrays.

An ADA function procedure has in-parameters only. Thus a function procedure cannot update variables supplied as arguments, but this is really only a half-hearted attempt to discourage side effects. The function's body can update global variables, a concealed and therefore more dangerous source of side effects.

ADA supports context-dependent overloading of procedures. In other words, two or more procedures may share the same identifier in the same scope provided only that they differ in their parameter or result types. Also, ADA treats its operators exactly like functions: we may overload any existing operator by providing an additional definition. (But we cannot invent new operator symbols.)

ADA procedures are not first-class values. In particular, a procedure P_1 cannot be passed as an argument to another procedure P_2. However, we can achieve essentially the same effect by passing a *pointer* to P_1 as an argument to P_2.

11.4.5   Data abstraction

ADA supports data abstraction principally by means of packages, as we saw in Section 6.1. Each package consists of a specification and a body. The ***package specification*** serves to declare the package's public components, and thus specify the package's API. The ***package body*** serves to provide implementation details: definitions of any public procedures, and declarations of any private components.

In general, the components of an ADA package may be anything that can be declared in the language: types and subtypes, constants and variables, exceptions, procedures, generic units, inner packages, and so on. Moreover, any subset of these components may be public. Thus ADA packages support encapsulation.

An important special case is a package that defines an abstract type. In this case the package specification declares the abstract type itself, and specifies the public procedures that operate on the abstract type. The *name* of the abstract type is public, but its representation is private. The package body defines the public procedures, and declares any private (auxiliary) procedures.

EXAMPLE 11.10   ADA abstract type

Program 11.6(a) shows the specification of a package named `Dictionaries`. This declares an abstract type `Dictionary`, and specifies public procedures that will operate on that abstract type.

Program 11.6(b) outlines the corresponding package body, which defines all the public procedures. The omitted details depend on the chosen representation for the abstract type (which could be a search tree, for instance).

Application code could use the `Dictionaries` package as follows:

```
use Dictionaries;
dict: Dictionary;
current_word: Word;
...
load(dict);
loop
   ...
   if not contains(dict, current_word) then
      ...
   end if;
   ...
end loop;
```

Values of type `Dictionary` can be manipulated *only* by calling the public operations of the `Dictionaries` package. The ADA compiler will prevent any attempt by the application code to access the `Dictionary` representation. Thus, without having to rely on the application programmer's self-discipline, the application code can be maintained independently of the package.

All ADA types, including abstract types, are by default equipped with the language's assignment and equality test operations, except for types defined as **limited**. Assignment of a static data structure (one constructed without pointers) entails copying all its components, which is copy semantics. On the other hand, assignment of a dynamic data structure (one constructed using pointers) entails copying the pointers but not their referents, which is reference semantics. This inconsistency creates a dilemma when we design an abstract type, since the type's representation is hidden and is not supposed to influence the behavior of the application code. Only if we are confident that the abstract type will always be represented by a static data structure should we declare it as simply **private**. If the abstract type might conceivably be represented by a dynamic data structure, we should declare it as **limited private**. (And if the abstract type needs assignment and/or equality test operations, we should make the package provide its own.)

Where a package defines an abstract type, the **private** part of the package specification defines the abstract type's representation. It would be more logical for the representation to be defined in the package *body*, along with the other implementation details. The reason for this design illogicality is that the ADA compiler must decide, using the package specification alone, how much storage space will be occupied by each variable of the abstract type. (Declarations of such variables might be compiled before the package body is compiled.) This is an example of a design compromise motivated by implementation considerations.

11.4.6   Generic abstraction

As we saw in Sections 7.1.1 and 7.2.1, ADA allows any package to be made generic, and then it can be parameterized with respect to values, variables, types, and procedures on which it depends. Here we give one further example.

EXAMPLE 11.11   ADA generic package with type and function parameters

Consider the following generic package specification:

```
generic
   type Row is private;
   type Key is private;
   with function row_key (r: Row) return Key;
package Tables is

   type Table is limited private;
   -- A Table value contains a number of rows, subject to the constraint
   -- that no two rows have the same key.

   exception table_error;

   procedure clear (t: out Table);
   -- Make table t contain no rows.

   procedure add (t: in out Table; r: in Row);
   -- Add row r to table t. Throw table_error if t already contains
   -- a row with the same key as r.

   function retrieve (t: Table; k: Key) return Row;
   -- Return the row in table t whose key is k. Throw table_error if
   -- t contains no such row.

private
```

```
capacity: constant Positive := ...;

type Table is
    record
        size: Integer range 0 .. capacity;
        rows: array (1 .. capacity) of Row;
    end record;

end Tables;
```

The generic package is parameterized with respect to the type Row, the type Key, and the function row_key.

The package body will use row_key to implement the add and retrieve operations:

```
package body Tables is

    procedure clear (t: out Table) is
    begin
        t.size := 0;
    end;

    procedure add (t: in out Table; r: in Row) is
        k: Key := row_key(r);
    begin
        for i in 1 .. t.size loop
            if row_key(t.rows(i)) = k then
                raise table_error;
            end if;
        end loop;
        t.size := t.size + 1;
        t.rows(t.size) := r;
    end;

    function retrieve (t: Table; k: Key) return Row is
    begin
        for i in 1 .. t.size loop
            if row_key(t.rows(i)) = k then
                return t.rows(i);
            end if;
        end loop;
        raise table_error;
    end;

end Tables;
```

Since both the type parameters Row and Key are declared as **private**, they are guaranteed to be equipped with assignment and equality-test operations.

Application code could use this generic package as follows:

```
subtype Short_Name is String(1 .. 6);
subtype Phone_Number is String(1 .. 12);
type Phone_Book_Entry is
    record
        name: Short_Name; number: Phone_Number;
    end record;

function entry_name (e: Phone_Book_Entry)
    return Short_Name is
```

```
begin
   return e.name;
end;

package Phone_Books is new Tables(
      Phone_Book_Entry, Short_Name, entry_name);

use Phone_Books;
phone_book: Table;
...
add(phone_book, "David", "+61733652378");
```

The instantiation generates an ordinary package by substituting Phone_Book_Entry for Row, Short_Name for Key, and entry_name for row_key. The generated package is named Phone_Books.

As well as a package, we can often make an ordinary procedure generic. A generic procedure gives us an extra level of abstraction.

EXAMPLE 11.12   ADA generic procedure with a type parameter

The following declares a swapping procedure, parameterized with respect to the type Item of the values being swapped:

```
generic
   type Item is private;
procedure swap (x, y: in out Item);
```

And here is the corresponding procedure body:

```
procedure swap (x, y: in out Item) is
   z: constant Item := x;
begin
   x := y;   y := z;
end;
```

We instantiate this generic procedure by supplying an argument type to be bound to the type parameter Item:

```
procedure swap_characters is new swap(Character);

procedure swap_integers is new swap(Integer);
```

Each instantiation of swap generates an ordinary (non-generic) procedure. The second instantiation generates an ordinary procedure named swap_integers, with two in-out-parameters of type Integer. The generated procedure can be called in the usual manner:

```
a: array (...) of Integer;
...
swap_integers(a(i), a(j));
```

Note that an ADA generic procedure must first be instantiated to generate an ordinary procedure, before the latter can be called. ADA does not allow the instantiation and call to be combined. (But see Exercise 11.5.)

11.4.7   Separate compilation

Separate compilation is similar to independent compilation (see Section 11.3.5), but with the important difference that type checking across compilation units is not compromised.

We have seen that an ADA package is declared in two parts: a package specification and a package body. Similarly, a procedure can be declared in two parts: a procedure specification (its heading) and a procedure body. In each case, the package or procedure has a *specification* of its interface, and a *body* containing implementation details.

An ADA compilation unit may be a single procedure specification, procedure body, package specification, or package body. Each compilation unit must name (in a *with-clause*) every separately compiled procedure or package on which it depends.

A procedure or package specification must be compiled before the corresponding procedure or package body, and before any compilation unit that depends on it. The ADA compiler ensures that compilation units are compiled (and recompiled) in a correct order. It also performs full type checks across compilation units, by the simple expedient of remembering the contents of every procedure and package specification.

EXAMPLE 11.13   ADA separate compilation

Consider an application program that uses the `Dictionaries` package of Program 11.6. Suppose that there are three compilation units: the package specification, the package body, and the application code. The application code might look like this:

```
with Dictionaries;  use Dictionaries;

procedure main is
   dict: Dictionary;
begin
   load(dict);
   ...
end;
```

We compile the `Dictionaries` package specification first, followed (in any order) by the `Dictionaries` package body and the application code.

If we subsequently modify the package specification (an API change), then we must recompile not only the package specification but also the package body and the application code.

If instead we modify the package body only (an implementation change), then we need recompile only the package body. Neither the package specification nor the application code is affected.

Notice that we derive this benefit *only* because the package is split into specification and body. If the whole package were a single compilation unit, then even a minor implementation change would force the whole package and the application code to be recompiled.

11.4.8   Package library

The ADA programming language comes with a modest package library. This supports character handling, string handling, dates and times, numerical (including complex) functions, input/output, storage deallocation, low-level programming, and so on.

The ADA package library is pre-compiled. The application program's compilation units must be linked with the library packages on which they depend.

11.4.9   A simple spellchecker

To conclude this overview of imperative programming in ADA, let us examine an ADA implementation of the simple spellchecker specified in Section 11.2.1. The program's architecture is shown in Figure 11.2. The program consists of several compilation units, and is outlined in Programs 11.5–11.7.

Program 11.5(a) shows the Words package specification, which declares the abstract type Word together with its operations. Program 11.5(b) outlines the Words package body, which defines these operations. Note that the package specification is prefixed by "**with** Ada.Text_IO;", because it depends on that library package.

```
with Ada.Text_IO;   use Ada.Text_IO;

package Words is

   type Word is private;
   -- Each Word value is a single word.

   procedure get_word (in_doc, out_doc: in out File_Type;
                wd: out Word);
   -- Read the next word from in_doc into wd, copying any preceding punctuation
   -- to out_doc. Raise end_error if there is no next word to be read.

   procedure put_word (out_doc: in out File_Type;
                wd: in Word);
   -- Write wd to out_doc.

private

   type Word is ...;   -- representation

end Words;
```

Program 11.5(a) Specification of the Words package in ADA (in outline).

```
package body Words is

    ...    -- auxiliary procedures

    procedure get_word (in_doc, out_doc: in out File_Type;
                        wd: out Word) is
    begin
        ...
    end;

    procedure put_word (out_doc: in out File_Type;
                        wd: in Word) is
    begin
        ...
    end;

end Words;
```

Program 11.5(b) Body of the Words package in ADA (in outline).

```
with Words;   use Words;

package Dictionaries is

    type Dictionary is limited private;
    -- Each Dictionary value is a set of words.

    procedure clear (dict: out Dictionary);
    -- Make dict empty.

    procedure add (dict: in out Dictionary; wd: in Word);
    -- Make wd a member of dict.

    function contains (dict: Dictionary; wd: Word)
        return Boolean;
    -- Return true if and only if wd is a member of dict.

    procedure load (dict: out Dictionary;
                    filename: in String);
    -- Load dict from filename.

    procedure save (dict: in Dictionary;
                    filename: in String);
    -- Save dict to filename.

private

    type Dictionary is ...;   -- representation

end Dictionaries;
```

Program 11.6(a) Specification of the Dictionaries package in ADA (in outline).

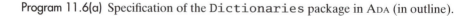

```
package body Dictionaries is

    ...   -- auxiliary procedures

    procedure clear (dict: out Dictionary) is
    begin
        ...
    end;

    procedure add (dict: in out Dictionary; wd: in Word) is
    begin
        ...
    end;

    function contains (dict: Dictionary; wd: Word)
         return Boolean is
    begin
        ...
    end;

    procedure load (dict: out Dictionary;
                    filename: in String) is
    begin
        ...
    end;

    procedure save (dict: in Dictionary;
                    filename: in String) is
    begin
        ...
    end;

end Dictionaries;
```

Program 11.6(b) Body of the Dictionaries package in ADA (in outline).

Program 11.6(a) shows the Dictionaries package specification, which declares the abstract type Dictionary together with its operations. Program 11.6(b) outlines the Dictionaries package body, which defines these operations. Note that the package specification is prefixed by "**with** Words;", because it depends on that package.

Program 11.7 outlines the high-level procedures consult_user, process_document, and main. The consult_user and process_document procedures are nested inside the main procedure. (Instead, they could have been compilation units in their own right.) Note that process_document repeatedly calls get_word within a loop; if get_word throws end_error, the corresponding exception handler exits the loop.

Compare this ADA program with its C counterpart (Programs 11.1–11.4). There is no doubt that the ADA program is better-engineered in every respect. It has a better architecture, due to its use of abstract types. It is more robust, due to its use of exceptions. It is less concise, but far more easily maintainable.

```ada
with Ada.Text_IO;    use Ada.Text_IO;
with Words;          use Words;
with Dictionaries;   use Dictionaries;
procedure main is

  procedure consult_user (current_word: in out Word;
                main_dict, ignored: in out Dictionary) is
  -- Ask the user what to do with current_word, which is unknown.
  -- If the user chooses to accept the word, make it a member of main_dict.
  -- If the user chooses to ignore the word, make it a member of ignored.
  -- If the user chooses to replace the word, get the user to enter a replacement word,
  -- and update current_word.
  begin
    ...
  end;

  procedure process_document (
                main_dict, ignored: in out Dictionary) is
  -- Copy all words and punctuation from the input document to the output
  -- document, but ask the user what to do with any words that are unknown (i.e.,
  -- not in main_dict or ignored).
    in_doc, out_doc: File_Type;
    current_word: Word;
  begin
    open(in_doc, in_file, "indoc.txt");
    open(out_doc, out_file, "outdoc.txt");
    loop
      get_word(in_doc, out_doc, current_word);
      if not contains(main_dict, current_word) and then
          not contains(ignored, current_word) then
        consult_user(current_word, main_dict, ignored);
      end if;
      put_word(out_doc, current_word);
    end loop;
  exception
    when end_error =>
      close(in_doc);  close(out_doc);
  end;

  main_dict, ignored: Dictionary;
begin
  load(main_dict, "dict.txt");
  clear(ignored);
  process_document(main_dict, ignored);
  save(main_dict, "dict.txt");
end;
```

Program 11.7 Definitions of the consult_user, process_document, and main procedures in ADA (in outline).

Summary

In this chapter:

- We have identified the key concepts of imperative programming: variables, commands, procedural abstraction, and (more recently) data abstraction.

- We have studied the pragmatics of imperative programming, comparing the disadvantages of programming with global variables with the advantages of data abstraction.

- We have studied the design of two major, but very different, imperative programming languages, C and ADA.

- We have compared two imperative implementations, in C and ADA, of a simple spellchecker.

Further reading

The classic text on C is KERNIGHAN and RITCHIE (1989), which served as a *de facto* standard that lasted until an internationally-recognized standard was developed. The most recent version of the standard is ISO/IEC (1999), and is covered in the textbook by HARBISON and STEELE (1995).

C has been heavily criticized for its idiosyncratic syntax, and for its many unsafe features such as weak type checking and pointer arithmetic. The dangers facing unwary C programmers are described in detail in KOENIG (1989).

The standard description of ADA83 is ICHBIAH (1983), and that of ADA95 is ISO/IEC (1995). Unusually, and commendably, the original ADA design team also published a design rationale (ICHBIAH 1979), which explores many important areas of programming language design and discusses the design decisions underlying the contemporary version of ADA.

ADA was designed to meet requirements set out by the US Department of Defense (1978). Their intention was to make ADA mandatory for all new software contracts (pure data processing software excepted). Unsurprisingly in view of ADA's predestined importance, the debate that accompanied and followed the design process was vigorous, sometimes generating more heat than light. Some of the more notable contributions were by HOARE (1981), LEDGARD and SINGER (1982), and WICHMANN (1984).

Exercises

Exercises for Section 11.1

11.1.1 Using your favorite imperative language, write both an iterative version and a recursive version of a function procedure that computes b^n, given b and n as arguments. What local variables do you need in each version?

Exercises for Section 11.2

*11.2.1 Choose a small or medium-sized imperative program that you have designed with global variables but without abstract types.
(a) Draw a diagram of your program's architecture, along the lines of Figure 11.1.
(b) Redesign your program systematically using abstract types. Draw a diagram of your program's new architecture, along the lines of Figure 11.2.

Exercises for Section 11.3

11.3.1 Consider the following C code:

```
p = 1;  m = n;  a = b;
while (m > 0) {
    if (m % 2 != 0) p = p * a;
    m = m / 2;
    a = a * a;
}
```

Write a more concise version of this code. Is the concise version more or less readable?

11.3.2 In a C switch command, control flows from the chosen subcommand to the following subcommand (unless prevented by a break or other sequencer). Can you think of a practical application where this feature is genuinely useful?

*11.3.3 Independent compilation compromises type checking of a C program, particularly if the program's compilation units are being developed by different members of a programming team. Explain how disciplined use of #include directives can mitigate the worst dangers of independent compilation. Could the discipline be enforced by suitable software management tools?

**11.3.4 C does not support data abstraction or generic abstraction. Nevertheless, it is possible to build a library of C program units that achieves some of the benefits of data abstraction and generic abstraction.

(a) Show how you would write a C program unit that achieves the effect of an abstract type. The program unit should provide a named type (such as Date), together with some operations on that type, without revealing how that type is defined.

(b) Now suggest how you might achieve the effect of a *generic* abstract type. You must enable a program unit that implements a generic abstract type (such as List) to be instantiated as required.

Application programmers should be able to link these program units to their programs. What software management tools would be needed, in addition to the C compiler?

11.3.5 Finish the coding of the C spellchecker of Programs 11.1–11.4.

11.3.6 Modify the C spellchecker of Programs 11.1–11.4 to use a third dictionary, the *user dictionary*. Any unknown words accepted by the user are to be added to the user dictionary, which must be saved when the program finishes. The main dictionary is no longer to be updated.

Exercises for Section 11.4

11.4.1 ADA formal parameter declarations do not directly reveal the underlying parameter mechanisms. What do they reveal? Summarize the advantages and disadvantages of this design decision.

11.4.2 An ADA package is divided into a package specification and a package body. Summarize the advantages and disadvantages of this design decision.

11.4.3 Consider the Dictionaries package of Program 11.6(a) and (b). Assume the following representation of the Dictionary type:

```
capacity: constant Positive := 1000;
type Dictionary is
   record
      size: Integer range 0 .. capacity;
      words: array (1 .. capacity) of Word;
   end record;
-- The words are stored in ascending order in words(1..size).
```

(a) If d1 and d2 are Dictionary variables, and w is a Word variable, which of the following ADA commands would be legal in the application code?

```
d1.words(1) := w;
add(d1, w);
d2 := (d1.size, d1.words);
d2 := d1;
if d1 = d2 then ... end if;
if d1.size > 0 then ... end if;
```

(b) How would your answers to (a) be affected if Dictionary were a *private* type rather than a *limited private* type?

*11.4.4 ADA insists that generic procedures are instantiated before being called.

(a) In principle, we could allow a generic proper procedure to be instantiated in the procedure call itself, e.g.:

```
swap(Integer)(a(i), a(i+1));
```

where swap is the generic procedure of Example 11.12. ADA does not actually allow this, but the same effect can be achieved (less concisely) by an ADA block command. Show how.

(b) A similar effect *cannot* be achieved for a generic function procedure. Why not?

(c) Investigate why ADA insists that generic procedures are instantiated before being called.

**11.4.5 When ADA was first designed, all of the following features were controversial: (a) exceptions; (b) overloading; (c) generic units. Was each feature well designed, or could it have been better designed, or should it have been omitted altogether?

11.4.6 Finish the coding of the ADA spellchecker of Programs 11.5–11.7.

11.4.7 Modify the ADA spellchecker of Programs 11.5–11.7 to use a user dictionary, as in Exercise 11.3.6. How easy are these modifications to make, compared to those of Exercise 11.3.6?

Chapter 12

Object-oriented programming

In this chapter we shall study:

- the key concepts that characterize object-oriented programming languages;
- the pragmatics of object-oriented programming;
- the design of two major object-oriented languages, C++ and JAVA;
- the object-oriented features of ADA95.

12.1 Key concepts

In Chapter 11 we saw that data abstraction has become an important concept in modern imperative languages. In fact, we can design entire programs in terms of abstract types or classes. If we go one step further and introduce class hierarchies, we reach a distinct programming paradigm, object-oriented programming.

The key concepts of object-oriented programming are:

- objects
- classes and subclasses
- inheritance
- inclusion polymorphism.

An *object* has one or more variable components, and is equipped with methods that operate on it. The object's variable components are typically private, and thus can be accessed *only* by the object's methods.

Objects give us a natural way to model real-world entities. Recall the example of an aircraft flight control program from Section 11.1. The aircraft's state includes its position, altitude, speed, payload, fuel load, and so on. Note that physical laws do not allow the aircraft's state to change suddenly: its position, altitude, and speed change gradually during flight, its fuel load decreases gradually, and (if it is an airliner) its payload does not change at all. The aircraft's state could be modeled by an object, equipped with methods that allow it to change only in accordance with physical laws. This is more reliable than modeling the aircraft's state by a group of ordinary variables, which the program could update arbitrarily.

Objects also give us a natural way to model cyber-world entities such as files, databases, Web pages, and user interface components. Consider a Web page that presents economic data derived from a database. The individual pieces of data are not supposed to be changed independently (because of the risk of inconsistency), and the fixed contents of the page (such as captions) are not supposed to change at all. The page could be modeled by an object equipped with methods to ensure that it is always updated atomically and with consistent data.

Classification of objects is a key characteristic of object-oriented languages. A *class* is a family of objects with similar variable components and methods. A *subclass* extends a class with additional components and/or additional (or overriding) methods. Each subclass can have its own subclasses, so we can build a hierarchy of classes.

Inheritance is also characteristic of object-oriented languages. A subclass inherits (shares) all the methods of its superclass, unless the subclass explicitly overrides any of these methods. Indeed, a whole hierarchy of classes can inherit methods from an ancestor class. Inheritance has a major impact on programmer productivity.

Inclusion polymorphism is a key concept, enabling an object of a subclass to be treated like an object of its superclass. This allows us, for instance, to build a heterogeneous collection of objects of different classes, provided that the collection is defined in terms of some common ancestor class.

Object-oriented programming has proved to be enormously successful, becoming the dominant programming paradigm in the 1990s. The reasons for its success are clear, at least in hindsight. Objects give us a very natural way to model both real-world and cyber-world entities. Classes and class hierarchies give us highly suitable (and reusable) units for constructing large programs. Object-oriented programming fits well with object-oriented analysis and design, supporting the seamless development of large software systems.

12.2 Pragmatics

The program units of an object-oriented program are classes. Classes may be related to one another by *dependency* (operations of one class call operations of another class), by *inclusion* or *extension* (one class is a subclass of another class), or by *containment* (objects of one class contain objects of another class).

A class is akin to a type, whose representation is determined by the class's variable components. If the variable components are public, they can be accessed directly by other classes, giving rise to tight coupling. If the variable components are private, the class is akin to an abstract type, ensuring loose coupling; a change to the class's representation will have little or no effect on other classes.

However, the inclusion relationship is a potential source of tight coupling, peculiar to object-oriented programs. If a subclass can access its superclass's variable components directly, the two classes are tightly coupled, since any change to the superclass's variable components will force changes to the subclass's implementation. (On the other hand, if the subclass *cannot* access its superclass's variable components directly, it must operate on them indirectly by calling the superclass's methods, which is an overhead.) In a large hierarchy of classes, the problem of tight coupling is significant: any change to an ancestor class's variable components could force changes to *all* of its subclasses' implementations.

Figure 12.1 illustrates the architecture of a (small) object-oriented program, showing dependency and inclusion relationships. Compare this with Figure 11.2,

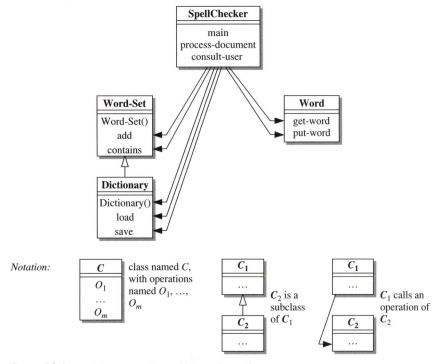

Figure 12.1 Architecture of an object-oriented program.

which shows the architecture of an imperative program with data abstraction. The major difference is that an object-oriented program may contain subclasses. A minor difference is that a (pure) object-oriented program consists entirely of classes, so the individual procedures of an imperative program become class methods in an object-oriented program.

12.3 Case study: C++

C++ was designed by Bjarne Stroustrup, who started in 1979 by extending C with classes. Thereafter, C++ gradually evolved by the addition of subclasses, overridable ("virtual") functions, overloading, and many other features. An internationally-recognized standard version of C++ was agreed in 1998. Standardization of C++ was coordinated with the contemporary standardization of C, ensuring that C remains a subset of C++ in all but a few minor respects (meaning that most C programs are also C++ programs).

It is notoriously difficult to extend an existing programming language successfully. The joins tend to be clearly visible. In this case, C++'s high-level data abstraction features sit uneasily with (and are indeed undermined by) the low-level features of C. Nevertheless, C++ has proved highly successful in practice, being widely used for both system and application programming, and introducing many imperative programmers to object-oriented programming.

We have already seen an overview of C in Section 11.3. To avoid repetition, the overview of C++ in this section concentrates on where it differs from C.

12.3.1 Values and types

C++ takes its primitive types largely from C. C++ does have a boolean type, **bool**, but it is classified as an integer type (with values 0 and 1), and it seems to be underused in practice.

C++ also takes its composite types largely from C. In addition C++ supports objects, but in fact it makes little distinction between structures and objects. Both structures and objects may be equipped with methods, but only objects support encapsulation.

C++'s expression repertoire is similar to C's. C++ is also an expression-oriented language.

C++'s type system is rather more complex, supporting inclusion polymorphism and overloading. Moreover, C++ has stronger type checking than C. In particular, C++ function calls are always type-checked, even if the called function is in a different compilation unit. Pointer arithmetic remains, however, and undermines type checking. For example, if p is of type **char***, the legal expression p+7 is also of type **char***, but the result could be a pointer to a variable of *any* type!

12.3.2 Variables, storage, and control

Like C, C++ supports global and local variables. Unlike C, C++ also explicitly supports heap variables, which are created by the **new** allocator and destroyed by the **delete** deallocator.

C++ includes all C's commands and sequencers. In addition, C++ supports exceptions, which are ordinary objects. Typically, an exception object is constructed just before being thrown; when the exception is caught, the handler can inspect it to determine what value it carries.

A C++ function may specify which classes of exceptions it may throw. A function with no exception specification could throw *any* exception. It is not possible to specify that a function *never* throws an exception.

12.3.3 Bindings and scope

A C++ program consists of declarations of global types, global variables, functions, classes, and generic units ("templates"). The main program is a function named main.

Within a C++ class declaration, we declare that class's components: variables, constructors, and methods.

Within a C++ function, constructor, or method, we may declare formal parameters, local variables, and local types.

A C++ parameter or variable may be declared with the specifier **const**, in which case it may be inspected but not updated. (Moreover, a pointer type may specify its referents **const**, in which case the referents may be inspected but not updated.)

12.3.4 Procedural abstraction

C++ supports function procedures, constructors, and methods. Methods differ from ordinary functions only in that they are attached to objects. The result type of a function or method may be **void** or any other type.

C++ supports both copy-in and reference parameters. Unlike C, C++ does not force us to pass an explicit pointer to achieve the effect of a reference parameter.

EXAMPLE 12.1 C++ function with reference parameters

In the following C++ function, min and max are reference parameters:

```
void minimax (int a[], int n, int& min, int& max) {
// Set min to the minimum, and max to the maximum, of the integers in
// a[0],...,a[n-1].
   min = max = a[0];
   int i;
   for (i = 1; i < n; i++) {
     int elem = a[i];
     if (elem < min)  min = elem;
     else if (elem > max)  max = elem;
   }
}
```

Here is a possible call to this function:

```
int[] temps = {13, 15, 20, 18, 21, 14, 12};
int low, high;
...
minimax(temps, 7, low, high);
```

The third and fourth arguments are (references to) the variables low and high, not their values.

Compare this example with Example 11.6.

C++ supports context-independent overloading of functions (and constructors and methods). In other words, two or more functions may share the same identifier in the same scope provided only that they differ in their parameter types or numbers. Also, C++ treats its operators exactly like functions: we may overload any existing operator by providing an additional definition. (But we may not invent new operator symbols.)

EXAMPLE 12.2 C++ overloaded functions

The following C++ functions are overloaded:

```
void put (ostream str, int i);
void put (ostream str, double r);
```

But it would be illegal to add the following overloaded function, because it differs from the second function above only in its result type:

```
int put (ostream str, double r);   // illegal!
```

EXAMPLE 12.3   C++ overloaded operators

The C++ library class `ostream` overloads the operator "`<<`" as follows:

```
class ostream : ... {
// An ostream object is a text output stream.
   ...
public:
   ostream& operator<< (char c);    // Write c to this stream.
   ostream& operator<< (int i);     // Write i to this stream.
   ostream& operator<< (double r);  // Write r to this stream.
   ...
}
```

Using this class we can write:

```
ostream out;
int n;
...
out << (n/100);   out << '%';
```

or, even more concisely:

```
out << (n/100) << '%';
```

12.3.5   Data abstraction

C++ supports data abstraction by means of classes. A class declaration names the class itself and its superclass(es), and declares the class's variable components and operations (constructors and methods).

In C++'s terminology, a subclass is called a "derived class", a superclass is called a "base class", and a method is simply called a "function".

A class declaration need only *declare* the class's operations. The class declaration may also *define* these operations, but more usually they are defined elsewhere.

The class declaration must also distinguish between public, private, and protected components. A public component can be accessed anywhere. A private component can be accessed only by the operations of the class itself. A protected component can be accessed only by operations of the class itself and its subclasses, and by "friend" functions of these classes. Full encapsulation is achieved by making the variable components private or protected, and making only the operations public.

The class declaration also distinguishes between two kinds of variable components: class variables and instance variables. An ***instance variable*** is a component of every object of the class, and a distinct copy of the instance variable exists for every object of that class. A ***class variable*** (distinguished by the specifier **static**) is global in the sense that it exists throughout the program's run-time, and only one copy of the class variable exists in the program.

Likewise, the class declaration distinguishes between two kinds of methods: instance methods and class methods. An ***instance method*** is attached to a particular object of the class, can access that object's instance variables, and thus operates on that object. A ***class method*** (also distinguished by the specifier **static**) is not attached to a particular object, and so cannot access the instance variables; however, it can access the class variables.

A ***constructor*** initializes a newly-created object of the class. Each constructor is named after the class to which it belongs. Overloading allows a class to have several constructors with the same name but different parameter types.

A C++ object may be a global, local, or heap variable. C++ adopts copy semantics for all values, including objects. However, the effect of reference semantics can be achieved by using pointers to objects.

EXAMPLE 12.4   C++ local and heap objects

Consider the following C++ class declaration (which defines all its operations):

```
class Person {
private:
    char* surname, forename;
    bool female;
    int birth_year;
public:
    Person (char* sname, char* fname, char gender,
                    int birth) {
        surname = sname;
        forename = fname;
        female = (gender == 'F' || gender == 'f');
        birth_year = birth;
    }
    char[] get_surname () {
        return surname;
    }
    void change_surname (char* sname) {
        surname = sname;
    }
    virtual void print () {
        ... //  print this person's name
    }
}
```

The following code declares three local `Person` variables:

```
{   Person pc("Curie", "Pierre", 'M', 1859);
    Person ms("Sklodowska", "Marie", 'F', 1867);
    Person mc;
    mc = ms;
    mc.change_surname(pc.get_surname());
}
```

The first declaration declares a local object pc (of class `Person`), and initializes it by calling the `Person` constructor with suitable arguments. The second declaration similarly declares a local object ms. The third declaration declares a local object mc, but does not initialize it. The assignment "mc = ms;" copies the object ms into mc. The subsequent call "mc.change_surname(...);" updates mc, but not ms.

The following code declares three *pointers* to `Person` variables:

```
{   Person* ppc =
        new Person("Curie", "Pierre", 'M', 1859);
    Person* pms =
        new Person("Sklodowska", "Marie", 'F', 1867);
    Person* pmc;
    pmc = pms;
    pmc->change_surname(ppc->get_surname());
    pms->print();
}
```

The first declaration allocates a heap object (of class `Person`), initializes it by calling the `Person` constructor, and makes the variable ppc point to that object. The second declaration similarly makes the variable pms point to a newly-allocated heap object. The third declaration declares a pointer variable pmc, but does not initialize it. The assignment "pmc = pms;" makes pmc point to the same object as pms (achieving the effect of reference semantics). The subsequent call "pmc->change_surname(...);" updates the object that both pms and pmc point to.

Although data abstraction is supported by C++ classes, it is undermined by other C++ features. For instance, if o is an object with a private variable component v, a malicious programmer who knows how the object is represented can access o.v by pointer arithmetic, starting with a pointer to o itself.

C++ supports multiple inheritance: a class may have any number of super-classes. A conceptual problem arises if a class inherits synonymous (but distinct) components from two or more superclasses: any references to such components will be ambiguous (or at least misleading). Moreover, multiple inheritance is awkward to implement efficiently. On the other hand, multiple inheritance is natural in some applications. The concept of multiple inheritance is therefore controversial.

C++ supports inclusion polymorphism in the sense that an object of a sub-class can be treated like an object of its superclass *when they are accessed through pointers*.

EXAMPLE 12.5   C++ inclusion polymorphism

Consider the Person class from Example 12.4 and the following subclass:

```cpp
class Student : public Person {

private:

    int student_id;
    char* degree;

public:

    Student (char* sname, char* fname, char gender,
                    int birth, int id, char* deg) {
      surname = sname;
      forename = fname;
      female = (gender == 'F' || gender == 'f');
      birth_year = birth;
      student_id = id;
      degree = deg;
    }

    void change_degree (char* deg) {
      degree = deg;
    }

    virtual void print () {
        ... // print this student's name and id
    }

}
```

The following code declares and uses an array of Person objects:

```cpp
Person p[10];
Person dw("Watt", "David", 'M', 1946);
Student jw("Watt", "Jeff", 'M', 1983, 0100296, "BSc");
p[0] = dw;
p[1] = jw;   // illegal!
```

The latter assignment is illegal because the types Person and Student are incompatible.

However, compare the following code, which declares and uses an array of *pointers* to Person objects:

```cpp
Person* pp[10];
Person* pdw = new Person("Watt", "David", 'M', 1946);
Student* pjw = new Student("Watt", "Jeff", 'M', 1983,
        0100296, "BSc");
pp[0] = pdw;
pp[1] = pjw;   // legal
for (int i = 0; i < 2; i++)
    pp[i]->print();   // safe
```

The assignment to pp[1] is legal because the types Person* and Student* are compatible. Moreover, the method call "pp[i]->print()" is safe, and will call either the Person class's print method or the Student class's print method, depending on the class of the object that pp[i] points to. This is dynamic dispatch.

12.3.6   Generic abstraction

As we saw in Sections 7.1.2 and 7.2.2, C++ supports generic classes. A generic class can be parameterized with respect to values, variables, types, and functions on which it depends. Here we give one further example, this time illustrating a function parameter.

EXAMPLE 12.6   C++ generic class with type and function parameters

The following generic class supports priority queues, where the queue elements are of *any* type equipped with a less function:

```
template
  <class Element,
   bool less (Element x, Element y)
  >
class Priority_Queue {

    // A Priority_Queue object is a priority queue, where the queue
    // elements are of any type Element equipped with a less function.

private:

    ... // representation

public:

    Priority_Queue ();
    // Construct an empty priority queue.

    void add (Element e);
    // Add e to this priority queue.

    Element remove ();
    // Remove and return the least element from this priority queue.

}
```

The class is parameterized with respect to the type Element and the function less. The definitions of the add and remove methods will use less to compare two Element values.

Application code could instantiate this package as follows:

```
struct Print_Job {
    int owner_id;
    int timestamp;
    char* ps_filename;
}

bool earlier (Print_Job job1, Print_Job job2) {
    return (job1.timestamp < job2.timestamp);
```

```
}
typedef Priority_Queue<Print_Job, earlier>
    Print_Queue;
```

This type definition generates an ordinary class, named `Print_Queue`, from the generic class by substituting `Print_Job` for `Element`, and `earlier` for `less`.

C++ also supports generic functions. A generic function gives us an extra level of abstraction.

EXAMPLE 12.7 C++ generic function with a type parameter

The following defines a swapping function that is parameterized with respect to the type `Item` of the values being swapped:

```
template
    <class Item>
void swap (Item& x, Item& y) {
    Item z = x;
    x = y;  y = z;
}
```

We can call this function without first instantiating it:

```
int a[];
...
swap(a[i], a[j]);
```

Here `swap` is called with two arguments of type `int&`. The C++ compiler infers that the generic function must be instantiated with `int` substituted for `Item`.

12.3.7 Independent compilation and preprocessor directives

C++ inherits independent compilation and preprocessor directives from C. However, C++ implementations have found ways to mitigate the worst of the problems mentioned in Section 11.3.5. In particular, type checking between compilation units can be achieved by encoding type information in each function's name. Programmers are still expected to use #include directives in a disciplined way, but accidental or deliberate departures from such discipline are not necessarily detected by the C++ compiler.

12.3.8 Class and template library

Like other object-oriented languages, C++ is well suited for writing class libraries. The C++ standard library comprises classes supporting general utilities, strings, numerical (including complex) computation, and input/output. There are also classes needed to support the language itself: storage allocation and deallocation, and exception handling.

There is also a C++ standard template library, which comprises generic container classes (stacks, queues, priority queues, lists, vectors, sets, multisets, maps, and multimaps) and generic functions (searching, sorting, merging, copying, and transforming).

12.3.9 A simple spellchecker

To conclude this overview of object-oriented programming in C++, let us examine a C++ implementation of the simple spellchecker specified in Section 11.2.1. The program consists of several compilation units, and is shown in Programs 12.1–12.4. Its architecture resembles Figure 12.1, except that its top-level program units are independent functions rather than methods.

Program 12.1(a) shows a header file for the Word class, which is equipped with a constructor and two class methods. Program 12.1(b) outlines definitions of the constructor and class methods. Note that get_word returns a status flag to indicate whether it has read a word or reached the end of the input document. (An alternative design would have been to make get_word throw an exception on reaching the end of the input document, but that would have been inconsistent with the design of C++'s input/output library.)

Program 12.2(a) shows a header file for the Word_Set class, which is equipped with a constructor and two methods. Program 12.2(b) outlines definitions of the Word_Set constructor and methods.

```
#include <fstreamio.h>

class Word {

    //  Each Word object is a single word.

private:

    ...  //  representation of a word

public:

    Word (String spelling);
    //  Construct a word with spelling.

    static int get_word (ifstream& in_doc,
                    ofstream& out_doc, Word& wd);
    //  Read the next word from in_doc, copying any preceding punctuation to
    //  out_doc.  Return nonzero if there is no next word to be read.

    static void put_word (ofstream& out_doc, Word wd);
    //  Write wd to out_doc.

};
```

Program 12.1(a) Header file for Word class in C++ (Word.h).

```
#include <fstreamio.h>
#include "Word.h"

Word::Word (String spelling) {
    ...
}

int Word::get_word (ifstream& in_doc,
                    ofstream& out_doc, Word& wd) {
    ...
}

void Word::put_word (ofstream& out_doc, Word wd) {
    ...
}
```

Program 12.1(b) Definitions of Word operations in C++ (in outline).

```
class Word_Set {
// Each Word_Set object is a set of words.

private:

    ... // representation of a set of words

public:

    Word_Set ();
    // Construct an empty set of words.

    void add (Word wd);
    // Make wd a member of this set of words.

    bool contains (Word wd);
    // Return true if and only if wd is a member of this set of words.

};
```

Program 12.2(a) Header file for Word_Set class in C++ (Word_Set.h).

Program 12.3(a) shows a header file for the Dictionary subclass, which is equipped with its own constructor and methods as well as methods inherited from its superclass Word_Set. Program 12.3(b) outlines definitions of the Dictionary constructor and methods.

Program 12.4 outlines the high-level functions consult_user, process_document, and main. Note that process_document tests the status flag returned by get_word, exiting the loop if the status flag indicates that the end of the input document has been reached.

```
#include "Word.h"
#include "Word_Set.h"
... // auxiliary functions
Word_Set::Word_Set () {
  ...
}
void Word_Set::add (Word wd) {
  ...
}
bool Word_Set::contains (Word wd) {
  ...
}
```

Program 12.2(b) Definitions of Word_Set operations in C++ (in outline).

```
class Dictionary : public Word_Set {
// Each Dictionary object is a set of words that can be loaded and saved.
public:
  Dictionary ();
  // Construct an empty dictionary.

  void load (char* filename);
  // Load this dictionary from filename.

  void save (char* filename);
  // Save this dictionary to filename.
};
```

Program 12.3(a) Header file for Dictionary class in C++ (Dictionary.h).

```
#include "Word_Set.h"
#include "Dictionary.h"
... //   auxiliary functions
Dictionary::Dictionary () {
  ...
}
void Dictionary::load (char* filename) {
  ...
}
void Dictionary::save (char* filename) {
  ...
}
```

Program 12.3(b) Definitions of Dictionary operations in C++ (in outline).

```
#include <fstreamio.h>
#include "Word.h"
#include "Word_Set.h"
#include "Dictionary.h"

void consult_user(Word& current_word,
                  Dictionary& main_dict,
                  Dictionary& ignored) {
// Ask the user what to do with current_word, which is unknown.
// If the user chooses to accept the word, make it a member of main_dict.
// If the user chooses to ignore the word, make it a member of ignored.
// If the user chooses to replace the word, get the user to enter a replacement word,
// and update current_word.
  ...
}

void process_document (Dictionary& main_dict,
                  Dictionary& ignored) {
// Copy all words and punctuation from the input document to the output document,
// but ask the user what to do with any words that are unknown (i.e., not in
// main_dict or ignored).
  Word current_word;
  ifstream in_doc(...);
  ofstream out_doc(...);
  for (;;) {
    if (Word::get_word(in_doc, out_doc, current_word)
        != 0)
      break;
    if (! main_dict.contains(current_word) &&
        ! ignored.contains(current_word))
      consult_user(current_word, main_dict, ignored);
    Word::put_word(out_doc, current_word);
  }
  in_doc.close();  out_doc.close();
}

int main () {
  Dictionary main_dict;
  Dictionary ignored;
  main_dict.load("dict.txt");
  process_document(main_dict, ignored);
  main_dict.save("dict.txt");
}
```

Program 12.4 Definitions of consult_user, process_document, and main functions in C++ (in outline).

12.4 Case study: JAVA

JAVA was designed in the mid-1990s by a SUN Microsystems team led by Bill Joy. Although originally intended for embedded system applications, JAVA soon evolved into a language suitable for Web applications. In particular, JAVA is well suited for writing *applets*. An applet is an application program located on a Web server; when selected by a user, the applet is downloaded and run on the user's (client) computer.

This application area imposes stringent requirements on both the programming language and its implementation. An applet must behave predictably and consistently on *all* computers. Even more importantly, it must be guaranteed safe. If malicious applets could disrupt other programs or corrupt files on the user's computer, the user would quickly learn not to trust *any* applets.

JAVA meets these stringent requirements. Although it is a descendant of C and C++, JAVA ruthlessly excludes unsafe and unpredictable features. Static type checking and dynamic checks (on array indexing, for example) ensure that erroneous operations are not performed. There are no explicit pointers. Unreachable objects are automatically deallocated. Moreover, JAVA is usually implemented in such a way (programs are compiled into virtual machine code) that even the object code is portable.

JAVA experienced explosive growth during the later 1990s, paralleling the growth of the Web itself. It is still used mainly for Web applications. Although the JAVA language is also suitable for general-purpose programming, the usual implementation makes execution of object code too slow for many applications.

Unlike C++, JAVA is a rather pure object-oriented language: all composite values are objects, and a program consists entirely of classes. JAVA also supports concurrent and distributed programming, although even these are built on object-oriented concepts. (See Section 13.4.)

12.4.1 Values and types

JAVA's primitive types are similar to those of C and C++. One important difference is that their representations and operations are precisely stipulated by JAVA. For instance, JAVA stipulates that **int** values are 32-bit two's complement integers. (C and C++ both allow their compilers to implement **int** in terms of the computer's native word length and arithmetic, insisting only that **int** has a wider range than **short int** but a narrower range than **long int**.) Similarly, JAVA stipulates that **float** values are IEEE standard 32-bit floating-point numbers.

All composite values in JAVA are objects. Even arrays are objects, although C-like notation is retained for constructing and indexing arrays. JAVA does not support records as such, but we can achieve the same effect by declaring a class with public instance variables. Likewise, JAVA does not support disjoint unions as such, but we can achieve the same effect by declaring a class and several subclasses (one subclass for each variant). JAVA supports recursive classes: an object of a given class may have variable component(s) of the same class.

JAVA complies only partially with the Type Completeness Principle. Constants, variables, parameters, and method results can be of any type. However, there are clear inconsistencies in the treatment of primitive values and objects. One inconsistency, which shows up in assignment and parameter passing, is that copy semantics is adopted for primitive values, while reference semantics is adopted for objects. The following example illustrates another inconsistency.

EXAMPLE 12.8   JAVA primitive values and objects

Consider the following method:

```
static boolean search (Object[] a, Object x) {...}
// Return true if and only if the array a contains an object that equals x.
```

Since every JAVA class is a subclass of Object, we can pass an array of objects of any class to this method:

```
String[] words = {"a", "aardvark", ...};
String word;
...
if (search(words, word)) ...
```

We can even pass a heterogeneous array containing objects of different classes. But we cannot pass an array of type **int**[] to this method, since **int** values are not objects. Instead we must pass an array of type Integer[]:

```
Integer[] ints = {new Integer(2), new Integer(3),
    new Integer(5), new Integer(7), ...};
int n;
...
if (search(ints, new Integer(n))) ...
```

Here "**new** Integer(n)" *wraps* the value of n in an Integer object. (Conversely, "intobj.intValue()" would *unwrap* the Integer object intobj to extract its **int** value.)

Since JAVA now provides a wrapping coercion, we can actually abbreviate the above code to:

```
Integer[] ints = {2, 3, 5, 7, ... };
int n;
...
if (search(ints, n)) ...
```

Here underlining shows the expressions where wrapping coercions take place.

JAVA provides a "wrapper" class for each of its eight primitive types: Integer for **int**, Float for **float**, and so on. Thus any primitive value can be wrapped in an object, and subsequently unwrapped. These wrapper objects can be used like any other objects, but wrapping and unwrapping are time-consuming.

JAVA's expression repertoire includes array constructions, constructor and method calls, and conditional expressions, but no iterative expressions or block expressions. An array construction allocates and initializes an array object, but is allowed only on the right-hand side of a constant or variable declaration, as in Example 12.8.

12.4.2   Variables, storage, and control

JAVA supports global, local, and heap variables. However, the only global variables in a JAVA program are class variables, which will be discussed in Section 12.4.5.

Heap variables are objects created by the **new** allocator; these are destroyed *automatically* when no longer reachable. Automatic deallocation (implemented by a garbage collector) simplifies the programmer's task and eliminates a common source of errors.

JAVA inherits all C++'s commands and sequencers, except jumps. JAVA exceptions are objects of a subclass of `Exception`.

A JAVA method may specify which classes of exceptions it may throw; a method with no exception specification may not throw any exception. The compiler rigorously checks this information: if a method M (or a method called by M) might throw an exception of class C, then either M must contain a handler for C or M's exception specification must include C. (At least, that is the basic principle. In practice, the JAVA designers believed that it would be counterproductive to insist on compile-time checking of low-level exceptions, such as those thrown by arithmetic and array indexing operations. So they decided on a design compromise: exceptions classified as low-level ("unchecked exceptions") may be omitted from exception specifications, and the compiler does not check them at all.)

12.4.3   Bindings and scope

A JAVA program consists of a number of class declarations, which may be grouped into packages. The user must designate a class equipped with a method named `main`, and that is the main program.

Within each class declaration we declare that class's variable components, constructors, methods, and inner classes. Within a constructor or method we may declare local variables.

Any JAVA variable may be declared with the specifier **final**, allowing it to be inspected but not updated. In effect it is a constant rather than a variable. The specifier **final** may also be used when declaring a method, indicating that the method is not overridable, or when declaring a class, indicating that the class may not have subclasses.

12.4.4   Procedural abstraction

JAVA supports constructors and methods, which are always components of a particular class. Unlike C++, JAVA does not support procedures that are independent of any class.

JAVA supports copy-in parameters only. In other words, the formal parameter acts like a local variable that is initialized with the argument value. Where the argument is a primitive value, it can be inspected but not updated. Where the argument is an object, however, it is accessed through a pointer; the pointer cannot be updated, but the object itself can. This gives us the effect of a reference parameter mechanism for objects only.

A JAVA method has a single result (unless its type is **void**). This, together with the copy-in parameter mechanism, makes it awkward to express a procedure with two or more results. In Example 12.1 we saw a procedure that computes both the minimum and the maximum of a given array of numbers. In most programming languages we could write a procedure with two copy-out or reference parameters; in JAVA we are forced into circumlocution. (See Exercise 12.4.2.)

JAVA supports context-independent overloading of methods. This must not be confused with method overriding. Suppose that a superclass and a subclass both define methods with the same name. If the methods have the same parameter types, the superclass's method is overridden by the subclass. If the methods have different parameter types, however, they are overloaded, and the superclass's method is inherited by the subclass.

12.4.5   Data abstraction

JAVA supports data abstraction by means of classes. A class declaration names the class itself and its superclass (Object by default), declares the class's variable components, and defines its constructors and methods.

Like C++, JAVA distinguishes between instance variables and class variables, and also between instance methods and class methods. Class variables and methods are distinguished by the specifier **static**.

A constructor initializes a newly-created object of the class. In JAVA each constructor is named after the class to which it belongs. Overloading allows a class to have several constructors with the same name but different parameter types.

The class declaration must distinguish between public, private, and protected components. A public component can be accessed anywhere. A private component can be accessed only by the operations of the class itself. A protected component can be accessed only by operations of the class itself, its subclasses, and other classes in the same package. Full encapsulation is achieved by making the variable components private (or at least protected), and making only the constructors and methods public.

All JAVA objects are heap variables. Unlike C++, a JAVA object cannot be a local or global variable.

JAVA supports inclusion polymorphism without restriction: an object of a subclass can be treated like an object of its superclass in all circumstances.

EXAMPLE 12.9   JAVA inclusion polymorphism

Consider the following class:

```
class Person {

    private String surname, forename;
    private bool female;
    private int birthYear;

    public Person (String sname, String fname,
                   char gender, int birth) {
        surname = sname;
        forename = fname;
        female = (gender == 'F' || gender == 'f');
        birthYear = birth;
```

```
        }

        public String getSurname () {
          return surname;
        }

        public void changeSurname (String sname) {
          surname = sname;
        }

        public void print () {
          ... // print this person's name
        }

    }
```

and the following subclass:

```
    class Student extends Person {

        private int student_id;
        private String degree;

        public Student (String sname, String fname,
                        char gender, int birth, int id,
                        String deg) {
          ...
        }

        void changeDegree (String deg) {
          degree = deg;
        }

        void print () {
          ... // print this student's name and id
        }

    }
```

The following code declares and uses an array of Person objects:

```
Person p = new Person[10];
Person dw = new Person("Watt", "David", 'M', 1946);
Student jw = new Student("Watt", "Jeff", 'M', 1983,
    0100296, "BSc");
p[0] = dw;
p[1] = jw;  // legal
for (int i = 0; i < 2; i++)
    p[i].print();  // safe
```

The assignment to p[1] is legal because types Person and Student are compatible. Moreover, the method call "p[i].print()" is safe, and will call either the Person class's print method or the Student class's print method, depending on the class of the object yielded by p[i]. This is dynamic dispatch.

12.4.6   Generic abstraction

Until 2004 JAVA did not support generic abstraction. This was a notable weakness, forcing programmers into over-reliance on inclusion polymorphism, as the following example illustrates.

EXAMPLE 12.10   JAVA collection class

Consider the following class:

```
class Stack {

    // A Stack object represents a stack whose elements are objects.

    private Object[] elems;
    private int depth;

    public Stack () { depth = 0; }

    public void push (Object x) { elems[depth++] = x;   }

    public Object pop () { return elems[--depth]; }

    public boolean isEmpty () { return (depth == 0); }

}
```

Since every JAVA class is a subclass of Object, a Stack object may contain objects of any class. It may even be heterogeneous, containing objects of different classes:

```
Stack stack = new Stack();
String s1 = ...;   Date d1 = ...;
stack.push(s1);
stack.push(d1);
...
Date d2 = (Date)stack.pop();
String s2 = (String)stack.pop();
```

But now consider the following code:

```
Stack stack = new Stack();
for (...) {
    String s = ...;
    stack.push(s);
}
while (! stack.isEmpty()) {
    String s = (String)stack.pop();
    ...
}
```

A human reader can easily see that only String objects are pushed on to stack, so only String objects can be popped. But the compiler cannot see that; it can infer only that the type of the method call "stack.pop()" is Object, hence the need to cast the result to type String.

Instead, we can implement stacks using a generic class, as follows:

```
class Stack <Item> {

    // A Stack<Item> object represents a stack whose elements are objects
    // of class Item.

    private Item[] elems;
    private int depth;

    public Stack () { depth = 0; }

    public void push (Item x) { elems[depth++] = x; }

    public Item pop () { return elems[--depth]; }

    public boolean isEmpty () { return (depth == 0); }

}
```

Now the above application code would be written as follows:

```
Stack<String> stack = new Stack<String>();
for (…) {
    String s = …;
    stack.push(s);
}
while (! stack.isEmpty()) {
    String s = stack.pop();
    …
}
```

12.4.7   Separate compilation and dynamic linking

A JAVA program is always compiled one class at a time. Each class is said to *import* the other classes on which it depends. (Classes in the same package are automatically imported, as are classes in the java.lang package. All other classes must be explicitly named in an import clause.) When a class is compiled, it is type-checked against the imported classes, which must have been compiled previously. Thus the entire program is statically type-checked. Type checking of a JAVA program includes enforcement of protections, for instance preventing any class from accessing the private variables and methods of an imported class.

JAVA implementations employ ***dynamic linking***. Consider an applet consisting of several compiled classes, located on some Web server. Initially only one class's object code is downloaded from the server, namely the class containing the main program, which immediately starts running. Each other class's object code is downloaded and linked to the running program only when (and if) needed. Dynamic linking spreads the overhead of downloading the classes that constitute the program. (Potentially it will *reduce* the overhead, if some of the classes are not needed in a particular run of the program.)

Unfortunately, dynamic linking undermines the security of static type checking, since there is no guarantee that the run-time environment (consisting of the classes that may be linked into the running program) is the same as the compile-time environment (consisting of the imported classes against which each class was type-checked). The JAVA dynamic linker attempts to repeat the type checks, but is unable to do so accurately.

EXAMPLE 12.11   JAVA dynamic linking

Assume that the following class is given:

```
class Widget {
    private ... secret;
    public Widget () {...} // constructor accessing secret
    public ... // methods accessing secret
}
```

Suppose that a malicious programmer wishes to write a main program that accesses w.secret directly:

```
class Malicious {
    public static void main (...) {
        Widget w = new Widget();
        ... w.secret ...
    }
}
```

Fortunately, the JAVA compiler will reject this illegal attempt to access a private instance variable.

However, if the programmer manages to obtain the Widget class's source code, he compiles a modified version:

```
class Widget {
    public ... secret;   // Now secret is public!
    public Widget () {...}
    public ... // methods
}
```

and then compiles Malicious importing the modified version of the Widget class. Finally, he arranges that the *original* version of the Widget class is in the program's run-time environment. The Malicious program then successfully accesses w.secret.

12.4.8 Class library

JAVA has an enormous class library, consisting of roughly 600 classes. For convenience they are grouped into about 130 packages, each package comprising a number of related classes and interfaces. These packages support applets, collections, component frameworks, cryptography, database access, distributed programming, events, exceptions, graphical user interfaces, images, input/output, mathematics, security, sound, threads, XML, and a great deal more.

Classes are particularly good as reusable program units, and most object-oriented languages have rich class libraries. Even so, JAVA's class library is exceptionally rich. In a typical JAVA program, most of the classes come from the class library, saving programmers the tedium of repeatedly reinventing wheels.

12.4.9   A simple spellchecker

To conclude this overview of object-oriented programming in JAVA, let us examine a JAVA implementation of the simple spellchecker specified in Section 11.2.1. The program's architecture is shown in Figure 12.1, and consists entirely of classes.

Program 12.5 outlines the Word class, which is equipped with a constructor and two class methods. Note that the getWord method throws an EOFException if it reaches the end of the input document, and this class is named in the method's exception specification.

```
import java.io.*;

class Word {

    // Each Word object is a single word.

    private ...;   // representation of a word

    public Word (String spelling) {
    // Construct a word with spelling.
        ...
    }

    public static Word getWord (BufferedReader inDoc,
                    BufferedWriter outDoc)
            throws EOFException {
    // Read the next word from inDoc and return it, copying any preceding
    // punctuation to outDoc. Throw an EOFException if there is no next word
    // to be read.
        ...
    }

    public static void putWord (BufferedWriter outDoc,
                    Word wd) {
    // Write word wd to outDoc.
        ...
    }

}
```

Program 12.5 Word class in JAVA (in outline).

```
class WordSet {

    // Each WordSet object is a set of words.

    private ...;   // representation of a set of words

    public WordSet () {
    // Construct an empty set of words.
        ...
    }

    public void add (Word wd) {
    // Make wd a member of this set of words.
        ...
    }

    public boolean contains (Word wd) {
    // Return true if and only if wd is a member of this set of words.
        ...
    }

}
```

Program 12.6   WordSet class in JAVA (in outline).

Program 12.6 outlines the WordSet class, which is equipped with a constructor and two methods.

Program 12.7 outlines the Dictionary class, which is equipped with its own constructor and methods as well as methods inherited from its superclass Word_Set.

Program 12.8 outlines the high-level SpellChecker class. This consists of methods consultUser, processDocument, and main. Note that process-Document catches any EOFException thrown by getWord, and the exception handler exits the loop.

This JAVA program with its C++ counterpart (Programs 12.1–12.4) highlight many of the similarities and differences between the two languages. JAVA is closer to being a pure object-oriented language, in that the program consists entirely of classes, all composite values are objects, objects are accessed uniformly through pointers (which effectively makes the pointers invisible), and so on. Thus JAVA programs tend to be easier to implement and to maintain. C++ is a multi-paradigm language, supporting both object-oriented programming and C-style imperative programming. Thus C++ is much more flexible than JAVA, but C++ programs tend to be harder to implement and to maintain. Finally, both JAVA and C++ enable programs to use exceptions to achieve robustness. While JAVA's class library consistently uses exceptions, however, C++'s input/output library still uses status flags, which tends to discourage the use of exceptions in application code.

```
class Dictionary extends WordSet {

    // Each Dictionary object is a set of words that can be loaded and saved.

    private ... // auxiliary methods

    public Dictionary () {
    // Construct an empty dictionary.
        ...
    }

    public void load (String filename) {
    // Load this dictionary from filename.
        ...
    }

    public void save (String filename) {
    // Save this dictionary to filename.
        ...
    }

}
```

Program 12.7   Dictionary class in JAVA (in outline).

12.5 Case study: ADA95

At the time when ADA83 was designed, the potential of object-oriented programming was not yet widely recognized. In the 1990s, however, the ADA designers made support for object-oriented programming a priority when they revised the language, which became known as ADA95.

Surprisingly few new features had to be added to ADA. The designers took the view that the key concepts of object-oriented programming (Section 12.1) are based on even more fundamental concepts. ADA83 already supported most of these fundamental concepts, particularly private types and subtypes. ADA95 adds a few new features: extensible tagged record types (to represent objects) and class-wide types (to achieve inclusion polymorphism). We can use these concepts to write object-oriented programs in ADA95, although with more effort than writing the corresponding object-oriented programs in C++ or JAVA.

ADA95 is a multi-paradigm language, in which we can write imperative programs, object-oriented programs, and hybrid programs. In Section 11.4 we examined ADA's support for imperative programming. In this section we briefly examine ADA95's support for object-oriented programming.

12.5.1 Types

In ADA95, a *tagged record* is like an ordinary record, except that it has an implicit tag field that can be tested at run-time. All records of a tagged record type T have the same components and the same tag.

```
import java.io.*;

class SpellChecker {

   public static Word consultUser (Word currentWord,
                 Dictionary mainDict, Dictionary ignored) {
   // Ask the user what to do with currentWord, which is unknown.
   // If the user chooses to accept the word, make it a member of mainDict.
   // If the user chooses to ignore the word, make it a member of ignored.
   // In either of these cases, return the same word.
   // If the user chooses to replace the word, get the user to enter a replacement word,
   // and return the replacement word.
      ...
   }

   public static void processDocument (Dictionary mainDict,
                 Dictionary ignored)
         throws IOException {
   // Copy all words and punctuation from the input document to the output
   // document, but ask the user what to do with any words that are unknown (i.e.,
   // not in mainDict or ignored).
      BufferedReader inDoc = new BufferedReader(...);
      BufferedWriter outDoc = new BufferedWriter(...);
      try {
        for (;;) {
          Word currentWord = getWord(inDoc, outDoc);
          if (! mainDict.contains(currentWord) &&
                ! ignored.contains(currentWord))
             currentWord = consultUser(currentWord,
                  mainDict, ignored);
          putWord(outDoc, currentWord);
        }
      }
      catch (EOFException e) {
        inDoc.close();  outDoc.close();
      }
   }

   public static void main () {
      Dictionary mainDict = new Dictionary();
      Dictionary ignored = new Dictionary();
      try {
        mainDict.load("dict.txt");
        processDocument(mainDict, ignored);
        mainDict.save("dict.txt");
      }
      catch (IOException e) { ... }
   }

}
```

Program 12.8   SpellChecker class in JAVA (in outline).

Tagged record types are *extensible*. That is to say, we can derive a new tagged record type *U* by extension of an existing tagged record type *T*. Tagged records of type *U* have all the components of tagged records of type *T*, plus additional components. Moreover, tagged records of type *U* have a different tag from tagged records of type *T*.

Of particular importance is the class-wide type *T*'class. The values of type *T*'class are tagged records of type *T* or any type derived from *T*.

EXAMPLE 12.12   ADA95 tagged records

Consider the following tagged record type:

```
type Point is
    tagged record
        x, y: Float;
    end record;
```

Each value of this type is a tagged tuple *Point(x, y)*.

Now consider the following tagged record type, which is derived from Point:

```
type Circle is new Point with
    record
        r: Float;
    end record;
```

Each value of this type is a tagged tuple *Circle(x, y, r)*. In the notation of Section 2.3:

$$\text{Point} = Point(\text{Float} \times \text{Float})$$
$$\text{Circle} = Circle(\text{Float} \times \text{Float} \times \text{Float})$$

The values of type Point'class include the values of type Point, Circle, and indeed any other type derived (directly or indirectly) from Point. In the notation of Section 8.1.2:

$$\text{Point}\ddagger = Point(\text{Float} \times \text{Float}) + Circle(\text{Float} \times \text{Float} \times \text{Float}) + \dots$$

The values of type **access** Point'class are pointers to variables of type Point, Circle, or any other type derived from Point. This is illustrated by the following code:

```
type Point_Access is access Point'class;
pp: Point_Access;
...
pp := new Point'(3.0, 4.0);        -- pp points to a point
pp := new Circle'(0.0, 0.0, 5.0);  -- pp points to a circle
```

In practice, tagged records are used to represent objects. A *private* tagged record type corresponds to a class, and a *private* extended tagged record type corresponds to a subclass.

Example 12.12 exposes an important difference between ADA95 and JAVA. ADA95 distinguishes between the type Point and the type Point'class. JAVA makes no such distinction, so a JAVA programmer cannot declare a variable that is constrained to point to an object of class Point.

12.5.2   Data abstraction

ADA95's treatment of classes is similar to its treatment of abstract types. To introduce a new class we declare a private type, together with public procedures, inside a package. In the package specification we declare the public procedures, and (after **private**) we define the private type's representation, which must be a tagged record type. In the corresponding package body we define the public procedures, and also any private procedures, in the usual way.

Each operation of an ADA95 class is an ordinary procedure. To enable the procedure to operate on an object, we pass that object as an ordinary argument in an ordinary procedure call "$P(..., O, ...)$". (This contrasts with C++ or JAVA, in which that object has a distinguished position in the method call: "$O \rightarrow M(...)$" or "$O.M(...)$".)

EXAMPLE 12.13   ADA95 class

Consider the following package specification:

```
package Persons is

    type Person is tagged private;

    procedure make_person (this: in out Person;
                    sname, fname: in Name;
                    gender: in Character;
                    birth: in Year_Number);

    function get_surname (this: Person) return Name;

    procedure change_surname (this: in out Person;
                    sname: in Name);

    procedure print (this: in Person);
    --  Print this person's name.

private

    type Person is
        tagged record
            surname, forename: Name;
            female: Boolean;
            birth_year: Year_Number;
        end record;

end Persons;
```

This declares a type Person, whose values will be objects represented by tagged records. This is revealed by the keyword **tagged** in the initial declaration of Person, although the details are (as usual) revealed only in the private part of the package specification.

The procedure make_person acts as a constructor. Each of the procedures get_surname, change_surname, and print operates on a Person object supplied as an argument.

Here is the corresponding package body:

```
package body Persons is

    procedure make_person (this: in out Person;
                    sname, fname: in Name;
                    gender: in Character;
                    birth: in Year_Number) is
    begin
       this := (sname, fname, (gender = 'F'), birth);
    end;

    function get_surname (this: Person) return Name is
    begin
       return this.surname;
    end;

    procedure change_surname (this: in out Person;
                    sname: in Name) is
    begin
       this.surname := sname;
    end;

    procedure print (this: in Person) is
    begin
       ...
    end;

end Persons;
```

Here is some possible application code:

```
use Persons;
pc, ms, mc: Person;
...
make_person(pc, "Curie", "Pierre", 'M', 1859);
make_person(ms, "Sklodowska", "Marie", 'F', 1867);
mc := ms;
change_surname(mc, get_surname(pc));
print(mc);
```

Note that changing mc's surname has no effect on ms, as a consequence of Ada's copy semantics.

To introduce a subclass we declare a private type, together with public procedures, inside a package. In the package specification we declare the public procedures, and (after **private**) we define the private type's representation, which must be an extension of the tagged record type used to represent objects of the superclass. (However, only additional procedures, and procedures intended to override those of the superclass, are declared in this way.) In the corresponding package body we define these public procedures, and also any private procedures, in the usual way.

It is usual (but not obligatory) to declare each class and subclass in a separate package. If we wish to allow a subclass's procedures direct access to the superclass's representation (i.e., the components of the tagged record), we can declare the subclass in a *child package*. A child package is logically contained within its parent package. It may access any component declared in the parent package specification, *including the private part*. The relationship between parent and child package is established by naming: if two packages are named *P* and *P.Q*, then *P.Q* is a child of *P*.

ADA95 supports inclusion polymorphism. An object of a subclass can be treated like an object of its superclass, since the superclass's class-wide type includes all such objects.

EXAMPLE 12.14   ADA95 subclass

Consider the `Person` class of Example 12.13. The following child package specification declares a subclass:

```
package Persons.Students is

    type Student is new Person with private;

    procedure make_student (this: in out Student;
                    sname, fname: in Name;
                    gender: in Character;
                    birth: in Year_Number;
                    id: in Student_Id;
                    deg: in Degree_Title);

    procedure change_degree (this: in out Student;
                    deg: in Degree_Title);

    procedure print (this: in Student);
    -- Print this student's name and id.

private

    type Student is new Person with
        record
            student_id: Student_Id;
            degree: Degree_Title;
        end record;

end Persons.Students;
```

We can tell from its name that the `Persons.Students` package is a child of the `Persons` package. We can also tell from its declaration that the `Student` type is derived from the `Person` tagged record type, although the details of the additional components are revealed only in the private part of the package specification.

Note that the `Student` class inherits the `Person` class's `get_surname` and `change_surname` procedures, but overrides the `print` procedure.

The following code declares and uses an array of *pointers* to Person objects:

```
use Persons, Persons.Students;
type Person_Access is access Person'class;
pp: array (1 .. 10) of Person_Access;
dw: Person;
jw: Student;
...
make_person(dw, "Watt", "David", 'M', 1946);
make_student(jw, "Watt", "Jeff", 'M', 1983,
    0100296, "BSc");
pp(1) := new Person'(dw);
pp(2) := new Student'(jw);   // legal!
for i in 1 .. 2 loop
  print(pp(i).all); // safe
end loop;
```

The assignment to pp(2) is legal because the types **access** Person and **access** Student are both compatible with the type **access** Person'class. Moreover, the procedure call "print(pp(i).all);" is safe, and will call either the Person class's print procedure or the Student class's print procedure, depending on the tag of the record that pp(i) points to. This is dynamic dispatch.

Summary

In this chapter:

- We have identified the key concepts of object-oriented programming: objects, classes and subclasses, inheritance, and inclusion polymorphism.

- We have studied the pragmatics of object-oriented programming, showing that an object-oriented program consists primarily of classes. Many classes are reusable.

- We have studied the design of two major object-oriented programming languages, C++ and JAVA. We have also studied the object-oriented features of the multi-paradigm language ADA95.

- We have compared two object-oriented implementations, in C++ and JAVA, of a simple spellchecker.

Further reading

SIMULA67 was the first programming language to introduce the concepts of objects, classes, and inheritance. However, SIMULA67 lacks encapsulation, so application code can access any of an object's components directly, resulting in tight coupling. SIMULA67 is described in BIRTWHISTLE et al. (1979).

SMALLTALK was the first pure object-oriented language, so pure in fact that *all* values are objects. Even commands are counted as objects (of class Block), and control structures like "if" and "while" are operations of that class. Thus SMALLTALK is very economical of concepts, but it is idiosyncratic with its strange syntax, dynamic typing, and dynamic scoping. See GOLDBERG and ROBSON (1989) for a very full account of SMALLTALK, including a language overview, programming examples, descriptions of all predefined classes, and implementation details.

EIFFEL was the first object-oriented language to demonstrate that the benefits of object-oriented programming can be achieved within a language that is statically typed and statically scoped. An overview of EIFFEL may be found in MEYER (1989), and a detailed account in MEYER (1988).

A full description of C++ may be found in STROUSTRUP (1997), and an extended account of its design and evolution in STROUSTRUP (1994). C++ is not a pure object-oriented language; indeed, it was deliberately designed to allow ordinary C-style programming. For an account of object-oriented programming as a discipline for programming in C++, see BOOCH (1987).

A whole library could be filled with all the books written about JAVA. The most accessible introduction is FLANAGAN (2002). The definitive description of JAVA is JOY et al. (2000).

For a fuller account of object-oriented programming in ADA95, see COHEN (1995).

For a more general overview of object-oriented programming, including its relationship to various programming languages, see COX (1986).

Exercises

Exercises for Section 12.1

*12.1.1 Using your favorite object-oriented language, design and implement a class Relation. Each Relation object should represent a finite binary relation, i.e., a set of pairs of objects. (See Section 15.1 for a discussion of relations.)

Exercises for Section 12.2

*12.2.1 Choose a small or medium-sized object-oriented program that you have designed. Diagram this program's architecture, along the lines of Figure 12.1.

Exercises for Section 12.3

12.3.1 Consider the C++ class Person of Example 12.4, the subclass Student of Example 12.5, and the following array:

```
Person* vets[100];
```

(a) Exactly what values may be stored in the array vets?

(b) Write a code fragment that prints the surname of every person in vets.

(c) Write a code fragment that prints the name and student id (where appropriate) of every person in vets.

(d) Write a code fragment that changes the degree program of every student in vets to "BVM".

12.3.2 Consider the C++ generic class Priority_Queue of Example 12.6.

(a) Modify the instantiation of the generic class to change the priority. Print jobs should be prioritized so that smaller jobs are serviced before larger ones.

(b) Using the following class:

```
class Date {
    int m, d;

    static bool before (Date date1, date2) {
        return (date1.m == date2.m ?
            date1.d < date2.d :
            date1.m < date2.m);
    }

    ...

}
```

instantiate the generic class to declare a priority queue q whose elements are Date objects prioritized by temporal order. Write code to add a few dates to q, in no particular order. In what order would these dates be removed from q?

12.3.3 Consider the C++ generic function swap of Example 12.7. If i1 and i2 are **int** variables, and p1 and p2 are Person variables, which of the following function calls are legal?

```
swap(i1, i2);
swap(p1, p2);
swap(i1, p1);
```

For each legal function call, state which type is substituted for the generic function's type parameter Item.

12.3.4 Finish the coding of the C++ spellchecker of Programs 12.1–12.4.

12.3.5 Modify the C++ spellchecker of Programs 12.1–12.4 to use a third dictionary, the *user dictionary*. Any unknown words accepted by the user are to be added to the user dictionary, which must be saved when the program finishes. The main dictionary is no longer to be updated.

Exercises for Section 12.4

*12.4.1 Every JAVA object is a heap variable (accessed through a pointer), while a C++ object may be either a global or local variable (accessed directly) or a heap variable (accessed through a pointer). What are the advantages and disadvantages of JAVA's inflexibility?

12.4.2 Write a JAVA method that computes both the minimum and maximum of an array of integers, like the C++ function of Example 12.1. Why is this awkward?

12.4.3 Consider the JAVA class Person and subclass Student of Example 12.9, and the following array:

```
Person[] vets = new Person[100];
```

(a) Exactly what values may be stored in the array vets?

(b) Write a code fragment that prints the surname of every person in vets.

(c) Write a code fragment that prints the name and student id (where appropriate) of every person in vets.

(d) Write a code fragment that changes the degree program of every student in vets to "BVM".

12.4.4 Finish the coding of the JAVA spellchecker of Programs 12.5–12.8.

12.4.5 Modify the JAVA spellchecker of Programs 12.5–12.8 to use a user dictionary, as in Exercise 12.3.5.

Exercises for Section 12.5

12.5.1 Consider the ADA95 class Person of Example 12.13, the subclass Student of Example 12.14, and the following array:

```
type Person_Access is access Person'class;
vets: array (0 .. 99) of Person_Access;
```

(a) Exactly what values may be stored in the array vets?

(b) Write a code fragment that prints the surname of every person in vets.

(c) Write a code fragment that prints the name and student id (where appropriate) of every person in `vets`.

(d) Write a code fragment that changes the degree program of every student in `vets` to "BVM".

*12.5.2 Design and implement an ADA95 spellchecker, along the lines of the C++ spellchecker (Programs 12.1–12.4) or the JAVA spellchecker (Programs 12.5–12.8).

Chapter 13

Concurrent programming

Concurrent programming is still quite immature, despite being nearly as old as programming itself, and many different approaches are being actively developed. One consequence is that concurrent programs must often be structured to suit a particular hardware architecture. Such programs do not usually adapt well to dissimilar architectures. Much research is aimed at solving this problem, which is one of the main obstacles in the way of much wider exploitation of concurrency.

This chapter presents what may be termed the "classical" approach to concurrent programming:

- It discusses issues arising from the interaction between concurrency and a number of other programming language features, particularly scope rules, exceptions, and object-orientation.

- It builds on the ideas of competition and communication introduced in Chapter 10, and shows how they are realized in ADA95 and JAVA.

- It illustrates the concurrency features of ADA95 in depth, by means of a case study: an implementation of the *banker's algorithm* for the avoidance of deadlock.

- It presents a number of issues in the practical implementation of concurrency on conventional computer hardware and operating systems.

13.1 Key concepts

Concurrent programming is so called because it allows the execution of commands to be overlapped, either by an arbitrary interleaving – multiprogramming – or by simultaneous execution on multiple CPUs – multiprocessing. (The word *concurrent* has Latin roots that literally mean "running together".)

The key concepts of concurrent programming are:

- parallel execution of two or more processes;
- inter-process synchronization;
- synchronized access to shared data by inter-process mutual exclusion;
- synchronized transfer of data by inter-process communication;

and, in more recent programming languages:

- concurrent control abstractions that support the above reliably.

Parallel execution is the essential difference between sequential and concurrent programming. Once we allow the ordering of events in the execution of a program to be weaker than a total ordering, all the consequences discussed in Section 10.3 can follow. The most profound among them are (i) the possibility that update operations on variables might fail to produce valid results, and (ii) the loss of determinism. These issues amplify each other, and have the potential for complete chaos.

Synchronization enables the programmer to ensure that processes interact with each other in an orderly manner, despite these difficulties. Lapses of synchronization are usually disastrous, causing sporadic and irreproducible failures.

Mutual exclusion of access to shared variables restores the semantics of variable access and update. This is achieved by synchronization operations allowing only one process to access a shared variable at any time. These operations are costly, and must be applied with total consistency; otherwise (eventual) program failure is inevitable. It is therefore desirable for high-level concurrent programming languages to offer a reliable, compiler-implemented means of mutual exclusion.

Communication provides a more general form of interaction between processes, because it applies as well in distributed systems as in centralized systems. Some concurrent programming languages (notably CSP and OCCAM) have been based entirely on communication, completely avoiding shared variables and their problems. However, in most concurrent languages, and in most language-independent frameworks for concurrent programming, communication is based on shared data and not *vice versa*.

Concurrent programming paradigms based on communication might dominate in the future, if CPU technology continues to outstrip storage technology, so that accessing a variable becomes, for all practical purposes, an exercise in data communication. Until then shared data will continue to be preferred, not least because it capitalizes on and extends (in a deceptively straightforward way) a conceptual model that all sequential programmers have thoroughly internalized.

Concurrent control abstractions promote reliable concurrent programming by taking much of the burden of synchronization into the programming language. The *conditional critical region* construct provides a high-level abstraction of both mutual exclusion and communication. The *monitor* construct offers similar advantages and adds data abstraction to the mix.

In this chapter we see how these key concepts are realized in ADA95 and in JAVA.

13.2   Pragmatics

The worst problems in concurrency arise from undisciplined access to shared variables by two or more processes. This adds synchronization problems to the other pragmatic issues created by *tight coupling*. The discussion in Section 11.2 touches on many relevant points, as they arise in the narrower context of sequential programming.

It is always a good idea to minimize the number of potentially shared variables. An ADA task module should be declared in the most global scope possible, so that the smallest set of nonlocal variables is accessible from within the task. When nonlocal data must be used within a task module, it may be possible to declare it constant. Since such data cannot be updated, it can always be accessed safely. A JAVA thread in a class nested within a method may safely access constant components and method parameters, but is not allowed to access other nonlocals.

In sequential programming the problems raised by global variables are mitigated by *encapsulation* and *data abstraction*.

Server processes offer services for use by other processes that are termed ***clients***. (Tasks that both offer and use services are also useful, for example to delegate work on a basis of "divide and conquer". We might call them ***brokers***.) Data is safest when it is totally encapsulated inside a server task, so that only the server has access to it and no issues of concurrent access can arise. This replaces competition and mutual exclusion by encapsulation and communication. (See Example 10.11.) However, the cost of running a task merely in order to serve up a set of data, and the cost of communication by rendezvous, may be high enough to discourage this program structure, despite its great advantages.

ADA packages (with their private types and private variables) and JAVA classes (with their protected and private components) provide powerful mechanisms by which encapsulation can be achieved in sequential programs. In concurrent programs we also need to be able to ensure that operations on encapsulated data are performed by only one process at a time. Combining encapsulation with mutual exclusion leads to the *monitor* concept (see Section 10.6.2). JAVA provides a restricted implementation of the monitor idea in the form of classes with *synchronized* operations. ADA95 goes a lot further, with its *protected types*. (In ADA95, the term *protected* implies automatic synchronization, not restricted scope as it does in JAVA.) These intrinsically concurrent features of the two languages are described in Sections 13.3 and 13.4, respectively.

Another issue in the design of concurrent programming languages is the treatment of exceptions. In sequential programs, exceptions are ***synchronous*** – they are thrown either explicitly, or as the immediate effect of executing a command that encounters some abnormal situation. Concurrent language designers must also deal with the possibility of ***asynchronous*** exceptions, thrown in one process by a command executed in a different process. In most respects an asynchronous exception has the properties of an interrupt, with all of the problems that implies. For that reason they have been excluded from the design of ADA. JAVA, too, does without asynchronous exceptions, apart from two peculiar inconsistencies described in Section 13.4.1.

The most complex and least developed aspect of present concurrent programming languages is the relationship between their concurrency features and their object-oriented features. Ideally, the two would be orthogonal, and capable of easy use in any reasonable combination. Neither ADA nor JAVA has attained this degree of integration, and, as a result, both languages still have a number of rough edges. Collectively, these are known as the ***inheritance anomaly***. The main problem is that there is no completely convincing model for inheriting synchronization properties. If a class inherits from its superclass, and either or both have synchronizing methods, it is often unclear whether that can be managed without conflicts that might cause deadlock, or that might force some of the methods of the superclass to be overridden, or even rewritten.

EXAMPLE 13.1   An inheritance anomaly

Suppose that we are given a class Q. Each object of class Q is a queue, equipped with add and remove methods, where remove throws an exception when the queue is empty.

We are now required to write a subclass WQ, with a remove method that waits until the queue is nonempty. Necessarily, Q's remove method must be overridden in WQ: WQ's remove method waits on a "queue nonempty" condition that must be signaled by add. However, Q's add method does not do any such thing, and so it must be overridden too. With both add and remove being overridden, one might wonder whether inheriting from Q offers any real advantage.

In ADA95 synchronization is dealt with, most naturally, using protected types. Object classes in ADA95 are represented by *tagged* types, which have no intrinsic synchronization properties. So, inheritance and mutual exclusion are disjoint features, making it cumbersome to apply both in the same data structure.

JAVA bases its thread model firmly on object-orientation: the Thread class, like every other, is a subclass of Object. If a class *C* inherits a synchronized method, that method is also synchronized in *C*. So far so good. Unfortunately, this does not preclude difficulties similar to that described in Example 13.1. And there are other issues.

- JAVA lacks multiple inheritance, so there is a problem if a subclass of Thread needs to inherit not only from Thread but also from a more application-specific superclass.

- Object has (invisible) components that are used to implement synchronization, and these are inherited by every object of every class. So the language imposes an overhead on all objects, in order to provide synchronization for the few that need it. This contravenes a basic principle of good programming language design.

In short, concurrency and object-orientation in both ADA95 and JAVA are rather like oil and water. They do not mix well, although they can be combined with the application of some hard work and the help of some extra ingredients.

13.3 Case study: ADA95

This section describes the most important concurrent control abstractions of ADA95: those that support the key concepts discussed in Section 13.1 – process creation and termination, mutual exclusion, and inter-process communication.

13.3.1 Process creation and termination

In ADA, a running task is created and started simply by declaring (or allocating) a value of a task type. A task terminates normally when it completes the last command in its body.

But server tasks often execute infinite loops, so as to be able to accept an unbounded number of entry calls, and they never stop in this way. A task can find out how many calls are queued on each of its entries, so a server could stop when all its entry queues are empty. The problem is that clients might be doing other things presently, but will later make more calls to these entries. If the server terminates in the meantime, such calls will fail. To deal with this "distributed termination" problem, ADA lets a task stipulate that, as an alternative to waiting for an entry call, it is willing to terminate – if, and only if, all potential clients are inactive, and therefore unable to make any further calls on its entries. All the tasks in this "willing" condition then terminate together.

EXAMPLE 13.2 An event task type

A way of proving the completeness of the concurrent features of a language is to show, somewhat perversely, that they can be used to implement the low-level concurrent primitives described in Chapter 10. Here we have a server task module that implements the Event type, with operations wait and signal, as defined in Section 10.5.4.

```
task type Event is
   entry wait;
   entry signal;
end Event;

task body Event is
begin
   loop
(1)    select
          accept signal;
          for i in 1 .. wait'count loop
(2)        select
              accept wait;
           else
              null;
           end select;
          end loop;
       or
(3)       terminate;
       end select;
    end loop;
end Event;
```

An Event task lets clients wait for the next occurrence of a signal, and then allows every client waiting for that signal to proceed. This is achieved by holding clients in the entry queue for wait. When signal is called, the wait entry queue is cleared by accepting every call.

The *selective wait* command starting at point (1) has a *terminate alternative* at point (3). If no potential client is active when this selective wait is executed, the terminate alternative is chosen and the Event server halts normally.

The value of wait'count is the number of tasks queued on wait, so the loop accepts every outstanding call. The accept command for wait is enclosed in a selective wait starting at point (2). The selective wait's else-part is executed if there is no outstanding call in the queue. In this case no action is taken. This is made necessary by the fact that a client might time-out or be aborted, thereby withdrawing its call on `wait`, after `wait'count` is evaluated but before its entry call is accepted.

It is sometimes necessary for a coordinator process to **cancel** other processes (i.e., make them terminate). One possibility is for each task to provide an entry that requests the task to stop. A difficulty here is that there might be pending calls from client tasks to some of its other entries, so that stopping is deferred until those calls are serviced. Another problem is that a rogue task might never accept calls on its "request-stop" entry. To deal with these issues, some way of *forcibly* terminating a task is needed.

The **abort command** lets one task cancel another. To prevent an aborted task from malfunctioning in a way that damages the rest of the system – as it might, if stopped while updating a system data structure such as an entry queue – ADA defines a set of *abort-deferred* constructs. These are operations that are guaranteed to complete before the abort takes effect. This in itself is not enough to ensure that application-level finalization (such as the closing of all the task's open files) is carried out, but it does ensure that killing a task does not cause unbounded havoc in the underlying system.

The parent of a process may need to await its completion. This is provided in many operating systems by the low-level `join` primitive (see Section 10.5.1). In ADA, each task has a *master*, which is the scope in which it was declared (roughly speaking). Control does not leave a master until all its child tasks have terminated; so task creation and termination are forced to be properly nested.

13.3.2   Mutual exclusion

ADA95 offers a powerful feature for mutual exclusion in its **protected modules**. These are similar in appearance to packages and tasks, and combine most of the advantages of monitors and conditional critical regions. Specifically, protected modules implement both automatic mutual exclusion and implicit signaling of conditions, together with simple encapsulation of data.

Encapsulated data may be operated on by public procedures of the protected module. Proper procedures of a protected object may inspect and/or update its encapsulated data, and automatically exclude each other. Function procedures of a protected object may only inspect the encapsulated data. (In this respect they are a much purer realization of the function concept than ordinary function procedures in ADA.) The benefit is that multiple protected function calls can be concurrently executed, in the same protected object, completely safely. However, protected procedure calls exclude protected function calls, and *vice versa*.

A protected module can be either a single protected object or a protected type, allowing many protected objects to be created. A protected module can declare only public procedures and entries, and its body may contain only the bodies of procedures and entries. The protected data is declared after **private**: it is therefore accessible only within the protected module's body.

EXAMPLE 13.3   A simple protected type

The following is a simple protected type that encapsulates a variable and provides operations to fetch and store its value. It can be used to make fetching and storing atomic, for types that cannot be declared to be atomic. Here is the protected type's specification:

```
protected type Protected_Item is

   procedure store (value : in Item);

   function fetch return Item;

private
   variable : Item;
end Protected_Item;
```

And here is the protected type's body:

```
protected body Protected_Item is

   procedure store (value: in Item) is
   begin
      variable := value;
   end store;

   function fetch return Item is
   begin
      return variable;
   end fetch;

end Protected_Item;
```

The variable declaration:

```
x, y : Protected_Item;
```

creates two variables of type Protected_Item. They can be used thus:

```
it : Item;
...
it := x.fetch;
y.store(it);
x.store(it);
```

Note that Protected_Item does not prevent a fetch operation on a variable that has no value stored in it.

Despite being similar to packages in overall structure, neither tasks nor protected objects can themselves be generic. However, they can be parameterized, in effect, by nesting within a generic package. For example, Protected_Item could be declared within a generic package taking Item as a parameter.

13.3.3   Admission control

Nondeterministic choice is provided in ADA by the selective wait command, which allows a task to rendezvous by accepting a call to any of several specified entries, with the possibility of taking alternative action when no call can be accepted.

Many entry calls can be accepted only when a precondition has been established. This need for **admission control** is met by allowing an alternative in a selective wait to have a **guard**, a boolean expression whose value determines whether the alternative is *open*. Only open alternatives (i.e., those with true guards) are taken into consideration when selecting the one to be executed. An alternative with no guard is always open. The task may execute any one of the open alternatives, so the selective wait command introduces bounded nondeterminism.

EXAMPLE 13.4   A semaphore task type

The following ADA task module implements a semaphore abstract type. Here is its specification:

```
task type Semaphore_Task is

    entry initialize (n : in Integer);

    entry wait;

    entry signal;

end Semaphore_Task;
```

And here is its body:

```
task body Semaphore_Task is
  count : Integer;
  -- On completion of each entry call, count = initial + signals − waits.
begin
  accept initialize (n : in Integer) do
    count := n;
    -- sets initial to n, signals to 0, and waits to 0
  end initialize;
  loop
    select
      when count > 0 => accept wait;
      count := count - 1;
      -- increments waits
    or
      accept signal;
      count := count + 1;
      -- increments signals
    end select;
  end loop;
end Semaphore_Task;
```

After accepting the priming call to initialize, a Semaphore_Task accepts calls to either wait or signal in any order, so long as the semaphore invariant (*waits ≤ initial + signals*) would not be violated by completing the call. When count is 0, completing a call to wait would violate the invariant; so the guard "**when** count > 0" defers acceptance of any pending calls. Calls on wait become acceptable again as soon as a call of `signal` is accepted that leaves `count` positive, making the guard condition true.

This task type could be used as follows:

```
nr_full, nr_free : Semaphore_Task;
...
nr_full.initialize(0);
nr_free.initialize(10);
...
nr_free.wait;
nr_full.signal;
```

Example 13.4 shows how easy it is to write server tasks that safely manage locally declared data on behalf of multiple clients. There is no need for mutual exclusion of access to the managed data, because it is never accessed concurrently.

Protected objects, also, can declare entries. Like a task entry, a protected entry can employ a guard to control admission. This provides automatic signaling, and ensures that when a protected entry call is accepted, its guard condition is true. Like a protected procedure, a protected entry operates under automatic mutual exclusion.

EXAMPLE 13.5   A single-slot buffer protected type

The task type shown in Example 10.11 implements a single-slot buffer abstract type. Here is the specification of a protected type with the same functionality:

```
protected type Protected_Buffer is

   entry send_message (item : in Message);

   entry receive_message (item : out Message);

private
   buffer : Message;
   bufferIsEmpty : Boolean := true;
end Protected_Buffer;
```

And here is the corresponding body:

```
protected body Protected_Buffer is

   entry send_message (item : in Message)
      when bufferIsEmpty is
   begin
      buffer := item;
      bufferIsEmpty := false;
   end send_message;

   entry receive_message (item : out Message)
      when not bufferIsEmpty is
```

```
        begin
           item := buffer;
           bufferIsEmpty := true;
        end receive_message;

    end Protected_Buffer;
```

Note how the guards, using the private state variable `bufferIsEmpty`, ensure that messages are alternately stored and fetched, and that no attempt can be made to fetch from an empty buffer. Note also the absence of explicit signaling and mutual exclusion constructs.

The variable declaration:

```
    urgent, pending : Protected_Buffer;
```

creates two variables of type `Protected_Buffer`. They can be used to store and fetch messages, thus:

```
    msg : Message;
    ...
    pending.send_message(msg);
    pending.receive_message(msg);
    urgent.send_message(msg);
```

where "`pending.send_message(msg);`" calls the entry `send_message` in the protected object `pending`, passing the value of `msg` as an argument.

The notation for calling a protected entry is exactly the same as that for calling a task entry. This makes it easy to replace one implementation of the abstract type by the other, the calling code being unaffected.

As an alternative to the server task shown in Example 13.4, a semaphore can be implemented as a protected object, with significant efficiency gains.

EXAMPLE 13.6   A semaphore protected type

The `initialize` and `signal` operations have no conditional component, so they are implemented as protected procedures, but the `wait` operation must be guarded and is therefore implemented as an entry. Here is the protected type's specification:

```
    protected type Semaphore_Protected_Type is

        procedure initialize (n : in Integer);

        entry wait;

        procedure signal;

    private
        count : Integer := 0;
        -- On completion of each entry call, count = initial + signals − waits.
    end Semaphore_Protected_Type;
```

And here is its body:

```
protected body Semaphore_Protected_Type is

    procedure initialize (n : in Integer) is
    begin
        count := n;
        -- sets initial to n , signals to 0, and waits to 0
    end initialize;

    entry wait
        when count > 0 is
    begin
        count := count - 1;
        -- increments waits
    end wait;

    procedure signal is
    begin
        count := count + 1;
        -- increments signals
    end signal;

end Semaphore_Protected_Type;
```

Unlike the task type in Example 13.4, this protected type does not enforce the requirement that initialize be called before any wait or signal operation. (Instead, count is given a default value.) Restoring this functionality is left as an exercise for the reader.

This protected type is used in the same way as the semaphore task type:

```
nr_full, nr_free : Semaphore_Protected_Type;
...
nr_full.initialize(0);
nr_free.initialize(10);
...
nr_free.wait;
nr_full.signal;
```

In Example 13.6, the guard on the wait entry accesses a private variable of the protected type. Sometimes an admission control criterion depends on the arguments of the entry, but guards cannot access entry parameters. (Allowing this would force the implementation to scan all of the entry queues in their entirety every time a protected operation terminated.) Instead, a means is provided by which an entry, having accepted a call it is unable to progress, can **requeue** the call (either in its own entry queue, or on another entry with a compatible parameter list). This provides the entry with a way of deferring the call until some later time, when it has more chance of being able to proceed.

Again for the sake of efficiency, a further rule (the "internal progress first" rule) is imposed on the acceptance of entry calls. It requires all calls to open entries that are made from inside the protected object to be accepted before any calls made to those entries from outside. Because of this rule, simply requeuing a call on the same entry could lead to an infinite loop. Requeuing instead on a private entry that exists solely to provide a "holding queue" is a common expedient.

EXAMPLE 13.7   A simple scheduler protected type

A scheduler maintains data structures modeling the allocation state of the managed resources. Processes may call scheduling operations concurrently, so it is natural to implement a scheduler as a protected object encapsulating the resource management data. The following package, Resource_Definitions, implements a simple scheduler, allowing processes to acquire resources for exclusive use.

The scheduling implemented by Resource_Definitions is trivial: a "first-come first-served" queuing policy is adopted, and free resources are granted on request. Requests for a busy resource are delayed until the resource is relinquished.

Here is the package specification; since the await_change entry is intended to be called only in the body of the scheduler, it is declared private:

```
package Resource_Definitions is

   type Resource_Name is (floppy, dvd, modem);

   protected Scheduler is

      entry acquire (resource : in Resource_Name);

      procedure relinquish (
                     resource : in Resource_Name);

   private

      entry await_change (resource : in Resource_Name);

      acquiring : Boolean := true;

   end Scheduler;

end Resource_Definitions;
```

Calling the acquire entry requests the allocation of a resource; if it is not available the calling task must be blocked. This is implemented by requeuing the call on a private entry, await_change.

The relinquish procedure releases a resource; it must unblock any task waiting to acquire it and does this by releasing all the tasks queued on await_change, which requeues them on acquire.

```
package body Resource_Definitions is

   is_free : array (Resource_Name) of Boolean
        := (Resource_Name => true);

   protected body Scheduler is

      entry acquire (resource : in Resource_Name)
        when acquiring is
```

```
begin
  if is_free(resource) then
     is_free(resource) := false;
  else
     requeue await_change;
  end if;
end acquire;

procedure relinquish (
                resource : in Resource_Name) is
begin
  is_free(resource) := true;
  acquiring := false;
end relinquish;

entry await_change (resource : in Resource_Name)
  when not acquiring is
begin
  if await_change'count = 0 then
     acquiring := true;
  end if;
  requeue acquire;
end await_change;

  end Scheduler;

end Resource_Definitions;
```

Note that the is_free array is not inside the protected object. But it *is* encapsulated within the package body, therefore it is accessible only to the protected operations of Scheduler, and thus is accessed safely.

In the Scheduler protected object of Example 13.7 there is a limited amount of busy waiting, as unsatisfied requests are shuttled from acquire to await_change and back. The fundamental reason for this is that several different conditions share the same acquire entry, which necessarily has a rather unspecific guard. A way to avoid this is to have a separate acquire entry for each resource, along the following lines:

```
entry acquire_floppy when is_free(floppy) is
begin
  is_free(floppy) := false;
end acquire_floppy;

...

entry acquire_modem when is_free(modem) is
begin
  is_free(modem) := false;
end acquire_modem;
```

In this very restricted case, with a small, fixed number of resources under control, such a solution is of unrivaled simplicity and elegance. But it does not scale well, and it would not be sensible to continue in this manner for hundreds (or even dozens) of different resources. What we need is something akin to an array of entries.

ADA provides just such a feature in the *entry family*. This is in effect an array of entries. Each entry family call computes a value that indexes the array and thus selects a particular entry to be called. The body of the entry contains an implicit iteration over the index range, binding a control variable to each value of the index range in turn. Unlike an ordinary parameter of an entry, this control variable can be used in a guard. This provides just the flexibility we need to code a simple `acquire` operation without busy waiting.

EXAMPLE 13.8   A protected type with an entry family

Here we use an entry family indexed by the `Resource_Name` type, so that there is one entry for each resource, however many of them there may be. (For the sake of later explanations, the code includes comments that we will use to trace its flow of control.) Here is the package specification (`Resource_Name` is the type of the `acquire` entry family's index range):

```
package Resource_Definitions is

    type Resource_Name is (floppy, dvd, modem);

    protected Scheduler is

        entry acquire (Resource_Name);

        procedure relinquish (
                        resource : in Resource_Name);

    end Scheduler;

end Resource_Definitions;
```

And here is the corresponding package body:

```
package body Resource_Definitions is

    is_free : array (Resource_Name) of Boolean
        := (Resource_Name => true);

    protected body Scheduler is

        entry acquire (for resource in Resource_Name)
        -- the process bids for the resource
            when is_free(resource) is
        begin
            is_free(resource) := false;
            -- the process has the resource
        end acquire;

        procedure relinquish (
                        resource : in Resource_Name) is
```

```
      begin
         is_free(resource) := true;
         -- the process has given up the resource
      end relinquish;

   end Scheduler;

end Resource_Definitions;
```

The scheduler can now be invoked as follows:

```
   use Resource_Definitions;
   ...
   Scheduler.acquire(floppy);
   Scheduler.acquire(dvd);
```

In summary, ADA95 task types and protected types combine and improve upon the best properties of monitors and conditional critical regions:

- Safe use of shared data is guaranteed by a combination of encapsulation and automatic mutual exclusion.
- Admission control is automatic, preconditions being made manifest in guards whose evaluation is driven by updates to the relevant variables, and without needing signaling operations that would create tight inter-task coupling.

13.3.4 Scheduling away deadlock

This section brings many of our themes together in an extended series of examples based on the banker's algorithm for the scheduled avoidance of deadlock. It provides a realistic setting in which to display the concurrent control abstractions of ADA95.

Firstly, here is an example showing how easy it is to cause deadlock.

EXAMPLE 13.9 Inevitable deadlock

The following procedure `trouble`, which is intended to be called concurrently by several tasks, uses the package `Resource_Definitions` of Example 13.8 to provide mutual exclusion:

```
   use Resource_Definitions;
   procedure trouble (res1, res2 : in Resource_Name) is
   begin
      Scheduler.acquire(res1);
      Scheduler.acquire(res2);
      ... -- here is the critical section
```

```
        Scheduler.relinquish(res2);
        Scheduler.relinquish(res1);
end trouble;
```

The following program calls `trouble` and deadlocks:

```
procedure main is
begin

    task worker1;
    task worker2;

    task body worker1 is
    begin
        -- worker 1 is getting into trouble ...
        trouble(floppy, modem);
        -- ... worker 1 is now out of trouble
    end worker1;

    task body worker2 is
    begin
        -- worker 2 is getting into trouble ...
        trouble(modem, floppy);
        -- ... worker 2 is now out of trouble
    end worker2;

begin
    null; -- at this point await termination of both workers
end;
```

The following trace is typical, and shows the program running into difficulties:

worker 2 is getting into trouble ...
worker 1 is getting into trouble ...
worker 2 bids for the modem
worker 1 bids for the floppy
worker 2 has the modem
worker 1 has the floppy
worker 2 bids for the floppy *(but worker 1 has it)*
worker 1 bids for the modem *(but worker 2 has it)*

Deadlock has struck!

The next example shows how to prevent deadlock by total resource ordering.

EXAMPLE 13.10   Deadlock prevention by resource ordering

As described in Section 10.3.3, we can prevent deadlocks by imposing a total ordering on resources and by insisting that they be acquired consistently with that ordering. Here we adapt the `trouble` procedure using this idea. It first sorts `res1` and `res2` into `r1` and `r2`, which can be used compatibly with the total ordering:

```
procedure trouble (res1, res2 : in Resource_Name) is
  r1 : constant Resource_Name
        := Resource_Name'min(res1, res2);
  r2 : constant Resource_Name
        := Resource_Name'max(res1, res2);
  -- the canonical ordering of resources is r1 followed by r2
begin
  Scheduler.acquire(r1);
  Scheduler.acquire(r2);
  ... -- here is the critical section
  Scheduler.relinquish(r2);
  Scheduler.relinquish(r1);

end;
```

Here is a typical trace of this version in action:

worker 2 is getting into trouble ...
worker 1 is getting into trouble ...
worker 2 bids for the floppy
worker 2 has the floppy
worker 1 bids for the floppy *(but worker 2 has it)*
worker 2 bids for the modem
worker 2 has the modem
worker 2 has given up the modem
worker 2 has given up the floppy
worker 1 has the floppy
... worker 2 is now out of trouble
worker 1 bids for the modem
worker 1 has the modem
worker 1 has given up the modem
worker 1 has given up the floppy
... worker 1 is now out of trouble
end of run

Now the program is deadlock-free and runs to completion.

The banker's algorithm is a more powerful resource management API than the simple package declared in Example 13.8, being capable of resolving conflicting demands for resources and ensuring that no deadlock results. It does this by suspending, temporarily, processes whose demands cannot yet be met without risking deadlock.

Program 13.1 declares the protected object Avoiding_Deadlock. It is nested in a generic package (see Section 7.1.1) named Banker. This allows it to be instantiated for a variety of different resource and process types, thus maximizing its reusability. (The notation "(<>)" in the specification of the generic formal type parameters Process_Id and Resource_Id indicates that the corresponding argument types used when instantiating the package must be *discrete primitive* types, such as integer or enumeration types.)

```
generic
  type Process_Id is (<>);
  type Resource_Id is (<>);
  type Inventory is array (Resource_Id) of Integer;
  capital : in Inventory;
  no_resource : in Resource_Id'Base; -- null id
package Banker is

    -- An implementation of E.W. Dijkstra's "banker's algorithm" for the scheduled
    -- avoidance of deadlock.

    protected Avoiding_Deadlock is

      procedure register (proc_id : in Process_Id;
                          claim : in Inventory);
      -- Inform the scheduler of the maximum amount of each resource that the
      -- task proc_id may claim.

      entry acquire (Process_Id) (res_id : in Resource_Id;
                          amount : in Positive);
      -- Wait, if necessary, for exclusive access to amount units of the resource
      -- identified by res_id.

      procedure relinquish (proc_id : in Process_Id;
                          res_id : in Resource_Id;
                          amount : in Positive);
      -- Give up exclusive access to amount units of the resource
      -- identified by res_id.

      procedure deregister (proc_id : in Process_Id);
      -- Inform the scheduler that the task proc_id is no longer in contention
      -- for resources.

    end Avoiding_Deadlock;

  end Banker;
```

Program 13.1 Specification of the banker's algorithm.

The acquire operation simulates the effect of allowing the demanded allocation of resource. If this leads to a state that cannot deadlock, that allocation is performed. Otherwise, the caller is suspended by a **requeue** operation until the state of the system changes and the caller's resource demand can be reconsidered. This is repeated as often as necessary. An outline of the algorithm might be sketched as follows:

```
entry acquire (for proc_id in Process_Id) (
              res_id : Resource_Id;
              amount : Positive)
  when the claim of process proc_id should be considered is
begin
  take amount of the resource res_id from the system state ;
```

```
        if the resulting state is deadlock-free then
            choose the next process with a claim to be considered;
            return; -- process proc_id has got the resource
        end if;
        -- The claim might deadlock, so abandon this attempt:
        give back amount of the resource res_id to the system state;
        choose the next process with a claim to be considered;
        -- N.B. process proc_id is now ineligible to be considered,
        -- so the following requeue does not cause an infinite loop:
        requeue acquire (proc_id); -- try again later
    end acquire;
```

Private procedures of Banker implement the pseudocode operations invoked above. They work on data describing the allocation state of the system that is also private to the body of Banker, and can therefore be accessed only by its private procedures. Since the latter can be called only via the public operations of Avoiding_Deadlock, they work safely.

Admission control is vital in acquire. Before requeuing a call that makes a presently unsatisfiable request, it is essential to ensure that it does not cause an infinite loop. This is also where fairness is brought to bear. Each time a new claim is made, or the allocation state changes, the scheduler chooses the next eligible process in turn, setting its identifier in the variable next_contender. (An eligible process is one that has registered and does not have a request known to be presently unsatisfiable.)

The guard condition of acquire (proc_id = next_contender) ensures that all processes are considered in a *round-robin* (which is inherently fair) and that no requeued call is considered until all competing demands are taken into account. See Program 13.2(a–e).

The code in Program 13.2 neither detects nor deals with a number of possible errors that might arise. Rectifying this defect is set as Exercise 13.3.3.

Using Banker we can program a version of trouble that is guaranteed to be deadlock-free. First we instantiate it with the types we need. See Program 13.3.

A typical trace from this version might go as follows:

```
worker 2 is getting into trouble . . .
worker 1 is getting into trouble . . .
worker 2 notifies its claim for floppy and modem
worker 1 notifies its claim for floppy and modem
worker 2 bids for the modem
worker 1 bids for the floppy
worker 2 has the modem
worker 1 waits for the floppy (because to grant it now might cause deadlock)
worker 2 bids for the floppy
worker 2 has the floppy
worker 2 has given up the floppy
worker 1 bids for the floppy
worker 2 has given up the modem
```

```
package body Banker is

  -- Two useful, but boring, procedures:

  procedure credit (quantity : in out Integer;
                    amount : in Positive) is
  begin
    quantity := quantity + amount;
  end credit;

  procedure debit (quantity : in out Integer;
                   amount : in Positive) is
  begin
    quantity := quantity - amount;
  end debit;

  -- The following data describe the system's current allocation state:

  none : constant Inventory := (Resource_Id => 0);

  type Process_Account is
       record
          claim : Inventory := none;
          -- sets a bound on the amount of each resource that the process may
          -- have on loan at any time
          loan : Inventory := none;
          -- gives the amounts allocated to the process
          can_complete : Boolean := false;
          -- true if the process can terminate
       end record;

  type Current_Account is
       array (Process_Id) of Process_Account;

  type System_State is
       record
          balance : Inventory := capital;
          -- gives the amounts not presently on loan
          exposure : Current_Account;
          -- gives the position of every process
       end record;

  system : System_State;

  procedure take_out_loan (proc_id : in Process_Id;
                   res_id : in Resource_Id;
                   amount : in Positive) is
  begin
    debit(system.balance(res_id), amount);
    credit(system.exposure(proc_id).loan(res_id), amount);
    debit(system.exposure(proc_id).claim(res_id), amount);
  end take_out_loan;
```

Program 13.2(a) Implementation of the banker's algorithm.

```
procedure give_back_loan (proc_id : in Process_Id;
             res_id : in Resource_Id;
             amount : in Positive) is
begin
 credit(system.balance(res_id), amount);
 debit(system.exposure(proc_id).loan(res_id), amount);
 credit(system.exposure(proc_id).claim(res_id), amount);
end give_back_loan;

function completion_is_possible (
             claim, balance : Inventory)
    return Boolean is
begin
  for r in Resource_Id loop
    if claim(r) > balance(r) then
       return false;
    end if;
  end loop;
  return true;
end completion_is_possible;

procedure simulate_future_demands (
             state : in out System_State) is
  stuck : Boolean;
begin
  loop
    stuck := true;
    for p in Process_Id loop
      declare
        a : Process_Account renames
            state.exposure(p);
      begin
        if not a.can_complete and then
            completion_is_possible(a.claim,
                state.balance)
        then
          for r in Resource_Id loop
            credit(state.balance(r), a.loan(r));
          end loop;
          a.can_complete := true;
          stuck := false;
        end if;
      end;
    end loop;   -- over Process_Id
    exit when stuck;
  end loop;
end simulate_future_demands;
```

Program 13.2(b) Implementation of the banker's algorithm (continued).

```
function cannot_deadlock return Boolean is
  state : System_State := system;
begin
  simulate_future_demands(state);
  return (capital = state.balance);
end cannot_deadlock;

type Set_Of_Process_Id is
    array (Process_Id) of Boolean;

all_processes : constant Set_Of_Process_Id
    := (Process_Id => true);
no_processes : constant Set_Of_Process_Id
    := (Process_Id => false);

is_ready : Set_Of_Process_Id := all_processes;
-- indicates whether each process must wait for a resource that was unavailable
-- at its last attempt

is_registered : Set_Of_Process_Id :=  no_processes;
-- shows whether each process has registered a claim

next_contender : Process_Id := Process_Id'first;
-- the next process to be admitted to the scheduler

procedure choose_next_contender (
              is_eligible : in Set_Of_Process_Id) is
  next : Process_Id := next_contender;
begin
  for p in Process_Id loop
    if next = Process_Id'last then
      next := Process_Id'first;
    else
      next := Process_Id'succ(next);
    end if;
    if is_eligible(next) then
      next_contender := next;
      return;
    end if;
  end loop;
end choose_next_contender;
```

Program 13.2(c) Implementation of the banker's algorithm (continued).

worker 1 has the floppy *(it cannot deadlock now)*
... worker 2 is now out of trouble
worker 1 bids for the modem
worker 1 has the modem
worker 1 has given up the modem
worker 1 has given up the floppy
... worker 1 is now out of trouble
end of run

```
-- The scheduler itself follows:

protected body Avoiding_Deadlock is

  procedure register (proc_id : in Process_Id;
                      claim : in Inventory) is
  begin
    system.exposure(proc_id).claim := claim;
    is_registered(proc_id) := true;
  end register;

  entry acquire (for proc_id in Process_Id) (
                    res_id : Resource_Id;
                    amount : Positive)
    when proc_id = next_contender is
  begin
    -- Grab the resource and update the system state:
    take_out_loan(proc_id, res_id, amount);
    -- Return if the result is deadlock-free:
    if cannot_deadlock then
      -- Progress the round-robin of contenders:
      choose_next_contender(is_ready and
          is_registered);
      return;
    end if;
    -- Abandon the attempt, restore the system state, and wait for a change:
    give_back_loan(proc_id, res_id, amount);
    is_ready(proc_id) := false;
    -- Progress the round-robin of contenders:
    choose_next_contender(is_ready and is_registered);
    -- Put the client back in the entry queue:
    requeue acquire (proc_id);
  end acquire;

  procedure relinquish (proc_id : in Process_Id;
                        res_id : in Resource_Id;
                        amount : in Positive) is
  begin
    give_back_loan(proc_id, res_id, amount);
    -- Make all waiting processes eligible to compete:
    is_ready := all_processes;
    -- Progress the round-robin of contenders:
    choose_next_contender(is_registered);
  end relinquish;
```

Program 13.2(d) Implementation of the banker's algorithm (continued).

13.4 Case study: JAVA

This section describes the concurrent control abstractions of JAVA. Like ADA95, JAVA takes inspiration from monitors and conditional critical regions. Unlike ADA95, JAVA builds its concurrency features on an object-oriented foundation.

```
      procedure deregister (proc_id : in Process_Id) is
      begin
        system.exposure(proc_id).claim := none;
        is_registered(proc_id) := false;
        if is_registered /= no_processes then
          -- Progress the round-robin of contenders, in case process proc_id
          -- was next_contender:
          choose_next_contender(is_ready and
              is_registered);
        else
          -- No processes remain in contention, so set the system back to its
          -- initial state:
          is_ready := all_processes;
          next_contender := Process_Id'first;
          return;
        end if;
      end deregister;

    end Avoiding_Deadlock;

  end Banker;
```

Program 13.2(e) Implementation of the banker's algorithm (continued).

13.4.1 Process creation and termination

A JAVA thread is an object. JAVA provides a Thread class equipped with a run method, and also a Runnable interface that specifies a run method. The class of a thread object must be a subclass of Thread, or a class that implements the Runnable interface; in either case, the thread's class must define its own run method. A thread is created like any object by the **new** allocator; this produces a dormant thread *t* that is activated by calling *t*.start(), which in turn calls the run method. The thread terminates normally when its run method returns.

A thread may be created with *daemon* status. The run-time environment kills all daemon threads without further ado, if it finds that all non-daemon threads have terminated. Nothing prevents a daemon thread from being killed when it is performing a critical operation, such as updating a file; so this feature is potentially very unsafe.

The *t*.join() method lets one thread await the termination of another thread.

As part of the recommended mechanism for cancellation, each thread has a boolean *interruption status* that indicates whether an attempt has been made to interrupt it. Normally, the method *t*.interrupt() has the effect of setting the interruption status of *t* to true, but if *t* is blocked in any of the wait, sleep, or join methods then it is forced to throw InterruptedException and its interruption status is set to false. (A thread awaiting entry to a synchronized construct is not so interrupted.) A thread is equipped with the interrupted() method, which returns its own interruption status, resetting it to false as a side effect. By checking its interruption status from time to time, and by catching

```
package Types is
  type Process_Name is (process1, process2);
  type Resource_Base is (nil_id, floppy, dvd, modem);
  subtype Resource_Name is
      Resource_Base range floppy .. modem;
  type Stock is array (Resource_Name) of Integer;
  wealth : constant Stock := (1, 1, 1);
end Types;

use Types;
package Manager is new Banker(
    Process_Id  => Process_Name,
    Resource_Id => Resource_Name,
    Inventory   => Stock,
    capital     => wealth,
    no_resource => nil_id);

use Manager;
procedure trouble (res1, res2 : in Resource_Name;
              proc_id : in Process_Name) is
begin
  Avoiding_Deadlock.register(proc_id,
      (floppy => 1, dvd => 0, modem => 1));
  Avoiding_Deadlock.acquire(proc_id) (res1, 1);
  Avoiding_Deadlock.acquire(proc_id) (res2, 1);
  -- ... here is the critical section
  Avoiding_Deadlock.relinquish(proc_id, res2, 1);
  Avoiding_Deadlock.relinquish(proc_id, res1, 1);
  Avoiding_Deadlock.deregister(proc_id);
end;
```

Program 13.3 Using the banker's algorithm.

InterruptedException, a thread can see whether its cancellation has been requested, and take appropriate action.

The history of cancellation mechanisms in JAVA is not a happy one:

- Originally, JAVA proposed the t.destroy() method to kill t immediately, but it was never implemented. Immediate termination of a thread with exclusive access to shared data would leave the data locked. Any other thread that later attempted exclusive access to that data would hang up.

- The t.stop() method, which forces t to throw the ThreadDeath exception, causes mutual exclusion to be prematurely relinquished. But the atomicity afforded by mutual exclusion is thereby lost, so other threads might see the shared data in an inconsistent state. Not surprisingly, stop has now been "deprecated".

These points emphasize that concurrency has a profound effect throughout a language. Lacking ADA's careful integration of design concepts, cancellation in JAVA requires the programmer to implement a nontrivial protocol, normally using the `interrupt` method. (To be fair, a programmer who wants *application-level* cancellation in ADA, with careful finalization of all nonlocal data, must make a similar effort.)

13.4.2   Mutual exclusion

Instead of providing a monitor construct, in the form of a class entailing automatic mutual exclusion, JAVA requires programmers to lock out concurrent access at the level of the method or the command. This is more flexible than a conventional monitor, but it is also more error-prone. The thread safety of a class depends on locks being consistently applied throughout all its methods. A JAVA compiler cannot offer the simple safety guarantee that comes with ADA95 protected types.

Every JAVA class (and therefore every object) is provided with a built-in mutual exclusion mechanism. A ***synchronized block*** is a composite command that enforces exclusive access to a designated object, O, for the duration of the command. It takes the form "**synchronized**(O) B", where B is a block command. The object is locked on entering the command (after blocking, if necessary), and unlocked when the command terminates, whether normally or by throwing an exception.

It is usually better to synchronize a whole method. In effect:

$$\textbf{synchronized}\ T\ M\ (\textit{FPs})\quad \equiv\quad T\ M\ (\textit{FPs})\ \{$$
$$F\qquad\qquad\qquad\qquad\qquad \textbf{synchronized(this)}\ B$$
$$\}$$

where T is the result type of method M, and FPs are its formal parameters.

If a subclass overrides a synchronized method the programmer must remember to respecify it as synchronized.

EXAMPLE 13.11   A synchronized variable class

Here is a simple JAVA class, analogous to Example 13.3, that encapsulates a variable and provides operations to fetch and store its value:

```
class Synchronized_Item {

  private Item variable;

  public synchronized void store (Item value) {
    variable = value;
  }

  public synchronized Item fetch () {
    return variable;
  }

}
```

And here is some application code:

```
Synchronized_Item x, y;
Item it;
```

```
...
it = x.fetch();
y.store(it);
x.store(it);
```

An error-prone consequence of object-based synchronization is that locking an object of class *C* does *not* give exclusive access to class variables of *C*. To achieve this it is necessary to lock the class object itself, either by using a synchronized class method, or in a synchronized block, thus: "**synchronized**(*C*.class){...}".

Each class has its own lock, separate from that of any other class, so a synchronized class method declared in a subclass (which uses the subclass lock) cannot safely access class variables of its parent class. Instead, the subclass programmer must remember to explicitly lock its parent.

13.4.3 Admission control

JAVA uses explicit signaling to implement admission control and guarded execution.

To delay a thread until a guarding condition has been established, JAVA provides constructs similar to events. Like its locking constructs, these are based on a built-in feature of every object – in this case its *wait set*.

The method *O*.wait() blocks until another thread calls *O*.notifyAll() to resume *all* threads waiting on *O* (if there are any). Unawaited notifications, like unawaited events, are lost. It is legal to call *O*.wait() only if a lock is held on *O*.

Atomically, *O*.wait() checks whether the current thread has been interrupted (throwing InterruptedException if need be); blocks the current thread; puts it in the wait set for *O*; and gives up its lock on *O*. A call of *O*.notifyAll() unblocks every thread in the wait set of *O* and they compete for processor time; when the scheduler chooses one to run, it restores its lock on *O*.

EXAMPLE 13.12 A single-slot buffer class

Here is a class with the same functionality as the protected type in Example 13.5.

```
class Synchronized_Buffer {

    private Message buffer;
    private boolean bufferIsEmpty = true;

    public synchronized void send_message (Message item)
            throws InterruptedException {
      while (! bufferIsEmpty) wait();
      buffer = item;
      bufferIsEmpty = false;
      notifyAll();
    }
```

```
       public synchronized Message receive_message ()
          throws InterruptedException {
       while (bufferIsEmpty) wait();
       bufferIsEmpty = true;
       notifyAll();
       return buffer;
       }

    }
```

And here is some application code:

```
    Synchronized_Buffer urgent, pending;
    Message msg;
    ...
    pending.send_message(msg);
    msg = pending.receive_message();
    urgent.send_message(msg);
```

By identifying events with objects, JAVA provides less functionality than traditional monitors. Notification alone does not distinguish between the "nonempty" and "nonfull" states of a buffer, for example. This is because there is no equivalent of MODULA's `signal` type, which allows a program to notify several distinct conditions separately. An object has only one wait set, so only one category of event can be communicated to a thread waiting on it. Unblocking conveys little information – no more, in fact, than the suggestion that there might have been a state change of interest.

When a thread exits a wait, it must therefore examine the object to find its new state, and block itself again if that is not yet satisfactory. The pattern is:

```
while (! E)
   O.wait();
```

The loop is necessary because the guarding condition E need not be true after unblocking. The `wait` might even have been unblocked by the notification of a completely different condition!

If all threads in a program wait for exactly the same state of an object, and if any one of them can deal with it appropriately, a possible optimization is to signal the condition by means of O.`notify()`, which resumes *one* thread in the wait set of O (at most).

In all other cases, programmers are well advised to play safe with `notifyAll`, despite the inefficiency due to threads needlessly blocking and unblocking.

It is possible to use `notify` in Example 13.12, instead of `notifyAll`, because the two circumstances in which notifications are issued cannot overlap. The notification in `receive_message` is issued if and only if the buffer is nonempty; in that case, and because of the locking due to the synchronized methods, the only possible members of the wait set are threads waiting in `send_message` (and *vice versa*). Compare this analysis with the transparency of the logic in Example 13.5.

Classes using `notify` give rise to inheritance anomalies if it is later discovered that their subclasses need to falsify the assumptions that justified the use of `notify`.

13.5 Implementation notes

This section concerns some practical issues that bear on the semantics and pragmatics of concurrent programming in ADA and JAVA. They are all to do with scheduling, in one way or another. Specifically, they concern the ways in which the actions of processes are scheduled by the underlying system, and how that can affect the performance (or even the correctness) of concurrent programs.

You might have wondered, when looking at the example code in this chapter, why none of the shared variables were declared volatile. The reason is that these algorithms have been carefully designed to access shared variables only within the synchronizing constructs of each language. The language designers have made us this promise: all prior updates are observable to a process on entry to a synchronized construct, and updates made within the synchronized construct are observable to other processes when it exits. The small print is different for ADA and for JAVA, but this is what it amounts to.

Few other languages can make comparable promises. Those that lack in-built concurrency, such as C and C++, are necessarily silent on the issue. This makes it very tricky indeed to write reliable, portable, concurrent code in these languages, despite the availability of thread libraries that give access to the concurrency features of the underlying operating system.

Shared variables accessed outside synchronized constructs are a very different case. Apart from providing atomic and volatile facilities, ADA washes its hands of such variables. Their timely update is the responsibility of the programmer, who must take all relevant compiler, architecture and operating system issues into account. This stance at least has the merit of clarity. JAVA tries to be more helpful, and defines a *memory model* that says how updates to shared variables become observable to unsynchronized accesses. The consensus among JAVA experts is that the memory model is an honorable failure. It is so obscure that few JAVA programmers understand it, and it significantly reduces efficiency, but it is still unable to prevent race conditions from giving pathological results. A major effort to improve the JAVA memory model is well under way.

The discussion of entry calls in ADA (Section 13.3.3), and the discussion of wait-set handling in JAVA (Section 13.4.3), glossed over the issue of *fairness*. In ADA, calls waiting to be admitted to an entry are put into the entry queue, and are taken from the entry queue, in order of arrival. This is inherently fair. JAVA does not define the policy under which threads, unblocking from a wait set, regain the object lock. It does not even require it to be fair. This makes it more difficult to guarantee the fairness of a concurrent algorithm in JAVA.

When more than one alternative (in a selective wait command) or more than one entry (in a protected object) has an open guard, ADA95 does not define how the choice between them is made. It need not be fair. However, the program's own admission control logic usually prevents this from being a problem. (When it is a problem, it is possible to specify an order of preference.)

Early operating systems for personal computers supported multiple threads by *non-preemptive* scheduling. This means that once a thread gains control, it stays in control until it voluntarily gives up the CPU. This approach has the virtue of simplicity. It also eliminates race conditions, as described in Section 10.5.2 in connection with interrupts.

Unfortunately, it is disastrous for reliability. If the running thread goes into an infinite loop, the effect is to freeze the whole system. It also makes it difficult to maintain responsiveness. Socially responsible threads voluntarily give up the CPU from time to time, so that other threads, some of which may be interacting with the user, are prevented from starving. However, nothing guarantees such altruistic behavior. For these reasons, preemptive priority scheduling is now used almost universally.

The idea of priority is crucial in concurrent programming, for it tells the scheduler which of the processes competing for resources should be preferred. Suppose that a high-priority process is blocked, and another process removes the blockage (e.g., by setting an entry guard true, or notifying a wait set). Can we be sure that the unblocked process will resume at once, in preference to any process of lower priority – the very essence of preemptive priority scheduling?

ADA does guarantee this. JAVA does not, permitting the implementation to resume an unblocked thread at a convenient later time. A programmer hoping to ensure snappy response times may try to work around this by forcing threads to give up the CPU from time to time, in non-preemptive style. At first sight, the `yield()` method seems to do what is wanted, but, again, JAVA provides no guarantee of useful behavior.

A difficulty that is *caused* by preemptive priority scheduling is *priority inversion*.

If a high-priority process, H, tries to acquire a resource, r, that has been obtained by a low-priority process, L, then H must wait until L relinquishes r. In effect, the priority of H has been temporarily reduced below that of L. This is an example of *bounded* priority inversion: the time H must wait is limited by the time for which L retains r. *Unbounded* priority inversion happens when a third process, M, of medium priority and having no interest in r, preempts L. That prevents L from relinquishing r in a timely manner. The progress of H is now at the mercy of M, which might even be stuck in an infinite loop.

Most notoriously, priority inversion was responsible for the repeated malfunction of a NASA Mars probe (fortunately cured by a software patch). This example shows that even meticulous design by skilled programmers can fail badly due to unpredictable timing effects. If a language can make such failures less likely, then it should do so.

An effective countermeasure to priority inversion is to find the highest priority, P_{max}, of any process that blocks on a given resource r. Then every process that acquires r is temporarily given the priority P_{max}, reverting to its usual priority when it relinquishes. This is the *ceiling priority protocol*. It lets all threads that acquire r run as speedily as those of the highest priority among them, so that the latter are not excessively delayed. This goes a long way to preventing priority inversion, although it is not totally foolproof. An ADA95 protected type normally uses the ceiling priority protocol, throwing an exception if any caller has higher priority than its given ceiling. In JAVA no such facility is provided, and the programmer must resort to explicit manipulation of thread priorities, or other expedients. Since JAVA does not ensure strict preemptive priority scheduling, these measures cannot be guaranteed to be effective.

In short, the designers of ADA have imposed scheduling requirements that permit efficient implementation, and also allow sound reasoning about the performance and responsiveness of concurrent programs.

The vagueness of JAVA in these matters makes things more difficult. As far as concurrent programs in JAVA are concerned, the slogan "write once, run anywhere" is more truthfully stated as "write once, run anywhere it works". This is a modest achievement for a language designed more than a decade after ADA made its début, and twenty years after CONCURRENT PASCAL.

Summary

ADA and JAVA, in their different ways, offer a variety of constructs and techniques for concurrency. Among these:

- We have seen how ADA *server* tasks can be used to implement a very simple model of data safety in a concurrent program organized around *communication*.
- We have seen how the *synchronized* feature of JAVA can be used to implement classes that are analogous to monitors, but less efficient and more error-prone.
- We have seen how the *protected object* feature of ADA combines most of the advantages of monitors and conditional critical regions in a single construct.
- We have seen how concurrency is implemented in conventional computer systems and how that relates to the more abstract concurrency features of ADA and JAVA.

Concurrency in ADA95 is comprehensively supported, at a high level of abstraction, and well integrated with the rest of the language. Moreover, this is achieved without sacrificing (too much) potential for good performance.

Concurrency in JAVA is provided by a set of rather low-level features, that tend nevertheless to inefficiency. Surprisingly, in view of the genesis of JAVA as a language for programming embedded systems, its handling of concurrency gives the impression of being an afterthought. Certainly, it is complicated and error-prone.

Further reading

The major concurrent programming paradigms are surveyed, with many examples, by PERROTT (1987). BUSTARD et al. (1988) discuss applications, including simulation, and are to be commended for addressing the question of testing concurrent programs. JONES and GOLDSMITH (1988) describe OCCAM. C and C++ programmers depend on "thread libraries" for concurrency facilities. The most important is the POSIX thread library, also known as "Pthreads"; see BUTENHOF (1997). BURNS and WELLINGS (1998) describe the ADA95 model of concurrency in detail. LEA (2000) does the same for JAVA, and illustrates many design patterns and library frameworks that attempt to insulate the JAVA programmer from the worst of its concurrency problems. DIBBLE (2002) describes a heroic effort to remedy the shortcomings of JAVA, aimed at making it feasible for use in real-time applications.

Exercises

Exercises for Section 13.3

13.3.1 Rewrite the monitor given in Example 10.10, as an ADA95 protected object.

13.3.2 Show that, using the buffer type given in Example 13.5, distributing n messages to n waiting tasks takes time of order $O(n)$. (Synchronization can be expected to dominate performance, if the Message type is not too large.)

*13.3.3 The ADA implementation of the banker's algorithm given in Programs 13.1 and 13.2 is less than ideally robust. This exercise sets out the changes needed to make it behave well in a number of boundary conditions.

(a) Add the following declarations to the declaration of Banker:

```
inventory_error : exception;
liveness_error  : exception;
safety_error    : exception;
```

(b) The intention for inventory_error is that it should be thrown by any call with a claim or an amount parameter that exceeds what is proper for the call; and that it should be thrown by deregister if the calling task has not yet relinquished all of its outstanding loans. Make the necessary changes to implement these checks.

(c) The intention for liveness_error is that it should be thrown if the system is found to be no longer live (i.e., if no process being scheduled can proceed, which can happen only if the scheduler has malfunctioned and failed to prevent deadlock). Make the necessary changes needed to throw this exception appropriately.

(d) The intention for safety_error is that it should be thrown if checks find that more resources have been allocated than were provided in capital (indicating that the scheduler has malfunctioned and failed to maintain mutual exclusion). Write the body of:

```
procedure check_validity_of_allocations
              (state : System_State);
```

It should throw safety_error if, in the given state, the balance of any resource is negative; or the system's capital of any resource is exceeded by its exposure to the loan and possible further claim of any process; or the total amount of any resource on loan exceeds the system's capital of that resource.

Find a suitable place to call check_validity_of_allocations.

*13.3.4 Five philosophers sit at a round table, with a bowl of spaghetti in the middle and a plate in front of each. They alternate between eating and thinking. Five forks are available, one placed between each two plates. Spaghetti is slippery stuff and must be taken with two forks to maintain good table manners. In order to eat, each philosopher must pick up both adjacent forks. Having picked up a fork, he will not put it down until he has eaten. There are not enough forks to let them all eat at once. Being devoted to the greatest good of the greatest number, each philosopher puts down both his forks when he has finished eating, then he starts to think.

(a) Construct a train of events in which the philosophers all deadlock and so die of hunger.

(b) Construct a train of events in which only some philosophers starve, both literally and technically!

(c) Instantiate the Banker generic package (Program 13.1) as necessary, and use it to program a solution in ADA that avoids both problems.

Exercises for Section 13.4

13.4.1 Show that neither the (deprecated) stop method in JAVA, nor the interrupt method, enables us to *guarantee* cancellation of a rogue thread.

13.4.2 In JAVA it is not possible to write a synchronized block protecting access to a component of primitive type.

(a) Explain why.

(b) Suggest two ways you might work around this problem.

13.4.3 Show that, using the buffer class of Example 13.12, distributing n messages to n waiting threads takes synchronization time of order $O(n^2)$.

13.4.4 Rewrite the monitor of Example 10.10 as a JAVA class.

*13.4.5 Rewrite the semaphore type of Example 13.6 as a JAVA class.

(a) Show that notify can be used reliably instead of notifyAll.

(b) Rewrite the buffer class in Example 13.12 to use your semaphore class for synchronization. Show that distributing n messages to n waiting threads now takes time of order $O(n)$.

(c) Comment on the synchronization features of JAVA.

*13.4.6 Write an implementation of the banker's algorithm in JAVA.

*13.4.7 In Exercise 10.5.4, we looked at *double-checked locking*, a technique that aims to avoid the overhead of mutual exclusion where possible. Lazy initialization is a common idiom in JAVA, and often liable to race conditions. Double-checked locking is often suggested as a palliative, along the following lines:

```
class Thing ... {

  private Other someOther;

  public void doSomething () {
    if (someOther == null) {
      synchronized (this) {
        if (someOther == null)
          someOther = new Other(...);
      }
    }
    someOther.op();
  }

}
```

(a) What can go wrong with this locking technique? How can it be made to work, and what are the implications for the reuse of the Other class?

(b) The programmer has attempted to ensure the efficiency and the safety of operations on Thing by totally encapsulating its components, synchronizing only where updates make that necessary. For example, the call "someOther.op();" is not synchronized, because the programmer assumes that it will not change someOther. Explain why that assumption is dangerous, and cannot be enforced in JAVA.

Exercises for Section 13.5

13.5.1 Why is *preemptive priority scheduling* important? To what extent do ADA95 and JAVA meet this need? Describe the yield method in JAVA and say why it is less useful than it might be. Find out the nearest equivalent in ADA95.

13.5.2 Explain *priority inversion*. Show that many cases of priority inversion can be automatically prevented in ADA. Suggest steps that a programmer can take to reduce the risk of priority inversion in JAVA programs.

Chapter 14

Functional programming

In this chapter we shall study:

- the key concepts that characterize functional programming languages;
- the pragmatics of functional programming;
- the design of a major functional language, HASKELL.

14.1 Key concepts

In functional programming, the model of computation is the application of functions to arguments. The key concepts of functional programming are therefore:

- expressions
- functions
- parametric polymorphism

and (in some functional languages):

- data abstraction
- lazy evaluation.

Expressions are a key concept of functional programming because their purpose is to compute new values from old, which quite simply is the very essence of functional programming.

Functions are a key concept of functional programming because functions abstract over expressions. Moreover, functions are typically first-class values. Thus functions can be passed as arguments, computed as results of other functions, built into composite values, and so on. A *higher-order* function is one that takes another function as an argument or computes another function as its result. For example, a higher-order function can traverse a list, applying an argument function to each component of the list.

Parametric polymorphism is a key concept of functional programming because it enables a function to operate on values of a family of types (rather than just one type). In practice, many useful functions are naturally polymorphic, and parametric polymorphism greatly magnifies the power and expressiveness of a functional language.

Data abstraction is a key concept in the more modern functional languages such as ML and HASKELL. As always, data abstraction supports separation of concerns, which is essential for the design and implementation of large programs. In a functional language, all the operations of an abstract type are constants and functions. Thus an abstract type may be equipped with operations that compute new values of the type from old. It is not possible for an abstract type to be equipped with an operation that selectively updates a variable of the type, as in an imperative language.

Lazy evaluation is based on the simple notion that an expression whose value is never used need never be evaluated. In order to understand this concept, we first explore a wider issue: the order in which expressions are evaluated.

14.1.1   Eager vs normal-order vs lazy evaluation

In this subsection we shall study the issue of when each actual parameter in a function call is evaluated to yield the argument. We start by studying the choice between eager and normal-order evaluation; later we shall see that lazy evaluation is a more practicable variation of normal-order evaluation.

Eager evaluation means that we evaluate the actual parameter once, at the point of call. In effect, we substitute the argument value for each occurrence of the formal parameter.

Normal-order evaluation means that we evaluate the actual parameter only when the argument is actually needed. In effect, we substitute the actual parameter itself (an unevaluated expression) for each occurrence of the formal parameter. (This is an over-simplification, however: see Exercise 14.1.3.)

Consider the function defined as follows:

```
sqr n = n * n
```

where n is the formal parameter. Consider also the function call "sqr(m+1)", and suppose that m's value is 6. Here are two different ways in which we could evaluate this function call:

- *Eager evaluation.* First we evaluate "m+1", yielding 7. Then we bind the formal parameter n to 7. Finally we evaluate "n * n", yielding $7 \times 7 = 49$.

- *Normal-order evaluation.* First we bind the formal parameter n to the unevaluated expression "m+1". Subsequently we (re)evaluate that expression every time that the value of n is required during the evaluation of "n * n". In effect, we evaluate "(m+1) * (m+1)", which yields $(6 + 1) \times (6 + 1) = 49$.

In the case of the sqr function, both eager and normal-order evaluation yield the same result (although eager evaluation is the more efficient). However, the behavior of certain functions does depend on the evaluation order. Consider the function defined as follows:

```
cand b1 b2 = if b1 then b2 else False
```

where b1 and b2 are formal parameters. Consider also the function call "cand (n>0) (t/n>50)". First suppose that n's value is 2 and t's value is 80.

- *Eager evaluation*: "n>0" yields *true* and "t/n>50" yields *false*; therefore the function call yields *false*.
- *Normal-order evaluation*: In effect, we evaluate "**if** n>0 **then** t/n>50 **else** False", which also yields *false*.

But now suppose that n's value is 0 and t's value is 80.

- *Eager evaluation*: "n>0" yields *false* but "t/n>50" fails (due to division by zero); therefore the function call itself fails.
- *Normal-order evaluation*: In effect we evaluate "**if** n>0 **then** t/n>50 **else** False", which yields *false*.

The essential difference between these two functions is as follows. The sqr function always uses its argument, so a call to this function can be evaluated only if its argument can be evaluated. On the other hand, the cand function sometimes ignores its second argument, so a call to the cand function can sometimes be evaluated even if its second argument cannot.

A function is **strict** in a particular argument if it always uses that argument. For example, the sqr function is strict in its only argument; the cand function is strict in its first argument, but nonstrict in its second argument.

Some programming languages possess an important property known as the **Church–Rosser Property**:

> *If an expression can be evaluated at all, it can be evaluated by consistently using normal-order evaluation. If an expression can be evaluated in several different orders (mixing eager and normal-order evaluation), then all of these evaluation orders yield the same result.*

The Church–Rosser Property is possessed by HASKELL. It is not possessed by any programming language that allows side effects (such as C, C++, JAVA, ADA, or even ML). In a function call "*F(E)*" where evaluating *E* has side effects, it certainly makes a difference when and how often *E* is evaluated. For example, suppose that "getint(f)" reads an integer from the file f (a side effect) and yields that integer. With eager evaluation, the function call "sqr(getint(f))" would cause one integer to be read, and would yield the square of that integer. With normal-order evaluation, the same function call would cause *two* integers to be read, and would yield their product!

In practice, normal-order evaluation is too inefficient to be used in programming languages: an actual parameter might be evaluated several times, always yielding the same argument. However, we can avoid this wasted computation as follows.

Lazy evaluation means that we evaluate the actual parameter when the argument is *first* needed; then we store the argument for use whenever it is *subsequently* needed. If the programming language possesses the Church–Rosser Property, lazy evaluation always yields exactly the same result as normal-order evaluation.

Eager evaluation is adopted by nearly all programming languages. Lazy evaluation is adopted only by pure functional languages such as HASKELL.

Lazy evaluation can be exploited in interesting ways. Evaluation of *any* expression can be delayed until its value is actually needed, perhaps never. In particular, we can notionally construct a large composite value (such as a list), and subsequently use only some of its components. The unused components will remain unevaluated. We shall explore some of the possibilities of lazy evaluation in Section 14.3.4.

14.2   Pragmatics

The basic program units of a functional program are functions. Typically, each function is composed from simpler functions: one function calls another, or one function's result is passed as an argument to another function. Programs are written entirely in terms of such functions, which are themselves composed of expressions and declarations. Pure functional programming does not use commands or proper procedures that update variables; these concepts belong to imperative and object-oriented programming. Instead, functional programming exploits other powerful concepts, notably higher-order functions and lazy evaluation.

A large functional program comprises a very large number of functions. Managing them all can be problematic. In practice, most functions can be grouped naturally into packages of some kind. Also, abstract types are just as advantageous in functional programming as in other paradigms. Thus the program units of a well-designed functional program are functions and *packages* (or *abstract types*).

Figure 14.1 shows the architecture of such a functional program. Two abstract types have been designed, each equipped with operations sufficient for this application. All the program units are loosely coupled to one another. In particular, since the representation of each abstract type is private, it can safely be changed without forcing modifications to the other program units.

14.3   Case study: HASKELL

HASKELL was designed in the 1980s by a large committee led by Simon Peyton Jones and John Hughes. It was strongly influenced both by ML, from which it took parametric polymorphism and type inference, and by MIRANDA, from which it took lazy evaluation. HASKELL was intended to be the world's leading functional language, and it has largely succeeded in that aim, although ML is also still popular.

HASKELL is a pure functional language, whose computational power derives largely from the use of higher-order functions and lazy evaluation. HASKELL does not provide variables, commands, or sequencers. Nevertheless, HASKELL programs can model state, and perform input/output, as we shall see in Section 14.3.7.

14.3.1   Values and types

HASKELL has a full repertoire of primitive types: Bool, Char, and various numeric types (both integer and floating point). Unusually, HASKELL provides not only a bounded integer type (Int) but also an unbounded integer type (Integer).

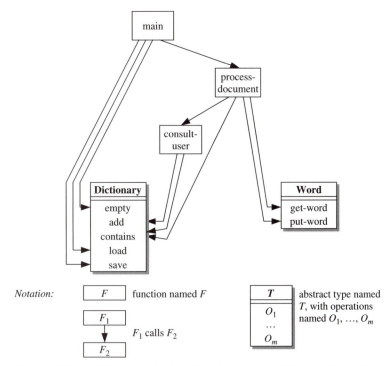

Figure 14.1 Architecture of a functional program with data abstraction.

HASKELL also has a full repertoire of composite types: tuples, algebraic types (disjoint unions), lists, and functions. Recursive types such as trees can be defined directly.

Lists are the most ubiquitous composite values in functional programs. The values of the HASKELL type [t] are lists whose elements are of type t. [] denotes the empty list, and "x : xs" constructs a list whose head (first element) is x and whose tail (list of remaining elements) is xs. (Note that ":" is an operator in HASKELL.)

HASKELL provides a rich library of useful functions on lists, such as:

```
head :: [t] -> t
-- head xs computes the head of list xs.

tail :: [t] -> [t]
-- tail xs computes the tail of list xs.

length :: [t] -> Int
-- length xs computes the length of list xs.

(++) :: [t] -> [t] -> [t]
-- xs ++ ys computes the concatenation of lists xs and ys.
```

Here the type variable t denotes an arbitrary type.

We can easily define other useful functions on lists, as the following example illustrates.

EXAMPLE 14.1   HASKELL list functions

Consider the following HASKELL functions:

```
sum :: [Int] -> Int
-- sum ns computes the sum of the components of list ns.

sum []       = 0
sum (n : ns) = n + sum ns

product :: [Int] -> Int
-- product ns computes the product of the components of list ns.

product []       = 1
product (n : ns) = n * product ns

through :: Int -> Int -> [Int]
-- through m n computes the list of integers m through n.

m 'through' n =
    if m > n
    then []
    else m : (m+1 'through' n)
```

(A binary function such as through can be used as an infix binary operator by writing it as 'through'.)

We could use the above functions to define the factorial function as follows:

```
factorial n = product (1 'through' n)
```

EXAMPLE 14.2   HASKELL list insertion

Consider inserting an integer into a sorted list of integers. In an imperative program we could define a procedure that inserts the new component by selective updating. In a HASKELL program we must instead define a function that computes a new list containing the new component as well as all the original components; the original list itself remains unchanged. The following function does this:

```
insert :: Int -> [Int] -> [Int]
-- insert i ns computes the list obtained by inserting i into the sorted list ns.

insert i [] =
    [i]
insert i (n : ns) =
    if i < n
    then i : n : ns
    else n : insert i ns
```

This function seems to copy the entire list in order to make a single insertion. On closer study, however, we see that the function actually copies only the nodes containing integers less than or equal to i; the remaining nodes are shared between the original list and the new list. Figure 14.2 illustrates the effect of inserting 7 in the list [2, 3, 5, 11, 13, 17].

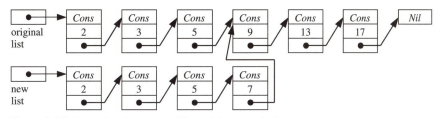

Figure 14.2 Insertion in a sorted list, without updating.

Figure 14.2 illustrates the representation of lists in a functional language, which is similar to the linked representation that might be chosen by an imperative programmer. The main difference is that a functional programmer never manipulates pointers explicitly. This is a useful simplification, and eliminates a major source of programming errors.

Figure 14.2 also illustrates the fact that parts of lists can be shared. In the absence of side effects, sharing does not affect the program's behavior, since the shared components cannot be updated. We can therefore ignore the existence of sharing, pretending that the lists are distinct. Again this is a useful simplification.

These points apply not only to lists but also to trees and other recursive types.

Recursive values such as lists can be manipulated with reasonable efficiency in a functional language, but not arrays. Two lists that differ in a single component can share much of their structure, but two arrays that differ in a single component cannot. Therefore any function that computes a modified array must copy it in its entirety, which is very costly if the function modifies a single component. For this reason, the HASKELL language does not provide built-in arrays. (However, a library module does support arrays for programs that really need them. For the sake of efficiency, this module provides functions capable of modifying *several* array components at a time.)

HASKELL complies well with the Type Completeness Principle. A constant, parameter, or function result can be of any type (including a function type).

As befits a functional language, HASKELL has a rich expression repertoire including constructions (for tuples, algebraic types, lists, and functions), function calls, conditional (if- and case-) expressions, iterative expressions (list comprehensions), and block expressions.

The simplest form of function construction is "\ I -> E". This constructs a function whose formal parameter is the identifier I and whose body is the expression E.

A HASKELL function call has the form "E_1 E_2", where the subexpression E_1 yields the function to be called, and the subexpression E_2 yields the argument. If f is a function whose result is another function, "f x" calls f to yield a function, and "f x y" (or "(f x) y") calls the yielded function.

A binary operator $\otimes$ denotes a function of type T_1 -> T_2 -> T, where T_1 and T_2 are the operand types and T is the result type. The expression "$E_1 \otimes E_2$" is equivalent to "$(\otimes)$ E_1 E_2".

Iteration over lists is so important that HASKELL provides an iterative expression for this purpose: the ***list comprehension***. For example, we can construct a list of integers, each one greater than the corresponding integer in ns, by writing:

```
[n + 1 | n <- ns]
```

If ns is the list [2, 3, 5, 7, 11], this list comprehension will yield the list [3, 4, 6, 8, 12]. Similarly, if ns is a list of integers, we can double just the odd integers from ns by writing:

```
[2 * n | n <- ns, n 'mod' 2 /= 0]
```

If ns is the list [2, 3, 5, 7, 11], this list comprehension will yield the list [6, 10, 14, 22].

The phrase "n <- ns" is an example of a *generator*. The occurrence of n to the left of the symbol "<-" is a binding occurrence: n is bound in turn to each component of the list ns.

The phrase "n 'mod' 2 /= 0" is an example of a *filter*, a boolean expression. Values of n for which this filter yields *false* are discarded.

In general, a list comprehension has the form $[E | Q_1, \ldots , Q_n]$, where each Q_i is either a generator or a filter. If Q_i is a generator, the scope of a binding occurrence in its left-hand side includes $Q_{i+1}, \ldots, Q_n$, and E.

List comprehensions are adapted from mathematical set notation. Compare the above list comprehensions with $\{n + 1 | n \in ns\}$ and $\{2n | n \in ns; n \bmod 2 \neq 0\}$, respectively.

EXAMPLE 14.3   HASKELL list comprehensions

The following function uses a list comprehension and the through function of Example 14.1:

```
sumsq :: Int -> Int
-- sumsq n computes the sum of the squares of the first n integers.

sumsq n = sum [i * i | i <- 1 'through' n]
```

Using list comprehensions we can code the quick-sort algorithm remarkably concisely:

```
sort :: [Int] -> [Int]
-- sort ns computes the list obtained by sorting list ns into ascending order.

sort [] = []
sort [x:xs] =
    sort [y | y <- xs, y < x]
        ++ [x]
        ++ sort [z | z <- xs, z >= x]
```

14.3.2   Bindings and scope

A HASKELL program is basically a collection of modules (packages). One of these modules must be named Main, and one of its components must be a function named main; that function is the main program.

Within a module we may define types, constants, and functions. There is no restriction on the order of the definitions, so a function may call other functions defined earlier or later. The functions may be directly or mutually recursive.

Inside a block expression we may define local constants and functions (but not types).

Both functions and case-expressions can be defined by pattern matching. A *pattern* resembles an expression, but may contain binding occurrences of identifiers. Given a value *v*, if there exist bindings for these identifiers such that the pattern (viewed as an expression) would yield *v*, then the pattern is said to *match* *v*. When the pattern matches a given value, it actually produces these bindings.

EXAMPLE 14.4 HASKELL pattern matching

Consider the following HASKELL type definition:

```
data Shape = Pointy | Circular Float
       | Rectangular(Float, Float)
```

The type defined here is a disjoint union.

Now consider the following function:

```
area :: Shape -> Float
-- area s computes the area of the shape s.
```

We can define this function by means of a case-expression:

```
area s =
   case s of
      Pointy            -> 0.0
      Circular r        -> pi * r * r
      Rectangular(h, w) -> h * w
```

This case-expression determines which of three alternative patterns matches the value of s. If the pattern "Pointy" matches the value of s, the result is 0.0. If the pattern "Circular r" matches the value of s, e.g., if that value is Circular 5.0, the identifier r is bound to 5.0 for the purpose of evaluating the expression "pi * r * r". If the pattern "Rectangular(h, w)" matches the value of s, e.g., if that value is Rectangular(2.0, 3.0), the identifiers h and w are bound to 2.0 and 3.0, respectively, for the purpose of evaluating the expression "h * w".

Alternatively, we can exploit pattern matching directly in the function definition:

```
area Pointy            = 0.0
area (Circular r)      = pi * r * r
area (Rectangular(h, w)) = h * w
```

This function determines which of three alternative patterns matches its argument value.

In general, a function may be defined by several equations. Each equation's left-hand side contains a different pattern in its formal parameter position. For an equation to be applied, its pattern must match the argument value, in which case the pattern produces bindings for the purpose of evaluating the right-hand side of the equation.

Defining functions by pattern matching is a popular functional programming idiom: it is concise, clear, and similar to mathematical notation.

We can declare a function's type:

```
length :: [t] -> Int
```

as well as define it:

```
length []      = 0
length (x : xs) = 1 + length xs
```

Declaring a function's type is optional; the HASKELL compiler can infer the function's type from its definition alone. However, declaring functions' types tends to make the program easier to understand.

14.3.3   Procedural abstraction

HASKELL supports only function procedures. It makes no distinction between parameterless functions and constants.

HASKELL functions are first-class values: they can be passed as parameters, computed as function results, built into composite values, and so on. This has a major impact on programming style.

A function with a functional parameter or functional result is called a ***higher-order function***. We frequently exploit higher-order functions to make code reusable, by abstracting over those parts of it that are specific to a particular application.

Allowing a function to compute another function as its result opens up many interesting possibilities, which are heavily exploited in functional programming. The simplest way to generate a new function is by composing two existing functions, as the following example illustrates.

EXAMPLE 14.5   HASKELL function composition

The " . " operator composes two given functions, and is defined as follows:

```
(.) :: (t -> u) -> (s -> t) -> (s -> u)
-- f . g computes a function h such that h(x) = f(g(x)).

f . g = \ x -> f(g(x))
```

Given the following library functions:

```
not :: Bool -> Bool
odd :: Int -> Bool
```

we can compose them as follows:

```
even = not . odd
```

This defines a function even whose type is Int -> Bool.

EXAMPLE 14.6   HASKELL curried function

Consider the following function:

```
power :: (Int, Float) -> Float
-- power(n, b) computes the nth power of b (assuming that n≥0).

power(n, b) =
   if n = 0 then 1.0 else b * power(n-1, b)
```

This function, when applied to a pair consisting of an integer and a real number, will compute a real number. For example, "power(2, x)" computes the square of x.

Now consider the following closely related function:

```
powerc :: Int -> Float -> Float
-- powerc n b computes the nth power of b (assuming that n≥0).

powerc n b =
   if n = 0 then 1.0 else b * powerc (n-1) b
```

This function, when applied to an integer n, will compute another function; the latter function, when applied to a real number, will compute the nth power of that real number. For example, "powerc 2 x" computes the square of x.

The advantage of powerc is that we can call it with only one argument. For example:

```
sqr  = powerc 2
cube = powerc 3
```

Here both sqr and cube are functions of type Float -> Float.

The function powerc of Example 14.6 is called a ***curried*** version of the function power. The technique of calling a curried function with fewer than the maximum number of arguments is called ***partial application***.

EXAMPLE 14.7   HASKELL higher-order functions

The following HASKELL library function is higher-order:

```
filter :: (t -> Bool) -> [t] -> [t]
-- filter f computes a new function that filters the components of a given
-- list, retaining only those components x for which f x yields true.

filter f [] = []
filter f (x : xs) =
   if f x then x : filter f xs else filter f xs
```

For instance, "filter odd" yields a function, of type [Int] -> [Int], that maps the list [2, 3, 5, 7, 11] to the list [3, 5, 7, 11].

The following HASKELL library function is also higher-order:

```
map :: (s -> t) -> [s] -> [t]
-- map f computes a new function that applies function f separately to each
-- component of a given list.
```

```
map f []        = []
map f (x : xs) = f x : map f xs
```

For instance, "map odd" is a function, of type `[Int] -> [Bool]`, that maps the list [2, 3, 5, 7, 11] to the list [*false, true, true, true, true*].

EXAMPLE 14.8   HASKELL generic sorting function

Let us parameterize the sorting function of Example 14.3 with respect to the function that compares two components:

```
genericSort :: (t -> t -> Bool) -> [t] -> [t]
-- genericSort before computes a function that sorts a given list
-- into ascending order, taking x 'before' y to mean that x should come
-- before y in the sorted list.

genericSort before =
    let
      sort [] = []
      sort (n : ns) =
          sort [i | i <- ns, i 'before' n]
              ++ [n]
              ++ sort [i | i <- ns, not (i 'before' n)]
    in sort
```

When applied to an appropriate comparison function, `genericSort` generates a specific sorting function. For instance:

```
intSort, reverseIntSort :: [Int] -> [Int]

intSort        = genericSort (<)

reverseIntSort = genericSort (>)
```

Each of these generated functions sorts a list of integers. (Recall that the operators "<" and ">" denote functions, each of type `Int -> Int -> Bool`.)

Here the comparison function is explicitly defined:

```
type String = [Char]

precedes :: String -> String -> Bool

cs1 'precedes' [] =
    False
[] 'precedes' (c2:cs2) =
    True
(c1:cs1) 'precedes' (c2:cs2) =
    if c1 == c2 then cs1 'precedes' cs2 else c1 < c2

lexicographicSort :: [String] -> [String]

lexicographicSort = genericSort precedes
```

As these examples illustrate, when we abstract over functions we very often also want to abstract over types. We benefit from being able to reuse a sorting function to sort lists of integers into a variety of different orders, but we benefit much more from reusing a sorting function to sort lists of many different types. Therefore HASKELL supports parametric polymorphism.

14.3.4   Lazy evaluation

In Section 14.1.1 we introduced lazy evaluation as a technique for delaying the evaluation of function arguments until they are needed.

The usefulness of lazy evaluation is greatly increased if we also allow unevaluated expressions as components of a list. Such expressions might eventually be evaluated, but only if and when they are selected from the list. A list containing unevaluated expressions is called a *lazy list*. A remarkable consequence of this is that we can build *infinite* lists, whose tails remain unevaluated.

This idea applies similarly to other composite types, so we can also build lazy (and infinite) trees, and so on.

EXAMPLE 14.9   HASKELL lazy lists (1)

Consider the following HASKELL function:

```
from :: Int -> [Int]
-- from n computes the list of all integers not less than n.

from n = n : from (n+1)
```

The list computed by the `from` function is infinite (if we ignore the bounded range of integers). With eager evaluation, this function would never terminate. But with lazy evaluation, the recursive call to the `from` function will be built into the list, and will be evaluated only if and when the tail of the list is selected.

Consider also the following function:

```
firstPrime :: [Int] -> Int
-- firstPrime ns computes the first prime number in the list ns.

firstPrime [] =
   0
firstPrime (n : ns) =
   if isPrime n then n else firstPrime ns
```

The following expression composes these two functions to compute the first prime number not less than m:

```
firstPrime (from m)
```

In principle, this expression first computes an infinite list of integers, then tests the first few integers in this list until it finds a prime number. In practice, the list always remains partially evaluated. Only when `firstPrime` selects the tail of the list does a little more evaluation of the list take place.

This example illustrates that the infinity of a lazy list is only potential. A lazy list is an active composite value that is capable of computing as many of its own components as needed.

A major benefit of lazy evaluation is that it supports a novel kind of modularity: the separation of control from calculation. The idea is to break an iterative or recursive computation into a pure *calculation part* and a *control part*. The calculation part computes all the necessary values and builds them into a composite value (such as a lazy list). The control part traverses all or part of this composite value, thus determining the flow of control. Often the calculation can be expressed more simply once control information is removed. And often the same calculation part can be reused with different control parts, or a control part can be reused with different calculation parts. (See also Exercises 14.3.9 and 14.3.10.)

EXAMPLE 14.10   HASKELL lazy lists (2)

Consider the problem of computing square roots by the Newton–Raphson method. This can naturally be decomposed into a calculation part that computes approximations, and a control part that decides when the process has converged sufficiently. Arbitrarily many approximations can be computed, so it is natural to build them into a lazy list. The following HASKELL function does that:

```
approxRoots :: Float -> [Float]
-- approxRoots x computes a list of converging approximations to the
-- square root of x.

approxRoots x =
   let
     rootsFrom r =
       r : rootsFrom (0.5 * (r + x/r))
   in rootsFrom 1.0
```

The following is a control function that interprets convergence in terms of the absolute difference between successive approximations:

```
absolute :: Float -> [Float] -> Float
-- absolute eps rs computes the first component of the list rs whose
-- absolute difference from its predecessor is at most eps.

absolute eps (r1 : r2 : rs) =
   if abs (r1 - r2) <= eps
   then r2
   else absolute eps (r2 : rs)
```

Now we can compose the square root function as follows:

```
sqrt = absolute 0.0001 . approxRoots
```

We could reuse the same list of approximations with a different control function: see Exercise 14.3.10. Conversely, we could reuse any one of these control functions with any numerical algorithm that generates a sequence of converging approximations.

The same idea can be exploited in search algorithms. The search space is calculated and built into a composite value such as a tree, and the search strategy is then expressed as a function on this tree. When both the computation of the search space and the search strategy are complex, separating the two can be a significant simplification. The explicit representation of the search space as a tree also makes it easy to add functions that manipulate the search space. For example, we could limit the search to a fixed depth by discarding deeper branches; or we could order branches so that regions of the search space in which the solution is likely to lie are explored first.

14.3.5 Data abstraction

HASKELL supports data abstraction by means of *modules*, which are similar to the packages of some other programming languages. A module groups together definitions of components such as types, constants, and functions. Each of these components may be either public or private.

An abstract type can be defined by a module that exports the type itself and its operations (constants and functions), but hides the type's representation.

EXAMPLE 14.11 HASKELL abstract type

The following module defines an algebraic type Date and several functions:

```
module Dates (Date, makeDate, advance, show) where

   data Date = Epoch Int
   -- A date is represented by the number of days since the first day of 2000.

   makeDate :: (Int, Int, Int) -> Date
   advance  :: Int -> Date -> Date
   show     :: Date -> String

   makeDate (y, m, d) =
     ...

   advance n (Epoch e) =
     Epoch (e + n)

   show (Epoch e) =
     let (y, m, d) = decompose (Epoch e)
     in show y ++ "-" ++ show m ++ "-" ++ show d

   decompose (Epoch e) =
     let
       y = ...
       m = ...
       d = ...
     in (y, m, d)
```

The module heading states that only the Date type and the makeDate, advance, and show functions are public. The decompose function is private. The tag Epoch is also private, so application code cannot use this tag to construct or pattern-match a Date value. Therefore application code can manipulate Date values only by calling the module's public functions. In other words, Date is an abstract type.

14.3.6   Generic abstraction

Generic abstraction is supported in HASKELL by parametric polymorphism, parameterized types, and type classes.

Parametric polymorphism allows us to define functions that operate over a family of types with similar structure. Consider the following polymorphic functions:

```
id      :: t -> t
second :: (s, t) -> t
length :: [t] -> Int

id x = x

second (x, y) = y

length []       = 0
length (x : xs) = 1 + length xs
```

The `id` function operates over all types, the `second` function operates over all tuple types with exactly two components, and the `length` function operates over all list types.

A type variable (such as `s` or `t` above) ranges over all types. In general, the definition of a polymorphic function can make no assumptions about the type denoted by a type variable.

However, the definitions of certain polymorphic functions must assume that the type denoted by a type variable is equipped with particular operations. For example, the function:

```
min :: t -> t -> t

min x y = if x < y then x else y    -- illegal!
```

cannot be defined unless we can assume that the type denoted by `t` is equipped with a "<" operator.

HASKELL uses type classes to resolve this problem. A *type class* is a family of types, all of which are equipped with certain required functions (or operators). When we declare a type class, we declare the required functions, and provide default definitions of them. Subsequently, we may declare any type to be an *instance* of the type class, meaning that it is equipped with the required functions of the type class; at the same time we may override any or all of the required functions' default definitions.

EXAMPLE 14.12   HASKELL type classes

The following type class Eq encompasses all types equipped with equality and inequality test operators, named "==" and "/=":

```
class Eq t where
    (==), (/=) :: t -> t -> Bool
    x /= y  =  not (x == y)
    x == y  =  not (x /= y)
```

These default definitions of "==" and "/=" define the operators in terms of each other. Every instance of this type class will have to override one or both of these default definitions (otherwise a call to either operator would never terminate).

The following defines a new algebraic type `Rational`:

```
data Rational = Rat(Int, Int)
--  The rational number m/n is represented by Rat(m,n), where n>0.
```

and the following specifies that the type `Rational` is an instance of the Eq type class:

```
instance Eq Rational where

   Rat(m1,n1) == Rat(m2,n2) =
      m1*n2 == m2*n1
```

Here the `Rational` "==" operator is redefined (in terms of the `Int` "==" operator), overriding its definition in the Eq type class declaration. However, the `Rational` "/=" operator is not redefined here, so its default definition (in terms of the `Rational` "==" operator) is retained.

The following type class Ord encompasses all types equipped with comparison operators named "<", "<=", ">=", and ">":

```
class Ord t where
    (<), (<=), (>=), (>) :: t -> t -> Bool

   x < y   =  y > x
   x <= y  =  not (y > x)
   x >= y  =  not (y < x)
   x > y   =  y < x
```

and the following specifies that the type `Rational` is an instance of the Ord type class:

```
instance Ord Rational where

   Rat(m1,n1) < Rat(m2,n2) =
      m1*n2 < m2*n1
```

The Eq type class of Example 14.12, and a richer version of the Ord type class, are actually in HASKELL's library. Nearly all HASKELL types (excepting mainly function types) are instances of the Eq type class, and so are equipped with "==" and "/=" operators.

A given type can be an instance of several type classes. For example, the `Rational` type of Example 14.12 is an instance of both Eq and Ord.

The following example illustrates how we can exploit a type class to define an interesting generic abstract type.

EXAMPLE 14.13   HASKELL generic abstract type

The following module defines a parameterized abstract type `PriorityQueue t`, with the restriction that the type denoted by t must be equipped with the "<" operator:

```
module PriorityQueues (PriorityQueue,
    empty, add, remove) where

data (Ord t) =>
    PriorityQueue t = PQ [t]
-- A priority queue is represented by a sorted list.

empty  :: PriorityQueue t
add    :: t -> PriorityQueue t -> PriorityQueue t
remove :: PriorityQueue t -> (t, PriorityQueue t)

empty = PQ []

add x (PQ xs) =
  let
      insert x [] = [x]
      insert x (y : ys) =
        if x < y
        then x : y : ys
        else y : insert x ys
  in PQ (insert x xs)

remove (PQ [x: xs]) = (x, PQ xs)
```

The "<" operator is used in the definition of the add function. The clause "(Ord t) =>" in the definition of the PriorityQueue t type guarantees that t is indeed equipped with a "<" operator (and other comparison operators not used here).

All instance types of a given type class are equipped with synonymous functions (or operators). Thus type classes support overloading (in a more systematic manner than the *ad hoc* overloading supported by other languages such as C++, JAVA, and ADA).

14.3.7 Modeling state

A pure functional language such as HASKELL has no explicit concept of storage and therefore no variables that can be updated. It might therefore seem that we cannot model real-world processes with inherent state. Actually we *can* model state, but we do so indirectly, without any explicit use of storage.

In HASKELL, an *action* is an abstract entity that effects a change of state (such as performing input/output) as well as producing a result. Actions can be composed sequentially, and we can predict the effect of performing a sequence of actions. (By contrast, we cannot predict the order in which HASKELL expressions will be evaluated, but that does not matter because evaluating an expression has no side effects.)

Actions are first-class values, and can therefore be passed as arguments, computed as function results, and built into composite values. IO t is the type of an action that performs input/output and produces a result of type t.

The primitive action "return E" simply evaluates the expression E. It has no effect other than producing the value of E. (Do not confuse this action with the return sequencer of imperative and object-oriented languages.)

Given two subactions, A_1 of type IO s, and A_2 of type IO t, we can form the following composite actions:

- "$A_1 >> A_2$" is an action that first performs A_1, discards its result, and then performs A_2. This composite action produces the result of A_2, so its type is IO t.

- "$A_1 >>= \ I -> A_2$" is an action that first performs A_1, binds identifier I to its result (of type s), and then performs A_2. This composite action also produces the result of A_2, so its type is IO t.

EXAMPLE 14.14   HASKELL input/output

The following program first reads from standard input the names of two text files, then copies the contents of the first text file to the second text file:

```
main =
   getLine                        >>= \ inName ->
   getLine                        >>= \ outName ->
   readFile inName                >>= \ inText ->
   writeFile outName inText >>
   putStr "Done!"
```

This uses several library functions:

```
getLine :: IO String
-- getLine reads a line of text from standard input, producing the line's
-- contents as a string.

putStr :: String -> IO ()
-- putStr str writes string str to standard output.

readFile :: FilePath -> IO String
-- readFile path reads the whole of the text file named path, producing
-- the file's contents as a string.

writeFile :: FilePath -> String -> IO ()
-- writeFile path str writes string str to the text file named path.
```

The following library functions enable us to throw and handle exceptions:

```
ioError :: IOError -> IO t
-- ioError e throws exception e.

catch :: IO t -> (IOError -> IO t) -> IO t
-- catch act handler performs action act. If act throws an exception,
-- handler is applied to that exception.
```

Note that IOError is a library abstract type whose values represent exceptions.

This technique for modeling state has limitations: it is not as expressive or natural as the assignments, input/output operations, and exception handling of an imperative language. It forces a two-level architecture on HASKELL programs:

the lower level consists of ordinary functions, which use values to compute new values; the upper level consists of actions that perform all the input/output, calling the lower-level functions to perform computation. HASKELL is a suitable language for implementing only those programs that naturally have such an architecture.

14.3.8   A simple spellchecker

To conclude this overview of functional programming in HASKELL, let us examine a HASKELL implementation of the simple spellchecker specified in Section 11.2.1. The program's architecture is shown in Figure 14.1. The program consists of several modules, and is outlined in Programs 14.1–14.3.

Program 14.1 outlines the Words module, which defines the abstract type Word together with its operations getWord and putWord, both of which are actions. Moreover, putWord will throw an exception if it reaches the end of the input document.

Program 14.2 outlines the Dictionaries module, which defines the abstract type Dictionary. The operations of this abstract type are a constant (empty) and some functions. For example, add is a function that computes the dictionary obtained by adding a word to an existing dictionary. (Contrast this with the imperative and object-oriented add operations in Programs 11.6, 12.2, and 12.6, each of which *updated* the dictionary to which it was applied.)

Program 14.3 outlines the Main module, which defines the high-level functions consultUser, processDocument, and main. The first two are parameterized actions, and the latter is the main program action. Note that processDocument reads a word from the input document and processes it, then calls itself recursively to process the remaining words. It also catches any exception thrown by getWord, in which case it returns immediately.

```
module Words (Word, getWord, putWord) where

    type Word = ...   -- representation
    -- Each Word value is a single word.

    getWord :: FilePath -> FilePath -> IO Word
    -- getWords inDoc outDoc reads a word from the file inDoc, copying any
    -- preceding punctuation to the file outDoc. It produces that word, or throws an
    -- exception if there is no next word.

    putWord :: FilePath -> Word -> IO ()
    -- putword outDoc word writes word to the file outDoc.

    getWord inDoc outDoc = ...

    putWord outDoc word = ...
```

Program 14.1   Words module in HASKELL (in outline).

```
module Dictionaries (Dictionary, empty, add, contains,
    load, save) where

import Words

type Dictionary = ...   -- representation
-- Each Dictionary value is a set of words.

empty :: Dictionary
-- empty is the empty dictionary.

add :: Word -> Dictionary -> Dictionary
-- add word dict yields the dictionary obtained by adding word to dict.

contains :: Dictionary -> Word -> Bool
-- dict 'contains' word yields true if and only if word is a member of
-- dict.

load :: FilePath -> IO Dictionary
-- load path loads a dictionary from the file named path, and produces that
-- dictionary.

save :: FilePath -> Dictionary -> IO ()
-- save path dict saves dict to the file named path.

empty = ...

add word dict = ...

dict 'contains' word = ...

load fn = ...

save fn dict = ...
```

Program 14.2   Dictionaries module in HASKELL (in outline).

Summary

In this chapter:

- We have identified the key concepts of functional programming: expressions, functions, parametric polymorphism, and (in some functional languages) data abstraction and lazy evaluation.
- We have studied the pragmatics of functional programming, noting that data abstraction is just as advantageous in functional programming as in other paradigms.
- We have studied the design of a major functional programming language, HASKELL. In particular, we found that lazy evaluation opens up novel ways of structuring programs. We also found that we can model state (such as input/output) without resorting to variables.
- We have seen a functional implementation, in HASKELL, of a simple spellchecker.

```
module Main where

  import Words
  import Dictionaries

  inDoc = "indoc.txt"
  outDoc = "outdoc.txt"

  consultUser :: Word -> Dictionary ->  Dictionary
       -> IO (Word, Dictionary, Dictionary)
  -- consultUser word mainDict ignored asks the user what to do with
  -- word, which is unknown.
  -- If the user chooses to accept the word, it is added to mainDict.
  -- If the user chooses to ignore the word, it is added to ignored.
  -- If the user chooses to replace the word, the user enters a replacement word.
  -- It produces (word', mainDict', ignored'), where word' is either
  -- word or its replacement, mainDict' is mainDict with word possibly
  -- added, and ignored' is ignored with word possibly added.

  processDocument :: Dictionary -> Dictionary
       -> IO Dictionary
  -- processDocument mainDict ignored copies all words and punctuation
  -- from the input document to the output document, but asks the user what to do
  -- with any words that are unknown (i.e., not in mainDict or ignored).
  -- It produces mainDict', which is mainDict with accepted words added.

  main :: IO ()

  consultUser currentWord mainDict ignored =
    ...

  processDocument mainDict ignored =
    catch (
      getWord inDoc outDoc                    >>= \ word ->
      consultUser word mainDict ignored  >>=
                        \ (word', mainDict', ignored') ->
      putWord outDoc word'                 >>
      processDocument mainDict' ignored'
    ) (
      \ ioexception -> return mainDict
    )

  main =
    load "dict.txt"                      >>= \ mainDict ->
    processDocument mainDict empty  >>= \ mainDict' ->
    save "dict.txt" mainDict'
```

Program 14.3   Main module in HASKELL (in outline).

Further reading

Several good introductions to functional programming in HASKELL are available. BIRD and WADLER (1988) place strong emphasis on proofs of correctness and program transformation. THOMPSON (1999) is a more elementary treatment.

WIKSTRÖM (1987) covers the purely functional subset of ML, emphasizing programming methodology; a definition of ML is included as an appendix.

ABELSON et al. (1996) describe SCHEME, a dialect of LISP. SCHEME supports higher-order functions and (to a limited extent) lazy evaluation, but also provides variables and side effects. Abelson et al. explore the potential of a hybrid functional–imperative style, concentrating heavily on the modularity of their programs.

The Church–Rosser Property is based on a theorem about the lambda-calculus, an account of which may be found in ROSSER (1982). (The lambda-calculus is an extremely simple functional language, much used as an object of study in the theory of computation.)

Exercises

Exercises for Section 14.1

14.1.1 The C++ expression "E_1 && E_2" yields *true* if and only if both E_1 and E_2 yield *true*; moreover, evaluation of E_2 is short-circuited if E_1 yields *false*. The ADA expression "E_1 **and then** E_2" behaves likewise. Explain why "&&" and "**and then**" cannot be defined as ordinary operators or functions in their respective languages.

14.1.2 (a) Define a HASKELL function cond such that "cond(E_1, E_2, E_3)" has *exactly* the same effect as the HASKELL expression "**if** E_1 **then** E_2 **else** E_3". Take advantage of lazy evaluation. (b) Explain why such a function cannot be defined using eager evaluation.

*14.1.3 Consider the function definition "$F\ I = E$" and the function call "$F\ A$". Normal-order evaluation might be characterized by:

$$F A \equiv E[I \Rightarrow A]$$

where $E[I \Rightarrow A]$ is the expression obtained by substituting A for all free occurrences of I in E. (a) Characterize eager evaluation in an analogous fashion. (b) Show that $E[I \Rightarrow A]$ must be defined carefully, because of the possibility of confusing the scopes of an identifier with more than one declaration. For example, consider:

```
let
    f n = let m = 7 in m * n
    m = 2
in f(m+1)
```

Exercises for Section 14.3

14.3.1 Draw a diagram, similar to Figure 14.2, that shows the effect of evaluating "ns1 ++ ns2", where ns1 is the list $[2, 3, 5]$, ns2 is the list $[7, 11, 13, 17]$, and "++" is the concatenation operator.

14.3.2 Suppose that an employee record consists of an employee's name (a string), age (an integer), gender (female or male), and grade (managerial, clerical, or manual). You are given employees, a list of employee records. Write list comprehensions to compute the following: (a) a list of all female employees; (b) a list of all male employees over 60 years of age; (c) a list of the names of all managers. Also write an expression to compute (d) the mean age of all female clerical employees.

14.3.3 (a) Define a HASKELL type whose values are binary search trees (BSTs) with integer components. (b) Define a function that inserts a given integer into a BST. (c) Define a function that maps a given unsorted integer list to a

BST, using your insertion function. (d) Define a function that maps a BST to an integer list using left–root–right traversal. (e) Form the composition of functions (c) and (d). What does it do?

14.3.4 Consider the type Shape of Example 14.4, and the following type:

```
type Point = (Float, Float)   -- x, y coordinates
```

Using pattern matching, define the following functions:

```
perimeter :: Shape -> Float
-- perimeter s computes the length of shape s's perimeter.

inside :: Point -> (Shape, Point) -> Bool
-- p 'inside' (s, c) computes true if and only if point p is inside
-- the shape s centered at point c.
```

14.3.5 The HASKELL operator ".'' composes any two compatible functions, as in Example 14.5. Give three reasons why "." cannot be defined in a language like C or PASCAL.

14.3.6 Example 14.6 uses the obvious algorithm to compute b^n (where $n \geq 0$). A better algorithm is suggested by the following equations:

$$b^0 = 1$$
$$b^{2n} = (b^2)^n$$
$$b^{2n+1} = (b^2)^n \times b$$

Write a HASKELL function to compute b^n using this better algorithm.

*14.3.7 (a) Consider a list comprehension of the form:

$$[E_1 \mid I <- E_2]$$

This uses the existing list, yielded by the expression E_2, to compute a new list. Each component of the new list is determined by evaluating E_1 with the identifier I bound to the corresponding component of the existing list. Show how the same effect can be achieved using the map function of Example 14.7. (b) Repeat with a list comprehension of the form:

$$[E_1 \mid I <- E_2, E_3]$$

which is similar, except that components of the existing list for which the expression E_3 yields *false* are discarded. Use the map and filter functions of Example 14.7.

14.3.8 Consider the genericSort function of Example 14.8. Use this to generate functions to sort lists of employee records (see Exercise 14.3.2). The lists are to be sorted: (a) by name; (b) primarily by grade and secondarily by name.

14.3.9 By replacing the calculation part and/or the control part of Example 14.9, write functions to compute the following: (a) the first power of 2 not less than m; (b) a list of all prime numbers between m and n.

14.3.10 Consider the calculation function approxRoots and the control function absolute of Example 14.10. Reuse the same calculation function with: (a) a control function that tests for convergence using relative difference between successive approximations; (b) a control function that chooses the fourth approximation regardless; (c) a control function that formats the approximations for debugging.

14.3.11 Finish the coding of the HASKELL spellchecker of Programs 14.1–14.3.

14.3.12 Modify the HASKELL spellchecker of Programs 14.1–14.3 to use a third dictionary, the *user dictionary*. Any unknown words accepted by the user are to be added to the user dictionary, which must be saved when the program finishes. The main dictionary is no longer to be updated.

Chapter 15

Logic programming

In this chapter we shall study:

- the key concepts of logic programming;
- the pragmatics of logic programming;
- the design of a major logic programming language, PROLOG.

15.1 Key concepts

Even paradigms as different as imperative and functional programming have one thing in common: a program reads inputs and writes outputs. Since the outputs are functionally dependent on the inputs, an imperative or functional program may be viewed abstractly as implementing a *mapping* from inputs to outputs.

A logic program, on the other hand, implements a *relation*. Since relations are more general than mappings, logic programming is potentially higher-level than imperative or functional programming.

Consider two sets of values S and T. We say that r is a **relation** between S and T if, for every x in S and y in T, $r(x, y)$ is either *true* or *false*.

For example, ">" is a relation between numbers, since for any pair of numbers x and y, $x > y$ is either *true* or *false*. (By convention, we write "$x > y$" rather than "$>(x, y)$".)

A simple geographical example is the relation "flows through" between rivers and countries: "the River Clyde flows through Scotland" is *true*, but "the Mississippi River flows through California" is *false*.

Figure 15.1 illustrates several different relations between two sets $S = \{u, v\}$ and $T = \{a, b, c\}$. A double-headed arrow connects each pair of values for which the relation is *true*. For example, $r_1(u, a)$ and $r_1(v, c)$ are *true*.

Compare Figure 15.1 with Figure 2.2, which illustrated mappings between sets S and T. In a mapping in $S \to T$, each value in S is mapped to exactly one value in T; but in a relation between S and T, a given value in S may be related to many values in T. In general, mappings are many-to-one, while relations are many-to-many. For example, the relation r_4 in Figure 15.1 is many-to-many.

Imperative and functional programming are essentially about implementing mappings. Having implemented a mapping m, we can make the following query:

$$\text{Given } a, \text{ determine the value of } m(a). \tag{15.1}$$

A query like (15.1) will always have a single answer.

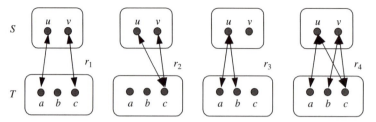

Figure 15.1 Four different relations between sets S and T.

Logic programming is about implementing relations. Having implemented a relation r, we can make queries like:

Given a and u, determine whether $r(a, u)$ is *true*.   (15.2)

Given a, find all y such that $r(a, y)$ is *true*.   (15.3)

Given u, find all x such that $r(x, u)$ is *true*.   (15.4)

Find all x and y such that $r(x, y)$ is *true*.   (15.5)

A query like (15.2) will have a single yes/no answer, but a query like (15.3), (15.4), or (15.5) could have any number of answers (perhaps none). Moreover, queries (15.3) and (15.4) show that a relation makes no distinction between inputs and outputs. Queries like these are characteristic of logic programming, and explain why it is potentially higher-level than imperative or functional programming.

For simplicity, so far we have talked about *binary* relations, i.e., relations between pairs of values. We can also talk about *unary* relations, written in the form $r(x)$, *ternary* relations, written $r(x, y, z)$, and so on.

EXAMPLE 15.1   Relations

Let Point = *point*(Float $\times$ Float) represent the set of all points on the xy plane.

Consider a relation *origin*(p), which is *true* if and only if point p is the origin. This is a unary relation on the set Point. It can be defined as follows:

origin(*point*(x, y)) if and only if $x = 0$ and $y = 0$

Now consider *inside*(p, r), which is *true* if and only if point p lies inside the circle of radius r centered at the origin. This is a binary relation between Point and Float. It can be defined as follows:

inside(*point*(x, y), r) if and only if $x^2 + y^2 < r^2$

Finally consider *collinear*(p_1, p_2, p_3), which is *true* if and only if points p_1, p_2, and p_3 all lie on a straight line. This is a ternary relation. It can be defined as follows:

collinear(*point*(x_1, y_1), *point*(x_2, y_2), *point*(x_3, y_3)) if and only if
$(x_1 - x_2)(y_2 - y_3) = (y_1 - y_2)(x_2 - x_3)$

Note that we can define relations in terms of other relations. We have defined the relations *origin*, *inside*, and *collinear* in terms of the relations "=" and "<" on numbers.

No logic programming language can exploit the full power of mathematical logic, for that formalism is unimplementable. We can use mathematical logic to specify solutions to problems such as this:

fermat(*n*) if and only if there exist positive integers a, b, c such that
$$a^n + b^n = c^n$$

but this "program" cannot be implemented (since the problem is incomputable).

Logic programming is therefore forced to employ a more restricted logic that can be implemented. It turns out that first-order predicate logic, further restricted to Horn clauses, is implementable. The key concepts of logic programming are therefore:

- assertions
- Horn clauses
- relations.

A simple **assertion** has the form $r(T_1, \ldots, T_m)$ where r is an m-ary relation, and where $T_1, \ldots, T_m$ are *terms* (expressions), possibly containing variables.

A **Horn clause** (or just *clause*) has the form:

$$A_0 \text{ if } A_1 \text{ and } \ldots \text{ and } A_n.$$

Informally, this clause means that, if the assertions $A_1, \ldots, A_n$ are all *true*, then we can infer that the assertion A_0 is also *true*. However, we cannot conversely infer that A_0 is *false* just because some A_i turns out to be *false*: a Horn clause is written in terms of "if" rather than "if and only if".

A **fact** is a special case of a Horn clause where $n = 0$:

$$A_0.$$

This fact states that the assertion A_0 is *true* unconditionally.

A logic program is a collection of Horn clauses. The restriction to Horn clauses ensures that an implementation is both possible and tolerably efficient.

Computation consists of testing a given **query** Q, which in its simplest form is just an assertion. If we can infer from the clauses of the program that Q is *true*, then we say that the query **succeeds**. If we cannot infer that Q is *true*, then we say that the query **fails**. This does not mean that Q is definitely *false*; it means simply that Q cannot be inferred to be *true* from the clauses of the program.

To test query Q, we use a technique known as **resolution**:

- If the program contains a fact "A_0." such that A_0 matches Q, then we immediately conclude that Q succeeds.
- If the program contains a clause "A_0 if A_1 and $\ldots$ and A_n." such that A_0 matches Q, then we test $A_1, \ldots, A_n$ separately as subqueries. If all succeed, then we conclude that Q succeeds. If any subquery fails, then we **backtrack**, i.e., give up the attempt to use this particular clause and try another clause instead.

Only when we have tried all clauses whose left-hand sides match Q can we conclude that query Q fails.

An assertion A **matches** a query Q if A and Q can be made equal by consistent substitution, i.e., by replacing each variable by the same value wherever it occurs in A or Q.

Relations abstract over assertions. We can define a relation r by one or more facts of the form "$r(\ldots)$." and/or clauses of the form "$r(\ldots)$ if $\ldots$.". We can call that relation from a clause of the form "$\ldots$ if $\ldots$ and $r(\ldots)$ and $\ldots$.".

Relations in logic programming play much the same role as procedures in other paradigms. Backtracking, however, gives logic programming a distinctive flavor, and is responsible for much of its power and expressiveness. Unfortunately, backtracking is time-consuming.

15.2   Pragmatics

The program units of a logic program are relations. Typically, each relation is composed from simpler relations. Programs are written entirely in terms of such relations. Pure logic programming does not use procedures (which belong to imperative and functional programming). Instead, logic programming uniquely exploits backtracking, which accounts for much of its power and expressiveness.

The very simple structure of Horn clauses forces individual relations to be rather small and simple. A procedure in an imperative or functional program can be as complex as desired, because its definition can include commands and/or expressions composed in many ways. The same is not true of the assertions in the definition of a relation. For this reason, logic programs tend to consist of a large number of relations, each of which has a rather simple definition.

Data abstraction, or at least a means to group relations into packages, would help to keep large logic programs manageable. Unfortunately, the only major logic programming language (PROLOG) has not followed the major imperative and functional programming languages, which have evolved in this way.

Figure 15.2 shows the architecture of a typical logic program.

15.3   Case study: PROLOG

PROLOG was gradually developed during the 1970s by Robert Kowalski and Alain Colmerauer, primarily as an experimental artificial intelligence tool. Lacking a standard definition, PROLOG evolved into several dialects, differing even in their basic syntax! Fortunately, the Edinburgh dialect became a *de facto* standard.

PROLOG received a major boost in 1981, when the Japanese Institute for New Generation Computing Technology selected logic programming as its enabling software technology, and launched the ten-year Fifth Generation Project to provide a complementary hardware technology in the shape of fast logical inference machines. That project did not achieve its very ambitious goals, but logic programming and PROLOG gained a high profile.

15.3.1   Values, variables, and terms

PROLOG's primitive values are numbers and atoms. **Atoms** can be compared with one another, but have no other properties. They are used to represent real-world

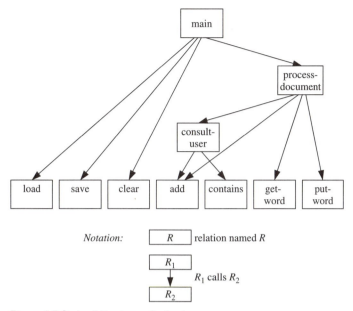

Figure 15.2 Architecture of a logic program.

objects that are primitive as far as the current application is concerned. Examples of atoms are red, green, and blue, which might represent colors, and jan, feb, mar, etc., which might represent months. Atoms resemble the enumerands of some other languages.

PROLOG's composite values are called ***structures***, but they are actually tagged tuples. For example, structures such as date(2000,jan,1) and date(1978,may,5) might be used to represent dates. The tags serve to distinguish structures that happen to have the same components but represent distinct real-world objects, such as point(2,3) and rational(2,3). The components of a structure can be any values, including substructures, for example:

```
person(name("Watt","Susanne"),
       female,
       date(1978,may,5))
```

A *list* in PROLOG is a special case of a structure. The atom [] denotes the empty list, and the structure ". (x,xs)" denotes the list whose head is x and whose tail is the list xs. More convenient notation for lists is also provided:

$$[x \mid xs] \quad \equiv \quad . (x, xs)$$

$$[x_1, \ldots, x_n] \quad \equiv \quad . (x_1, \quad \ldots \quad . (x_n, []) \ldots)$$

A *string* in PROLOG is a list of integers, where each individual integer represents a character. For example, the string literal "Susanne" denotes a list of seven integers.

PROLOG is a dynamically typed language. Values of all types (numbers, atoms, and structures) can be used interchangeably. Thus we can construct heterogeneous lists containing values of different types. We can also compare values of different types using the equality relation "=", but such a comparison always yields *false*.

A PROLOG term is a variable, numeric literal, atom, or structure construction. Terms occur as arguments to relations.

A PROLOG variable (written with an initial uppercase letter to distinguish it from an atom or tag) denotes a fixed but unknown value, of any type. Thus PROLOG variables correspond to mathematical variables, *not* the updatable variables of an imperative language. A variable is declared implicitly by its occurrence in a clause, and its scope is just the clause in which it occurs.

15.3.2   Assertions and clauses

A PROLOG assertion has the form $r(T_1, \ldots, T_m)$, where r is an m-ary relation and $T_1, \ldots, T_m$ are terms.

An assertion A matches a query Q if there is a substitution of terms for variables that makes A and Q the same. For example, born(P, 1978) matches born("Susanne", 1978) under the substitution P = "Susanne". Likewise, born(P, Y) matches born("Jeffrey", 1983) under the substitution P = "Jeffrey" and Y = 1983. Clearly, an assertion can match a query only if they refer to the same relation.

A PROLOG clause is a Horn clause written in one of the following forms:

A_0 .
A_0 :- A_1 , ..., A_n .

The first of these is a fact. The second is read as "A_0 succeeds if A_1 succeeds and ... and A_n succeeds".

A PROLOG clause may also contain the symbol ";", which means "or". For example:

A_0 :- A_1; A_2, A_3 .

is read as "A_0 succeeds if either A_1 succeeds or A_2 succeeds and A_3 succeeds". This is just an abbreviation for a pair of Horn clauses, "A_0 :- A_1." and "A_0 :- A_2, A_3.".

15.3.3   Relations

A PROLOG relation is defined by one or more clauses.

EXAMPLE 15.2   PROLOG relations

The following PROLOG facts together define a unary relation star on celestial bodies, where each celestial body is represented by an atom (such as sun):

```
% star(B) succeeds if and only if B is a known star.
star(sirius).
star(sun).
```

```
star(vega).
% ... and similarly for other stars.
```

Here are some possible queries:

`?- star(sun).`	This succeeds.
`?- star(jupiter).`	This fails.

The following PROLOG facts together define a binary relation `orbits`:

```
% orbits(B1, B2) succeeds if and only if B1 is known to orbit around B2.
orbits(mercury, sun).
orbits(venus, sun).
orbits(earth, sun).
orbits(mars, sun).
orbits(moon, earth).
orbits(phobos, mars).
orbits(deimos, mars).
% ... and similarly for other planets and their satellites.
```

Here are some possible queries:

`?- orbits(mars, sun).`	This succeeds.
`?- orbits(moon, sun).`	This fails.
`?- orbits(phobos, B).`	This asks which body or bodies Phobos orbits. It succeeds yielding a single answer: `B = mars`.
`?- orbits(B, mars).`	This asks which body or bodies orbit Mars. It succeeds yielding the answers `B = phobos` and `B = deimos`.
`?- orbits(B, venus).`	This fails, since there is no substitution for B that would make this query match any of the facts.

The following clause defines a unary relation `planet`:

```
% planet(B) succeeds if and only if B is a known planet of the Sun.
planet(B) :-
    orbits(B, sun).
```

Here are some possible queries:

`?- planet(mars).`	This succeeds.
`?- planet(P).`	This succeeds yielding the answers `P = mercury`, `P = venus`, `P = earth`, `P = mars`, etc.

The following clause defines a unary relation `satellite`:

```
% satellite(B)  succeeds if and only if B is a known satellite of a known
%     planet of the Sun.
satellite(B) :-
    orbits(B, P), planet(P).
```

This clause says that a body B is a satellite if it orbits some celestial body P and that same P is a planet. Here are some possible queries:

```
?- satellite(phobos).       This succeeds.
?- satellite(S).            This succeeds yielding the answers
                            S = moon, S = phobos, S =
                            deimos, etc.
```

Finally, the following clause defines a unary relation `solar`:

```
% solar(B) succeeds if and only if B is a known member of the Solar System.
solar(sun).
solar(B) :-
      planet(B);
      satellite(B).
```

The first clause says that the Sun is a member of the solar system. The second clause says that a body B is a member of the solar system if it is a planet or if it is a satellite. Here are some possible queries:

```
?- solar(venus).        This succeeds.
?- solar(moon).         This succeeds.
?- solar(sirius).       This fails.
?- solar(B).            This succeeds yielding the answers B =
                        sun, B = mercury, B = venus, B
                        = earth, B = mars, B = moon, B
                        = phobos, B = deimos, etc.
```

Not all relations defined in PROLOG have such straightforward logical meanings. The following example illustrates one way in which PROLOG departs from our logical intuition.

EXAMPLE 15.3   PROLOG arithmetic relations

The relations of Example 15.3.1 might be expressed in PROLOG as follows. Assume that the point (x, y) is represented by the structure $point(x,y)$.

```
origin(point(X,Y)) :-
      X = 0, Y = 0.

inside(point(X,Y), R) :-
      X*X+Y*Y < R*R.
```

Here are some possible queries:

```
?- origin(point(0,2)).      This fails.
?- origin(P).               This succeeds yielding the answer P =
                            point(0,0).

?- inside(point(1,2), 3).   This succeeds.
?- inside(point(1,2), R).   This query is erroneous.
```

The last query attempts to ask for the radii of all circles that enclose the point (1, 2). It amounts to finding every value for R such that 5 < R*R, but PROLOG's built-in relation "<" succeeds only when both its arguments are known numbers. In consequence, the relation inside behaves correctly only when both its arguments are known.

The only way to repeat a computation in PROLOG is by defining a recursive relation. Relations on lists are typically recursive.

EXAMPLE 15.4   PROLOG recursive relations

The following clauses define a binary relation contains:

```
% contains(L, Y) succeeds if and only if Y is an element of list L.
contains([X|Xs], X).
contains([X|Xs], Y) :-
     contains(Xs, Y).
```

The first clause says that X is an element of a list with head X and tail Xs. The second clause says that Y is an element of a list with head X and tail Xs if Y is an element of Xs. Here are some possible queries:

?- contains([2,3,5], 3).	This succeeds.
?- contains([2,3,5], 4).	This fails.
?- contains([2,3,5], V).	This succeeds yielding the answers V = 2, V = 3, and V = 5.
?- contains([], 4).	This fails.

The last query fails simply because there is no clause that matches it.
The following clauses define a ternary relation addlast:

```
% addlast(X, L1, L2) succeeds if and only if adding X to the end of list
%     L1 yields the list L2.
addlast(X, [], [X]).
addlast(X, [Y|Ys], [Y|Zs]) :-
     addlast(X, Ys, Zs).
```

The first clause says that adding X to the end of the empty list yields [X]. The second clause says that adding X to the end of [Y|Ys] yields [Y|Zs], if adding X to the end of Ys yields Zs. Here are some possible queries:

?- addlast(7, [], L).	This succeeds yielding the answer L = [7].
?- addlast(7, [2,3,5], L).	This succeeds yielding the answer L = [2, 3, 5, 7].
?- addlast(V, L, [2,3,5]).	This succeeds yielding the answer V = 5 and L = [2, 3].
?- addlast(V, L, []).	This fails.

The following clauses define a ternary relation `concat`:

```
% concat(L1, L2, L3) succeeds if and only if concatenating the lists L1
%    and L2 yields the list L3.
concat([], Ys, Ys).
concat([X|Xs], Ys, [X|Zs]) :-
    concat(Xs, Ys, Zs).
```

The first clause says that concatenating the empty list and Ys yields Ys. The second clause says that concatenating [X|Xs] and Ys yields [X|Zs], if concatenating Xs and Ys yields Zs. Here are some possible queries:

?- concat([2,3], [5,7], L).	This succeeds yielding the answer L = [2, 3, 5, 7].
?- concat([2,3], L, [2,3,5,7]).	This succeeds yielding the answer L = [5, 7].
?- concat(L1, L2, [5,7]).	This finds all possible ways of splitting [5, 7]. It succeeds yielding the answers: (1) L1 = [] and L2 = [5, 7] (2) L1 = [5] and L2 = [7] (3) L1 = [5, 7] and L2 = []

Thus the relation `concat` can be used to concatenate two given lists, or to remove a given list from the front (or back) of another list, or to find all ways of splitting a given list. In an imperative or functional language, we would need to write several procedures or functions to accomplish all these computations.

15.3.4 The closed-world assumption

An assertion *A* might fail. This does not mean that *A* is definitely *false*; it simply means that we cannot infer from the clauses of the program that *A* is *true*. In fact, only assertions using built-in relations (such as "chalk = cheese" and "2 > 3") are definitely *false* in PROLOG. When an assertion is tested, therefore, success means *true* and failure means either *unknown* or *false*.

As this is rather inconvenient, PROLOG bends the rules of logic by ignoring the distinction between *unknown* and *false*. In other words, an assertion is assumed to be *false* if it cannot be inferred to be *true*. This is called the **closed-world assumption** – the PROLOG processor assumes that the program encodes all relevant information about the application domain (the "world").

In Example 15.2, a query like "?- orbits(halley, sun)." would fail, simply because the program asserted nothing at all about halley. A query like "?- comet(halley)." would also fail, simply because the program did not define a unary relation comet.

This of itself is not too serious: PROLOG programmers are well aware that the closed-world assumption obliges them to encode all relevant information. However, PROLOG compounds the problem by providing a form of negation. If *A* is an assertion, then "not(A)" is an assertion that negates the assumed truth value of *A*. Thus the negation of *unknown* is taken to be *true*! Using negation, it is easy to write clauses that are truly misleading.

EXAMPLE 15.5   PROLOG **negation**

Suppose that we add the following clause to Example 15.2:

```
comet(B) :-
    not(star(B)), not(planet(B)), not(satellite(B)).
```

Here are some possible queries:

?- comet(halley).	This succeeds.
?- comet(apollo).	This succeeds.
?- orbits(halley, sun).	This fails.

The first query succeeds, but only by coincidence! This is highlighted by the fact that the second query also succeeds.

15.3.5   Bindings and scope

A PROLOG program consists of one or more relations. Each relation, as we have seen, is defined by one or more clauses.

The scope of every relation is the entire program. It is not possible in PROLOG to define a relation locally to another relation, nor to group relations into packages.

The scope of each variable is the whole of the clause (or query) in which it occurs. This clause from Example 15.2:

```
planet(B) :-
    orbits(B, sun).
```

has the following meaning in predicate logic:

For all B, `planet(B)` succeeds if `orbits(B, sun)` succeeds.

This clause:

```
satellite(B) :- orbits(B, P), planet(P).
```

has the following meaning:

For all B, `satellite(B)` succeeds if there exists P such that
`orbits(B, P)` and `planet(P)` both succeed.

This query:

```
?- satellite(S).
```

has the following meaning:

Does there exist S such that `satellite(S)` succeeds?

In general, every PROLOG variable *V* is either *universally quantified* ("for all *V*: …") or *existentially quantified* ("there exists *V* such that …"), according to the following rules:

- A variable that occurs on the left-hand side of a clause is universally quantified.
- A variable that occurs on the right-hand side (but not on the left-hand side) of a clause is existentially quantified.
- A variable that occurs in a query is existentially quantified.

Quantification is always implicit in PROLOG.

15.3.6   Control

In principle, the order in which resolution is done should not affect the set of answers yielded by a query (although it will affect the order in which these answers are found). In practical logic programming, however, the order is very important.

The main consideration is nontermination, which is a possible consequence of recursive clauses. The following example illustrates the problem.

EXAMPLE 15.6   Nontermination

Suppose that we add the following relation to Example 15.2:

```
% neighbor(A, B) succeeds if and only if A or B is a satellite of the other.
neighbor(A, B) :-
     planet(A), orbits(B, A).
neighbor(A, B) :-
     neighbor(B, A).
```

In principle, queries like the following:

```
?- neighbor(earth, moon).
?- neighbor(moon, earth).
```

should both succeed. If we consistently apply the *nonrecursive* clause first, both queries will indeed give the correct answers. But if we consistently apply the *recursive* clause first, both queries will loop forever, due to repeated application of the recursive clause.

Consider the clause "A_0 :- A_1, A_2.". Assume that A_1 loops forever but A_2 fails. If we test A_2 first, it fails and we can immediately conclude that A_0 fails. (This is consistent with a predicate logic interpretation of the clause.) But if we test A_1 first, it will loop forever and the computation will make no further progress.

Thus the actual behavior of a logic program depends on the order in which resolution is done. To allow the programmer control over the computation, PROLOG defines the resolution order precisely:

- The assertions on the right-hand side of a clause are tried in order from left to right.
- If a relation is defined by several clauses, these clauses are tried in order from first to last.

Together with backtracking, these rules define the control flow of PROLOG programs. A consequence of these rules is that every PROLOG program is deterministic. If a query has multiple answers, we can even predict the order in which these answers will be found.

Backtracking is very time-consuming. If we know in advance that a query will have only one answer (say), then it would be wasteful to allow the PROLOG processor to continue searching for more answers once the first answer has been found.

In Example 15.2, we know that a query like "?- orbits(deimos, P)." will have just one answer, but the PROLOG processor does not know that (since the program cannot declare that orbits is a many-to-one relation). So even when the answer P = mars has been found, the PROLOG processor will try all the remaining clauses in a fruitless attempt to find other answers.

PROLOG provides a kind of sequencer, called the **cut**, that suppresses backtracking whenever it is encountered. The cut is written as "!".

Suppose that we are testing a query Q using the following clause:

$$A_0 \; :\text{-} \; A_1, \; !, \; A_2.$$

If A_1 fails, then the PROLOG processor backtracks and tries another clause, as usual. But if A_1 succeeds, the processor accepts the first answer yielded by A_1, passes the cut, and goes on to test A_2. Passing the cut has the effect that, if A_2 subsequently fails, then the processor immediately concludes that Q itself fails – the PROLOG processor will make no attempt to find any further answers from A_1, and will not try any further clauses to test Q.

Or suppose that we are testing a query Q using the following clause:

$$A_0 \; :\text{-} \; !.$$

If A_0 matches Q, the PROLOG processor will not try any further clauses to test Q.

EXAMPLE 15.7   PROLOG cut

Suppose that a phone-book is represented by a list of entries, in which each entry is a structure of the form entry(Name, Number), and in which no two entries contain the same name.

The following clauses define a ternary relation lookup1:

```
% lookup1(PhoneBook, Name, Num) succeeds if and only if
%     PhoneBook contains entry(Name, Num).
lookup1([entry(Name1,Num1)|Ents], Name1, Num1).
lookup1([entry(Name2,Num2)|Ents], Name1, Num1) :-
     lookup1(Ents, Name1, Num1).
```

Let PhoneBook be the following list:

```
[entry("Ali",6046),
 entry("Carol",6742),
 entry("David",6742)]
```

Then the following query:

```
?- lookup1(PhoneBook, "Carol", Number).
```

yields the single answer Number = 6742. This answer is correct, but to find it the PROLOG processor examines *every* entry in PhoneBook!

Queries like this can be answered more efficiently if we cut off the search as soon as we have a match:

```
% lookup2(PhoneBook, Name, Num) succeeds if and only if
%     PhoneBook contains entry(Name,Num).
lookup2([entry(Name1,Num1)|Ents], Name1, Num1) :-
       !.
lookup2([entry(Name2,Num2)|Ents], Name1, Num1) :-
       !, lookup2(Ents, Name1, Num1).
```

The cuts do not affect the answers yielded by queries like the one mentioned above. However, they eliminate possible answers to other kinds of query. For instance, this query:

```
?- lookup1(PhoneBook, Name, 6742).
```

yields two answers, Name = "Carol" and Name = "David", while this query:

```
?- lookup2(PhoneBook, Name, 6742).
```

yields only the first of these answers. (See also Exercise 15.3.4.)

The cut is an *ad hoc* feature, added to PROLOG to make execution of queries tolerably efficient. Cuts cannot be understood in terms of predicate logic, but only in terms of PROLOG's control flow. Cuts often have unexpected effects, as illustrated by Example 15.7. Thus cuts are low-level sequencers, somewhat analogous to jumps in imperative languages.

15.3.7   Input/output

A simple PROLOG program might consist entirely of ordinary relations. The inputs to the program are queries; its outputs are the corresponding answer(s) to these queries (including substitutions for variables that occur in the queries), formatted by the PROLOG processor.

More realistic programs need to read data from files, and write data to files, in formats chosen by the program designer. For this purpose PROLOG provides a number of built-in relations:

see(F)	Opens the file named F, making it the current input file.
read(T)	Reads a term from the current input file; T is that term (or the atom end_of_file if no term remains to be read).
seen	Closes the current input file.
tell(F)	Opens the file named F, making it the current output file.
write(T)	Writes the term T to the current output file.
nl	Writes an end-of-line to the current output file.
told	Closes the current output file.

Of course these are not relations in the proper sense of the word. A program that uses these relations is not a pure logic program, and its behavior can be understood only in terms of PROLOG's control flow (Section 15.3.6).

15.3.8   A simple spellchecker

To conclude this overview of logic programming in PROLOG, let us briefly examine a spellchecker with the architecture shown in Figure 15.2. This program is outlined in Programs 15.1–15.4.

Program 15.1 outlines relations concerned with words, which are here represented by strings. The get_word and put_word relations perform input/output of individual words. Note that get_word's result is either a word or the atom end_of_file. An additional relation less is defined here, since PROLOG does not support lexicographic comparison of strings.

Program 15.2 outlines relations concerned with dictionaries. For example, add is a ternary relation that can be used to compute the dictionary obtained by adding a word to an existing dictionary. A dictionary is here represented by a binary search tree. PROLOG does not support data abstraction, so it is not possible to keep the representation private. (In this program, however, the higher-level relations are defined exclusively in terms of the dictionary relations, thus avoiding tight coupling.)

Program 15.3 outlines the higher-level relations consult_user, process_document, and main. Program 15.4 shows several auxiliary relations (known, handle_word, and process_words) that are needed to assist in the definition of process_document. These relations make liberal use of cuts, for the sake of efficiency. The relation process_words calls get_word, and uses pattern matching on its result to decide what to do next: if the result is end_of_file, process_words succeeds immediately; if the result is a word,

```
%  A word is here represented by a string.

%  get_word(W) reads the next word from the current input file, copying any
%  preceding punctuation to the current output file. W is either that word or
%  end_of_file if there is no next word to be read.
get_word(W) :-
     ...

%  put_word(W) writes word W to the current output file.
put_word(W) :-
     ...

%  less(W1, W2) succeeds if and only if word W1 precedes word W2 in alphabetical
%  order.
less(W1, W2) :-
     ...
```

Program 15.1 Word relations in PROLOG (in outline).

```
% A dictionary is a set of words. Here it is represented by a binary search tree: either
% empty or dict(Dl, W, Dr), where W is a word and Dl and Dr are dictionaries.

% clear(D) succeeds iff D is the empty dictionary.
clear(empty).

% add(D, W, D1) succeeds iff D1 is the dictionary obtained by adding W to D.
add(empty, W, dict(empty,W,empty)).
add(dict(Dl,W,Dr), W, dict(Dl,W,Dr)).
add(dict(Dl,Wd,Dr), W, dict(Dl1,Wd,Dr)) :-
    less(W, Wd), !,
    add(Dl, W, Dl1).
add(dict(Dl,W,Dr), W, dict(Dl,Wd,Dr1)) :-
    less(Wd, W), !,
    add(Dr, W, Dr1).

% contains(D, W) succeeds iff D is W is a member of D.
contains(dict(Dl,W,Dr), W).
contains(dict(Dl,Wd,Dr), W) :-
    less(W, Wd), !,
    contains(Dl, W).
contains(dict(Dl,Wd,Dr), W) :-
    less(Wd, W), !,
    contains(Dr, W).

% load(F, D) reads all words from the file named F into the dictionary D.
load(F, D) :-
    see(F),
    loadwords(empty, D),
    seen.

% save(F, D) writes all words in dictionary D to the file named F.
save(F, D) :-
    tell(F),
    savewords(D),
    told.

% loadwords(D, D1) reads all words from the current input file and adds them to
% the dictionary D, yielding the dictionary D1.
loadwords(D, D) :-
    read(end_of_file), !.
loadwords(D, D2) :-
    read(W),
    add(D, W, D1),
    loadwords(D1, D2).

% savewords(D) writes all words in dictionary D to the current output file.
savewords(empty).
savewords(dict(Dl,W,Dr)) :-
    write(W),
    savewords(Dl),
    savewords(Dr).
```

Program 15.2 Dictionary relations in PROLOG.

```
% consult_user(Word, MainDict, Ignored, Word1, MainDict1,
% Ignored1) asks the user what to do with Word, which is unknown.
% If the user chooses to accept the word, it is added to MainDict.
% If the user chooses to ignore the word, it is added to Ignored.
% If the user chooses to replace the word, the user enters a replacement word.
% Word1 is either Word or its replacement, MainDict1 is mainDict with Word
% possibly added, and Ignored1 is Ignored with Word possibly added.
consult_user(Word, MainDict, Ignored,
                 Word1, MainDict1, Ignored1) :-
     ...

% process_document(MainDict, Ignored, MainDict1) copies all words
% and punctuation from the input document to the output document, but asks the user
% what to do with any words that are unknown. MainDict1 is MainDict with
% accepted words added.
process_document(MainDict, Ignored, MainDict1) :-
     see("indoc.txt"),
     tell("outdoc.txt"),
     process_words(MainDict, Ignored, MainDict1),
     seen,
     told.

main :-
     load("dict.txt", MainDict),
     clear(Ignored),
     process_document(MainDict, Ignored, MainDict1),
     save("dict.txt",  MainDict1).
```

Program 15.3 Definitions of the consult_user, process_document, and main relations in PROLOG (in outline).

process_words processes that word and then calls itself recursively to process the remaining words.

Summary

In this chapter:

- We have identified the key concepts of logic programming: assertions, Horn clauses, and relations.

- We have studied the pragmatics of logic programming. We noted that data abstraction would be as advantageous in logic programming as in other paradigms.

- We have studied the design of a major logic programming language, PROLOG. We found that programming in PROLOG benefits from the power of backtracking, but in practice also needs impure features like the cut and input/output, which cannot be understood in terms of mathematical logic.

- We have seen a logic programming implementation, in PROLOG, of a simple spellchecker.

```
% known(Word, MainDict, Ignored) succeeds if and only if Word is known
% (i.e., in MainDict or Ignored).
known(Word, MainDict, Ignored) :-
    contains(MainDict, Word), !;
    contains(Ignored, Word).

% handle_word(Word, MainDict, Ignored, Word1, MainDict1,
% Ignored1) asks the user what to do with Word if it is unknown.
handle_word(Word, MainDict, Ignored,
            Word, MainDict, Ignored) :-
    known(Word, MainDict, Ignored), !.
handle_word(Word, MainDict, Ignored,
            Word1, MainDict1, Ignored1) :-
    not(known(Word, MainDict, Ignored)), !,
    consult_user(Word, MainDict, Ignored,
        Word1, MainDict1, Ignored1).

% process_words(MainDict, Ignored, MainDict1) copies all words
% and punctuation from the current input file to the current output file, but asks the user
% what to do with any words that are unknown. MainDict1 is MainDict with
% accepted words added.
process_words(MainDict, Ignored, MainDict) :-
    get_word(end_of_file), !.
process_words(MainDict, Ignored, MainDict2) :-
    get_word(Word), !,
    handle_word(Word, MainDict, Ignored,
        Word1, MainDict1, Ignored1),
    put_word(Word1),
    process_words(MainDict1, Ignored1, MainDict2).
```

Program 15.4 Definitions of auxiliary relations in PROLOG.

Further reading

This chapter has given only a very brief outline of the logic programming paradigm. For a much fuller account of logic programming in general, and of PROLOG in particular, see BRATKO (1990) or MALPAS (1987).

Exercises

Exercises for Section 15.1

15.1.1 Consider the sets Country = {*China, Egypt, Greece, India, Italy, Russia, Spain, Turkey*} and Continent = {*Africa, Asia, Europe*}. Draw a diagram, similar to Figure 15.1, showing the relation "is located in" between countries and continents.

Exercises for Section 15.3

15.3.1 Consider the relation *collinear* of Example 15.1. Define this relation in PROLOG.

15.3.2 Consider the list relations defined in Example 15.4. (a) Give an alternative definition of `addlast` in terms of `concat`. (b) Define a relation `last(L, X)` that succeeds if and only if X is the last element of the list L. (c) Define a relation `reverse(L1, L2)` that succeeds if and only if L2 is the reverse of the list L1. (d) Define a relation `ordered(L)` that succeeds if and only if the list of integers L is in ascending order.

15.3.3 Consider the `lookup1` and `lookup2` relations of Example 15.7.

(a) Using the example PhoneBook, what answers would you expect from the following queries? Explain these answers.

```
?- lookup1(PhoneBook, "David", 9999).
?- lookup1(PhoneBook, "Susanne", Number).
?- lookup1(PhoneBook, Name, 6041).
?- lookup1(PhoneBook, Name, Number).
```

(b) Repeat with the `lookup2` relation.

(c) Repeat with the following relation:

```
% lookup3(PhoneBook, Name, Num)  succeeds if and only if
%       PhoneBook  contains  entry(Name,Num).
lookup3([entry(Name1,Num1)|Ents], Name1, Num1).
lookup3([entry(Name2,Num2)|Ents], Name1, Num1) :-
        Name1 \= Name2, lookup3(Ents, Name1, Num1).
```

Note that the built-in relation "`\=`" succeeds if and only if its operands are unequal; both operands must be known values.

(d) Define a relation `insert(Book1, Name, Num, Book2)` that succeeds if and only if Book2 is the phone-book obtained by adding `entry(Name,Num)` to Book1, or fails if Book1 already contains an entry for Name.

15.3.4 Use cuts to improve the efficiency of queries in Example 15.2. Make reasonable assumptions about which kinds of query are most likely. What queries will have their answers affected by your cuts?

15.3.5 Finish the coding of the Prolog spellchecker of Programs 15.1–15.3.

15.3.6 Modify the Prolog spellchecker of Programs 15.1–15.3 to use a third dictionary, the *user dictionary*. Any unknown words accepted by the user are to be added to the user dictionary, which must be saved when the program finishes. The main dictionary is no longer to be updated.

Chapter 16

Scripting

In this chapter we shall study:

- the pragmatics of scripting;
- the key concepts of scripting languages;
- the design of a major scripting language, PYTHON.

16.1 Pragmatics

Scripting is a paradigm characterized by:

- use of scripts to glue subsystems together;
- rapid development and evolution of scripts;
- modest efficiency requirements;
- very high-level functionality in application-specific areas.

Scripting is used in a variety of applications, and scripting languages are correspondingly diverse. Nevertheless, the above points influence the design of all scripting languages.

A software system often consists of a number of subsystems controlled or connected by a script. In such a system, the script is said to *glue* the subsystems together. One example of gluing is a system to create a new user account on a computer, consisting of a script that calls programs to perform the necessary system administration actions. A second example is an office system that uses a script to connect a word processor to a spellchecker and a drawing tool. A third example is a system that enables a user to fill a Web form, converts the form data into a database query, transmits the query to a database server, converts the query results into a dynamic Web page, and downloads the latter to the user's computer for display by the Web browser.

Each subsystem could be a complete program designed to stand alone, or it could be a program unit designed to be part of a larger system, or it could be itself a script. Each subsystem could be written in a different programming or scripting language.

Gluing exposes the problem of how to pass data between a script and a subsystem written in a different language. In some systems only strings can be passed directly; for example, a UNIX command script manipulates only strings, and a C program accepts an array of strings as its argument, so the script can call

413

the program without difficulty. Nowadays subsystems are often classes written in object-oriented languages, in which case the script should be able to pass objects around, and perhaps call methods with which these objects are equipped.

Scripts are characterized by *rapid development and evolution.* Some scripts are written and used once only, such as a sequence of commands issued by the user, one at a time, to a system that presents a command-line interface. Other scripts are used frequently, but also need to be modified frequently in response to changing requirements. In such circumstances, scripts should be easy to write, with concise syntax. (This does not imply that scripts need be cryptic. Many of the older scripting languages have extremely cryptic and irregular syntax, and scripts written in such languages are very hard to read.)

Script development typically entails a lightweight edit–run cycle (as opposed to the heavyweight edit–compile–link–run cycle of conventional program development). In some scripting languages, source code is interpreted directly; compilation and linking are omitted altogether. In other scripting languages (including PYTHON), source code is automatically compiled into virtual machine code, which is then interpreted; compilation and linking do take place, but only behind the scenes.

Efficiency is not an essential requirement for scripts. Clearly a once-used script need not be particularly fast, but that is less obvious for a frequently-used script. When a script is used as glue, however, the system's total running time tends to be dominated by the subsystems, which are typically written in programming languages and can be tuned as much as desired. (If the running time is dominated by the glue, the system's architecture should be reconsidered.) Since the script's execution speed is not critically important, the overheads of interpretation and of dynamic type checking can be tolerated.

Scripting languages all provide *very high-level functionality* in certain application-specific areas. For instance, many scripts are required to parse and translate text, so all scripting languages provide very high-level facilities for processing strings. This point will be amplified in the following section.

16.2 Key concepts

Scripting is similar to imperative programming in many respects. Thus all scripting languages support variables, commands, and procedures, which are the key concepts of imperative programming.

Scripting languages are so diverse that it is difficult to identify any concepts that they all share with one another but do not share with imperative programming languages. Nevertheless, the following concepts are characteristic of scripting languages:

- very high-level string processing;
- very high-level graphical user interface support;
- dynamic typing.

All scripting languages provide very high-level support for *string processing.* The justification for this is the ubiquity of textual data, such as e-mail messages, database queries and results, XML documents, and HTML documents. Generation of text is easy enough, even with simple string operations, but parsing of text (i.e., discovering its internal structure) is more troublesome. To solve this kind of problem a powerful tool is the *regular expression*, which we shall study in Section 16.2.1.

Many scripting languages provide very high-level support for building *graphical user interfaces* (*GUIs*). One justification for this is to ensure loose coupling between the GUI and the application code; the GUI is especially likely to evolve rapidly as usability problems are exposed. Another justification is a potentially large productivity gain. For example, a single line of code in the scripting language TCL suffices to create a button, fix its visual appearance and label, and identify a procedure in the application code (or in the script itself) that will be called when a user clicks the button. To achieve the same effect takes many lines of code in a conventional programming language (even assuming that the language has a suitable GUI library).

Many scripting languages are *dynamically typed*. When used as glue, scripts need to be able to pass data to and from subsystems written in different languages, perhaps with incompatible type systems. Scripts often process heterogeneous data, whether in forms, databases, spreadsheets, or Web pages. For scripting applications, a simple type system would be too inflexible, while an advanced type system such as parametric polymorphism or generic classes would sit uneasily with the pragmatic need for rapid development and evolution.

Of course, dynamic typing is not an unmixed blessing. Scripts can indeed be written more quickly when the types of variables and parameters need not be declared, but the absence of type information makes scripts harder to read. A dynamically typed scripting language does indeed avoid the need for a complicated type system, but type errors can be detected only by the vagaries of testing, and some type errors might remain undetected indefinitely. (Recall that static typing enables the compiler to certify that type errors will *never* cause run-time failure.)

Just because some scripts are used once only, it does not follow that maintenance of scripts is not a problem. If a script is useful and will be used frequently, its very success condemns it to be maintained just like any program written in a conventional language. To be maintainable, a script or program must be readable, well documented, designed for change, and as error-free as possible. Fortunately, the designers of the more modern scripting languages such as PYTHON clearly understand the importance of maintenance, but even they have not yet found a way to reconcile the conflicting goals of flexibility and elimination of run-time type errors.

16.2.1   Regular expressions

A *regular expression* (or *RE*) is a kind of pattern that *matches* some set of strings. Here are some simple examples of regular expressions.

- The regular expression M(r|s|iss) means "M" followed by either "r" or "s" or "iss". Thus it matches the strings "Mr", "Ms", and "Miss" (but no others).

Table 16.1   Forms of regular expressions: (a) basic forms; (b) derived forms.

(a)

Basic form	What it matches
c	"c" (where c is a single character)
$RE_1|RE_2$	any string matched by either RE_1 or RE_2
RE_1RE_2	any string obtained by concatenating a string matched by RE_1 and a string matched by RE_2
$RE*$	any string obtained by concatenating zero or more strings, each of which is matched by RE
(RE)	any string matched by RE (the parentheses being used for grouping)

(b)

Derived form	What it matches
.	"c" (where c is a single character)
$RE^?$	either the empty string or any string matched by RE
RE^+	any string obtained by concatenating *one* or more strings, each of which is matched by RE
RE^n	any string obtained by concatenating exactly n strings, each of which is matched by RE (where n is a nonnegative integer)

- The regular expression ba*n means "b" followed by zero or more "a"s followed by "n". Thus it matches the strings "bn", "ban", "baan", "baaan", and so on.
- The regular expression (em|in)* means zero or more occurrences of either "em" or "in". Thus it matches the strings "", "em", "in", "emem", "emin", "inem", "inin", "ememem", "eminem", and so on.

Table 16.1 summarizes the various forms of regular expression, showing what each means in terms of the strings it matches. The basic forms c, $RE_1|RE_2$, RE_1RE_2, $RE*$, and (RE) are sufficient to express everything we want. However, we find it convenient in practice also to use derived forms such as ". ", $RE^?$, RE^+, and RE^n. All the derived forms can be expressed in terms of the basic forms. (See Exercise 16.2.3.)

EXAMPLE 16.1   Regular expressions in practice

The UNIX command language employs a dialect of regular expressions in which "*" matches *any* string of characters, and ". " matches itself. The following command:

```
print *.txt
```

contains a regular expression "*.txt", and is interpreted as follows. First, the regular expression is replaced by a sequence of all filenames in the current directory (folder) that are matched by the regular expression. Second, the print program is called with these filenames as arguments. The command's net effect is to print all files in the current directory whose names end with ".txt".

The following script:

```
(1) for f in *
    do
       case $f in
(2)      *.ps)
             print $f; rm $f;;
(3)      *.txt)
             print $f;;
(4)      *)
             ;;
       esac
    done
```

contains a case-command within a for-command. In line (1), the regular expression "*" matches *all* filenames in the current directory, so the for-command's control variable f is set to each filename in turn. The case-command tests the regular expressions at lines (2), (3), and (4) until it finds one that matches $f (the value of f). The regular expression "*.ps" matches any filename ending with ".ps"; "*.txt" matches any filename ending with ".txt"; and "*" matches any filename at all. The script's net effect is to print and remove all POSTSCRIPT files in the current directory, print all text files, and ignore all other files.

This script is typical of the kind of application for which scripting languages are intended. It calls existing programs, such as print and rm. It is short but useful, automating a sequence of actions that would be tedious to perform manually.

Almost all scripting languages employ regular expressions in string matching operations. A simple operation might test whether a given regular expression matches a given string *s*. A more powerful operation might discover which parts of *s* are matched by certain parts of the regular expression. (This is a form of *parsing*.) Typically the matching operation yields a tuple or list of substrings of *s* that are matched by the parenthesized parts of the regular expression. For example, the regular expression "{(.*),(.*)}" matches the string "{one,two}", and yields the substrings "one" and "two".

16.3   Case study: PYTHON

PYTHON was designed in the early 1990s by Guido van Rossum. It has been used to help implement the successful Web search engine GOOGLE, and in a variety of other application areas ranging from science fiction (visual effects for the *Star Wars* series) to real science (computer-aided design in NASA).

PYTHON borrows ideas from languages as diverse as PERL, HASKELL, and the object-oriented languages, skillfully integrating these ideas into a coherent whole. PYTHON scripts are concise but readable, and highly expressive. PYTHON is a compact language, relying on its library to provide most of its very high-level functionality such as string matching (unlike older scripting languages such as PERL, in which such features are built-in). PYTHON is dynamically typed, so scripts contain little or no type information.

16.3.1   Values and types

PYTHON has a limited repertoire of primitive types: integer, real, and complex numbers. It has no specific character type; single-character strings are used instead. Its boolean values (named False and True) are just small integers. However, *any* value can be tested: zero, the empty tuple, the empty string, the empty list, and so on, are treated like False; all other values are treated like True.

PYTHON has a rich repertoire of composite types: tuples, strings, lists, dictionaries, and objects. A PYTHON list is a heterogeneous sequence of values. A *dictionary* (sometimes called an associative array) is a heterogeneous mapping from keys to values, where the keys are distinct immutable values. Components of tuples, strings, lists, and dictionaries may be inspected, and components of lists and dictionaries may be updated, using a uniform notation that resembles conventional array-indexing notation. Also, list and dictionary components may be inserted and deleted.

PYTHON counts procedures as first-class values, along with all primitive and composite values. Thus PYTHON conforms well to the Type Completeness Principle.

PYTHON is dynamically typed. The value of any variable, parameter, or component may be of any type. All operations are type-checked at run-time. The expression "isinstance(E, T)" yields True if the value yielded by E is of type T, and "type(E)" yields the type of the value yielded by E.

PYTHON's expression repertoire includes procedure calls, constructions (for tuples, lists, dictionaries, objects, and procedures), and iterative expressions (list comprehensions). Surprisingly, there are no conditional expressions.

EXAMPLE 16.2   PYTHON tuples, lists, and dictionaries

The following code illustrates tuple construction:

```
date = 1998, "Nov", 19
```

Now date[0] yields 1998, date[1] yields "Nov", and date[2] yields 19.

The following code illustrates two list constructions, which construct a homogeneous list and a heterogeneous list, respectively:

```
primes = [2, 3, 5, 7, 11]
years = ["unknown", 1314, 1707, date[0]]
```

Now primes[0] yields 2, years[1] yields 1314, years[3] yields 1998, "years[0] = 843" updates the first component of years, and so on. Also, "years.append(1999)" adds 1999 at the end of years.

The following list comprehension:

```
[n + 1  for n in primes]
```

yields the list [3, 4, 6, 8, 12] whose components are one greater than the corresponding components of `primes`. The following list comprehension:

```
[2 * n  for n in primes  if n % 2 != 0]
```

yields the list [6, 10, 14, 22] whose components are double the corresponding components of `primes`, after discarding even components. (Compare the HASKELL list comprehensions in Example 14.3.1.)

The following code illustrates dictionary construction:

```
phones = {"David": 6742, "Carol": 6742, "Ali": 6046}
```

Now `phones["Carol"]` yields 6742, `phones["Ali"]` yields 6046, "`phones ["Ali"] = 1234`" updates the component of `phones` whose key is "Ali", and so on. Also, "`"David" in phones`" returns True, and "`phones.keys()`" returns a list containing "Ali", "Carol", and "David" (in no particular order).

16.3.2   Variables, storage, and control

PYTHON supports global and local variables. Variables are not explicitly declared, simply initialized by assignment. After initialization, a variable may later be assigned any value of any type, as a consequence of dynamic typing.

PYTHON adopts reference semantics. This is especially significant for *mutable* values, which can be selectively updated. Primitive values and strings are immutable; lists, dictionaries, and objects are mutable; tuples are mutable if any of their components are mutable. In practice reference semantics behaves much like copy semantics for immutable values, so operations on numbers and strings behave as we would expect.

PYTHON's repertoire of commands include assignments, procedure calls, conditional (if- but *not* case-) commands, iterative (while- and for-) commands, and exception-handling commands.

PYTHON assignments are similar to those of C, including the form "$V \otimes = E$" (abbreviating "$V = V \otimes E$") for each binary operator $\otimes$. However, PYTHON differs from C in not allowing an assignment to be used as an expression.

PYTHON additionally supports simultaneous assignment. For example:

```
y, m, d = date
```

assigns the three components of the tuple `date` (Example 16.2) to three separate variables. Also:

```
m, n = n, m
```

concisely swaps the values of two variables m and n. (Actually, it first constructs a pair, then assigns the two components of the pair to the two left-side variables.)

PYTHON if- and while-commands are conventional. PYTHON for-commands support definite iteration, the control sequence being the components of a tuple, string, list, dictionary, or file. In fact, we can iterate over any value equipped with an operation that generates a sequence. We can easily achieve the conventional iteration over a sequence of numbers by using the library procedure $range(m,n)$, which returns a list of integers from m through $n-1$.

PYTHON supports break, continue, and return sequencers. It also supports exceptions, which are objects of a subclass of Exception, and which can carry values.

EXAMPLE 16.3   PYTHON iterative commands

The following code computes the greatest common divisor of two integers, m and n:

```
p, q = m, n
while p % q != 0:
    p, q = q, p % q
gcd = q
```

Note the elegance of simultaneous assignment. Note also that indentation is required to indicate the extent of the loop body.

The following code sums the numeric components of a list row, ignoring any nonnumeric components:

```
sum = 0.0
for x in row:
    if isinstance(x, (int, float)):
        sum += x
```

EXAMPLE 16.4   PYTHON exceptions

The following code prompts the user to enter a numeric literal, and stores the corresponding real number in num:

```
while True:
    try:
        response = raw_input("Enter a numeric literal: ")
        num = float(response)
        break
    except ValueError:
        print "Your response was ill-formed."
```

This while-command keeps prompting until the user enters a well-formed numeric literal. The library procedure raw_input(...) displays the given prompt and returns the user's response as a string. The type conversion "float(response)" attempts to convert the response to a real number. If this type conversion is possible, the following break sequencer terminates the loop. If not, the type conversion throws a ValueError exception, control is transferred to the ValueError exception handler, which displays a warning message, and finally the loop is iterated again.

16.3.3   Bindings and scope

A PYTHON program consists of a number of modules, which may be grouped into packages. Within a module we may initialize variables, define procedures, and declare classes. Within a procedure we may initialize local variables and define local procedures. Within a class we may initialize variable components and define procedures (methods).

During a PYTHON session, we may interactively issue declarations, commands, and expressions from the keyboard. These are all acted upon immediately. Whenever we issue an expression, its value is displayed on the screen. We may also import a named module (or selected components of it) at any time.

PYTHON was originally a dynamically-scoped language, but it is now statically scoped.

16.3.4   Procedural abstraction

PYTHON supports function procedures and proper procedures. The only difference is that a function procedure returns a value, while a proper procedure returns nothing.

Since PYTHON is dynamically typed, a procedure definition states the name but not the type of each formal parameter. The corresponding argument may be of different types on different calls to the procedure.

PYTHON supports the reference parameter mechanism. Thus a mutable argument can be selectively updated.

EXAMPLE 16.5   PYTHON procedures

The following function procedure returns the greatest common divisor of its two arguments:

```
def gcd (m, n):
    p, q = m, n
    while p % q != 0:
        p, q = q, p % q
    return q
```

Here p and q are local variables.

The following proper procedure takes a date represented by a triple (as in Example 16.2), and prints that date in ISO format (e.g., "2000-01-01"):

```
def print_date (date):
    y, m, d = date
    if m = "Jan":
        m = 1
    elif m = "Feb":
        m = 2
    ...
    elif m = "Dec":
        m = 12
    print "%04d-%02d-%02d" % (y, m, d)
```

Here y, m, and d are local variables.

EXAMPLE 16.6   PYTHON procedure with dynamic typing

The following function procedure illustrates the flexibility of dynamic typing. It returns the minimum and maximum component of a given sequence:

```
def minimax (vals):
    min = max = vals[0]
    for val in vals:
        if val < min:
            min = val
        elif val > max:
            max = val
    return min, max
```

In a call to this procedure, the argument may be either a tuple or a list. Moreover, the components of that tuple or list may be of any type equipped with "<" and ">": integers, real numbers, strings, tuples, lists, or dictionaries.

Note that this procedure returns a pair. In effect it has two results, which we can easily separate using simultaneous assignment:

```
readings = [...]
low, high = minimax(readings)
```

Some older languages such as C have library procedures with variable numbers of arguments. PYTHON is almost unique in allowing such procedures to be defined by programmers. This is achieved by the simple expedient of allowing a single formal parameter to refer to a whole tuple (or dictionary) of arguments.

EXAMPLE 16.7   PYTHON procedure with a variable number of arguments

The following proper procedure accepts any number of arguments, and prints them one per line:

```
def printall (*args):
    for arg in args:
        print arg
```

The notation "*args" declares that args will refer to a *tuple* of arguments.

All of the following procedure calls work successfully:

```
printall(name)
printall(name, address)
printall(name, address, zipcode)
```

16.3.5 Data abstraction

PYTHON has three different constructs relevant to data abstraction: packages, modules, and classes. Modules and classes support encapsulation, using a naming convention to distinguish between public and private components.

A *package* is simply a group of modules. A *module* is a group of components that may be variables, procedures, and classes. These components (or a designated subset of them) may be imported for use by any other module. All components of a module are public, except those whose identifiers start with "_" which are private.

A *class* is a group of components that may be class variables, class methods, and instance methods. A procedure defined in a class declaration acts as an instance method if its first formal parameter is named self and refers to an object of the class being declared. Otherwise the procedure acts as a class method. To achieve the effect of a constructor, we usually equip each class with an *initialization method* named "__init__"; this method is automatically called when an object of the class is constructed. Instance variables are named using the usual "." notation (as in self.attr), and they may be initialized by the initialization method or by any other method. All components of a class are public, except those whose identifiers start with "__", which are private.

EXAMPLE 16.8   PYTHON class

Consider the following class:

```
class Person:
    def __init__ (self, sname, fname, gender, birth):
        self.__surname = sname
        self.__forename = fname
        self.__female = (gender == "F" or gender == "f")
        self.__birth = birth

    def get_surname (self):
        return self.__surname

    def change_surname (self, sname):
        self.__surname = sname

    def print_details (self):
        print self.__forename + " " + self.__surname
```

This class is equipped with an initialization method and three other instance methods, each of which has a self parameter and perhaps some other parameters. In the following code:

```
dw = Person("Watt", "David", "M", 1946)
```

the object construction on the right first creates an object of class Person; it then passes the above arguments, together with a reference to the newly-created object, to the initialization method. The latter initializes the object's instance variables, which are named __surname, __forename, __female, and __birth (and thus are all private). The following method call:

```
dw.change_surname("Bloggs")
```

has the same effect as:

```
Person.change_surname(dw, "Bloggs")
```

which shows clearly that the method's formal parameter self refers to the object dw.

Now consider the following subclass of `Person`:

```
class Student (Person):
    def __init__ (self, sname, fname,      \
                    gender, birth, id, deg):
        Person.__init__(self,      \
            sname, fname, gender, birth)
        self.__studentid = id
        self.__degree = deg

    def change_degree (self, deg):
        self.__degree = deg

    def print_details (self):
        Person.print_details(self)
        print "id " + str(self.__studentid)
```

This class provides its own initialization method, provides an additional method named `change_degree`, and overrides its superclass's `print_details` method. We can see that each object of class `Student` will have additional variable components named `__studentid` and `__degree`. The following code:

```
jw = Student("Watt", "Jeff", "M", 1983, 100296, "BSc")
```

creates and initializes an object of class `Student`. The following code illustrates dynamic dispatch:

```
for p in [dw, jw]:
    p.print_details()
```

PYTHON supports multiple inheritance: a class may designate any number of superclasses. Ambiguous references to class components are resolved by searching the superclasses in the order in which they are named in the class declaration. As explained in Section 6.3.4, this tends to make it difficult to understand large class hierarchies.

PYTHON's support for object-oriented programming is developing but is not yet mature. The use of the "__" naming convention to indicate privacy is clumsy and error-prone; class components are public by default. Still more seriously, variable components can be created (and deleted) at any time, by any method and even by application code! For example, in Example 16.8 the assignment "`dw.height = 1.8`" would create an extra public instance variable in the object `dw` (without affecting any other `Person` object, nor any `Student` object). This undermines a fundamental assumption of object-oriented programming, that all objects of the same class have the same structure.

16.3.6   Separate compilation

PYTHON modules are compiled separately. Each module must explicitly import every other module on which it depends.

Each module's source code is stored in a text file. For example, a module named `widget` is stored in a file named `widget.py`. When that module is first imported, it is compiled and its object code is stored in a file named `widget.pyc`. Whenever the module is subsequently imported, it is recompiled only if the source code has been edited in the meantime. Compilation is completely automatic.

The PYTHON compiler does not reject code that refers to undeclared identifiers. Such code simply fails if and when it is executed.

Nor does the PYTHON compiler perform type checking: the language is dynamically typed. The compiler will not reject code that might fail with a type error, nor even code that will certainly fail, such as:

```
def fail (x):
   print x+1, x[0]
```

16.3.7   Module library

PYTHON is equipped with a very rich module library, which supports string handling, markup, mathematics, cryptography, multimedia, GUIs, operating system services, Internet services, compilation, and so on.

Unlike older scripting languages, PYTHON does not have built-in high-level string processing or GUI support. Instead, the PYTHON module library provides such functionality. For example, the `re` library module provides powerful string matching facilities using regular expressions.

EXAMPLE 16.9   HTML parsing

An HTML document contains a number of headings. A level-1 heading, for instance, has the form "`<H1>`*title*`</H1>`". Here "H1" is an example of a *tag*.

Suppose that a table of contents is to be printed for a given HTML document, with each heading's title indented according to its level. For instance, if the document contained the text of this chapter expressed in HTML, the table of contents should look like this:

```
16 Scripting
     16.1 Pragmatics
     16.2 Key concepts
          16.2.1 Regular expressions
     16.3  Case study: Python
     ...
     Exercises
```

PYTHON actually provides an `HTMLParser` class that is suitable for this application. For the sake of illustration, however, let us suppose that we must write a script from scratch.

The following regular expression will match an HTML heading at any level up to 6:

```
<(H[1-6])>(.*?)</\1>
```

Note the following points:

- "`[1-6]`" matches any one of the characters "1" through "6".
- "`.*?`" matches the *shortest* possible substring (which is what we want here), whereas "`.*`" would match the *longest* possible substring.

- The two parenthesized subexpressions, namely "(H[1-6])" and "(.*?)", will match the heading's tag and title, respectively. That tag and that title will be remembered by the matching algorithm.

- "\1" matches the same substring as the *first* parenthesized subexpression, namely the tag. This prevents unmatched opening and closing tags as in "<H1>*title*</H2>".

The following procedure prints the table of contents:

```
      def print_toc (docname):
(1)     doc = open(docname)
(2)     html = doc.read()
(3)     pattern = re.compile("<(H[1-6])>(.*?)</\\1>")
(4)     matches = pattern.findall(html)
(5)     for (tag, title) in matches:
(6)         level = int(tag[1])
(7)         print "\t" * (level-1) + title
```

Line (1) opens the named document, and line (2) stores its entire contents in html, as a single string. Line (3) "compiles" the regular expression in such a way as to make subsequent matching efficient. Line (4) finds all substrings of html that are matched by the regular expression, storing a list of (tag, title) pairs in matches. Line (5) iterates over matches, setting tag and title to the components of each pair in turn. Line (6) extracts the level number from the tag, and line (7) prints the title preceded by the appropriate number of tabs.

The solution in Example 16.9 is extraordinarily clear and concise. Probably no other (programming or scripting) language could match it.

EXAMPLE 16.10   CGI argument parsing

When a Web form is completed, the data is encoded as a string of the form:

$$\text{“}key_1 = value_1 \& \dots \& key_n = value_n\text{”}$$

where each key is the name of a field and each value is the field's content. A given key may be repeated (e.g., if the form contains a list box and multiple selections are possible). Moreover, for technical reasons, any space in a value is encoded as "+", and any other non-alphanumeric character is encoded in hexadecimal ("%*dd*"). For example, the following string:

```
"name=Watt%2C+David&gender=M&child=Susanne&child=Jeff"
```

encodes the following data:

```
name        Watt, David
gender      M
child       Susanne|Jeff
```

PYTHON actually provides a cgi module for processing CGI data. For the sake of illustration, however, let us suppose that we must write a script from scratch.

The following procedure takes CGI data encoded as a string, and returns that data structured as a dictionary:

```
       def parse_cgi (encoding):
         hex_pattern = re.compile("%([0-9A-Fa-f]{2})")
         hex_replacement =     \
             lambda match: chr(int(match.group(1), 16))
         dictionary = {}
(1)      for pair in encoding.split("&"):
(2)        key, value = pair.split("=")
(3)        value = value.replace("+", " ")
(4)        value = hex_pattern.sub(hex_replacement, value)
(5)        if key in dictionary:
             dictionary[key] += "|" + value
           else:
             dictionary[key] = value
         return dictionary
```

Line (1) splits the encoding string into a list of substrings of the form "*key=value*", and iterates over that list. Line (2) splits one of these substrings into its key and value. Line (3) replaces each occurrence of "+" in the value by a space, and line (4) replaces each occurrence of "*%dd*" by the character whose hexadecimal code is *dd*. The if-command starting at line (5) either adds a new entry to the dictionary or modifies the existing entry as appropriate.

Summary

In this chapter:

- We have surveyed the pragmatic issues that influence the design of scripting languages: gluing, rapid development and evolution, modest efficiency requirements, and very high-level functionality in relevant areas.

- We have surveyed the concepts common to most scripting languages: very high-level support for string processing, very high-level support for GUIs, and dynamic typing.

- We have studied the design of a major scripting language, PYTHON. We saw that PYTHON resembles a conventional programming language, except that it is dynamically typed, and that it derives much of its expressiveness from a rich module library.

Further reading

BARRON (2000) surveys the "world of scripting" and the older scripting languages, such as JAVASCRIPT, PERL, TCL, and VISUAL BASIC. Interestingly, Barron omits PYTHON from his survey, classifying it as a programming language rather than a scripting language (although on grounds that are highly debatable). Example 16.10 is based on a PERL example in Barron's book.

OUSTERHOUT (1998) is a short article that vividly describes the advantages of scripting, and the enthusiasm of its advocates. Ousterhout was the designer of TCL.

Exercises

Exercises for Section 16.1

16.1.1 Consider a spreadsheet used by a small organization (such as a sports club) to keep track of its finances. Would you classify such a spreadsheet as a script? Explain your answer.

Exercises for Section 16.2

16.2.1 This exercise is a drill for readers unfamiliar with regular expressions.

    (a) Does abc|de match "abc", "abce", "abcde", "bcde", or "de"?

    (b) Does ab(c|d)e match "abc", "abce", "abcde", "bcde", or "de"?

    (c) Does abb*c match "abbbb", "abbc", "abc", "ac", or "bbc"?

    (d) Does a(bc)*c match "abbbc", "abc", "abcbcc", "abcc", or "ac"?

16.2.2 The following HTML includes an example of a link to another document:

```
See Acme's
<A HREF="http://www.acme.com/mission.html">
mission statement</A>.
```

The simplest form of HTML link is <A HREF="*URL*">*link-text*</A>. Write down a regular expression that matches this form of link.

16.2.3 Consider the derived forms of regular expressions in Table 16.1. Express the derived forms $RE^?$, RE^+, and RE^2 in terms of the basic forms.

Exercises for Section 16.3

16.3.1 Write a PYTHON procedure that neatly tabulates the components of a dictionary.

16.3.2 Write a PYTHON module that supports the "phone-book" operations of your mobile phone. Represent the phone-book by a dictionary, as in Example 16.2.

16.3.3 Using your answer to Exercise 16.2.2, write a PYTHON procedure that returns a list of all the URLs to which a given HTML document is linked.

*16.3.4 Design and implement a simple spellchecker (as specified in Section 11.2.1) in PYTHON.

PART V

CONCLUSION

Part V concludes the book by suggesting guidelines for selecting languages for software development projects, and guidelines for designing new languages.

Chapter 17

Language selection

In this chapter we shall:

- identify technical and economic criteria that should be considered when selecting languages for software development projects;
- illustrate how to use these criteria to evaluate candidate languages for a particular project.

17.1 Criteria

At some stage in every software development project, the selection of a language becomes an important decision.

All too often, languages are selected for all the wrong reasons: fanaticism ("... is brilliant"), prejudice ("... is rubbish"), inertia ("... is too much trouble to learn"), fear of change ("... is what we know best, for all its faults"), fashion ("... is what everyone is using now"), commercial pressures ("... is supported by MegaBuck Inc."), conformism ("no-one ever got fired for choosing ... "). That such social and emotional influences are often decisive is a sad reflection on the state of the software engineering profession.

Professional software engineers should instead base their decisions on relevant technical and economic criteria, such as the following.

- *Scale:* Does the language support the orderly development of large-scale programs? The language should allow programs to be constructed from compilation units that have been coded and tested separately, perhaps by different programmers. Separate compilation is a practical necessity, since type inconsistencies are less common within a compilation unit (written by one programmer) than between compilation units (perhaps written by different programmers), and the latter are not detected by independent compilation.

- *Modularity:* Does the language support the decomposition of programs into suitable program units, such that we can distinguish clearly between *what* a program unit is to do (the application programmer's view) and *how* it will be coded (the implementer's view)? This separation of concerns is an essential intellectual tool for managing the development of large programs. Relevant concepts here are procedures, packages, abstract types, and classes.

- *Reusability:* Does the language support effective reuse of program units? If so, the project can be accelerated by reusing tried-and-tested program units; it might also develop new program units suitable for future reuse. Relevant concepts here are packages, abstract types, classes, and particularly generic units.

- *Portability:* Does the language help or hinder writing of portable code? In other words, can the code be moved from one platform to a dissimilar platform without major changes?

- *Level:* Does the language encourage programmers to think in terms of high-level abstractions oriented to the application? Or does it force programmers to think all the time in terms of low-level details such as bits and pointers? Low-level code is notoriously error-prone, especially when pointers are involved. It is, however, necessary in some parts of some applications.

- *Reliability:* Is the language designed in such a way that programming errors can be detected and eliminated as quickly as possible? Errors detected by compile-time checks are guaranteed absent in the running program, which is ideal. Errors detected by run-time checks are guaranteed to cause no harm other than throwing an exception (or at worst terminating the program), which is second-best. Errors not detected at all can cause unlimited harm (such as corrupting data) before the program crashes. While reliability is always important, it is absolutely essential in safety-critical systems.

- *Efficiency:* Is the language capable of being implemented efficiently? Some aspects of object-oriented programming entail run-time overheads, such as class tags and dynamic dispatch. Run-time checks are costly (although some compilers are willing to suppress them, at the programmer's own risk). Garbage collection is also costly, slowing the program down at unpredictable times. Interpretive code is about ten times slower than native machine code. If critical parts of the program must be highly efficient, does the language allow them to be tuned by resort to low-level coding, or by calls to procedures written in a lower-level language?

- *Readability:* Does the language help or hinder good programming practice? A language that enforces cryptic syntax, very short identifiers, default declarations, and an absence of type information makes it difficult to write readable code. The significant point is that code is read (by its author and other programmers) more often than it is written.

- *Data modeling:* Does the language provide types, and associated operations, that are suitable for representing entities in the relevant application area? Examples would be records and files in data processing; real numbers and arrays in scientific computation; strings in text processing; lists, trees, and mappings in translators; and queues in operating systems and simulators. If the language itself lacks the needed types, does it allow programmers to define new types and operations that accurately model entities in the application area? Relevant concepts here are abstract types and classes.

- *Process modeling:* Does the language provide control structures that are suitable for modeling the behavior of entities in the relevant application area? In particular, we need concurrency to model simultaneous processes in simulators, operating systems, and real-time process controllers.

- *Availability of compilers and tools:* Are good-quality compilers available for the language? A good-quality compiler enforces the language's syntax and type rules, generates correct and efficient object code, generates run-time checks (at least as an option) to trap any errors that cannot be detected at compile-time, and reports all errors clearly and accurately. Also, is a good-quality integrated development environment (IDE) available for the language? An IDE enhances productivity by combining a program editor, compiler, linker, debugger, and related tools into a single integrated system.

- *Familiarity:* Are the available programmers already familiar with the language? If not, is high-quality training available, and will the investment in training justify itself in future projects?

17.2   Evaluation

In this section we illustrate how to evaluate candidate languages for particular software development projects. We shall consider two possible projects: a word processor and an automatically driven road vehicle. For each project we shall evaluate four candidate languages: C, C++, JAVA, and ADA.

We can make at least a preliminary evaluation of the candidate languages against all of the selection criteria summarized in the previous section. In addition, we should re-evaluate the languages against the *data modeling* and *process modeling* criteria (and also perhaps the *scale, level*, and *efficiency* criteria) for each particular project.

EXAMPLE 17.1   Preliminary evaluation of C, C++, JAVA, and ADA

- *Scale:* All four languages allow a program to be constructed from compilation units. C's independent compilation is a very shaky basis for large-scale programming: only the disciplined use of header files provides any protection against type inconsistencies between compilation units, and such discipline cannot be enforced by the compiler. C++ also exhibits some of the weaknesses of independent compilation. ADA's separate compilation rigorously enforces type consistency between compilation units. JAVA's separate compilation does likewise, but it is partly undermined by dynamic linking.

- *Modularity:* All four languages of course support procedural abstraction. More importantly, C++ and JAVA support data abstraction by means of classes, and ADA by means of both abstract types and classes, but C does not support data abstraction at all.

- *Reusability:* C++, JAVA, and ADA support both data abstraction and generic abstraction, enabling us to write reusable program units. Both C++ and JAVA provide large class libraries that can be reused by all programmers. C supports neither data abstraction nor generic abstraction, making it very poor for reuse.

- *Portability:* C and C++ have many features that make programs unportable, such as pointer arithmetic and even ordinary arithmetic. (For instance, even using C++ exceptions it is not possible to handle overflow.) ADA programs are much more portable; for instance, programmers can easily employ platform-independent arithmetic. JAVA programs are exceptionally portable: even object code can be moved from one platform to another without change.

- *Level:* C is a relatively low-level language, characterized by bit-handling operations and by the ubiquitous use of pointers to achieve the effect of reference parameters and to define recursive types. C++ relies on pointers for recursive types and object-oriented programming, although disciplined use of data abstraction makes it possible to localize most pointer handling. Similar points can be made about pointer handling in ADA. ADA is generally high-level, but also supports low-level programming in clearly signposted program units. JAVA is also high-level, avoiding all explicit pointer handling. (All objects are implicitly accessed through pointers, but that is evident only in the language's reference semantics.)

- *Reliability:* C and C++ are very unreliable, setting numerous traps for unsuspecting programmers. Great care is needed to avoid dangling pointers to deallocated heap variables or to dead local variables. Especially in C, the feeble type system permits meaningless type conversions and pointer arithmetic, and does not enforce type checks between compilation units, thus exposing programs to a variety of run-time type errors. Moreover, the lack of run-time checks allows these errors, and others such as out-of-range array indexing, to go undetected until unlimited harm has been done. JAVA and ADA are much more reliable: dangling pointers cannot arise; full compile-time type checks automatically detect a large proportion of programming errors; and automatic run-time checks ensure that other errors such as out-of-range array indexing are detected before serious harm is done.

- *Efficiency:* C and C++ can be implemented very efficiently. JAVA and ADA are slowed down by run-time checks. More significantly, JAVA depends heavily on garbage collection (since all objects are heap variables), and JAVA programs are usually compiled into interpretive code; the resulting performance penalties are acceptable for applets, but not for computationally intensive programs.

- *Readability:* All of these languages make it possible to write readable software. Unfortunately it is common practice among C and C++ programmers to write very cryptic code. This, combined with use of low-level features like pointer arithmetic, makes programs hard to maintain.

- *Data modeling:* In all four languages it is easy to define the data types needed in different application areas. Data abstraction in C++, JAVA, and ADA makes it possible to equip each type with necessary and sufficient operations, and to ensure that application code uses only these operations, but C has no such safeguards.

- *Process modeling:* C provides only basic control structures, while C++, JAVA, and ADA provide exceptions. Most importantly, JAVA and ADA support concurrency directly using high-level abstractions. C and C++ instead rely on the underlying operating system to support concurrency (which impairs portability).

- *Availability of compilers and tools:* Currently there is a wide choice of low-cost good-quality compilers and IDEs for all four languages. However, most JAVA compilers generate interpretive code, which in turn can be translated into (inefficient) native machine code by a "just-in-time" compiler. (There is no reason why JAVA compilers could not generate efficient native machine code directly, but that is currently unusual.)

- *Familiarity:* Currently, most professional programmers are familiar with C, C++, or JAVA, but ADA is much less well known. C and JAVA, being relatively small languages, can quickly be mastered by professional programmers. (The JAVA class library is another matter!) C++ and ADA, being large languages, take a long time to master.

EXAMPLE 17.2   Evaluation of languages for a word processor

Let us evaluate C, C++, JAVA, and ADA for a project to design and implement a new word processor. Following up on the preliminary evaluation of Example 17.1, we should re-evaluate the languages against the following criteria.

- *Data modeling:* The word processor will need data types such as paragraphs, style sheets, and dictionaries.
- *Process modeling:* The word processor will have no special process modeling requirements. (Actually, concurrency would help to keep the graphical user interface responsive while the application is computing the effects of an insertion or deletion, but for simplicity we shall ignore that here.)
- *Scale:* The word processor will be a medium-size program.
- *Level:* The word processor will have no need for low-level coding.
- *Efficiency:* The word processor must be reasonably efficient, because of the computation involved in refreshing the window after inserting, deleting, or reformatting text.

Overall, we might reasonably come to the following conclusions. C would be less than ideal, scoring well on efficiency, but scoring badly on scale, modularity, and reliability. C++ would be preferable, scoring better than C on scale and modularity. JAVA might be suitable, scoring well on everything except efficiency. ADA would be suitable, scoring well on everything except probably familiarity.

EXAMPLE 17.3   Evaluation of languages for an automatically driven road vehicle

Let us evaluate C, C++, JAVA, and ADA for a project to design and implement the control system for an automatically driven road vehicle. This system must be able to recognize road hazards such as junctions, bends, other vehicles, and so on, using suitably positioned cameras. Following up on the preliminary evaluation of Example 17.1, we should re-evaluate the languages against the following criteria.

- *Data modeling:* The control system will need data types such as images.
- *Process modeling:* The control system will need concurrency so that it can simultaneously steer, accelerate or brake, watch other vehicles, and so on. For instance, it must not suspend steering while braking or while processing a camera image.
- *Scale:* The control system will be a large program.
- *Level:* Some parts of the control system, such as image processing, will need low-level coding capability.
- *Reliability:* The control system is a safety-critical system, so it must be extremely reliable and fail-safe.

- *Efficiency:* The control system will be a real-time system, and must be able to process its camera images fast enough to react appropriately. For instance, it must be able to recognize obstacles fast enough to avoid collisions.

Overall, we might reasonably come to the following conclusions. Both C and C++ should be ruled out on reliability grounds. JAVA should be ruled out on efficiency grounds. ADA would be suitable in every respect.

Summary

In this chapter:

- Having dismissed some of the more irrational arguments that tend to be used when selecting a language for a particular software development project, we have identified a number of technical and economic criteria that should properly be taken into account.
- We have used these criteria to evaluate the suitability of C, C++, JAVA, and ADA for two possible projects, a word processor and an automatically driven road vehicle.

Exercises

Exercises for Section 17.1

*17.1.1 Recall your own experience of a software development project in which a careful selection of language was required. Were all the criteria of Section 17.1 taken into account? Were any additional criteria taken into account?

Exercises for Section 17.2

*17.2.1 Choose a language other than C, C++, JAVA, or ADA, and evaluate its suitability for implementing a word processor, along the lines of Example 17.2.

*17.2.2 Choose a language other than C, C++, JAVA, or ADA, and evaluate its suitability for implementing an automatically driven road vehicle, along the lines of Example 17.3.

*17.2.3 Consider a software development project in which you are currently involved. Evaluate several candidate languages for this project.

*17.2.4 What additional selection criterion should be taken into account when selecting a language suitable for writing *applets*? Evaluate C++ and JAVA for this purpose.

*17.2.5 What additional selection criterion should be taken into account when selecting a language suitable for writing *macros* in a word processor or spreadsheet system? Evaluate C++, JAVA, and VISUAL BASIC for this purpose.

Chapter 18

Language design

This chapter addresses the difficult question of how we should design programming and scripting languages. While few of us will ever be involved in the design of a new language or even the extension of an existing language, all of us should be able to analyze critically the design of existing languages.

18.1 Selection of concepts

The main purpose of this book has been to show that a large variety of languages can be understood in terms of a relatively small number of concepts. Nevertheless, these concepts still are too numerous to be incorporated in any single language. The language designer's first problem, therefore, is a judicious selection of concepts. What to omit is just as important a decision as what to include.

The concepts of values and types, variables and storage, bindings and scope, and procedural abstraction are so fundamental that they are found in almost every language. Nevertheless the pure functional languages demonstrate that many useful problems can be solved elegantly by defining functions, without resort to updatable variables. A similar point could be made about logic languages.

Every modern language should support data abstraction in some form. All programs benefit from being decomposed into suitable program units, and large programs are manageable only if they are decomposed in this way. Experience has shown that the most useful program units are packages, abstract types, and classes. The lack of data abstraction is therefore a serious weakness in any language.

An important goal of software engineering is reuse. New programs should be able to include existing tried-and-tested program units. Reusable program units must be self-contained, and in particular should make no unnecessary assumptions about the types of data that they manipulate. Thus a language intended for serious software engineering should support generic units, inclusion polymorphism, or parametric polymorphism. Currently these concepts are associated mainly with imperative, object-oriented, and functional languages, respectively, but it is not clear why this should be so.

Concurrency is also important in some applications. But concurrent programming is significantly more difficult than sequential programming, and is justified only when large efficiency gains are possible (such as when an inherently parallel algorithm can be distributed), or when the application is naturally concurrent (such as a simulator, process controller, or operating system). Designers can reasonably omit concurrency in languages not intended for such applications.

18.2 Regularity

How should concepts be combined to design a language? Simply piling feature upon feature is not a good approach, as PL/I vividly demonstrated. Even smaller languages sometimes betray similar symptoms. FORTRAN and COBOL provide baroque input/output facilities, but every programmer encounters situations where these facilities are not quite right. Surely it is preferable to provide a small set of basic facilities, and allow programmers to build more elaborate facilities on top of these as required? Abstract types and classes support and encourage this approach.

To achieve maximum power with a given number of concepts, the programmer should be able to combine these concepts in a regular fashion, with no unnecessary restrictions or surprising interactions. The semantic principles discussed in this book help the language designer to avoid irregularities.

The Type Completeness Principle (Section 2.5.3) suggests that all types in the language should have equal status. For example, parameters and function results should not be restricted to particular types. Nevertheless, some languages insist that function results are of primitive type. In such a language it would be very awkward to program complex arithmetic, for example, since we could not write function procedures to compute complex sums, differences, and so on.

The Abstraction Principle (Section 5.1.3) invites the language designer to consider abstraction over syntactic categories other than the usual ones: function procedures abstract over expressions, and proper procedures abstract over commands. The language designer should also consider generic units, which abstract over declarations, and parameterized types, which abstract over types.

The Correspondence Principle (Section 5.2.3) states that for each form of declaration there exists a corresponding parameter mechanism. This principle helps the language designer to select from the bewildering variety of possible parameter mechanisms. To the extent that the language complies with this principle, programmers can easily and reliably generalize blocks into procedures.

The Qualification Principle (Section 4.4.3) invites the language designer to consider including blocks in a variety of syntactic categories. Many languages have block commands, but few (other than functional languages) have block expressions, and still fewer have block declarations.

18.3 Simplicity

Simplicity should always be a goal of language design. The language is our most basic tool as programmers, so must be mastered thoroughly. The language should help us to solve problems: it should allow us to express solutions naturally, and indeed should help us discover these solutions in the first place. A large and complicated language creates problems by being difficult to master. Tony Hoare has expressed this point succinctly: large and complicated languages belong not to the solution space but to the problem space.

PASCAL demonstrated that a language designed with limited aims can be very simple. Indeed its success was due largely to its simplicity. It included a small but judicious selection of concepts; it was easily and quickly mastered, yet it was powerful enough to solve a wide variety of problems.

Nevertheless, there is a tension between the goal of simplicity and the demands of a truly general-purpose language. A general-purpose language will be used in a wide variety of application areas, including those demanding concurrent programming. It will be used to construct large programs consisting of numerous program units written by different programmers, and to construct libraries of program units likely to be reused in future programs. Such a language must include most of the concepts studied in this book, and must inevitably be much more complicated than a language like PASCAL.

The most promising way to resolve this tension is to compartmentalize the language. An individual programmer then has to master only those parts of the language needed to solve the problem on hand. For this approach to work, the language designer must avoid any unexpected interactions between different parts of the language, which could cause an unwary programmer to stray into unknown territory.

PL/I was heavily and justifiably criticized for failing to control its complexity. A notorious example is the innocent-looking expression "$25 + 1/3$", which yields 5.3! PL/I used complicated (and counterintuitive) fixed-point arithmetic rules for evaluating such expressions, sometimes truncating the *most* significant digits! An unwary programmer familiar only with the rules of integer arithmetic might easily stumble into this trap.

ADA has also been criticized for its size and complexity. In many respects, however, ADA makes a good job of controlling its complexity. Suppose, for example, that a PASCAL programmer is learning ADA, but is not yet aware of the existence of exceptions. The programmer might write an ADA program that unintentionally throws an exception but, in the absence of a handler, the program will simply halt with an appropriate error message (just as the corresponding PASCAL program would do).

Even HASKELL, a much simpler language, has traps for unwary programmers. Polymorphic type inference is complicated, and it is possible that the type inferred for a function might be different from the one intended by the programmer. Such a discrepancy might be buried in the middle of a large program, and thus escape notice. To avoid such confusion, the programmer can voluntarily declare the type of every function. That type information is redundant (since it could be inferred by the compiler), but it makes the programmer's intentions explicit and thus makes the program easier to read. Redundancy is often a good thing in language design.

Parametric polymorphism, inclusion polymorphism (inheritance), overloading, and coercions are all useful in their own right, but combining two or more of these in a single language can lead to unexpected interactions. For instance, C++ and JAVA combine overloading and inheritance. Consider the following JAVA class and subclass:

```
class Line {
   private int length;
(1) public void set (int newLength) {
     length = newLength;
   }
   ...
}
class ColoredLine extends Line {
   public static final RED = 0, GREEN = 1, BLUE =  2;
   private int color;
(2) public void set (int newColor) {
     color = newColor;
   }
   ...
}
```

In the programmer's mind, lengths and colors are different types, so method (2) should *overload* method (1). But in the actual code, lengths and colors are both integers, so method (2) *overrides* method (1).

To return to our theme of controlling complexity, the language designer cannot, and should not attempt to, anticipate all facilities that the programmer will need. Rather than building too many facilities into the language, the language should allow programmers to define the facilities they need in the language itself (or reuse them from a library). The key to this is abstraction. Each new function procedure, in effect, enriches the language's expression repertoire; each new proper procedure enriches its command repertoire; and each new abstract type or class enriches its type repertoire.

We can illustrate this idea in the area of input/output. Older languages such as FORTRAN, COBOL, and PL/I have complicated built-in input/output facilities. Being built-in and inextensible, they make a vain attempt to be comprehensive, but often fail to provide exactly the facilities needed in a particular situation. By contrast, modern languages such as C++, JAVA, and ADA have no built-in input/output at all. Instead their libraries provide input/output units (classes or packages) that cater for most needs. Programmers who do not need these units can ignore them, and programmers who need different facilities can design their own input/output units. These programmers are not penalized (in terms of language or compiler complexity) by the existence of facilities they do not use.

We can also illustrate this idea in the area of scripting. The older scripting languages such as PERL and TCL have built-in string matching using regular expressions. The newer scripting language PYTHON avoids this language complexity by providing library classes with similar functionality. Again, programmers are free to ignore these classes and to provide their own.

Taken to its logical conclusion, this approach suggests a small core language with powerful abstraction mechanisms, together with a rich library of reusable program units. The language could provide a small repertoire of primitive and composite types, together with the means to define new types equipped with

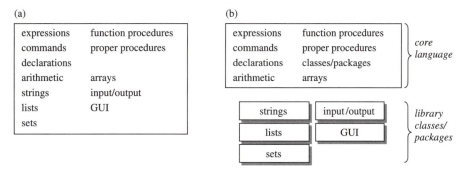

Figure 18.1 (a) A monolithic language; (b) a core language plus library.

suitable operations. The library could include program units for things like strings, lists, and input/output that are needed in many but not all programs. All this is summarized in Figure 18.1. The effect is that necessary complexity is devolved from the language itself to its library. Furthermore, programmers can develop their own more specialized libraries to complement the standard library. (See also Exercise 18.3.1.)

JAVA exemplifies this approach extraordinarily well. The JAVA core language is very simple (no larger than C, and far smaller than C++), and easy to learn. The JAVA standard class library includes an enormous number of classes grouped into packages. JAVA's core language and class library together provide an enormous wealth of facilities, and the productivity of JAVA programmers is unmatched.

18.4 Efficiency

In the early days of computing, when computers were extremely slow and short of storage, languages like FORTRAN and COBOL were designed with numerous restrictions to enable them to be implemented very efficiently. Much has changed since then: computers are extremely fast and have vast storage capacities; and compilers are much better at generating efficient object code.

Moreover, we now understand that seeking optimum efficiency is unproductive. Typically 90% of a program's run-time is spent in 10% of the code. It is therefore more productive to identify the critical 10% of the code and make it run as fast as required, rather than waste effort on speeding up the noncritical 90% of the code.

Nevertheless, every language should be capable of an acceptably efficient implementation. What is acceptable depends on what is required of programs in the application area for which the language is intended. A language intended for system programming must be highly efficient. A language intended for ordinary application programming must be reasonably efficient. A language intended for programming applets or for scripting need not be particularly efficient.

A language's efficiency is strongly influenced by its selection of concepts. Some concepts such as dynamic typing, parametric polymorphism, object orientation, and automatic deallocation (garbage collection) are inherently costly. Logic programming is inherently less efficient than functional programming, which in turn is inherently less efficient than imperative programming. The language designer must decide whether the benefits of each concept outweigh its cost.

Sometimes an interaction of concepts has paradoxical effects on efficiency. For example, in an imperative language selective updating of an array is cheap, while in a functional language an array-transforming operation would be costly (having to copy all the unaffected components). Conversely, in an imperative language sharing of list components is inhibited (by the possibility of selective updating), while in a functional language sharing is always possible. Therefore imperative languages prefer arrays while functional languages prefer lists.

Friedrich Bauer has suggested a useful principle: a language should not include a concept if it imposes significant costs on programs that do not use it. This principle is respected by ADA and JAVA exceptions: we can implement exceptions in such a way that a program that throws no exceptions runs as fast as it would do if exceptions did not exist. This principle is also respected by ADA's concurrency control abstractions. It is not respected by JAVA's synchronization features, which are designed to support concurrency, but which impose a cost on every object, even in a sequential program.

18.5   Syntax

This book has deliberately concentrated on semantic concepts, because they are of primary importance in designing, understanding, and using languages. Syntactic issues are of secondary importance, but they are certainly important enough to deserve a short discussion here.

Numerous articles have been written on surface syntactic issues. Should semicolons separate or terminate commands? Should keywords be abbreviated? Should composite commands be fully bracketed? (See Exercises 18.5.1 and 18.5.2.) Such aspects of a language's syntax might affect the number of syntactic errors made by novice programmers, but experienced programmers easily cope with such syntactic differences.

A much more important criterion for a language's syntax is that programs should be readable. A program is written once but read many times, both by its author and by other programmers. So the language designer should choose a syntax that permits and encourages programmers to write programs fit to be read by others. Programmers should be free to choose meaningful identifiers (an obvious point, perhaps, but one ignored in older languages like FORTRAN and BASIC). Keywords should generally be preferred to unfamiliar symbols. It should be easy to mingle commentary with the program text, and to lay out the text in such a way as to suggest its syntactic (and semantic) structure.

Another important criterion is that finger slips should not radically change the code's meaning. This possibility was notoriously illustrated by the software controlling an early Venus probe, in which the intended FORTRAN code "DO1I =1,25" (which introduces a loop with control variable I ranging from 1 through 25) was mistyped as "DO1I =1.25" (which assigns 1.25 to an undeclared variable named DO1I), causing the probe to be lost. It is better that a finger slip should be detected by the compiler as a syntactic error than that it should change the code's meaning.

The language's syntax should use familiar mathematical notation wherever possible. For example, in mathematics "=" means "is equal to". The use of "=" in HASKELL definitions, and its use in ADA to denote the equality test, are consistent with the mathematical meaning. But the use of "=" in C, C++, and JAVA to mean "*becomes* equal to" (assignment) is not consistent with the mathematical meaning. It is notoriously common for C novices to write:

```
if (x = y) printf("...");
```

expecting to print something if the value of x equals the value of y. In fact, this code assigns the value of y to the variable x, then tests the assigned value, then prints something if the assigned value is nonzero. (This is another example in which a finger slip, here writing "=" instead of "==", radically changes the code's meaning.)

A deeper point is that the language's syntax should be transparent. It should be obvious from a syntactic form what semantic concept is being used. The syntactic forms and semantic concepts should be (more or less) in one-to-one correspondence.

C and C++ declarations illustrate bad syntactic design. Type definitions come in four different forms (introduced by **enum**, **struct**, **typedef**, and **union**). Variable and parameter declarations are even more confusing. For example:

```
char * x, y;
char s, t[];
```

declares x to be of type **char*** (pointer to **char**), y to be of type **char**, s also to be of type **char**, and t to be of type **char[]**! Type information is smeared all over each declaration. By contrast, JAVA variable and parameter declarations concentrate the type information in one place. For example:

```
char[] s, t;
```

declares both s and t to be of type **char[]**.

The same syntactic form should not mean different things in different contexts. For example, the C syntactic form "(**char**)x" violates this dictum: in one context this is a variable declaration, declaring x to be of type **char**; in another context this is a cast, converting the value of x to type **char**.

Here is a more complicated example of confusing syntax from C++. Suppose that a class Widget has two constructors, one with a single **int** parameter, the other being parameterless. Then we can create and initialize two heap objects:

```
Widget* w1 = new Widget(7); // calls the first constructor
Widget* w2 = new Widget();  // calls the second constructor
```

But suppose that we want to create two similar local objects on the stack:

```
Widget w3(7); // calls the first constructor
Widget w4();  // intended to call the second constructor!
```

The declaration of w3 works as expected. But the declaration of w4 does not create a `Widget` object; it declares a function with a `Widget` result!!

A single syntactic form should not confuse two distinct concepts. For example, C and C++ make no clear syntactic distinction between function procedures and proper procedures. Another example is that ADA record types confuse the distinct concepts of Cartesian products and disjoint unions; by contrast, HASKELL's tuple types support Cartesian products, while its algebraic types separately support disjoint unions.

Each concept should preferably be supported by a single syntactic form. Providing alternative forms for the same concept makes the language larger and more complicated, and is rarely justified. A fairly harmless example is PYTHON's syntactic form "**unless** E:", which is an alternative to "**if** ! E:". More seriously, ADA has a tendency to allow programmers to achieve the same effect in several different ways. For example, consider the following procedure:

```
procedure draw_box (x, y: Integer;
                    width: Integer := 1;
                    depth := 1);
```

This procedure can be called not only in the conventional positional notation:

```
draw_box(0, 0, 1, 2);
```

but also in so-called "keyword notation":

```
draw_box(depth => 2, width => 1, x => 0, y => 0);
```

and also with some actual parameters omitted if their default values are to be used:

```
draw_box(y => 0, x => 0, depth => 2);
```

The advantage of keyword notation is that the programmer writing the procedure call need not remember the order of the parameters. The disadvantage is that the flexible order of actual parameters, together with the possibility of mixing positional and keyword notation, the existence of default arguments, and the existence of overloading, make the rules for interpreting (and understanding) procedure calls uncomfortably complicated.

A program is essentially a semantic structure, specifying how a computation should be performed. The syntax is merely a notation by which the programmer selects the semantic concepts to be used in that computation. The most important properties of the syntax are that it should be easy to learn, and make programs easy to understand.

18.6   Language life cycles

Each new language passes through a number of stages from its initial design to routine use by programmers:

- The requirements for the new language are identified. What is its intended application area? Will it be used to write long-lived reusable software, or short-lived "throw-away" programs?

- The language's syntax and semantics are designed. As discussed above, the primary decisions are which semantic concepts to select, and how to combine them to make the language regular and simple, yet powerful. Design of the syntax is secondary, and should be left until last.

- A specification of the new language is prepared. The specification must be clearly written, complete, consistent, and unambiguous. This allows programmers to review and comment on the new language.

- Using the specification, an initial implementation of the new language is constructed. This allows programmers to gain experience with the new language.

- The specification, implementation, and programmers' experience all provide feedback to the designer, drawing attention to any unsatisfactory aspects of the design, which can then be improved.

- If the new language is successful, improved implementations are constructed, textbooks are written, and a community of programmers is built up. In due course, the language might become an international standard. It will also undergo revision as its requirements change over time.

There are strong analogies between the above stages and the stages of the familiar software life cycle (requirements, design, specification, prototyping, implementation, testing, documentation, and maintenance). So we see that not only software systems but also languages have life cycles.

18.7 The future

We started this book with a brief history of programming and scripting languages. Let us conclude with some brief speculations on how programming and scripting languages might develop in the future.

At the time of writing, the dominant paradigm is object-oriented programming (together with the complementary object-oriented analysis and design methods). New object-oriented languages are being designed, and object-oriented facilities are being grafted on to imperative and scripting languages. This situation seems likely to continue for the foreseeable future.

Functional and logic programming will remain important, but only within their established niches. Functional and logic languages are hampered by their inability to model state in a natural way, except by more-or-less *ad hoc* extensions that destroy these languages' conceptual clarity.

Scripting will remain important, since it enables nonprofessional programmers to customize software to their own requirements. However, the conceptual distance between scripting and programming is narrower than the scripting enthusiasts claim. So scripting languages will continue to converge with programming languages. In fact the gap between programming and scripting languages will surely come to be seen as a historical accident.

It is possible that new paradigms will become more prominent in the future. *Aspect-oriented programming* emerged in the late 1990s as a promising way to build large programs with multiple "aspects", which tend to cut across the functional units of such programs. In an object-oriented distributed system, for example, the aspects might be the objects' functionality, locations, communications, and synchronization. Aspect-oriented programming allows such aspects to be programmed separately, then woven together by a special compiler.

The Internet will continue to pose difficult challenges for language designers, in terms of distributed programming and especially security. Existing language technology allows us to download applets in full confidence that they are harmless. So why cannot we open office documents attached to e-mails without worrying that their macros might contain viruses? For that matter, why cannot we have operating systems that are far more resistant to viral infections? Appropriate language technology could make our systems more secure, but its development and deployment are currently inhibited by commercial forces and resistance to change. We should all *insist* on change!

Summary

In this chapter:

- We have seen that a judicious selection of concepts is essential in any language design.

- We have seen that, given a selection of concepts, we can maximize the language's power and expressiveness by combining these concepts in a regular manner. The Type Completeness, Abstraction, Correspondence, and Qualification Principles suggest some ways to achieve this goal.

- We have seen that languages designed with limited aims can be very simple. On the other hand, general-purpose languages are inevitably complicated, but they should control their complexity by devolving as much functionality as possible to a package or class library.

- We have seen that every language should be capable of acceptably efficient implementation, employing only concepts whose costs are justified by their benefits and preferably are borne only by programs that actually use them.

- We have seen that a language's syntax should be designed so that programs are readable, mistakes are quickly detected, and the syntactic forms in a program transparently reveal the underlying semantic concepts.

- We have seen that each language has a life cycle, which is similar to the software life cycle.

- We have speculated on the future development of programming and scripting languages.

Further reading

Useful commonsense advice on language design has been offered by HOARE (1973) and WIRTH (1974). Both Hoare and Wirth place strong emphasis on simplicity, security, efficiency (at both compile-time and run-time), and readability. Hoare recommends that the language designer should select and consolidate concepts already invented and tested by others, and avoid the temptation to introduce new and untried concepts. Wirth emphasizes the importance of

making the inherent cost of using each concept clearly visible to the programmer.

McIVER and CONWAY (1996) examine aspects of programming language design that tend to cause difficulties for novices in particular.

For a brief introduction to aspect-oriented programming, see ELRAD et al. (2001).

Exercises

Exercises for Section 18.1

18.1.1 (Revision) Consider the following concepts: static typing, variables, bindings, procedural abstraction, data abstraction, generic abstraction, concurrency. Which of these concepts are supported by each of the following languages: C, C++, JAVA, ADA, HASKELL, PROLOG, and PYTHON?

Exercises for Section 18.2

*18.2.1 Consider the following languages: C, C++, JAVA, ADA, HASKELL, PROLOG, and PYTHON. Assess each language's compliance with:

(a) the Type Completeness Principle;

(b) the Abstraction Principle (consider expressions, commands where applicable, and declarations);

(c) the Correspondence Principle;

(d) the Qualification Principle (consider expressions, commands where applicable, and declarations).

Exercises for Section 18.3

*18.3.1 Consider the approach to managing language complexity suggested at the end of Section 18.3, and illustrated in Figure 18.1. It might be argued that this is a recipe for chaos. A monolithic language forces all programmers to work with a common set of facilities, while a core language plus library encourages programmers to design and use their own program units (rather than those in the library), encouraging egotistic programming and ultimately hindering portability. Develop this argument, and also develop a counterargument.

*18.3.2 Which (if any) built-in features of C++ and ADA might reasonably be supported by program units in the library?

Exercises for Section 18.5

18.5.1 Consider the use of semicolons as command separators or terminators. As illustrated below, PASCAL commands are separated by semicolons when composed sequentially, ADA (and C) commands are terminated by semicolons, and PYTHON commands are each terminated by an end-of-line:

PASCAL:	ADA:	PYTHON:
`if x < y then`	`if x < y then`	`if x < y:`
`begin`	`    z := x;`	`    z = x`
`    z := x;`	`    x := y;`	`    x = y`
`    x := y;`	`    y := z;`	`    y = z`
`    y := z`	`end if;`	
`end`		

What are the advantages and disadvantages of each syntax?

18.5.2 Consider the syntax of composite (conditional and iterative) commands in various languages. As illustrated below, C requires each subcommand to be enclosed in braces (unless the subcommand is very simple), ADA composite commands provide their own bracketing, and PYTHON requires subcommands to be indented:

C:

```
l = 0;
r = n - 1;
while (l <= r) {
  m = (l + r)/2;
  if (x == xs[m])
    break;
  if (x < xs[m])
    r = m + 1;
  else
    l = m + 1;
}
```

ADA:

```
l = 0;
r = n - 1;
while l <= r loop
  m = (l + r)/2;
  if x = xs[m] then
    exit;
  end if;
  if x < xs[m]
    r = m - 1;
  else
    l = m + 1;
  end if;
end loop;
```

PYTHON:

```
l = 0
r = n - 1
while l <= r:
  m = (l + r)/2
  if x == xs[m]:
    break
  if x < xs[m]:
    r = m - 1
  else:
    l = m + 1
```

What are the advantages and disadvantages of each syntax?

Bibliography

ABELSON, H., SUSSMAN, G. J., AND SUSSMAN, J. (1996) *Structure and Interpretation of Computer Programs*, 2nd edn, MIT Press, Cambridge, MA; also McGraw-Hill, New York.

AHO, A. V., SETHI, R., AND ULLMAN, J. D. (1986) *Compilers: Principles, Techniques, and Tools*, Addison-Wesley, Reading, MA.

ANSI (1994) *Information Technology – Programming Language – Common LISP*, ANSI INCITS 226–1994 (R1999), American National Standards Institute, Washington, DC.

APPEL, A. (1998) *Modern Compiler Implementation in JAVA*, Cambridge University Press, Cambridge, UK.

ATKINSON, M. P. AND BUNEMAN, O. P. (1987) Database programming languages, *ACM Computing Surveys* **19**, 105–90.

BARRON, D. (2000) *The World of Scripting Languages*, Wiley, Chichester, UK.

BEAZLEY, D. M. (2001) *PYTHON Essential Reference*, 2nd edn, New Riders Publishing, Indianapolis, IN.

BIRD, R. A. AND WADLER, P. L. (1988) *Introduction to Functional Programming*, Prentice Hall International, Hemel Hempstead, UK.

BIRTWHISTLE, G. M., DAHL, O. -J., MYHRHAUG, B., AND NYGAARD, K. (1979) *SIMULA Begin*, Petrocelli Charter, New York.

BÖHM, C. AND JACOPINI, G. (1966) Flow diagrams, Turing machines, and languages with only two formation rules, *Communications of the ACM* **9**, 366–71.

BOOCH, G. (1987) *Software Engineering with ADA*, 2nd edn, Addison-Wesley, Reading, MA.

BRACHA, G., ODERSKY, M., STOUTAMIRE, D., AND WADLER, P. (1998) Making the future safe for the past: adding genericity to the JAVA programming language, in *ACM SIGPLAN Conference on Object-Oriented Programming Systems, Languages, and Applications (OOPSLA'98)*, 183–200.

BRATKO, I. (1990) *PROLOG: Programming for Artificial Intelligence*, Addison-Wesley, Wokingham, UK.

BRINCH HANSEN, P. (1973) *Operating System Principles*, Prentice Hall, Englewood Cliffs, NJ.

BRINCH HANSEN, P. (1977) *The Architecture of Concurrent Programs*, Prentice Hall, Englewood Cliffs, NJ.

BURNS, A. AND WELLINGS, A. J. (1998) *Concurrency in ADA*, Cambridge University Press, Cambridge, UK.

BUSTARD, D., ELDER, J., AND WELSH, J. (1988) *Concurrent Program Structures*, Prentice Hall International, Hemel Hempstead, UK.

BUTENHOF, D. R. (1997) *Programming with POSIX Threads*, Addison-Wesley, Reading, MA.

CARDELLI, L. (1986) *Amber, in Combinators and Functional Programming*, Springer, Berlin, pp. 21–47.

CARDELLI, L. AND WEGNER, P. (1985) On understanding types, data abstraction, and polymorphism, *ACM Computing Surveys* **17**, 471–522.

COHEN, N. H. (1995) *ADA as a Second Language*, McGraw-Hill, New York.

COULOURIS, G., DOLLIMORE, J., AND KINDBERG, K. (2000) *Distributed Systems: Concepts and Design*, 3rd edn, Addison-Wesley, Reading, MA.

COX, B. (1986) *Object-Oriented Programming: an Evolutionary Approach*, Addison-Wesley, Reading, MA.

DIBBLE, P. (2002) *Real-Time JAVA Platform Programming*, Sun Microsystems Press, Santa Clara, CA.

DIJKSTRA, E. W. (1968a) Cooperating sequential processes, in *Programming Languages* (ed. F. Genuys), Academic Press, New York, pp. 43–112.

DIJKSTRA, E. W. (1968b) Go to statement considered harmful, *Communications of the ACM* **11**, 147–8.

DIJKSTRA, E. W. (1976) *A Discipline of Programming*, Prentice Hall, Englewood Cliffs, NJ.

DRAYTON, P., ALBAHARI, B., AND NEWARD, E. (2002) *C# in a Nutshell*, O'Reilly, Sebastopol, CA.

ELRAD, T., FILMAN, R. E., AND HADER, A. (eds) (2001) Aspect-oriented programming, *Communications of the ACM* **44**, 29–41.

FLANAGAN, D. (2002) *JAVA in a Nutshell*, 3rd edn, O'Reilly, Sebastopol, CA.

GEHANI, N. AND MCGETTRICK, A. D. (eds) (1988) *Concurrent Programming*, Addison-Wesley, Wokingham, UK.

GHEZZI, C. AND JAZAYERI, M. (1997) *Programming Language Concepts*, 3rd edn, Wiley, New York.

GOLDBERG, A. AND ROBSON, D. (1989) *SMALLTALK-80*: the Language, Addison-Wesley, Reading, MA.

HARBISON, S. P. AND STEELE, G. L. (1995) *C: a Reference Manual*, Prentice Hall, Englewood Cliffs, NJ.

HINDLEY, J. R. (1969) The principal type-scheme of an object in combinatory logic, *Transactions of the AMS* **146**, 29–60.

HOARE, C. A. R. (1972) Notes on data structuring, in *Structured Programming* (eds O. -J. Dahl, E. W. Dijkstra, and C. A. R. Hoare), Academic Press, London, pp. 83–174.

HOARE, C. A. R. (1973) Hints on programming language design, in *Proceedings of ACM Symposium on Principles of Programming Languages 1973*, ACM Press, New York.

HOARE, C. A. R. (1975) Recursive data structures, *International Journal of Computer and Information Sciences* **4**, 105–32.

HOARE, C. A. R. (1978) Communicating sequential processes, *Communications of the ACM* **21**, 666–77.

HOARE, C. A. R. (1981) The emperor's old clothes, *Communications of the ACM* **24**, 75–83.

HOARE, C. A. R. (1986) *Communicating Sequential Processes*, Prentice Hall International, Hemel Hempstead, UK.

HOROWITZ, E. (ed.) (1995) *Programming Languages: a Grand Tour*, 3rd edn, Freeman, New York.

ICHBIAH, J. (ed.) (1979) Rationale for the design of the *ADA* programming language, *ACM SIGPLAN Notices* **14**, no. 6B (special issue).

ICHBIAH, J. (ed.) (1983) *ADA Programming Language*, ANSI/MIL-STD-1815A, ADA Joint Program Office, Department of Defense, Washington, DC.

ISO (1979) *Programming Languages – PL/I*, ISO 6160:1979, International Organization for Standardization, Geneva, Switzerland.

ISO (1990) *Information Technology – Programming Languages – PASCAL*, ISO 7185:1990, International Organization for Standardization, Geneva, Switzerland.

ISO/IEC (1995) *Information Technology – Programming Languages – ADA*, ISO/IEC 8652:1995, International Organization for Standardization, Geneva, Switzerland.

ISO/IEC (1997) *Information Technology – Programming Languages – FORTRAN, Part 1:* Base Language, ISO/IEC 1539-1:1997, International Organization for Standardization, Geneva, Switzerland.

ISO/IEC (1998) *Programming Languages – C++*, ISO/IEC 14882:1998, International Organization for Standardization, Geneva, Switzerland.

ISO/IEC (1999) *Programming Languages – C*, ISO/IEC 9899:1999, International Organization for Standardization, Geneva, Switzerland.

ISO/IEC (2002) *Programming Languages – COBOL*, ISO 1989:2002, International Organization for Standardization, Geneva, Switzerland.

JONES, G. AND GOLDSMITH, M. (1988) *Programming in OCCAM2*, Prentice Hall International, Hemel Hempstead, UK.

JOY, W., STEELE, G., GOSLING, J., AND BRACHA, G. (2000) *JAVA Language Specification*, 2nd edn, Addison-Wesley, Reading, MA.

KERNIGHAN, B. W. AND RITCHIE, D. M. (1989) *C Programming Language*, 2nd edn, Prentice Hall, Englewood Cliffs, NJ.

KNUTH, D. E. (1974) Structured programming with goto statements, *ACM Computing Surveys* **6**, 261–302.

KOENIG, A. (1989) *C Traps and Pitfalls*, Addison-Wesley, Reading, MA.

LANDIN, P. J. (1966) The next 700 programming languages, *Communications of the ACM* **9**, 157–64.

LEA, D. (2000) *Concurrent Programming in JAVA: Design Principles and Patterns*, Addison-Wesley, Reading, MA.

LEDGARD, H. F. AND SINGER, A. (1982) Scaling down ADA, *Communications of the ACM* **25**, 121–5.

LISKOV, B. H. AND ZILLES, S. N. (1974) Programming with abstract data types, *ACM SIGPLAN Notices* **9**, 50–9.

MALPAS, J. (1987) *PROLOG: a Relational Language and its Applications*, Prentice Hall International, Hemel Hempstead, UK.

McCARTHY, J. (1965) A basis for a mathematical theory of computation, in *Computer Programming and Formal Systems* (eds P. Braffort and D. Hirschberg), North-Holland, Amsterdam, pp. 33–70.

McCARTHY, J., ABRAHAMS, P. W., EDWARDS, D. J., et al. (1965) *LISP 1.5 Programmer's Manual*, 2nd edn, MIT Press, Cambridge, MA.

McIVER, L. AND CONWAY, D. M. (1996) Seven deadly sins of introductory programming language design, in *Proceedings of Software Engineering Education and Practice 1996*, IEEE Computer Society, pp. 309–16.

MEYER, B. (1988) From structured programming to object-oriented design: the road to EIFFEL, *Structured Programming* **10**, 19–39.

MEYER, B. (1989) *Object-Oriented Software Construction*, Prentice Hall International, Hemel Hempstead, UK.

MILNER, R. (1978) A theory of type polymorphism in programming, *Journal of Computer and System Science* **17**, 348–75.

MILNER, R., TOFTE, M., HARPER, R., AND McQUEEN, D. (1997) *The Definition of Standard ML – Revised*, MIT Press, Cambridge, MA.

NAUR, P. (ed.) (1963) Revised report on the algorithmic language ALGOL60, *Communications of the ACM* **6**, 1–20; also *Computer Journal* **5**, 349–67.

OUSTERHOUT, J. K. (1998) Scripting: higher level programming for the 21st century, *IEEE Computer* **31**, 3, 23–30.

PARNAS, D. L. (1972) On the criteria to be used in decomposing systems into modules, *Communications of the ACM* **15**, 1053–8.

PERROTT, R. H. (1987) *Parallel Programming*, Addison-Wesley, Wokingham, UK.

PRATT, T. W. AND ZELCOWITZ, N. V. (2001) *Programming Languages: Design and Implementation*, 4th edn, Prentice Hall, Englewood Cliffs, NJ.

REYNOLDS, J. C. (1985) Three approaches to type structure, in *Mathematical Foundations of Software Development* (eds H. Ehrig, C. Floyd, M. Nivat, and J. Thatcher), Springer, Berlin, pp. 97–138.

ROSSER, J. B. (1982) Highlights of the history of the lambda-calculus, *Conference Record of 1982 ACM Symposium on Lisp and Functional Programming, Pittsburgh*, ACM, New York, pp. 216–25.

SEBESTA, R. W. (2001) *Concepts of Programming Languages*, 5th edn, Addison-Wesley, Reading, MA.

SETHI, R. (1996) *Programming Languages: Concepts and Constructs*, Addison-Wesley, Reading, MA.

SIMPSON, H. R. (1990) Four-slot fully asynchronous communication mechanism, *IEE Proceedings* **137** (Part E), 17–30.

STRACHEY, C. (1967) Fundamental concepts in programming languages, in *Proceedings of International Summer School in Computer Programming* 1967, Copenhagen.

STROUSTRUP, B. (1994) *The Design and Evolution of C++*, Addison-Wesley, Reading, MA.

STROUSTRUP, B. (1997) *The C++ Programming Language*, 3rd edn, Addison-Wesley, Reading, MA.

SUTTER, H. (2002) A pragmatic look at exception specifications, *C/C++ Users Journal* **20** (7).

TENNENT, R. D. (1977) Language design methods based on semantic principles, *Acta Informatica* **8**, 97–112.

TENNENT, R. D. (1981) *Principles of Programming Languages*, Prentice Hall International, Hemel Hempstead, UK.

THOMPSON, S. (1999) *HASKELL: The Craft of Functional Programming*, 2nd edn, Addison-Wesley, Harlow, UK.

US Department of Defense (1978) *Requirements for high-order computer programming languages*, ADA Joint Program Office, Department of Defense, Washington, DC.

VAN ROSSUM, G. AND DRAKE, F. L. (eds) (2003) *PYTHON reference manual*, Release 2.3, www.python.org/doc/current/ref/.

VAN WIJNGAARDEN, A., et al. (1976) *Revised Report on the Algorithmic Language ALGOL68*, Springer, Berlin.

WALL, L., CHRISTIANSEN, T., AND ORWANT, J. (2000) *Programming PERL*, 3rd edn, O'Reilly, Sebastopol, CA.

WATT, D. A. (1991) *Programming Language Syntax and Semantics*, Prentice Hall International, Hemel Hempstead, UK.

WATT, D. A. AND BROWN, D. F. (2000) *Programming Language Processors in JAVA*, Prentice Hall, Harlow, UK.

WEXELBLAT, R. L. (ed.) (1980) *ACM History of Programming Languages Conference, Los Angeles*, ACM Monograph, Academic Press, New York.

WICHMANN, B. A. (1984) Is ADA too big? – a designer answers the critics, *Communications of the ACM* **27**, 98–103.

WIKSTRÖM, Å. (1987) *Functional Programming using Standard ML*, Prentice Hall International, Hemel Hempstead, UK.

WIRTH, N. (1974) On the design of programming languages, in *Proceedings of IFIP Congress* 1974, North-Holland, Amsterdam, pp. 386–93.

WIRTH, N. (1977) MODULA: a programming language for modular multiprogramming, *Software Practice and Experience* **7**, 3–35.

ZAHN, C. T. (1974) A control statement for natural top-down structured programming, *Symposium on Programming Languages*, Paris.

Glossary

Abnormal situation An abnormal situation is one in which a program cannot continue normally. The program signals this situation by setting a status flag or by throwing an exception.

Abort-deferred In ADA95, an abort-deferred construct is an operation that must complete before cancellation of a task takes effect.

Abstract class An abstract class is one in which no object can be constructed. Its operations may include abstract methods, but no constructor. It must have one or more non-abstract subclasses.

Abstract method An abstract method is an undefined method of an abstract class. It must be overridden by all non-abstract subclasses.

Abstract type An abstract type is one whose representation is private. It must be equipped with some operations, which have exclusive access to the representation.

Abstraction Principle The Abstraction Principle states: It is possible to design procedures that abstract over any syntactic category, provided only that the constructs in that syntactic category specify some kind of computation. For example, proper procedures abstract over commands, and function procedures abstract over expressions.

Accept command In ADA, an accept command is a composite command that services an entry call. A serving task blocks at an accept command for an entry with no outstanding call.

Activation An activation of a block is the time interval during which that block is being executed. An activation of a procedure is the time interval between call and return.

Actual parameter An actual parameter is an expression (or other construct) that determines an argument to be passed to a procedure or method.

Address The address of a storage cell or variable is its location in storage.

Admission control In concurrent programming, admission control logic ensures that an operation is delayed until its precondition has been established.

Algebraic type In HASKELL, an algebraic type is a disjoint union.

Aliasing Aliasing occurs when a variable can be accessed using two or more different names. Aliasing is a consequence of variable parameters and variable renaming declarations.

Allocator An allocator is a construct that creates a heap variable. Examples are **new** in C++, JAVA, and ADA.

Application program interface (API) In software engineering, the application program interface of a program unit is the minimum information that application programmers need to know in order to use the program unit successfully.

Applied occurrence An applied occurrence of an identifier is one where the identifier is used. See also *binding occurrence*.

Architecture The architecture of a program is the way in which it is decomposed into program units.

Argument An argument is a value, variable, or other entity that is passed to a procedure or method when it is called.

Array An array is a collection of components, each of which is indexed by a distinct value in the array's index range.

Assertion In a logic language, an assertion is a "call" to a relation. The assertion either succeeds or fails.

Assignment An assignment is a command that evaluates an expression and stores its value in a variable. In an expression-oriented language, however, an assignment is itself an expression.

Atom In PROLOG, an atom is a primitive value other than a number.

Atomic An operation is atomic if no intermediate stage in its execution is observable by any process. A variable is atomic if accessing it is an atomic operation.

Await command In concurrent programming, an await command blocks within a conditional critical region until a boolean expression involving the shared variable of the region yields *true*. While waiting, a process relinquishes its exclusive use of the shared variable. When it resumes, exclusive access is restored.

Backtrack In logic programming, backtracking occurs when an attempt to test a query against a particular clause fails, and the query is instead tested against some other clause.

Bindable   A bindable entity is one that may be bound to an identifier in a particular programming language.

Binding   A binding is a fixed association between an identifier and a bindable entity. Bindings are produced by declarations.

Binding occurrence   A binding occurrence of an identifier is one where the identifier is declared. See also *applied occurrence*.

Block   A block is a program construct that delimits the scope of any declarations within it. See also *block command, block expression*.

Block command   A block command consists of declarations and a subcommand. The subcommand is executed in the scope of the declarations. An example is "{...}" in C, C++, and JAVA.

Block expression   A block expression consists of declarations and a subexpression. The subexpression is evaluated in the scope of the declarations. An example is "let ... in ..." in HASKELL.

Block structure   Block structure is the textual relationship between blocks in a particular programming language. See also *flat block structure, monolithic block structure, nested block structure*.

Body   The body of an iterative command is a subcommand that is to be executed repeatedly. The body of a procedure is a command (or expression) that is to be executed (evaluated) when the procedure is called.

Bounded   In a generic unit, a bounded type parameter is one that restricts the corresponding argument type. For instance, the argument might have to be a subtype of a specified type, or it might have to be a type equipped with specified operations. An unbounded type parameter allows the argument to be any type whatsoever.

Boundedly nondeterministic   A computation is boundedly nondeterministic if its sequence of steps and its outcome are not entirely predictable, but there are only a limited number of possible outcomes, all of which may be equally acceptable.

Break sequencer   In C, C++, and JAVA, a break sequencer terminates execution of an enclosing command.

Cardinality   The cardinality of a set is the number of members of that set. The cardinality of a type is the number of values of that type.

Carry   A sequencer may carry a value to its destination. Examples are return sequencers in most programming languages, and exceptions in JAVA.

Cartesian product   A Cartesian product is a set of tuples. Examples are C structure types and ADA record types.

Case command   A case command consists of a condition (expression) and several subcommands. The condition's value determines which of these subcommands is chosen to be executed.

Case expression   A case expression consists of a condition (expression) and several other subexpressions. The condition's value determines which of these subexpressions is chosen to be evaluated.

Cast   A cast is an explicit type conversion.

Catch   When an exception is thrown, it may be caught by an exception handler for that particular exception.

Ceiling priority protocol   In concurrent programming, the ceiling priority protocol prevents priority inversion by temporarily giving every process that acquires a resource the highest priority of *any* process using that resource.

Church–Rosser Property   A programming language possesses the Church–Rosser Property if the following holds: If an expression can be evaluated at all, it can be evaluated by consistently using normal-order evaluation; if an expression can be evaluated in several different orders (mixing eager and normal-order evaluation), then all of these evaluation orders yield the same result. Only pure functional languages (such as HASKELL) possess the Church–Rosser Property.

Class   A class is a set of similar objects. All objects of a given class have similar variable components, and are equipped with the same operations.

Class method   A class method is attached to a class (not to a particular object). It can access class variables only.

Class variable   A class variable is a component of a class (not a component of a particular object). Its lifetime is the program's whole run-time.

Class-wide type   The values of a class-wide type are the objects of a particular class and all of its subclasses.

Clause   See *Horn clause*.

Closed-world assumption   In logic programming, the closed-world assumption is that an assertion is *false* if it cannot be inferred to be *true*. This assumption is justified only if the program encodes all relevant information about the application domain.

Coercion A coercion is an implicit type conversion.

Collateral command A collateral command consists of two or more subcommands, which are executed in any order, possibly in interleaved order.

Collateral declaration A collateral declaration consists of two or more subdeclarations, whose bindings are combined. The scope of each subdeclaration includes none of the others.

Command A command is a program construct that is executed in order to update variables.

Command expression A command expression consists of a command and a subexpression. The latter is evaluated after the command is executed.

Communication In concurrent programming, there is communication from process P to process Q if P produces data that Q consumes.

Compatible Two types are compatible if they have values in common.

Competing commands In concurrent programming, two or more commands compete if each needs exclusive access to the same resource for some of its steps.

Compilation unit A compilation unit is a part of a program that can be compiled on its own.

Composite type A composite type is one whose values are composite. See also *Cartesian product, disjoint union, mapping, recursive type*.

Composite value A composite value (or data structure) is a value that is composed from simpler values.

Composite variable A composite variable is one that is composed from simpler variables.

Concept A concept is an idea that underlies the design of one or more programming languages.

Concurrent program A concurrent program specifies the possible state changes of two or more sequential processes.

Concurrent programming Concurrent programming is a paradigm whose key concepts are processes and their interactions.

Conditional command A conditional command consists of a condition (expression) and two or more subcommands. The condition's value determines which of these subcommands is chosen to be executed. See also *if-command, case command*.

Conditional critical region In concurrent programming, a conditional critical region is a composite command that provides both automatic mutual exclusion and implicit communication.

Conditional expression A conditional expression consists of a condition (expression) and two or more subexpressions. The condition's value determines which of these subexpressions is chosen to be evaluated. See also *if-expression, case expression*.

Constant access A constant access is a simple expression that takes the value of a constant.

Constant declaration A constant declaration binds an identifier to a value.

Constant parameter A constant parameter is a formal parameter that is bound to the corresponding argument value.

Construction A construction is an expression that constructs a composite value such as an array, record, or object.

Constructor A constructor is an operation of an abstract type or class, which constructs a value or object.

Context-dependent overloading Context-dependent overloading occurs when two or more procedures have the same identifier in the same scope, but differ in their parameter types and/or their result types.

Context-independent overloading Context-independent overloading occurs when two or more procedures have the same identifier in the same scope, but differ in their parameter types.

Continue sequencer In C, C++, and Java, a continue sequencer terminates the current iteration of an enclosing loop body.

Control sequence In an Ada for-command, the control sequence is the sequence of values assigned to the control variable.

Control variable In an Ada for-command, the control variable is used for counting the iterations.

Copy parameter mechanism A copy parameter mechanism allows for a value to be copied into and/or out of a procedure. See also *copy-in parameter, copy-in-copy-out parameter, copy-out parameter*.

Copy semantics Copy semantics means that, when a value is assigned to a variable, that variable is made to contain a copy of that value.

Copy-in parameter A copy-in parameter allows for a value to be copied into a procedure when it is called.

Copy-in-copy-out parameter A copy-in-copy-out parameter allows for a value to be copied into a procedure when it is called and out of the procedure when it returns.

Copy-out parameter   A copy-out parameter allows for a value to be copied out of a procedure when it returns.

Correspondence Principle   The Correspondence Principle states: For each form of declaration there exists a corresponding parameter mechanism. For example, a constant declaration corresponds to a constant parameter, and a variable declaration with initialization corresponds to a copy-in parameter.

Coupling   Coupling is the degree of interdependence between program units. Two program units are tightly (loosely) coupled if changes to one are likely (unlikely) to force major changes to the other.

Create   When a variable is created, one or more storage cells are allocated to it.

Critical section   In concurrent programming, parallel commands that must access the same resource *r* under mutual exclusion are critical sections with respect to *r*.

Curried   A curried function is a function, with *n* parameters, that can be called with fewer than *n* arguments. The result of such a call is itself a function.

Cut   In PROLOG, a cut is a kind of sequencer that prevents future backtracking.

Daemon thread   In JAVA, the run-time environment kills all daemon threads if it finds that all non-daemon threads have terminated.

Dangling pointer   A dangling pointer is one that points to a variable that has been destroyed.

Deadlock   In concurrent programming, deadlock is when a set of processes are unable to continue because of their mutually incompatible demands for resources.

Deallocator   A deallocator is a program construct that destroys a heap variable.

Declaration   A declaration is a program construct that is elaborated to produce bindings. It might also have side effects such as creating variables.

Definite iteration   An iterative command supports definite iteration if the number of iterations is known in advance. An example is the ADA for-command.

Definition   A definition is a declaration that produces bindings but has no side effects.

Denote   In an environment that binds an identifier to an entity, the identifier is said to denote that entity.

Dereferencing   Dereferencing is a coercion that takes a variable and yields its current value.

Destination   The destination of a sequencer is the program point to which control is transferred by the sequencer.

Destroy   When a variable is destroyed, the storage cells previously allocated to it can be deallocated and used for some other purpose.

Deterministic   A computation is deterministic if its sequence of steps and therefore its outcome are entirely predictable and reproducible.

Direct file   A direct file is one whose components may be accessed randomly using their unique position numbers.

Discrete primitive type   A discrete primitive type is a primitive type other than a floating-point type. Its values can be mapped on to a range of integers.

Discriminated record   In ADA, a discriminated record is a kind of disjoint union. It has a component (the ''discriminant'') whose current value determines which other components the record contains.

Disjoint union   A disjoint union of two or more types consists of a tag and (depending on the tag) a value of one of these types. Examples are HASKELL algebraic types and ADA discriminated record types.

Distributed system   In a distributed system, processes run on a network of computers that do not share primary storage.

Do-while-command   In C, C++, and JAVA, a do-while-command consists of a condition (boolean expression) and a body (subcommand). It repeatedly executes the body and then evaluates the condition, terminating as soon as the condition yields *false*.

Dynamic array   A dynamic array is one whose index bounds are computed at run-time, but remain fixed throughout the array's lifetime.

Dynamic dispatch   Dynamic dispatch occurs in a method call where the version of the method to be called cannot be determined at compile-time: the target object could be either an object of a class that is equipped with the method, or an object of a subclass that overrides the method.

Dynamic linking   Dynamic linking means that each program unit is linked into a program only when the program unit is first needed during the program's run-time.

Dynamically scoped   A programming language is dynamically scoped if each procedure's body is executed in the environment of the procedure call.

Dynamically typed   A programming language is dynamically typed if values have types but variables and expressions do not. Each operation is type-checked at run-time, immediately before the operation is applied.

Eager evaluation   With eager evaluation, an operation is applied as soon as its operands are known.

Effectively deterministic   A computation is effectively deterministic if its sequence of steps is unpredictable but its outcome is predictable.

Elaborate   When a declaration is elaborated, it produces bindings.

Empty list   An empty list is a list with no components.

Empty string   An empty string is a string with no characters.

Encapsulation   Encapsulation means that a program unit such as a package may distinguish between its public and private components.

Entry   In ADA, an entry of a task (or protected object) is a service provided by the task.

Entry call   In ADA, an entry call invokes an entry of a task (or protected object) and may pass arguments to the entry. The entry call is queued until the task is ready to accept it.

Entry family   In ADA95, an entry family is a set of entries indexed by a value that may be used in a guard controlling admission to the entry.

Enumerand   An enumerand is a value of an enumeration type.

Enumeration type   An enumeration type is a type whose values (enumerands) are explicitly listed when the type is declared.

Environment   An environment is a set of bindings that are fixed in a given scope.

Equivalent   Two types are equivalent if the programming language allows them to be used interchangeably. Both types must have the same set of values.

Escape   An escape is a sequencer that terminates execution of an enclosing command, procedure, or program.

Evaluate   When an expression is evaluated, it yields a value.

Event   An event is an entity that represents a category of system state changes, and is used for signaling the occurrence of such changes between processes.

Exception   An exception is an entity that represents an abnormal situation. When an exception is thrown, it can be caught by an enclosing command or calling procedure that contains a suitable exception handler. In some programming languages, an exception may carry a value that may be accessed by the exception handler.

Exception handler   An exception handler is a program construct, labeled by an exception (or class of exceptions), to which control may be transferred when such an exception is thrown.

Exception specification   An exception specification of a procedure (or method) specifies which exceptions a call to that procedure (method) might throw.

Exception-handling command   An exception-handling command consists of a subcommand and one or more exception handlers. If the subcommand (or a procedure called by it) throws an exception, the corresponding exception handler if any is executed.

Execute   When a command is executed, it updates variables.

Exit sequencer   In ADA, an exit sequencer terminates execution of an enclosing loop.

Expression   An expression is a program construct that is evaluated to yield a value. It might also have side effects such as updating variables.

Expression-oriented   An expression-oriented programming language is one that makes no distinction between expressions and commands.

Fact   In logic programming, a fact is an unconditional Horn clause.

Fail   In logic programming, a query fails if it cannot be inferred from the clauses in the program that the query is *true*.

Fairness   A concurrent system has the fairness property if it ensures that no process needing a resource is indefinitely prevented from obtaining it by the demands of competing processes.

File   A file is a data structure held in persistent secondary storage.

First-class value   A first-class value is one that can be manipulated in unrestricted ways. Typically, it can be passed as an argument, used as a component of a composite value, assigned, and so on.

Flat block structure   In a programming language with flat block structure, each program is partitioned into one or more non-overlapping blocks.

Flexible array   A flexible array is one whose index bounds are computed at run-time, and may be changed during the array's lifetime.

For-command   In ADA, a for-command is an iterative command in which a control variable is assigned a predetermined sequence of values. In C, C++, and JAVA, a for-command is an abbreviation for a while-command with initialization.

Formal parameter   A formal parameter is an identifier through which a procedure can access an argument. The formal parameter is bound either to the argument itself, or to a local variable containing a copy of the argument, depending on the parameter mechanism.

Free   An identifier is free in a program construct if the construct contains an applied occurrence of that identifier with no corresponding binding occurrence.

Function   In mathematics, a function is a mapping from one set to another. See also *function procedure*.

Function call   A function call is an expression that calls a function procedure. It passes arguments, and yields the function procedure's result.

Function definition   A function definition is a declaration that binds an identifier to a function procedure.

Function procedure   A function procedure is a procedure that, when called, returns a value as its result.

Function specification   A function specification declares the identifier, formal parameters, and result type of a function procedure.

Functional programming   Functional programming is a paradigm whose key concepts are expressions and functions.

Generic unit   A generic unit is a program unit that is parameterized with respect to values, types, procedures, etc., on which it depends. It can be instantiated to generate an ordinary program unit. Examples are ADA generics and C++ templates.

Global variable   A global variable is one declared in the program's outermost block. Its lifetime is the program's entire run-time.

Guard   In ADA95, a guard is a boolean expression that controls admission to an entry.

Halt sequencer   A halt sequencer is one that terminates execution of the program.

Heap variable   A heap variable is one that is created by an allocator. Its lifetime extends until it is destroyed or it becomes unreachable.

Heterogeneous   A collection of values is heterogeneous if they are not all of the same type.

Hidden   In nested block structure, a declaration of an identifier may be hidden by a declaration of the same identifier in an inner block.

Higher-order function   A higher-order function is one whose parameter or result is itself a function.

Homogeneous   A collection of values is homogeneous if they are all of the same type.

Horn clause   In logic, a Horn clause is a clause of the form "A_0 if A_1 and ... and A_n", where $n \geq 0$. All variables occurring in A_0 are taken to be existentially quantified, and all other variables occurring in the clause are taken to be universally quantified.

If-command   An if-command consists of a condition (a boolean expression) and two subcommands. The value of the expression determines which subcommand is chosen to be executed.

If-expression   An if-expression consists of a condition (a boolean expression) and two other subexpressions. The condition's value determines which of these subexpressions is chosen to be evaluated.

Imperative programming   Imperative programming is a paradigm whose key concepts are variables, commands, and procedures.

Implementable   A programming language must be implementable, meaning that every program in the language can be executed on a computer.

Inclusion polymorphism   Inclusion polymorphism is a type system in which each type (or class) may have subtypes (subclasses) that inherit the type's (class's) operations.

Indefinite iteration   An iterative command supports indefinite iteration if the number of iterations is not known in advance. An example is the while-command.

Independent commands   Two commands are independent if no step of one command can affect the outcome of any step of the other command.

Independent compilation   Independent compilation means that each compilation unit is compiled on its own, with no type information from the other compilation units in the same program. Type inconsistencies between compilation units cannot be detected.

Index range   An array's index range is the range of values used to index that array's components.

Indexing   Indexing is the operation that uses a value in an array's index range to access a particular component of that array.

Infix notation   In infix notation, a binary operator is written between its operands, as in "$x + y$".

Inherit If a type (or class) is equipped with an operation, and that same operation is applicable to a subtype (subclass), the subtype (subclass) is said to inherit that operation.

Inheritance anomaly An inheritance anomaly is a language design weakness resulting in poor support for the inheritance of synchronization properties.

In-out-parameter In ADA, an in-out-parameter is one that permits a procedure to inspect and update the value of an argument variable.

In-parameter In ADA, an in-parameter is one that permits a procedure to inspect an argument value.

Instance In HASKELL, an instance of a type class is a type equipped with all the operations of that type class.

Instance method An instance method is a method attached to a particular object. The instance method accesses that object using a keyword such as `this`.

Instance variable An instance variable is a variable component of each object of a given class.

Instantiation Instantiation of a generic unit generates an ordinary program unit, in which each of the generic unit's formal parameters is replaced by an argument.

Interface An interface is a kind of program unit that specifies (but does not define) operations that will have to be provided by other program units that claim to implement the interface.

Interruption status The interruption status of a JAVA thread indicates whether an attempt has been made to interrupt it.

Iteration An iteration of an iterative command is a single execution of its body.

Iterative command An iterative command is one which causes repeated execution of its body.

Iterative expression An iterative expression is one which causes repeated execution of a subexpression. An example is the HASKELL list comprehension.

Jump A jump is a sequencer that transfers control to a labeled command elsewhere in the program.

Label A label is an identifier attached to a command.

Language processor A language processor is a system that executes a program, or prepares a program for execution. Examples are compilers, interpreters, and program editors.

Lazy evaluation With lazy evaluation, an operation is applied when its result is needed for the first time.

Lazy list A lazy list is one whose components are evaluated and added only when they are needed. A lazy list may be of infinite length.

Length The length of an array or list is the number of components in it. The length of a string is the number of characters in it.

Lifetime The lifetime of a variable is the time interval between its creation and its destruction. A variable occupies storage cells only during its lifetime.

List A list is a sequence of components. Only the first of these components need be directly accessible.

List comprehension A list comprehension is an iterative expression that computes a list from one or more other lists.

Literal A literal is a program construct that always denotes the same value.

Liveness A concurrent system has the liveness property if it guarantees both fairness and freedom from deadlock.

Local variable A local variable is one that is declared inside a block, and whose lifetime is an activation of that block.

Logic programming Logic programming is a paradigm whose key concepts are assertions, Horn clauses, and relations.

Loop See *iterative command*.

Lower bound An array's lower bound is the minimum value of its index range.

Mapping A mapping takes each value in one set S to a value in another set T. Examples are arrays (where S is the index range and T is the component type) and functions (where S is the parameter type and T is the result type).

Match In functional programming, a pattern P matches a value v if there exist bindings for all unbound identifiers in P that would make P equal v.

In logic programming, an assertion A matches a query Q if A and Q can be made equal by consistent substitution, i.e., by replacing each variable by the same value wherever it occurs in A or Q.

In string processing, a regular expression matches a string according to the rules defined in Table 16.1.

Method A method is an operation (other than a constructor) of a class.

Module Depending on the context, a module is a synonym for a program unit or for a package.

Monitor In concurrent programming, a monitor is a program unit that combines encapsulation with automatic mutual exclusion and explicit communication.

Monolithic block structure   In a programming language with monolithic block structure, each program is a single block.

Monomorphic   Each parameter and result of a monomorphic procedure has a single type.

Monotype   A monotype denotes a single type. It contains no type variables.

Multiple assignment   A multiple assignment stores several values in several variables at the same time.

Multiple inheritance   Multiple inheritance allows a class to have any number of superclasses.

Name equivalence   Two types are name-equivalent if they were defined in the same place.

Nested block structure   In a programming language with nested block structure, blocks may be nested within other blocks.

New-type declaration   A new-type declaration binds an identifier to a type that is not equivalent to any existing type.

Nondeterministic   A computation is nondeterministic if its sequence of steps and its outcome are unpredictable.

Non-preemptive scheduling   Non-preemptive scheduling allows a running thread to stay in control until it voluntarily gives up the CPU.

Normal-order evaluation   With normal-order evaluation, an operation is applied every time that its result is needed.

Null pointer   A null pointer is a special pointer value that has no referent.

Object   An object is a tagged tuple. Typically an object is equipped with methods that have exclusive access to the object's components.

Object-oriented programming   Object-oriented programming is a paradigm whose key concepts are objects, classes and subclasses, inheritance, and inclusion polymorphism.

Observable   An action is observable to a later operation if it affects the operation's flow of control, or if it updates a variable that the operation inspects.

Operation   An operation is a procedure (or method or constructor) that constructs, inspects, or updates values of a given type (objects of a given class).

Operator   An operator is a symbol that denotes a function. Calls to that function are written in infix notation. In some programming languages, operators can be defined or redefined.

Out-parameter   In ADA, an out-parameter is one that permits a procedure to update (but not inspect) the value of an argument variable.

Overloading   Overloading occurs when two or more procedures legally have the same identifier in the same scope.

Overridable   A method of a class is overridable if it may be overridden by any subclass of that class.

Override   If a class is equipped with one version of a method, but a subclass is equipped with a different version of the method, the subclass is said to override that method.

Package   A package is a program unit that declares several (typically related) components, which may be types, constants, variables, procedures, exceptions, and so on.

Package body   In ADA, a package body declares private components of a package. It also defines public procedures specified in the corresponding package specification.

Package specification   In ADA, a package specification declares public components of a package. It specifies but does not define any public procedures.

Paradigm   A paradigm is a distinctive style of programming. Each paradigm is characterized by the predominance of certain key concepts.

Parallel command   A parallel command consists of two or more subcommands, which are executed concurrently.

Parameter mechanism   A parameter mechanism is the mechanism by which each formal parameter of a procedure enables access to the corresponding argument. See also *copy parameter mechanism, reference parameter mechanism*.

Parameterized type   A parameterized type is a type that has other types as parameters. Examples are array and list types.

Parametric polymorphism   Parametric polymorphism is a type system that enables polymorphic procedures to be written.

Partial application   Partial application means calling a curried function with fewer than the maximum number of arguments. The result of such a call is itself a function.

Pattern   A pattern a program construct that resembles an expression, but may contain binding occurrences of identifiers. When a pattern matches a given value, it produces bindings for these identifiers.

Persistent variable A persistent variable is one whose lifetime may transcend the run-time of a program.

Pointer A pointer is a value that is either null or refers to a variable.

Polymorphic Each parameter and result of a polymorphic procedure has a family of types.

Polytype A polytype denotes a family of types. It contains type variables.

Pragmatics A programming language's pragmatics is concerned with the way in which the language is intended to be used in practice.

Prefix notation In prefix notation, an operator is written before its operands, as in "$+(x, y)$". In most programming languages, prefix notation is used only for calls to procedures whose names are identifiers.

Primitive type A primitive type is one whose values are primitive.

Primitive value A primitive value is one that cannot be decomposed into simpler values.

Priority inversion In concurrent programming, a priority inversion happens when a high-priority process is forced to wait until a low-priority process leaves a critical section.

Private A private component of a program unit is one that is visible only inside that unit.

Procedural parameter A procedural parameter is a formal parameter that is bound to the corresponding argument procedure.

Procedure A procedure is an entity that embodies a computation. See also *function procedure, proper procedure*.

Procedure definition A procedure definition is a declaration that binds an identifier to a procedure. See also *function definition*.

Process In concurrent programming, a heavyweight process is the execution of a complete program, supported by an operating system that allocates an address space, a share of main storage, a share of the CPU time, and so on. For lightweight process, see *thread*.

Program unit A program unit is a named part of a program that can be designed and implemented more-or-less independently. Examples are procedures, packages, and classes.

Programming linguistics Programming linguistics is the study of programming languages.

Projection Projection is an operation that recovers a particular variant of a disjoint union.

Proper procedure A proper procedure is a procedure that, when called, updates variables.

Proper procedure call A proper procedure call is a command that calls a proper procedure. It passes arguments, and executes the proper procedure's body to update variables.

Protected A protected component of a program unit is one that is visible both inside that unit and inside certain related units. In particular, a protected component of a class is visible inside all subclasses.

Protected module In Ada95, a protected module is a program unit that implements automatic mutual exclusion, implicit signaling of conditions, and simple encapsulation of data.

Public A public component of a program unit is one that is visible both inside and outside that unit.

Qualification Principle The Qualification Principle states: It is possible to include a block in any syntactic category, provided that the constructs in that syntactic category specify some kind of computation.

Query A query is an assertion (or sequence of assertions) that is to be tested against the clauses of a logic program.

Reachable A heap variable is reachable if it can be accessed by following pointers from a global or local variable. An unreachable heap variable may safely be destroyed.

Record A record is a tuple of named components.

Recursive declaration A recursive declaration is one whose scope includes itself.

Recursive type A recursive type is one defined in terms of itself. The representation of a recursive type always uses pointers.

Reference parameter mechanism A reference parameter mechanism allows for an argument to be accessed indirectly through the corresponding formal parameter.

Reference semantics Reference semantics means that, when a value is assigned to a variable, that variable is made to contain a reference to that value.

Referent The referent of a non-null pointer is the variable to which it points.

Regular expression A regular expression is a kind of pattern that matches a set of strings.

Relation In logic, r is a relation between two sets S and T if, for every x in S and y in T, $r(x, y)$ is either *true* or *false*. In logic programming, a relation may be defined by one or more Horn clauses.

Rendezvous   In concurrent programming, a rendezvous is an unbuffered interaction between two processes. In order to rendezvous, each process executes a command indicating its willingness to interact. Each process waits if the other one has not yet reached its rendezvous point. When both processes are ready, a message may be copied from one to the other; then both continue independently.

Requeue command   In ADA95, a requeue command puts back an accepted entry call (either in its own queue, or on the queue of another entry with a compatible parameter list). This provides the entry with a way of deferring an accepted call, so implementing admission control that depends on parameters of the call.

Resolution   In logic programming, resolution is a technique used for testing a query Q. If the program contains a clause whose left-hand assertion matches Q, test the clause's right-hand assertions separately as subqueries. If all subqueries succeed, then conclude that Q succeeds. If any subquery fails, then backtrack and try some other clause.

Result   A function procedure's result is the value it returns to the function call.

Return sequencer   A return sequencer is one that terminates execution of a procedure. If the latter is a function procedure, the return sequencer carries a result.

Safety   A concurrent program has the safety property if its accesses to a shared resource r never overlap in time, so that all of the commands it applies to r have their normal, sequential, effect.

Scheduling   In concurrent programming, scheduling is the allocation of resources to processes over time, aiming to further some objective (such as good response time).

Scope   The scope of a declaration is the part of the program in which the bindings produced by the declaration are available.

Scripting   Scripting is a paradigm characterized by gluing together of subsystems, rapid development and evolution, modest efficiency requirements, and very high-level functionality.

Second-class value   A second-class value is one that is restricted in the operations that may be applied to it. Typically, a second-class value may be passed as an argument, but may not be stored or used as a component of a composite value. Examples are C, C++, and ADA procedures (although pointers to procedures are first-class values).

Selection   Selection is an operation that accesses a particular component of a tuple.

Selective update   Selective update is an operation that updates one component of a composite variable, without affecting its other components.

Selective wait command   A selective wait is an ADA composite command allowing a task bounded nondeterministic choice between accepting entry calls and executing alternative courses of action.

Selector procedure   A selector procedure is a procedure that, when called, returns a variable as its result.

Semantics   A programming language's semantics is concerned with the meaning of programs in the language, i.e., how they are expected to behave when executed.

Semaphore   In concurrent programming, a semaphore is a variable used for inter-process mutual exclusion and communication.

Separate compilation   Separate compilation means that each compilation unit is compiled on its own, but with full type information from the other compilation units in the same program. Type inconsistencies between compilation units can be detected.

Sequencer   A sequencer is a program construct that transfers control to another point in the program. See also *escape, exception, jump*.

Sequential command   A sequential command consists of two or more subcommands, which are executed in order from first to last.

Sequential declaration   A sequential declaration consists of two or more subdeclarations, whose bindings are combined. The scope of each subdeclaration includes the following subdeclarations.

Sequential file   A sequential file is one whose components may be accessed only in order from first to last.

Sequential process   A sequential process is a totally ordered set of actions, each of which changes the state of a component of a computing system.

Sequential program   A sequential program specifies the possible state changes of a sequential process, which take place in an order determined by the program's control structures and its inputs.

Share   Two composite variables share components if these components can be accessed by following pointers from both composite variables. If the shared components can be selectively updated, the composite variables are updated simultaneously.

Side effect   A side effect occurs if evaluation of an expression updates a variable, or if elaboration of a declaration creates a variable.

Simple variable   A simple variable is one that occupies a single storage cell. It cannot be selectively updated.

Single inheritance   Single inheritance allows a class to have at most one superclass.

Skip   A skip is a command that has no effect whatsoever.

Speed-dependent   A concurrent program is speed-dependent if its outcome depends on the relative speeds at which its constituent sequential processes run.

Spin lock   In concurrent programming, a spin lock is a busy-waiting loop, in which a process waits for access to a shared resource by repeatedly testing a flag that indicates whether the resource is free.

Starvation   In concurrent programming, a process is said to starve when it is deprived of needed resources by scheduling rules that do not ensure fairness.

Static array   A static array is one whose index bounds are fixed at compile-time.

Static variable   A static variable is one whose scope is restricted but whose lifetime is the program's entire run-time. Examples are C static variables and C++ or JAVA class variables.

Statically scoped   A programming language is statically scoped if each procedure's body is executed in the environment of the procedure definition. For each applied occurrence of an identifier in the program, there is a unique binding occurrence.

Statically typed   A programming language is statically typed if every variable and expression has a fixed type. Every operation is type-checked at compile-time.

Storable   A value is storable if it can be stored in a single storage cell.

Storage   Storage is a collection of storage cells, each of which has a unique address.

Storage cell   Each storage cell has a current status, which is either allocated or unallocated. Each allocated storage cell has a current content, which is either a storable value or *undefined*.

Strict   A function is strict in a particular argument if that argument is always used.

String   A string is a sequence of characters.

Structural equivalence   Two types are structurally equivalent if they have the same set of values.

Structure   In C or C++, a structure is a tuple of named components. In PROLOG, a structure is a tagged tuple.

Subclass   Given a class C, a subclass of C is a set of objects that are similar to one another but richer than the objects of class C. An object of the subclass may have extra variable components and may be equipped with extra methods.

Subtype   Given a type T, a subtype of T is a subset of the values of T, equipped with the same operations as T.

Succeed   In logic programming, a query succeeds if it can be inferred from the clauses in the program that the query is *true*.

Superclass   If S is a subclass of C, then C is a superclass of S.

Synchronized   In JAVA, a synchronized method or block automatically enforces mutually exclusive access to a designated object.

Syntax   A programming language's syntax is concerned with the form of programs in the language, i.e., how they are composed of expressions, commands, declarations, and other constructs.

Tag test   Tag test is an operation that checks the tag of a disjoint union.

Tagged record   In ADA95, a tagged record is a record that is tagged with an indication of its type. Tagged record types can be extended.

Target object   Each method call names a method and identifies a target object, which must be an object equipped with an instance method of that name. The instance method accesses the target object using a keyword such as **this**.

Task   See *thread*.

Task module   In ADA, a task module is a program unit that executes concurrently, as a task.

Template   In C++, a template is a generic function or class.

Terminate abruptly   A command terminates abruptly if it executes a sequencer that transfers control out of it.

Terminate normally   A command terminates normally if it reaches its normal end.

Thread   In concurrent programming, a thread is a flow of control through a program, but it does not possess independent computational resources. Instead, a thread exists within a process and uses the resources of the process. A JAVA thread is created as an object whose class is a subclass of `Thread` or implements the `Runnable` interface.

An Ada thread is created by declaring or allocating a task object.

Throw   Throwing an exception transfers control to a corresponding exception handler.

Total update   Total update is an operation that updates all components of a composite variable at the same time.

Transient variable   A transient variable is one that is not persistent. Its lifetime is bounded by the program's run-time.

Type   A type is a set of values, equipped with one or more operations that can be applied uniformly to all these values. See also *composite type, primitive type, recursive type*.

Type check   A type check ensures that the operands of an operation have the expected types. Type checks can be performed at compile-time if the programming language is statically typed, but must be performed at run-time if the programming language is dynamically typed.

Type class   In Haskell, a type class is a family of types all of which are equipped with specified operations.

Type Completeness Principle   The Type Completeness Principle states: No operation should be arbitrarily restricted in the types of its operands.

Type conversion   A type conversion is a mapping from values of one type to corresponding values of a different type.

Type declaration   A type declaration is a declaration that binds an identifier to a new or existing type. See also *new-type declaration, type definition*.

Type definition   A type declaration is a declaration that binds an identifier to an existing type.

Type error   A type error is an inconsistency exposed by a type check.

Type inference   In a statically typed language, type inference must be performed wherever the type of a variable or expression is not explicitly stated.

Type system   A programming language's type system groups values into types.

Type variable   A type variable is an identifier that stands for any one of a family of types.

Union   In C and C++, a union is a group of variants without a tag.

Universal   A programming language must be universal, meaning that every solvable problem has a solution expressible in the language.

Untyped   A programming language is untyped if its values are not grouped into types.

Upper bound   An array's upper bound is the maximum value of its index range.

Value   A value is an entity that can be manipulated by a program. Values can be evaluated, stored, passed as arguments, returned as function results, and so on.

Variable   In imperative and object-oriented programming, a variable is a container for a value, which may be inspected and updated. In functional and logic programming, a variable stands for an unknown value.

Variable access   A variable access is a simple expression that accesses a variable.

Variable declaration   A variable declaration is a declaration that creates and binds an identifier to a variable, and possibly also initializes that variable.

Variable parameter   A variable parameter is a formal parameter that is bound to the corresponding argument variable.

Variable renaming definition   A variable renaming definition is a declaration that binds an identifier to an existing variable.

Visible   A declaration of an identifier is visible throughout its scope, except where hidden by a declaration of the same identifier in an inner block.

Volatile   In concurrent programming, a variable that is used by more than one process may be declared volatile, to inhibit optimizations that might prevent some processes from observing an up-to-date value.

Wait set   In Java, a wait set is the set of threads blocked on an object in a synchronized method or block.

While-command   A while-command consists of a condition (boolean expression) and a body (sub-command). It repeatedly evaluates the condition and then executes the body, terminating as soon as the condition yields *false*.

Index